MARKET PRACTICE IN
FINANCIAL
MODELLING

MARKET PRACTICE IN
FINANCIAL
MODELLING

Chia Chiang Tan

DBAnalytics, Deutsche Bank

World Scientific

NEW JERSEY · LONDON · SINGAPORE · BEIJING · SHANGHAI · HONG KONG · TAIPEI · CHENNAI

Published by

World Scientific Publishing Co. Pte. Ltd.

5 Toh Tuck Link, Singapore 596224

USA office: 27 Warren Street, Suite 401-402, Hackensack, NJ 07601

UK office: 57 Shelton Street, Covent Garden, London WC2H 9HE

Library of Congress Cataloging-in-Publication Data
Tan, Chia Chiang.
    Market practice in financial modelling / by Chia Chiang Tan.
    p. cm.
    Includes bibliographical references and index.
    ISBN-13: 978-981-4366-54-0
    ISBN-10: 981-4366-54-4
    1. Derivative securities--Mathematical models. 2. Finance--Mathematical models.
3. Finance. I. Title.
    HG6024.A3T327 2012
    332.64'57015195--dc23

                                                        2012014667

British Library Cataloguing-in-Publication Data
A catalogue record for this book is available from the British Library.

In-house Editor: Alisha Nguyen

Typeset by Stallion Press
Email: enquiries@stallionpress.com

Printed in Singapore.

To my father and
in memory of my mother.

"Chia Tan's book provides a refreshing introduction to concepts of quantitative finance applied to real world financial markets. He intuitively explains and guides the reader to tackle problems in financial engineering with practical solutions in mind, and is mindful to point out which issues each model can address and also the problems and limitations. Whereas mathematical elegance often overshadowed important issues prior to the financial crisis of 2008, this is one of the first books with a chapter explaining, in simple terms, such issues as counterparty risk, balance sheet and funding costs, and basis risk that have become important topics to many financial institutions these days. This book will be a valuable resource for hedge fund managers and buy-side institutions who plan to use over-the-counter derivative products, and also as a refresher for the sell-side dealers who trade them."

David Ha
Interest Rates Trader, Goldman Sachs Japan

Preface

Picking up this book suggests that you probably have some interest in financial modelling. This book is about market practice on the modelling of financial derivatives, a sort of consensus body of knowledge that a seasoned derivatives professional would possess. It is not on statistical modelling to predict exchange rates, or relative value analysis of different stocks, or optimal portfolio construction.

A student of quantitative finance is typically taught courses in probability and stochastic calculus, corresponding numerical techniques, as well as the foundations of derivatives pricing and the main ideas behind certain key models. To supplement his knowledge, various good books exist on specific subject areas, e.g. equities, foreign exchange or interest rates, although they sometimes contain far too much detail for someone interested in a general grounding in the subject. Beyond this, our student will be confronted with an ocean of academic and practitioner papers.

However, a student should not be daunted by the gulf between foundational derivatives pricing and market practice financial modelling. Financial professionals are practical people, who would not seek a more complex model, unless it is useful for more accurately pricing or better capturing the risks of the products at hand. And whilst beyond material covered in foundational courses, typical models used for exotic pricing are certainly not beyond the comprehension of someone with a decent background in derivatives pricing.

Thus, assuming foundational knowledge, I intend in this book to distil the relevant material found in specific subject texts in quantitative finance, and help a student navigate through the ocean of papers, so that he may reach the faraway shores in good time and high spirits. And along the way, of course, I shall relate the theory of financial modelling to its practical application. By the end of the journey, I hope to have assisted our student in gaining a better understanding of market practice in financial modelling, so that he may utilise it effectively.

I am not proposing to cover cutting edge financial modelling. For one, this is more appropriately left to the realm of papers. By their nature, such advances are unpredictable and so are best made available when their authors are ready. Furthermore, research in financial modelling can produce interesting results which may subsequently prove less useful than thought, so there is little point in collating together a general body of up-to-date cutting edge research. And it is unlikely that quantitative professionals have a consensus on some of the findings of the latest research. Actually, some of this research in financial institutions is rightly viewed as proprietary and will not be available for years in any event.

What will this book cover? First, I will touch on no-arbitrage principles as a brief reminder of the basics of derivatives pricing and also discuss market quantities and standard market instruments to set up the context for the rest of the material. Next, I shall cover replication, a topic not always discussed in texts, but used extremely commonly in financial institutions (e.g. for CMS products), in keeping with the principle to use models only where necessary. Moving on, I shall briefly discuss the use of copula techniques for valuing contracts dependent on 2 underlyings observed at one point in time (e.g. the CMS spread option).

Thereafter, things get more interesting. Local volatility is examined in terms of its theoretical basis, smile dynamics and parameterisations (e.g. the implications of a normal versus lognormal model). Its counterpart stochastic volatility follows naturally, with a discussion of its dynamics and the more popular models (e.g. SABR, Heston). And of course, the natural extension is to combine local and stochastic volatility. The reader should understand the implications of local or stochastic volatility, and an illustration will help, e.g. by considering simple barrier products.

In the realm of interest rates, I shall begin with short rate models. It is not really useful to go into the history of such models, rather, I shall cover the practical requirements for such models to be useful (e.g. existence of quasi-analytic form of discount bond as function of state variables), and practical constraints on these (e.g. number of state variables). I shall illustrate based on some of the popular flavours (e.g. Hull–White, Cheyette). Moving on to the Libor Market Model, I shall explore why market models have initially captured much interest from financial professionals and the myriad of issues that have made them slow to receive acceptance as the dominant models for interest rates. Specifically, the huge number of state variables and hence computational expense, and the suboptimal treatment of early exercise in a Monte Carlo setup (by either the Andersen or Longstaff–Schwartz approaches) will be examined. Having considered local and stochastic volatility earlier, the discussion of interest rate models is extended to include consideration of these features.

I continue with a discussion of long-dated foreign exchange and the effect of interest rate volatility on forward foreign exchange volatility. On the topic of forward smile products (e.g. the cliquet), once again the discussion of local versus stochastic volatility from earlier becomes relevant. An analysis of the effect of mean reversion on forward volatility also follows. And the book wraps up by exploring the practical issues where a dealer can no longer fund at the risk-free rate post 2008 — whilst certainly complicating the theoretical underpinnings of derivatives pricing, we shall see that fortunately the framework can be extended to accommodate this new reality.

At the end of each chapter, there is a summary of the topics which hopefully will help you consolidate your understanding of the material. There are also exercises (some of which are quite involved) for the interested reader to explore the topic further and better acquaint himself with the material. They are not really necessary and omitting them will not interrupt the flow of the discussion. The intention after all is for the text to be self-contained.

This book is aimed at helping the reader acquire familiarity with market practice in financial modelling. For reasons of general applicability, I have focused on the core areas of equities, foreign exchange

and interest rates. Credit and commodities are more specialised topics, which require treatment of their own peculiarities.

This book is aimed at a student with a background in stochastic
calculus, numerical techniques (e.g. PDE, Monte Carlo methods) and
foundational derivatives pricing. However, it is a practitioner's text
intended to help the student bridge the gulf with market practice and
not an academic discourse. Where possible, I have tried to portray
the bigger picture with how models relate to each other and are
relevant to considerations in the product of interest.

I hope that this book would be useful in helping a student of
quantitative finance get a headstart in understanding how financial
modelling is used in practice for derivatives pricing in financial institutions. The rest is up to you.

Foreword

Financial derivatives pricing must appear daunting to the uniniti-
ated these days — with so much jargon, and so much background
assumed of the new entrant. Beginning with foundations lying in the
calculus of Brownian motion, you may be expected to appreciate the
implications of local volatility versus stochastic volatility, or you may
have to come to grips with the concept of mean reversion for which
not only traders have a weird affinity. It all seems too intimidating
doesn't it? In times when the industry is shrinking but yet many
aspiring students attempt to enter into the complex world of derivatives, it is more important than ever to demonstrate the ability to
connect the formal mathematical apparatus on the one hand with
the reality of products and its behaviour on the other.

These challenges however not only apply to new entrants but
interestingly to the exact opposite end of the spectrum as well: senior
management and hence the main decision makers of large financial
institutions. I believe that the general under-representation of mathematically skilled staff at this end has contributed to the severity
of the financial crisis to some extent. This is because the application of "rigorous" mathematics in deriving the price of a complex
credit derivative transaction may give a senior decision maker the
wrong sense of comfort into the risk she is taking in the name of her
institution.

I think if you have, at some point in your life, looked into the
derivation of the asymptotic formula for the SABR expansion for
example and considered its limitations, you will more likely retain

a "constructive scepticism" towards models and their applications. Thus you will be better equipped to make the right decisions even when you are at the stage of your career where management consumes the bulk of your time.

It is very crucial to develop a sense of what type of questions a model is good at answering, and what sort of questions it may fail miserably to answer. For example, the Heston model and in particular its extensions that incorporate local vol provide an excellent framework to adequately describe trades that exhibit vol-convexity. However, the same model may completely undervalue out-of-the money call options on the VIX, a popular volatility index, as a result of the mean reversion considerations mentioned above.

In short, what I am saying is this: Mastering all the mathematics well but lacking intuition when applying it to the context of specific products is just as dangerous as having too little mathematical knowledge but a good understanding of innovating product features. I found that it is exactly when these two ends meet and start influencing each other that real progress is made. It occurs when intuition drives the mathematical and numerical developments but, at the same time, mathematical results help to further shape and skill the intuition behind a problem.

For example, I found it very fruitful to think about a variety of insurance products that are traditionally priced and innovated by the actuarial department within an insurance firm in terms of exotic derivative transactions. Once you master this skill you may even start to think about high-frequency market-making as a trading operation that sells option strangles at various levels in the limit order book and derive useful ways of thinking about the risks.

In my opinion the explicit appetite for exotic products will diminish for the foreseeable future, as a result of the crisis and enhanced capital requirements. However the world in which we live in will remain complex and interconnected. As a result seemingly "harmless" transactions may turn out significantly more complex when taking a second look. In this sense the "derivative way of thinking" will always remain a fruitful concept that is here to stay even if exotic derivatives should not.

Having said all that, it is unfortunate that many books out there do not attempt to relate abstract financial concepts with their real world applications, leaving the reader a rather large gap to fill. Hopefully, this book will be more amenable for developing a reader's intuition, and the reader would be able to see that financial mathematics is not really so inaccessible after all.

Alex Langnau
Global Head of Quantitative Analytics
Allianz Investment Management
Visiting Scientist, Ludwig-Maximillians University, Munich

Contents

Acknowledgements

I am indebted to various friends and colleagues (present and former), whose support and encouragement have made the completion of this book possible. Also, I am grateful to the management of DB Analytics for their understanding and support of this endeavour.

In no particular order, I would like to thank Oleg Soloviev for a detailed review of the contents and various helpful suggestions, as well as for spotting errors in the manuscript. I would also like to thank Alain Chebanier for his review of parts of the manuscript, which has influenced the nature of the ideas presented. Jagjit Dhaliwal deserves thanks for his review of sample chapters, which has highlighted areas which need clearer explanation.

I am grateful to Ani Banerjee for his enthusiastic support of the project and his review of the overall coherence and relevance of the material. I owe it to Alex Langnau for his support and overview of the contents of the manuscript, as well as his earlier review of a previous manuscript which has helped me develop consciousness for the need to reach out to the reader. I am also grateful to Iain Clark, who supplied me with some material from his book Foreign Exchange Option Pricing pre-publication as reference, which helped guide the contents of my chapter on Local Stochastic Volatility.

I should also thank Yves-Richard Hong and Kevin Le Tenoux, who as target readers, have spotted errors in parts of the manuscript, as well as indicated areas which need clarification and elaboration.

In addition, I am grateful to Andy Tran and Danish Siddiqui for supplying data which was necessary for me to produce some of the graphs for the text. I should also thank Lars Schouw and Shiv Madan who had helped me obtain data when writing a previous book, some of which made it into this book.

Finally, I must thank the staff at World Scientific for their under-standing and support throughout the project and their confidence in this book.

Any errors in the material are solely my responsibility.

1

Introduction

"When you are hungry, you go to the kitchen."

This book is about market practice in the modelling of financial derivatives. The intent is to discuss the essential features that a model needs to capture to appropriately treat various financial products. But we must start somewhere. To avoid boring the initiated, basic familiarity with stochastic calculus and a good grounding in mathematics is assumed. But for clarity, it will nevertheless be useful to go through a few key ideas that are fundamental to the pricing of derivatives.

This chapter breezes through the basics of derivatives pricing and various key considerations, as well as introduces various market quantities, so that the reader can relate the discussion to market observables, rather than see it from only an abstract sense.

1.1 The Theory

Derivatives pricing is theoretically anchored in the concept of replication. Basically, the premise is that if you have two portfolios whose payoffs are equivalent at a future date, then their values must be equivalent today. If we ignore the possible need to liquidate these portfolios prior to that future date, the possibility of the counterparty of one of the portfolios defaulting, and the potential cost differentials of funding these two portfolios, this statement is uncontroversial.

It follows that to price a derivative, it is sufficient if you could come up with a replicating portfolio. Notice that in this case, we are not concerned about what happens to the underlying itself, or indeed if it is overpriced.

Further, if this replicating portfolio can be constructed today (independent of model assumptions), then you can price the derivative with confidence, since it is just a combination of existing traded market products. That is the realm of static replication, which we shall cover in Chapter 3.

More frequently, it is necessary for the replicating portfolio to be dynamic, i.e. you may have to rebalance it over time, and the rebalancing is dependent on certain model assumptions. In this way, pricing of derivatives becomes dependent on the model chosen for the underlying.

Let us now investigate what this means in practical terms.

1.1.1 *Ito's Lemma*

Let us start with a Wiener process W_t. Amongst its properties, it is continuous and has independent random increments that are normally distributed, i.e. for $s < t < S < T$:

$$E[W_t - W_s] = 0,$$
$$\text{var}[W_t - W_s] = E[(W_t - W_s)^2] = t - s,$$
$$E[(W_T - W_S)(W_t - W_s)] = 0,$$

and

$$W_t - W_s \sim N(0, t - s).$$

There are arguments that a continuous process cannot properly represent market quantities since they tend to jump. For example, negative shocks (e.g. a major disaster or credit event) can cause stock prices to drop sharply instantaneously. And interest rates at the short end tend to be changed by 25 basis points (from central bank action) or nothing at all. But for longer expiries and for hedging considerations for derivatives where we are worried about how the 10-year euro swap rate moves or changes in the forward value of the S&P 500 over the next three years, jumps are not very meaningful, since they disproportionately affect the short term but their effect is smoothed out over time. To this end, it is beyond the scope of this book to investigate jump processes, and because of their practical utility, we shall focus on processes constructed out of Wiener processes instead.

So, let us now consider the following stochastic differential equation (SDE) for the process of an asset

$$dS_t = \mu(S_t, t)dt + \sigma(S_t, t)dW_t.$$

Consider a function $f(S_t, t)$ of S_t and t. Ito's Lemma gives

$$df_t = \frac{\partial f_t}{\partial t} + \frac{\partial f_t}{\partial S_t} dS_t + \frac{1}{2}\frac{\partial^2 f_t}{\partial S_t^2}(dS_t)^2$$

$$= \frac{\partial f_t}{\partial t}dt + \frac{\partial f_t}{\partial S_t}(\mu(S_t, t)dt + \sigma(S_t, t)dW_t) + \frac{1}{2}\frac{\partial^2 f_t}{\partial S_t^2}\sigma^2(S_t, t)dt$$

$$= \left[\frac{\partial f_t}{\partial t} + \mu(S_t, t)\frac{\partial f_t}{\partial S_t} + \frac{1}{2}\sigma^2(S_t, t)\frac{\partial^2 f_t}{\partial S_t^2}\right]dt + \sigma(S_t, t)\frac{\partial f_t}{\partial S_t}dW_t.$$

As in standard calculus, $(dt)^2 = dtdW_t = 0$. But in contrast, $dW_t^2 = dt$.

To see this, consider (for $t_i = \frac{iT}{N}$):

$$V(T) = \left[\int_0^T \sigma(S_t, t)dW_t\right]^2$$

$$= \lim_{N\to\infty}\left[\sum_{i=1}^{N}\sigma(S_{t_i}, t_i)(W_{t_i} - W_{t_{i-1}})\right]^2$$

$$= \lim_{N\to\infty}\left[\sum_{i=1}^{N}\sigma^2(S_{t_i}, t_i)(W_{t_i} - W_{t_{i-1}})^2\right.$$

$$\left. + 2\sum_{i=1}^{N}\sum_{j=1}^{i-1}\sigma(S_{t_i}, t_i)\sigma(S_{t_j}, t_j)(W_{t_i} - W_{t_{i-1}})(W_{t_j} - W_{t_{j-1}})\right].$$

Then the expectation is given by

$$E[V(T)] = \lim_{N\to\infty} \left[\sum_{i=1}^{N} \sigma^2(S_{t_i}, t_i) E[(W_{t_i} - W_{t_{i-1}})^2] \right.$$

$$+ 2 \sum_{i=1}^{N} \sum_{j=1}^{i-1} \sigma(S_{t_i}, t_i) \sigma(S_{t_j}, t_j) E[(W_{t_i} - W_{t_{i-1}})$$

$$\left. \times (W_{t_j} - W_{t_{j-1}})] \right]$$

$$= \lim_{N\to\infty} \left[\sum_{i=1}^{N} \sigma^2(S_{t_i}, t_i) \frac{T}{N} + 2 \sum_{i=1}^{N} \sum_{j=1}^{i-1} \sigma(S_{t_i}, t_i) \sigma(S_{t_j}, t_j) 0 \right]$$

$$= \int_0^T \sigma^2(S_t, t) dt$$

since

$$E[(W_{t_i} - W_{t_{i-1}})^2] = \frac{iT}{N} - \frac{(i-1)T}{N} = \frac{T}{N} \quad \text{and}$$

$$E[(W_{t_i} - W_{t_{i-1}})(W_{t_j} - W_{t_{j-1}})] = 0 \quad \text{for } i \neq j.$$

Further, it can be shown[1] that

$$\lim_{N\to\infty} E\left[\left\{ \left(\sum_{i=1}^{N} \sigma(S_{t_i}, t_i)(W_{t_i} - W_{t_{i-1}}) \right)^2 \right. \right.$$

$$\left. \left. - \int_0^T \sigma^2(S_t, t) dt \right\}^2 \right] = 0.$$

Thus, the stronger condition

$$V(T) = \int_0^T \sigma^2(S_t, t) dt$$

holds in a mean square convergence sense.

---

[1] See Neftci in [Nef96].

1.1.2 *The Black–Scholes Partial Differential Equation (PDE)*

Given our discussion earlier, if we can come up with a self-financing and predictable trading strategy that attains a particular payoff, then that trading strategy gives the price of that payoff. We would like to replicate a derivative with value given by $f(S_t, t)$ above where

$$df_t = \frac{\partial f_t}{\partial t} + \frac{\partial f_t}{\partial S_t} dS_t + \frac{1}{2} \frac{\partial^2 f_t}{\partial S_t^2} (dS_t)^2.$$

Our trading strategy involves holding $\Delta(S_t, t)$ units of the underlying S_t at time t, and financing by borrowing or lending at the risk-free rate r_t.[2]

A portfolio of the derivative and our replicating strategy is worth

$$\Pi(S_t, t) = \Delta(S_t, t) S_t - f(S_t, t).$$

For it to be self-financing, we require

$$d\Pi(S_t, t) = \Delta(S_t, t) dS_t - df(S_t, t).$$

Now, if we choose $\Delta(S_t, t) = \frac{\partial f_t}{\partial S_t}$, notice that

$$d\Pi(S_t, t) = -\frac{\partial f_t}{\partial t} dt - \frac{1}{2} \frac{\partial^2 f_t}{\partial S_t^2} (dS_t)^2$$

$$= \left(-\frac{\partial f_t}{\partial t} - \frac{1}{2} \frac{\partial^2 f_t}{\partial S_t^2} \sigma^2(S_t, t) \right) dt.$$

Since our portfolio only involves dt terms and not dW_t terms, it is risk-free and hence must grow at the risk-free rate r_t. This gives

$$d\Pi(S_t, t) = r_t \Pi(S_t, t) dt$$

$$= r_t (\Delta(S_t, t) S_t - f(S_t, t)) dt$$

$$= \left(r_t S_t \frac{\partial f_t}{\partial S_t} - r_t f(S_t, t) \right) dt$$

---

[2]This is predictable and hence a valid strategy in a sense that at time t, our trading strategy does not require knowing S_T for $T > t$.

from which we obtain the celebrated Black–Scholes PDE for the price of a derivative

$$\frac{\partial f_t}{\partial t} + r_t S_t \frac{\partial f_t}{\partial S_t} + \frac{1}{2}\frac{\partial^2 f_t}{\partial S_t^2}\sigma^2(S_t, t) = r_t f(S_t, t).$$

1.1.3   *Martingale Representation Theorem*

More generally, Harrison and Pliska [HP81] show that in an economy free of arbitrage opportunities, the price of every derivative based on continuous processes is attainable by a self-financing trading strategy involving relative asset prices. To be more precise, we need the framework below. Much of the rest of Section 1.1 is inspired by Pelsser [Pel00].

A numeraire asset is any asset that has strictly positive prices. A numeraire can be seen as a unit of measuring value. For example, the domestic money market account (i.e. a notional interest-bearing risk-free account B_t with SDE $dB_t = r_t B_t dt$) is a typical candidate for a numeraire, as it means we are measuring value in terms of our domestic currency. However, it is legitimate (and can be convenient for pricing purposes[3]) to measure wealth in terms of units of Walmart stock or ounces of gold.

Let A_t be a numeraire asset and S_t^i be the prices of underlying assets. We can construct trading strategies based on holding $\Delta_i(t)$ units of relative assets $\frac{S_t^i}{A_t}$, with value V_t given by

$$\frac{V_t}{A_t} = \frac{V_0}{A_0} + \sum_{i=1}^{N}\int_0^t \Delta_i(u)d\left(\frac{S_u^i}{A_u}\right).$$

If these trading strategies are self-financing, then the relative value $\frac{V_t}{A_t}$ is a martingale. Specifically,

$$E_t\left[\frac{V_T}{A_T}\right] = E\left[\frac{V_T}{A_T}|F_t\right]$$

$$= \frac{V_t}{A_t}$$

---

[3]We shall encounter examples of the above in Sections 1.2.4, 2.2.1 and 2.2.2.

for $T > t$, where F_t is the filtration (i.e. all available information up to time t).

The above claim is that no arbitrage requires that all derivatives can be attained by self-financing trading strategies. This leads to the Martingale Pricing Equation for pricing a derivative security:

$$\frac{V_t}{A_t} = E_t^A \left[\frac{V_T}{A_T} \right].$$

Note that our expectation is with respect to a measure induced by the numeraire asset A_t. Probabilities of various events depend on this measure (and should not be thought of as real world probabilities). Recall that in derivatives pricing, what matters is the cost of replicating a payoff rather than the true probabilities of various scenarios being realised.

1.1.4 *Radon–Nikodym Transform*

But what forces us to use a particular numeraire asset A_t? Our above equation holds independent of our choice of numeraire, so that for a different numeraire asset B_t, we have

$$V_t = A_t E_t^A \left[\frac{V_T}{A_T} \right] = B_t E_t^B \left[\frac{V_T}{B_T} \right].$$

It follows that

$$\frac{V_t}{A_t} = E_t^A \left[\frac{V_T}{A_T} \right]$$

$$= E_t^B \left[\frac{V_T}{A_T} \frac{A_T B_t}{B_T A_t} \right]$$

$$= E_t^B \left[\frac{V_T}{A_T} \frac{dQ_t^A}{dQ_t^B} \right],$$

where $\frac{dQ_t^A}{dQ_t^B} = \frac{A_T B_t}{B_T A_t}$ is the definition of the Radon–Nikodym derivative.

Thus, to change from measure Q^B (with numeraire B_t) to measure Q^A (with numeraire A_t), we multiply by the Radon–Nikodym derivative $\frac{dQ_t^A}{dQ_t^B}$.

1.1.5   *Girsanov Theorem*

Girsanov's Theorem is a useful tool for dealing with change of measure. In brief, it states that for a Wiener process, a change of measure only affects the drift term.

Consider now the Radon–Nikodym derivative

$$R_t = \frac{dQ_t^A}{dQ_t^B}.$$

Suppose it satisfies for some $\eta(t)$ the SDE

$$dR_t = \eta(t) R_t dW_t^B,$$

where W_t^B is a Wiener process with respect to measure Q^B.

Then Girsanov's Theorem gives

$$dW_t^A = dW_t^B - \eta(t)dt.$$

An implication of Girsanov's Theorem is that when we change measure, volatility is unaffected. For example, as will be seen in Section 9.1.3, change of measure in the Libor Market Model still allows us to use the same caplet volatilities as per a Black model for our Libor rates.

1.1.6   *Feynman–Kac Theorem*

Another essential tool in our complement is the Feynman–Kac Theorem. This relates the no-arbitrage martingale equation in Section 1.1.3 to the pricing PDE.

Specifically, the equation

$$\frac{V_t}{A_t} = E_t^A \left[\frac{V_T}{A_T} \right]$$

is equivalent to

$$\frac{\partial V_t}{\partial t} + r_t S_t \frac{\partial V_t}{\partial S_t} + \frac{1}{2} \frac{\partial^2 V_t}{\partial S_t^2} \sigma^2(S_t, t) = r_t V(S_t, t)$$

by taking $V_t = V(S_t, t)$ and $A_t = B_t = e^{\int_0^t r_u du}$ (our money market account in Section 1.1.3 above).

Let the drift of V_t be $\mu_V(t)$. The above can be seen easily because

$$
\begin{aligned}
d\left(\frac{V_t}{B_t}\right) &= \left(\frac{V_t + dV_t}{B_t + dB_t} - \frac{V_t}{B_t}\right) \\
&= \frac{V_t}{B_t}\left(\frac{1 + \frac{dV_t}{V_t}}{1 + \frac{dB_t}{B_t}} - 1\right) \\
&= \frac{V_t}{B_t}\left(1 + \frac{dV_t}{V_t} - \frac{dB_t}{B_t} - 1\right) \\
&= \frac{V_t}{B_t}(1 + \mu_V(t)dt + \cdots dW_t - r_t dt - 1) \\
&= \frac{V_t}{B_t}((\mu_V(t) - r_t)dt + \cdots dW_t)
\end{aligned}
$$

where we do not have $\frac{dV_t}{V_t}\frac{dB_t}{B_t}$ or $(\frac{dB_t}{B_t})^2$ terms in the third equality because there is no dW_t term in dB_t. Further,

$$
E_t^B\left[d\left(\frac{V_t}{B_t}\right)\right] = 0
$$

since $\frac{V_t}{B_t}$ is a martingale, so that $\mu_V(t) = r_t$, and

$$
E_t^B[dV_t] = r_t V_t dt.
$$

The theorem extends easily to processes dependent on multiple Wiener processes.

1.1.7 *Reflection Principle*

It would be fitting to conclude this brief theoretical section with the Reflection Principle, which is very useful for visualising barrier products.

Specifically, consider a Wiener process W_t. Then we have that the probability

$$
P\left(\max_{0 < t \le T} W_t \ge M \text{ and } W_T < K\right) = P(W_T \ge 2M - K).
$$

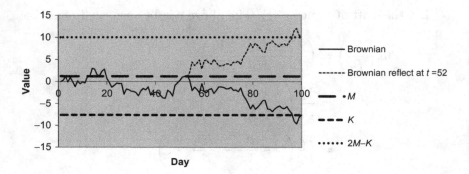

Figure 1.1:   Reflection of Brownian Motion.
Note: Path of Brownian variate and its counterpart reflected at $W_t = M$.

This can be seen from Figure 1.1, since after crossing M at time t $(0 < t < T)$, a Wiener process has equal likelihood of following the path that drops to K at time T or rises to $2M - K$.

In a similar way, we obtain

$$P\left(\min_{0<t\leq T} W_t < m \text{ and } W_T \geq K\right) = P(W_T < 2m - K).$$

The Reflection Principle leads to the following conclusion

$$P\left(\max_{0<t\leq T} W_t \geq M\right) = P\left(\max_{0<t\leq T} W_t \geq M \text{ and } W_T < M\right)$$

$$+ P\left(\max_{0<t\leq T} W_t \geq M \text{ and } W_T \geq M\right)$$

$$= P(W_T \geq M) + P(W_T \geq M)$$

$$= 2P(W_T \geq M).$$

This leads to the intuition that a one-touch option (i.e. an option that pays 1 if an asset breaches a barrier at any time during its life) is approximately worth two digital options (i.e. an option that pays 1 if an asset breaches a barrier at expiry itself). This is only an approximation since in practice discounting matters, and also the process for the underlying is unlikely to be normal.

However, the above illustrates how the Reflection Principle may be useful for understanding barrier products in a normal model. It also has applications for understanding barrier pricing in a lognormal model. We shall cover barrier products in more detail in Chapter 3 on replication and then further in Chapter 7 on the local stochastic volatility model.

1.2 Market Quantities

We will consider standard market instruments in detail in Chapter 2. Standard market instruments form the basis of hedges used to offset the risks for derivatives and exotic products. As such, it is necessary for models to be calibrated so that they recover the prices of standard market instruments. For now, it is however useful to give the reader a flavour as to the types of quantities of interest for different asset classes. For example, in order to price an interest rate derivative, what quantity does a model need to generate at any given future time? What about in the foreign exchange world?

1.2.1 *Interest Rates*

Consider a payment of €1 (or $1, £1, etc.) due at a future point in time T. This is usually worth less than €1 today, since if you have €1 today, you can lend it and receive interest. Furthermore, the longer the maturity (i.e. time at which payment is due), the lower the value is today.

In this way, we can define the discount curve $D(t, T)$ as the value at time t of future payments due at time T. (See Figure 1.2 for an example of a discount curve.) In particular, the current discount curve $D(0, T)$ is determined from the prices of linear traded instruments (deposits, futures and swaps) to be discussed in Chapter 2.

Now, let us consider a typical interest rate derivative. It would involve a payoff dependent on either the forward rate or swap rate as seen at a future point in time.

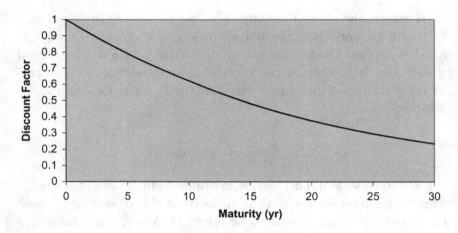

Figure 1.2:   Euro discount curve (June 2007).

Note: This is monotonically decreasing as a function of maturity, reflecting positive interest rates.

Source: Bloomberg data.

A forward rate from period T to period $T+\tau$ is set at time T and paid at time $T+\tau$. The benchmarks are Euribor for euros and Libor for dollars, sterling and yen (for which Tibor is also used), based on the average of rates quoted for interbank lending.[4] Its value at time t is given by

$$f(t,T,T+\tau) = \frac{\left(\dfrac{D(t,T)}{D(t,T+\tau)} - 1 \right)}{\tau}.$$

This follows from no-arbitrage arguments. After all, if we deposit up to time $T + \tau$ or deposit up to time T and enter into a forward rate agreement to deposit from time T to time $T + \tau$, these two approaches must yield the same result at time $T + \tau$ giving

$$D(T,T) = D(T,T+\tau)(1 + f(T,T,T+\tau)\tau),$$

from which our equation above for the value at time t follows.[5]

---

[4]For convenience, we shall hereafter refer to the above benchmark rates generically as the Libor rate.

[5]Note that $D(T,T) = 1$.

A standard swap comprises an exchange of payments between two counterparties. One party pays a fixed rate, and the other pays a floating rate based on Libor (or Euribor). A (par) swap rate is the fair value fixed rate that causes the swap to be worth 0 at inception.

Let the floating payments be at dates $\{T_i^*\}_{i=1}^M$ with $\tau_i^* = T_i^* - T_{i-1}^*$, then the floating leg is worth

$$\sum_{i=1}^M f(t, T_{i-1}^*, T_i^*) \tau_i^* D(t, T_i^*) = \sum_{i=1}^M \left(\frac{D(t, T_{i-1}^*)}{D(t, T_i^*)} - 1 \right) D(t, T_i^*)$$

$$= \sum_{i=1}^M (D(t, T_{i-1}^*) - D(t, T_i^*))$$

$$= D(t, T_0^*) - D(t, T_M^*).$$

Typically, the fixed leg and floating leg do not have the same frequency (e.g. for dollar swaps, the fixed leg pays semi-annually whilst the floating leg pays quarterly). Let the fixed payments be at dates $\{T_i\}_{i=1}^N$ with $\tau_i = T_i - T_{i-1}$, $T_0 = T_0^*$, $T_N = T_M^*$ and R be the fixed rate. Then the fixed leg is worth

$$R \sum_{i=1}^N \tau_i D(t, T_i).$$

Thus, the par swap rate (from setting the value of the fixed leg equal to the floating leg) is

$$R(t) = \frac{D(t, T_0) - D(t, T_N)}{\sum_{i=1}^N \tau_i D(t, T_i)}.$$

It follows that both the Libor rate and swap rate at a future point in time t are fully determined by the discount curve at that time. Thus, it is sufficient for any interest rate model to produce the discount curve $D(t, T)$ at any future point in time t.

1.2.2 *Spot Quantities*

In equities, a derivative contract typically has terms that refer to the spot price, i.e. the price for immediate purchase of the stock. In foreign exchange, the spot FX rate is usually the referenced underlying.[6] To this end, a model of the underlying directly makes sense.

However, even if a contract refers to a forward price as underlying, it can be seen that this can be obtained by no arbitrage from spot prices and interest rates. For example, let S_t be the spot FX rate[7] at time t, $D(t,T)$ be the domestic discount factor for maturity T, and $D^f(t,T)$ be the foreign discount factor for maturity T. Then the forward FX rate for delivery at T is

$$F(t,T) = S_t \frac{D^f(t,T)}{D(t,T)}.$$

This can easily be seen. If you have $D(t,T)$ of foreign currency, you can convert it to $S_t D(t,T)$ in domestic currency immediately and deposit up to maturity T so that it is worth S_t at time T. Alternatively, you can deposit it and earn foreign interest so that it is worth $\frac{D(t,T)}{D^f(t,T)}$ in foreign currency at time T, and agree to sell it at the forward rate of F. These two approaches must yield the same result, hence our equation above for the forward FX rate.

In equities, the consideration is similar but we now have to deal with discrete dividends. After all, in the real world, a stock pays dividends on discrete dates, e.g. twice a year. If you enter into a forward on the stock, you are not entitled to the dividends. Thus, the value of the forward must be adjusted (reduced) for dividends. For example, if dividends of amount a_i are due at times $\{T_i\}_{i=1}^N$ prior to the delivery time T of the forward, then the value of the forward is

$$F_S(t,T) = \frac{1}{D(t,T)} \left(S_t - \sum_{i=1}^N a_i D(t,T_i) \right).$$

In practice, dividends in the near term are treated discretely but over longer horizons (e.g. after two years), it is difficult to accurately forecast dividends on the stock (and this may change depending on

---

[6] Although spot often means for settlement in two business days in FX.
[7] I.e. number of units of domestic currency per unit of foreign currency.

the fortunes of the company). So, it is often the case that a continuous dividend yield is assumed beyond a certain horizon. Alternatively, discrete dividends are treated but the amounts are taken as proportional to the prevailing stock price.

From the above, for equities and foreign exchange, it is only necessary to model the spot price process (together with stochastic rates if necessary). It is never necessary to model the entire forward price process of equity or FX for different maturities.

For liquid market instruments (i.e. equity and FX options),[8] it is the volatility of the forward that affects the price. Provided we are not dealing with very long expiries and concerned with the possibility of early exercise and how stochastic rates affect forward volatility and terminal correlations, it is often acceptable to ignore stochastic rates (or rather incorporate them in the forward process for a given delivery date which we model instead of spot). Chapter 10 discusses the effect of stochastic rates in more detail.

1.2.3   *Asset Forward Prices*

It is tempting to extend our argument of Section 1.2.2 to the context of commodities. However, the buy and hold argument above does not work so well. For example, agricultural products are perishable. So, it is not possible to borrow money, buy some wheat and hold to whatever maturities desired. Electricity cannot even be stored, and if too much electricity is generated, it may even be necessary to pay to give away electricity or risk having the generator burn down! In this way, the relationship between spot and forward prices in commodities is much looser and we cannot just treat forwards as being spot grown over time at some appropriate funding and with some deterministic adjustments (e.g. for storage cost).

Instead, it is necessary to model the whole of the forward curve $F_C(t, T)$, i.e. the price of forward contracts in a commodity with delivery at time T as seen at time t. This makes commodities modelling similar to interest rates modelling. Indeed, for really liquid

---

[8]As will be discussed in Chapter 2.

commodities (e.g. oil), an adaptation of the Health-Jarrow-Morton (HJM) framework for rates (as discussed in Chapter 8) is often used.

We should not however belittle the importance of accepting the differences in the two markets. For one, commodities tend to have far higher volatilities and also be subject to seasonality effects.[9] Further, commodities are generally far less liquid than rates, so there is less data to inform a calibration of the models, nor is there always a market to reliably hedge various aspects of risk. We shall not dwell much further on the topic of commodities in this book, but hopefully an appreciation of the nature of commodities modelling will help.

It is worth remarking that for FX, we cannot actually posit a model for the entire forward curve $F(t, T)$ since the dynamics are fully specified by the dynamics of spot FX and the domestic and foreign rates. In equities, positing a model for the forward curve $F_S(t, T)$ will require stochastic dividends with sufficient volatility (too much in practice) to account for any discrepancies with the dynamics of spot and the domestic rate. In this sense, commodities modelling is different from equity or FX modelling.

1.2.4 *Volatilities*

Section 1.1.2 discussed how hedging leads to the elimination of the random component in the value of a hedged portfolio, and hence the Black–Scholes PDE for the price f_t of a derivative

$$\frac{\partial f_t}{\partial t} + r_t S_t \frac{\partial f_t}{\partial S_t} + \frac{1}{2} \frac{\partial^2 f_t}{\partial S_t^2} \sigma^2(S_t, t) = r_t f(S_t, t).$$

Notice that this equation does not have a term based on the 'true' drift $\mu(S_t, t)$ of the underlying S_t, i.e. it is irrelevant if we think the underlying is likely to appreciate or depreciate in value. That is what hedging is about.

However, the volatility term $\sigma(S_t, t)$ appears in the equation. This is not entirely surprising, since hedging involves maintaining at all times an amount $\Delta(S_t, t) = \frac{\partial f_t}{\partial S_t}$ of the underlying, this amount

---

[9]E.g. higher prices of oil in winter due to increased consumption for heating.

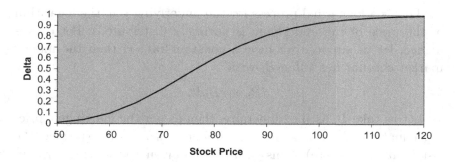

Figure 1.3:   Delta for call option (Strike 80, Expiry 1.5y).
Note: The delta of a call option increases from 0 for very low spot and approaches 1 as spot increases to infinity.

changing with S_t. It follows that the higher the volatility, the more frequent and larger the amount of rebalancing of the portfolio we need.

It should be noted that when hedging, we are buying high and selling low. For example, Figure 1.3 shows the delta profile of a European call option on a stock below (i.e. an instrument giving one the right to buy the stock at a given strike on the expiry date). The higher the value of the underlying, the greater the value of the option. Hence, to hedge our option, we need to hold a greater amount of the underlying. This means we have to buy more of the stock when its price increases and sell more of the stock when its price decreases.

Now, even ignoring transaction costs, and assuming we can trade continuously in size and time,[10] we still need to know when to buy and sell. Suppose we buy if stock increases by an infinitesimal dS and sell when stock drops by the same. Then we will always be buying at $S + dS$ and selling at $S - dS$. This is guaranteed to cost us money whenever the stock moves. In this way, the value of the option can be seen to be the result of hedging, the cost of which depends on the volatility of the underlying.

Let us concern ourselves with the dynamics

$$dS_t = \mu S_t dt + \sigma S_t dW_t.$$

---

[10]I.e. we can rebalance infinitesimally small amounts instantaneously.

This is a lognormal process for the underlying (i.e. the logarithm of the price of the underlying is normally distributed). For convenience, let us suppose we have a constant rate r, then the money market account has value B_t with

$$dB_t = rB_t dt.$$

Let us take B_t as the numeraire, then as per the martingale pricing equation, $\frac{S_t}{B_t}$ is a martingale under this measure (termed the risk-neutral measure). This means that given the Wiener process W_t^B under the new measure, we have

$$d\left(\frac{S_t}{B_t}\right) = \frac{S_t}{B_t}\left(\frac{dS_t}{S_t} - \frac{dB_t}{B_t}\right) = (\mu - r)\frac{S_t}{B_t}dt + \sigma\frac{S_t}{B_t}dW_t^B$$

$$= \sigma\frac{S_t}{B_t}dW_t^B.$$

This gives $\mu = r$, so that $dS_t = rS_t dt + \sigma S_t dW_t^B$ and $d\log S_t = (r - \frac{1}{2}\sigma^2)dt + \sigma dW_t^B$ (via Ito's Lemma).

A call option has payoff $C_T = \max(S_T - K, 0)$ at time T. This has value

$$\frac{C_t}{B_t} = E_t^B\left[\frac{C_T}{B_T}\right]$$

$$= e^{-r(T-t)}E_t^B[\max(S_T - K, 0)]$$

$$= e^{-r(T-t)}\int_{-\infty}^{\infty}\max\left(S_t e^{(r-\frac{1}{2}\sigma^2)(T-t)+\sigma z\sqrt{T-t}} - K, 0\right)$$

$$\times\frac{1}{\sqrt{2\pi}}e^{-\frac{1}{2}z^2}dz$$

$$= e^{-r(T-t)}\int_{z^*}^{\infty}\left(S_t e^{(r-\frac{1}{2}\sigma^2)(T-t)+\sigma z\sqrt{T-t}} - K\right)\frac{1}{\sqrt{2\pi}}e^{-\frac{1}{2}z^2}dz$$

$$= e^{-r(T-t)}\left[S_t e^{(r-\frac{1}{2}\sigma^2)(T-t)}\int_{z^*}^{\infty}e^{\sigma z\sqrt{T-t}}\frac{1}{\sqrt{2\pi}}e^{-\frac{1}{2}z^2}dz\right.$$

$$\left. - K\int_{z^*}^{\infty}\frac{1}{\sqrt{2\pi}}e^{-\frac{1}{2}z^2}dz\right]$$

$$= e^{-r(T-t)}\left[S_t e^{r(T-t)}\int_{z^*}^{\infty}\frac{1}{\sqrt{2\pi}}e^{-\frac{1}{2}(z-\sigma\sqrt{T-t})^2}dz - KN(-z^*)\right]$$

$$= e^{-r(T-t)} \left[S_t e^{r(T-t)} \int_{z^*-\sigma\sqrt{T-t}}^{\infty} \frac{1}{\sqrt{2\pi}} e^{-\frac{1}{2}y^2} dy - KN(-z^*) \right]$$

$$= e^{-r(T-t)} [S_t e^{r(T-t)} N(-z^* + \sigma\sqrt{T-t}) - KN(-z^*)],$$

where

$$S_t e^{\left(r-\frac{1}{2}\sigma^2\right)(T-t)+\sigma z^*\sqrt{T-t}} = K$$

$$\Rightarrow z^* = \frac{\log\left(\frac{K}{S_t}\right) - \left(r - \frac{1}{2}\sigma^2\right)(T-t)}{\sigma\sqrt{T-t}}$$

and we have used the change of variable $y = z - \sigma\sqrt{T-t}$.

This gives the celebrated Black–Scholes formula for the price of a call option as

$$C_t = S_t N(-z^* + \sigma\sqrt{T-t}) - e^{-r(T-t)} KN(-z^*).$$

It is more common to write this as

$$C_t = S_t N(d_1) - e^{-r(T-t)} KN(d_1 - \sigma\sqrt{T-t}),$$

where

$$d_1 = \frac{\log\left(\frac{S_t}{K}\right) + \left(r + \frac{1}{2}\sigma^2\right)(T-t)}{\sigma\sqrt{T-t}}.$$

For completeness, it is worth mentioning that the Black–Scholes formula for a put option with payoff $P_T = \max(K - S_T, 0)$ is

$$P_t = e^{-r(T-t)} KN(-d_1 + \sigma\sqrt{T-t}) - S_t N(-d_1),$$

which we could obtain in the same manner.

Whereas we have used deterministic interest rates above, this is not required. If we had stochastic interest rates, it is convenient to work under the T-forward measure, i.e. with the numeraire being the discount bond $D(t,T)$ maturing at time T. This is convenient since at time T, the value of a forward with delivery T is simply the value of the underlying, so that we have

$$C_T = \max(S_T - K, 0) = \max(F(T,T) - K, 0)$$

and $D(T,T) = 1$.

This gives via the martingale pricing equation:

$$\frac{C_t}{D(t,T)} = E_t^T \left[\frac{C_T}{D(T,T)} \right]$$

$$= E_t^T [\max(F_T - K, 0)]$$

$$= \int_{-\infty}^{\infty} \max \left(F(t,T)e^{-\frac{1}{2}\sigma^2(T-t)+\sigma z\sqrt{T-t}} - K, 0 \right) \frac{1}{\sqrt{2\pi}} e^{-\frac{1}{2}z^2} dz$$

$$= F(t,T)N(-z^* + \sigma\sqrt{T-t}) - KN(-z^*),$$

where

$$z^* = \frac{\log\left(\frac{K}{F(t,T)}\right) + \frac{1}{2}\sigma^2(T-t)}{\sigma\sqrt{T-t}},$$

and our derivation is along the same lines as before, so we get the similar looking equation

$$C_t = D(t,T)[F(t,T)N(-z^* + \sigma\sqrt{T-t}) - KN(-z^*)].$$

This explains the earlier remark that to price a vanilla option in equities or FX, it is only the volatility of the forward process that matters. Incidentally, our use of the forward process means we have incorporated equity dividends and the effect of the domestic and foreign rates in our new formulation.

It is worth pointing out that whereas the market has long since moved away from a pure lognormal model for equity and FX options, it is common to quote option prices in terms of implied volatilities. This can be seen as an input into a Black box, since a given implied volatility will give a unique price given the rest of the market data (e.g. rates, spot, dividends). After all, the price of a call or put is a monotonic function of implied volatility. There is logic to quoting implied volatilities rather than prices since prices for options of different strikes obviously vary a lot more than implied volatilities, so it is easier to visualise an implied volatility surface. Figure 1.4 shows an example of an equity volatility surface. The fact that implied volatilities are different for different strikes suggests that the lognormal model does not adequately capture market dynamics. (We shall explore implied volatility and the models needed to capture

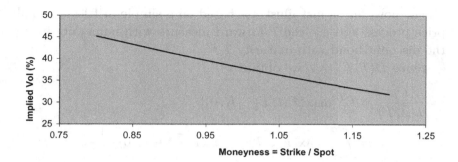

Figure 1.4: Implied vol for 6-month option on S&P 500 (25 February 2009).
Note: Notice how implied vols are higher for lower strikes.
Source: Bloomberg data.

different volatility behaviours in subsequent chapters, particularly from Chapter 5 onwards.)

Whilst in equity and FX, it has been common to quote in terms of lognormal volatilities, in interest rates it is more common to assume that absolute volatility remains the same, regardless of the level of rates. Rebonato and de Guillaume [RdG10] show in a study of historical data that for levels of rates between 2% and 6%, dynamics of rates are approximately normal, whereas outside this region, dynamics of rates are approximately lognormal. In any case, it is common to quote normal implied volatilities to represent the prices of swaptions.[11]

To this end, let us consider the normal process for the forward of the underlying with SDE

$$dF(t,T) = \mu dt + \sigma dW_t.$$

As before, we can show via the martingale pricing equation that using the generic numeraire A_t, we obtain for the corresponding Wiener process W_t^A the SDE

$$d\left(\frac{F(t,T)}{A_t}\right) = \sigma dW_t^A.$$

---

[11]More on swaptions in Chapter 2.

For now, let us just illustrate based on a simple driftless normal price process and use the T-forward measure with numeraire being the discount bond with maturity T.[12]

Since $D(T, T) = 1$, we obtain

$$\frac{C_t}{D(t, T)} = E_t^T[\max(F(t, T) - K, 0)]$$

$$= \int_{-\infty}^{\infty} \max(F(t, T) + \sigma z\sqrt{T - t} - K, 0)\frac{1}{\sqrt{2\pi}}e^{-\frac{1}{2}z^2}dz$$

$$= \int_{z^*}^{\infty} (F(t, T) + \sigma z\sqrt{T - t} - K)\frac{1}{\sqrt{2\pi}}e^{-\frac{1}{2}z^2}dz$$

$$= (F(t, T) - K)N(-z^*) + \sigma\sqrt{\frac{T - t}{2\pi}}\int_{z^*}^{\infty} ze^{-\frac{1}{2}z^2}dz$$

$$= (F(t, T) - K)N(-z^*) + \sigma\sqrt{\frac{T - t}{2\pi}}\left[-e^{-\frac{1}{2}z^2}\right]_{z^*}^{\infty}$$

$$= (F(t, T) - K)N(-z^*) + \sigma\sqrt{\frac{T - t}{2\pi}}e^{-\frac{1}{2}(z^*)^2},$$

where

$$F(t, T) + \sigma z^*\sqrt{T - t} = K$$

$$\Rightarrow z^* = \frac{K - F}{\sigma\sqrt{T - t}}.$$

So, the price of a call option under the normal model is given by

$$C_t = D(t, T)\left[(F(t, T) - K)N(-z^*) + \sigma\sqrt{\frac{T - t}{2\pi}}e^{-\frac{1}{2}(z^*)^2}\right].$$

1.2.5   *Correlations*

Derivatives are contracts that depend on some underlying. These contracts can depend on more than one underlying. In this case, the

---

[12]We shall see in Chapter 2 that for a caplet, we need to choose the $T + \tau$-forward measure whilst for a swaption (i.e. option on a swap) we need to choose the annuity as numeraire.

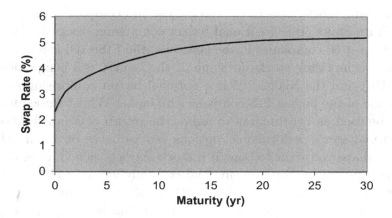

Figure 1.5: US swap curve (4 January 2005).

Note: Notice how interest rates tend to be higher for longer maturities. This is often the case.

Source: Bloomberg data.

correlations between the underlyings can be relevant. There can be good reasons for a derivative to depend on multiple underlyings.

Consider for example a contract that pays $\max(10y\text{Rate} - 2y\text{Rate}, 0)$. Such a contract can be relevant because, for example, interest rate curves have historically tended to be upward sloping, i.e. rates for longer maturities tend to be higher. (See Figure 1.5 for an illustration.) And perhaps an investor wishes to take a position that benefits if rates remain upward sloping.

Our spread option has variance

$$\begin{aligned}
\text{var}(R_1 - R_2) &= \text{var}(R_1) + \text{var}(R_2) - 2\text{cov}(R_1, R_2) \\
&= \text{var}(R_1) + \text{var}(R_2) \\
&\quad - 2\text{corr}(R_1, R_2)\sqrt{\text{var}(R_1)\text{var}(R_2)}.
\end{aligned}$$

So clearly its volatility depends on the correlation between the two interest rates. In particular, the volatility (and hence price) will be much lower if correlation is close to 100%.

Consider next an option on a basket of stocks. These are not uncommon. For example, the S&P 500 is a notional basket comprising stocks in some of the largest 500 companies in the US, the Euro Stoxx 50 is a notional basket comprising stocks in some of the largest 50 companies in the eurozone, the FtSe 100 is a notional basket comprising stocks in some of the largest 100 companies in the UK, and the Nikkei 225 is a notional basket comprising stocks in some of the largest 225 companies in Japan. Whilst these indices can be used as benchmarks to assess the return of a portfolio or a fund manager's performance, options can be based on them. After all, perhaps you want to benefit if stock markets rallied, even if you do not know whether an individual company will do well. Or more likely, an investor with a large portfolio of stocks may want some protection against a general decline in the markets (e.g. via a put option on Euro Stoxx 50).

In the same manner, it is possible to have an option written on a bespoke basket of stocks. This will lower the volatility (and hence price) of the option[13] since correlation between the components is invariably less than 100%. Specifically, if $H_t = \sum_{i=1}^{N} w_i S_t^i$ is a basket comprising the stocks S_t^i with weights w_i, then

$$\mathrm{var}(H_t) = \sum_{i=1}^{N} w_i^2 \mathrm{var}(S_t^i) + 2 \sum_{i=1}^{N} \sum_{j=1}^{i-1} w_i w_j \mathrm{cov}(S_t^i, S_t^j)$$

$$= \sum_{i=1}^{N} w_i^2 \mathrm{var}(S_t^i) + 2 \sum_{i=1}^{N} \sum_{j=1}^{i-1} w_i w_j \mathrm{corr}(S_t^i, S_t^j)$$

$$\times \sqrt{\mathrm{var}(S_t^i)\mathrm{var}(S_t^j)}.$$

For illustration, take $w_i = \frac{1}{N}$, $\mathrm{var}(S_t^i) = \sigma^2$, then

$$\mathrm{var}(H_t) = \frac{\sigma^2}{N} + \frac{2\sigma^2}{N^2} \sum_{i=1}^{N} \sum_{j=1}^{i-1} \mathrm{corr}(S_i, S_j)$$

$$< \frac{\sigma^2}{N}\left(1 + \frac{2}{N}\frac{N(N-1)}{2}\right) = \sigma^2.$$

---

[13]Versus a weighted average of the vols of the underlyings.

In a different context, correlation can be relevant when considering long-dated products dependent on equity or FX options, since the correlation between interest rates and spot equity/FX can affect the terminal correlation between spot and forward rates at future times, and hence the value of certain termination features. This is the province of Chapter 10.

1.2.6   *Calibration*

Derivatives pricing is heavily based on the concept of hedging. In Section 1.2.4, we discussed how the drift of the underlying is not important for purposes of pricing an option. On the other hand, since we hedge derivatives via simpler instruments, we must recover the prices of these instruments. At a basic level, any model must consistently price linear products. As discussed in Section 1.2.1 and 1.2.2, we can obtain no-arbitrage prices for equity and FX forwards and also for forward rate agreements and forward starting swaps. It follows that their prices must be consistent with the discount curve as well as spot equity and FX rates.

Books in rates modelling have historically tended to discuss equilibrium (i.e. where interest rates will tend towards some 'equilibrium' level not necessarily consistent with forward rates) and no-arbitrage models (i.e. where the discount curve today is recovered). For example, the original Vasicek model $dr_t = \kappa(L - r_t)dt + \sigma dW_t$ comes under the former whilst the Hull–White model $dr_t = \kappa(\theta(t) - r_t)dt + \sigma dW_t$ comes under the latter. After all, a single L cannot be used to fit the entire discount curve today, whereas $\theta(t)$ has been introduced to exactly fit the discount curve today. However, whatever the merits of forward Libor and swap rates as predictors of future interest rates, a model cannot be used to hedge exotics with simpler products unless it can recover the prices of linear instruments above.

At the next level, we are interested in hedging exotic options with simpler options. For example, vanilla equity and FX options are the basic instruments in their respective markets. So, a model should aim to recover the prices of these products to a fair degree of accuracy, since this determines the price of the exotic option. This is the essence of calibration. We shall see in Chapters 5 to 7 that recovering the prices of vanilla products is not sufficient to correctly price exotics, as different models could recover these prices, but some can imply unrealistic dynamics for the underlying that affect the prices of exotic options accordingly.

On the other hand, in the interest rates world, it is not always possible to calibrate to the prices of all liquid instruments. For example, swaptions are liquid but in interest rates, swaptions exercise into swaps of different maturities, in addition to having different expiries. This leads to a proliferation of the number of swaptions whose prices we seek to recover, and hence far greater difficulty in recovering these prices. We shall see in Chapters 8 and 9 that it is not necessary for the pricing of various exotics to calibrate to the entire swaption grid. Indeed, it may not be desirable, since with the sheer abundance of points in an entire swaption grid, it is likely that some price information is stale, and calibration to the whole grid can thus lead to aberrant model parameters (and hence dynamics) when we try to recover both up-to-date and stale prices simultaneously.

Throughout the rest of the book, the reader shall see that calibration is quite an art as is modelling. For example, if we wish to fully describe the dynamics of a stock, perhaps we need jumps to explain short end behaviour, stochastic volatility and (its correlation *vis-à-vis* the underlying) to explain the downward sloping volatility skew (i.e. lower vol for higher strike) and skew persistence over time, and even jumps in the stochastic volatility to explain how volatility tends to remain elevated after a crisis. But how can one realistically implement such a model with a robust method of calibrating parameters to reflect changes in market conditions, as well as achieve pricing within the timescales needed for trading these products? Ultimately, the art of modelling and calibration involves compromises and understanding when one needs to take account of certain features and when one is justified to ignore these.

I hope to be able to provide some insights on this to the reader in subsequent chapters.

1.3   Consolidation

1.3.1   *Summary*

This chapter has two distinct parts. In the first, we set out the fundamental theory behind the pricing of derivatives — i.e. if you can set up a replicating portfolio for a derivative's payoff, then the value of the portfolio gives the value of the derivative, since risk-free profits (arbitrage) should not persist. We have also discussed the various machinery for setting up the pricing framework. First, we have introduced the Wiener process — being continuous with independent random increments that are normally distributed. This is a key building block (namely the random component) of stochastic calculus, and Ito's Lemma gives the key difference between stochastic calculus and standard calculus. We then moved on to derive the Black–Scholes PDE by eliminating the random component in the process for a financial derivative via holding a suitable amount of the hedge instrument. Thereby, we have shown that the drift of the underlying is irrelevant when pricing a derivative. We have generalised the formulation via the martingale representation theorem — i.e. any derivative can be attained by self-financing trading strategies, so a relative asset (i.e. asset over numeraire) is a martingale in the measure corresponding to that numeraire.

We have then introduced the Radon–Nikodym derivative (basically a ratio of numeraire assets) that should be multiplied onto a payoff to effect a change of measure. Girsanov's Theorem tells us a change of measure just involves a change of drift (based on the volatility of the Radon–Nikodym derivative), whereas the volatility of the underlying remains unchanged. We then showed how the Feynman–Kac Theorem relates the martingale pricing equation to the Black–Scholes PDE. We concluded this part by describing the Reflection Principle, which relates the probability of the maximum/minimum of a Wiener process over a period being below/above some value to the probability of the Wiener process itself at the end of the period — the latter being easier to evaluate.

The second part is a lot less theoretical. The focus is on what quantities a model must produce to be adequate for pricing derivatives. Starting with interest rates, we showed how knowing discount factors for all future maturities at a given time point is necessary and sufficient to price any security. In particular, contracts tend to refer to Libor and swap rates, which are functions of discount factors. It follows that an interest rate model must be able to produce discount factors for all maturities at a future time. In contrast, in the equities and FX worlds, we generally need only the spot price/FX rate — which forms the basis of most contracts. In FX, the spot FX rate and domestic and foreign discount curves determine all forward FX rates. In equities, the spot price, domestic curve and dividends schedule determine all forward prices. For an asset (e.g. oil, wheat) however, it may be necessary to model the entire forward curve (*a la* interest rates) since cash-and-carry may not work (e.g. agricultural products being perishable).

We then discussed volatilities. Notice that volatility remains as a term in the Black–Scholes PDE. Indeed, it increases the cost of hedging and hence the price of the derivative, since it increases the frequency of hedge rebalancing required to maintain an amount of underlying according to the derivative's delta. We derived the formula for the price of a call option under the Black–Scholes model and also under the normal model — the latter being particularly used in the interest rates world. We then came to correlations which are important for products on multiple underlying. For payoffs based on the difference between two rates, higher correlation lowers the price; for baskets based on a (weighted) sum, higher correlation increases the price. We end with a brief discussion of the main considerations in calibration. Basically, any model must reproduce forwards exactly (i.e. forward FX rates, equity prices and the forward discount curve); as for options, we want a reasonably good fit to vanillas that form the hedges for the exotic product at hand, since that will be the cost of implementing the hedge. And calibration needs to be stable — i.e. the model parameters should not be too different if the market has not changed.

1.3.2 *Exercises*

(1) Find $\text{cov}(W_t, W_T)$ for $t < T$.

(2) Find $P(\min_{0 < t \leq T} W_t \leq m)$.

(3) Show that the formula for the price of a put option with payoff of $P_T = \max(K - S_T, 0)$ at time T is $P_t = e^{-r(T-t)} KN(-d_1 + \sigma\sqrt{T-t}) - S_t N(-d_1)$, where

$$d_1 = \frac{\log\left(\frac{S_t}{K}\right) + \left(r + \frac{1}{2}\sigma^2\right)(T - t)}{\sigma\sqrt{T - t}}.$$

(4) Consider a derivative $V(S_t, r_t, t)$ dependent on the (non-dividend-paying) stock price S_t and short rate r_t with SDEs given by $dS_t = \mu(t)S_t dt + \sigma S_t dW_t$ and $dr_t = \kappa(\theta(t) - r_t)dt + \lambda dU_t$ respectively with $dW_t dU_t = \rho dt$. Using a hedging argument (say with a stock and a discount bond), find the PDE for $V(S_t, r_t, t)$. (We will discuss the short rate model in Chapter 8.)

(5) Consider the SDE $dX_t = \mu X_t dt + \sigma X_t dW_t$ for the FX rate. By considering the domestic and foreign money market accounts with SDEs $dB_t = r_t B_t dt$ and $dB_t^f = r_t^f B_t^f dt$ and using Girsanov's Theorem, show that the drift under the domestic risk-neutral measure is $\mu = r_t - r_t^f$.

2

Standard Market Instruments

"A swaption is a rare type of goose found only in Peru."

Derivatives pricing is best understood in the context of traded products. After all, the main underpinning of pricing theory is that a derivative costs as much as the replicating portfolio. So, naturally, the question one must ask is: What products can we use to create this replicating portfolio?

When an institution sells flow options (i.e. liquidly traded plain vanilla options), it hedges by dynamically trading in the underlying linear products (i.e. products with no optionality). Therefore, any model must fully recover the prices of linear products in the market. When an institution sells exotic options, it hedges with the underlying linear products and the flow options as well. As such, it is necessary for a pricing model to be calibrated (i.e. by choosing the model parameters) so that it recovers the prices of flow options reasonably well.

This chapter covers the more liquid linear and options products traded in the derivatives markets, partly as they are of practical relevance, but also to anchor the discussion in a real-world setting. We start with a discussion of the yield curve, since discounting affects the prices of all assets, and move on naturally to interest rates options. We then consider foreign exchange options and market conventions related to these. And we conclude by considering equities. When I did my Masters degree, a fellow student once remarked, "I know how to price a swaption but I do not know what it is." And another replied, "A swaption is a rare type of goose found only in Peru." Hopefully, the reader will not be left with the same sentiments.

2.1   Linear Interest Rates

Interest rates products exist since institutions need to manage the cost of borrowing. Typically, interest rates are not static but vary based on economic circumstances. They tend to fall during a recession as central banks try to stimulate the economy and tend to rise in times of a boom as a consequence of greater demand for money and also since central banks will raise rates to control inflation. Also, borrowing for different maturities tends to attract different rates. Some investors have a natural demand for products with long maturities (e.g. pension funds) due to their long-term liabilities and others more naturally prefer shorter term deposits (e.g. general insurers with frequent claims to meet).

In this section, we will consider some of the products used by institutions to manage their interest rates risk. We are referring to borrowing between counterparties with high credit rating (AA), rather than borrowing by risky counterparties which attracts higher rates of interest. Prior to the credit crunch of 2008, it was possible for AA counterparties to borrow at Libor, but these days collateralisation is necessary and Libor is merely a benchmark. We shall ignore these subtleties for most of the book as their treatment introduces an unnecessary complexity into our discussion, but the topic is sufficiently important to warrant treatment in a separate chapter (Chapter 12). As such, we shall assume in the remainder of the chapters that it is possible for an AA-rated counterparty to borrow and lend at Libor, and discussions regarding interest rates shall be based on this borrowing.

2.1.1   *Deposits, Futures, and Swaps*

Deposits, futures, and swaps are amongst the most liquid instruments in the interest rates market. Whilst futures are exchange traded, deposits and swaps tend to be traded mainly via the over-the-counter (OTC) market (i.e. bilateral deals between a client and a financial institution).

Deposits

Deposits are short-term lending (of less than 1 year). They are quoted at a rate r (e.g. 3%) for a fixed term τ (e.g. 1 month, 3 months or 6 months) based on simple compounding, so that accrued interest is $r\tau$.

Futures

Futures are standardised exchange traded products. They tend to be for 3-month terms and have maturities mostly on specific IMM[1] dates (i.e. third Wednesday) in the months March, June, September, and December. They represent the forward rate for a 3-month period starting from the maturity of the contract and based on an accrual fraction of $\tau = 0.25$ and a notional $N = 1,000,000$. The quoted price of a future is $1 - f$, where f is the future rate. Since they are exchange traded, there is daily margining. Specifically, if the future rate is f^* at the end of the day, then if you are long the future, you are due to receive from the exchange $N(1 - f^*)\tau - N(1 - f)\tau = N(f - f^*)\tau$ (or pay the exchange if the amount is negative).

Notice that in a future, there is no discounting. If the Libor rate at maturity T (and for period from T to $T + \tau$) is L_T, the value of a long future contract with price $1 - f$ is

$$E^B[(1 - L_T) - (1 - f)] = E^B[f - L_T],$$

where our numeraire is the money market account $B_t = e^{\int_0^t r_u du}$ which reflects the accrual of interest up to time t. Note that in contrast to typical OTC derivatives, we do not discount,[2] since the undiscounted changes in the future prices are settled daily.

---

[1]Abbreviation of International Monetary Market.
[2]I.e. divide the payoff by B_T.

This gives the fair value futures rate as

$$f = E^B[L_T]$$
$$= D(0,T)E^T[L_T B_T].$$

where the second equality is from a change to the T-forward measure[3] as per Section 1.1.4.

To simplify our discussion, let us first consider the case where we have to settle (i.e. receive the payoff) at time T instead of the natural payment time $T + \tau$ for a Libor rate.

Specifically, our fair value rate is $f^* = E^T[L_T]$. Notice that we are considering the measure with discount bond of maturity T as numeraire whereas $L_T = (\frac{1}{D(T,T+\tau)} - 1)/\tau$, so L_T is not a martingale under this measure.

We can utilise a change of measure to get

$$f^* = \frac{D(0,T+\tau)}{D(0,T)} E^{T+\tau}\left[L_T \frac{D(T,T)}{D(T,T+\tau)}\right]$$
$$= \frac{1}{1+L_0\tau} E^{T+\tau}[L_T(1+L_T\tau)]$$
$$= \frac{1}{1+L_0\tau}(L_0 + E^{T+\tau}[L_T^2]\tau)$$
$$= L_0 \frac{(1 + E^{T+\tau}[L_T^2]\tau/L_0)}{1+L_0\tau}.$$

The multiplier to the fair value Libor rate L_0 is greater than one and represents a convexity adjustment (more on this in Chapter 3). Suppose you are long the Libor rate. For this contract, you will be paid at time T. In contrast, for the standard forward contract, the payoff is at the end of $T + \tau$, so that its value at time T needs to be discounted via $\frac{1}{1+L_T\tau}$. Clearly, as rates rise, the discounting increases. Thus, a contract paying Libor at time T has a more desirable payoff then the standard forward contract. (Similarly, if rates fall, you lose more in a standard forward, since you discount your loss at a lower rate.) This means the fair value rate for a contract

---

[3]I.e. numeraire is discount bond with maturity T.

paying at time T must be higher than the fair value forward Libor rate, justifying our convexity adjustment.

For your futures contract, you settle the undiscounted difference daily, i.e. you get paid today rather than at time T or at time $T + \tau$. L_T and B_T are likely to be highly correlated.[4] Under the circumstances, the above argument means that the convexity adjustment is further increased, making the fair value futures rate f even higher than f^*, which is higher than the fair value forward rate. In fact, this effect is much bigger since a future tends to be on a 3-month rate (i.e. $\tau = 3m$) but maturity T can be a few years.

In practice, a simple model[5] is used to obtain the futures convexity adjustment or the trading desk just estimates it since the future is such a liquid market instrument.

Swaps

A swap is amongst the most liquid of interest rates instruments. Prior to the credit crunch, the bid offer spread for euro swap rates has been as low as a miniscule 0.2 basis point (although it has since increased these days).

A standard swap involves an exchange of cash flows between two counterparties, each paying one of the legs of the swap. One leg pays a fixed rate R and another leg pays a floating rate based on Libor. The floating and fixed legs do not typically have the same frequency. In euros, the fixed leg pays annually and the floating leg pays semi-annually. In US dollars, the fixed leg pays semi-annually and the floating leg pays quarterly.

The daycount fractions involved are based on different conventions for each leg. For US dollars and euros, it is 30/360 for the fixed leg and Act/360 for the floating leg. These conventions can differ for other currencies, e.g. in sterling Act/365 is used.[6]

---

[4]The high correlation is because it is likely that when the Libor rate moves up, so does the rest of the curve, and vice versa.

[5]E.g. the Ho–Lee model as discussed in Question 2 of the exercises.

[6]The daycount 30/360 is roughly translated to 30 days a month and 360 days a year, so that a 3-months interval typically has daycount fraction of 0.25. Act/360 is calculated as number of calendar days in period divided by 360, so that the daycount fraction

Swaps exist for a whole spectrum of expiries: 1 year, 2 years, 3 years, 5 years, 7 years, 10 years, 12 years, 15 years, 20 years, 25 years, 30 years, 40 years and even 50 years (for some currencies). Valuation of a swap has been discussed in Section 1.2.1.

2.1.2   *The Yield Curve*

The yield curve represents the cost of borrowing across various maturities. The idea is that given the most liquid market instruments (i.e. deposits, futures, and swaps), we wish to obtain discount factors for all maturities which reprice these instruments exactly. As discussed in Section 1.2.1, this provides the necessary information to price any other interest rate products that involve no optionality.

Typically, the yield curve is built from deposits with maturities up to between 1 month and 3 months (dependent on the nearest future maturity), futures thereafter up to a maturity of about 2 years, and swaps for longer maturities. See Figure 2.1 for a diagrammatic illustration of the various instruments used to build a yield curve.

Curve building requires us to obtain discount factors coupled with a means of interpolation that will ensure that all of the liquid

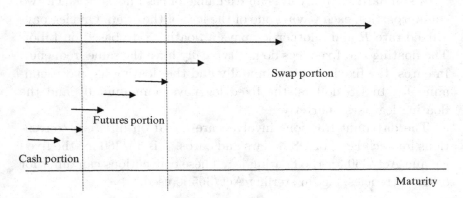

Figure 2.1:   The above diagram illustrates how various instruments are used to construct the yield curve. The maturity date of each instrument gives a point of the yield curve. We can obtain these points consecutively via a bootstrap technique.

---

depends on which months comprise the interval. Act/365 is calculated as number of calendar days in period divided by 365.

market instruments are repriced. Define a zero rate with maturity T via $z_T = -\frac{\log D(0,T)}{T}$ and a continuous forward rate between T_1 and T_2 (with $T_1 < T_2$) via $f_{T_1 T_2} = \frac{\log D(0,T_1) - \log D(0,T_2)}{T_2 - T_1}$. Then typical methods of curve building include having linear zero rates or constant forward rates between maturities of our instruments used to build the curve. These are local interpolation methods. However, the above approaches are not smooth (i.e. forward rates over each period tend to jump a lot). Spline techniques (and global interpolation) tend to produce smooth forwards but are undesirable because the risk obtained by such techniques is globalised (e.g. a change in the 30-year swap rate will affect the 1-month rate). See Figure 2.2 for the forward rates from different build methods. To this end, various hybrid approaches have been investigated.

Suppose we have a local interpolation method. Then we could build our curve by a bootstrap technique, i.e. we obtain the discount factors for successive expiries one at a time. Starting with deposits, notice that if the deposit rate is r_i for maturity T_i^D, then the discount factor is obtained by $D(0, T_i^D) = \frac{1}{1 + r_i T_i^D}$.

Going on to futures, suppose that the i-th future has expiry T_i^F, accrual fraction τ, futures rate f_i, and futures convexity c_i, then we need to choose $D(0, T_i^F + \tau)$ such that $f_i - c_i = (\frac{D(0,T_i^F)}{D(0,T_i^F + \tau)} - 1)/\tau$. This can be done by root finding since we know all discount factors

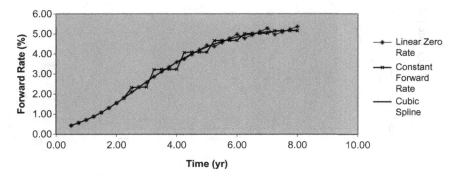

Figure 2.2: The continuous forward rates in the graph are obtained from the above interpolation schemes. Notice how the linear zero rate and constant forward rate schemes lead to jagged profiles, whilst the cubic spline scheme is much smoother.

up to $T_{i-1}^F + \tau$, and choosing $D(0, T_i^F + \tau)$ will fully determine all discount factors in between (where we interpolate as necessary based on our chosen interpolation method).

Now, we consider fitting swaps. Here, for a swap with maturity $T_i^S = T_j$, accrual periods $\{\tau_k\}_{k=1}^j$ for the fixed leg, and fixed rate R_i, the relevant equation is $R_i = \dfrac{1 - D(0, T_j)}{\sum_{k=1}^j \tau_k D(0, T_k)}$. We now have to solve for $D(0, T_i^S)$ assuming we know all discount factors up to T_{i-1}^S, with the discount factors in between obtained via interpolation.

Figures 2.3a–c show some examples of the shapes of the yield curves of the different currencies over the years.

2.1.3   *Overnight Index Swaps and Basis Swaps*

Unfortunately, the idea of borrowing and lending at Libor is not a true reflection of reality, and certainly after the credit crunch of 2008, it no longer holds. In particular, there is a premium for borrowing based on floating rates of longer periods.

Let us consider the overnight index swap (OIS). This is an instrument where one leg pays the OIS rate, defined as the geometric average of the overnight rate over the period. So, for example, for a

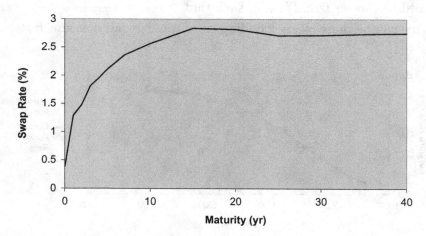

Figure 2.3a: US swap curve as of 2 January 2009. This is a steeply upward sloping curve, which flattens for maturities over 15 years.
Source: Bloomberg data.

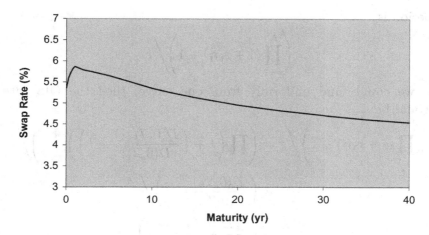

Figure 2.3b: Sterling (i.e. UK) swap curve as of 31 January 2007. Apart from maturities less than 1 year, this is clearly a downward sloping curve.
Source: Bloomberg data.

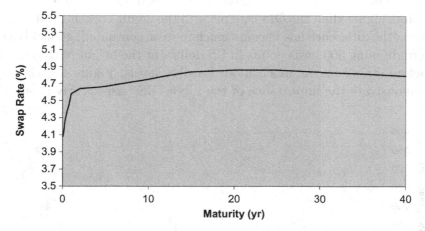

Figure 2.3c: Euro swap curve as of 31 July 2007. Apart from maturities less than one year, this curve is rather flat.
Source: Bloomberg data.

period $T = T_0$ to $T + \tau = T_N$ divided into subintervals $\{\tau_i\}_{i=1}^{N}$ of one business day each with overnight rate r_i, the OIS rate[7] for the

---

[7]Some markets use a variation of the definition for the OIS rate. For example, the Fed Funds rate (US OIS rate) is based on arithmetic averaging instead, so strictly it does not simplify to exactly the libor rate even in the absence of the libor-OIS basis.

period is

$$\left(\prod_{i=1}^{N} (1 + r_i \tau_i) - 1 \right) \Big/ \tau.$$

If we could fund uniformly from one curve, then the OIS rate would be

$$\left(\prod_{i=1}^{N} (1 + r_i \tau_i) - 1 \right) \Big/ \tau = \left(\prod_{i=1}^{N} \left(1 + \left(\frac{D(0, T_{i-1})}{D(0, T_i)} - 1 \right) \right) - 1 \right) \Big/ \tau$$

$$= \left(\frac{D(0, T_0)}{D(0, T_N)} - 1 \right) \Big/ \tau$$

$$= \left(\frac{D(0, T)}{D(0, T + \tau)} - 1 \right) \Big/ \tau,$$

which is the Libor rate for the period.

However, typically, the Libor rate tended to be about 8 basis points higher than the OIS rate prior to the credit crunch. And these days, the difference has become much more accentuated, going above a frightening 300 basis points in US dollars at the height of the crisis, before stabilising at much more sensible levels. Figure 2.4 should demonstrate the importance of the Libor-OIS basis clearly enough.

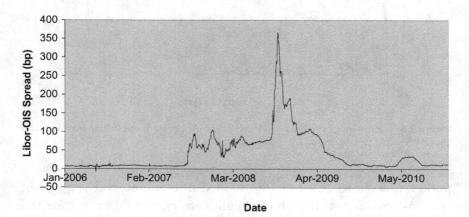

Figure 2.4: The graph shows the US 3-month Libor-OIS spread (i.e. Libor rate — OIS rate) from 2006 to 2010. Note how it spiked from a stable value of about 8bp prior to July 2007 to a peak of 366bp at the height of the crisis, and has now stabilised at about 16bp. *Source*: Bloomberg data.

In the same token, a floating 3-month rate versus a floating 6-month rate cannot be obtained from the same curve. Prior to the crisis, the 6-month rate tended to be higher than the 3-month rate but the difference was less than 1 basis point. Now, it can be over 10 basis points at the short end. For that reason, basis swaps provide important information regarding discount factors. These are swaps where one leg pays Libor for one tenor (e.g. 6 months) and another leg pays Libor for another tenor (e.g. 3 months) plus a spread so that the value of the swap is zero at inception.

There is a philosophical argument as to why the OIS rate should be much lower than Libor, and why the 3-month floating rate should be lower than the 6-month floating rate. This is attributed to Morini [Mor10]. Basically, Libor is based on quotes from banks with certain attributes (e.g. AA rating). Now, a counterparty that is Libor-eligible (i.e. suitable to contribute to Libor) today will most likely be Libor-eligible tomorrow. However, will it be Libor-eligible in 3-months' time? (Things can and do change for each institution.) In this sense, Libor is safer than each of the counterparties contributing to the Libor quote. But if you enter into a contract with floating rate based on a given tenor (say 3 months), you are stuck with the credit rating of all the counterparties responsible for that Libor quote over the given tenor (i.e. 3 months period) until the next fixing, and so do not benefit from the true risk rating of Libor. Thus, only the OIS rate corresponds to the true risk rating of Libor (i.e. as close to a risk-free rate as you can get — one day exposure to changes in your counterparties' risk profiles). In the US, the OIS rate refers to the Fed Funds rate, in the eurozone it is EONIA, and in the UK it is SONIA.

There is thus a need to recognise that funding cannot be obtained from a single curve. We would build a curve for forecasting (i.e. to obtain Libor rates) for the appropriate Libor term (e.g. 3 months or 6 months) and another curve for discounting. Under these circumstances, we obtain the value of a basis swap as

$$\sum_{i=1}^{N} f_i^A \tau_i^A D(0, T_i^A) = \sum_{i=1}^{M} (f_i^B + s) \tau_i^B D(0, T_i^B),$$

where $f_i^A = (\frac{D^A(0,T_i^A)}{D^A(0,T_{i+1}^A)} - 1)/\tau_i^A$ is the value of the forward rate of tenor A obtained from a forecasting curve $D^A(0,\ldots)$ constructed based on swaps of tenor A,

f_i^B is similarly obtained from a forecasting curve constructed based on swaps of tenor B,

$D(0,\ldots)$ is a uniform discounting curve obtained by considering the OIS rate, and s is a fixed spread.

This makes things a lot more complicated even for pricing a swap in the present world. For the purposes of understanding various aspects of derivatives pricing, it adds little value to consider the above details. As such, we shall ignore the implications of funding for most of the book. We shall however briefly consider the topic in Chapter 12, so that the reader is aware of the real world implications of funding being no longer an issue to neglect.

2.2   Interest Rate Options

Now that we have discussed basic linear instruments in interest rates, it is worth considering the vanilla options market next. These comprise caplets and swaptions, with swaptions being by far more important than caplets in most markets.

2.2.1   *Caplets*

These are just options on the Libor rate. A caplet with strike K and accrual fraction τ has payoff $\max(L_T - K, 0)\tau$ at time $T + \tau$ where L_T is the Libor rate observed at time T.

Similarly, a floorlet has payoff $\max(K - L_T, 0)\tau$ at time $T + \tau$.

The value of a caplet is given by

$$C_0 = D(0,T)\tau E^T[\max(L_T - K, 0)D(T, T + \tau)]$$
$$= D(0, T + \tau)\tau E^{T+\tau}[\max(L_T - K, 0)]$$

using a simple measure change to the $T+\tau$-forward measure (where the numeraire is the discount bond with maturity $T + \tau$).

But $L_T = (\frac{D(T,T)}{D(T,T+\tau)} - 1)/\tau$ and so is a martingale under the measure with numeraire being the discount bond with maturity $T + \tau$.

So, assuming a lognormal distribution for the Libor rate, we obtain the Black formula for a caplet as

$$C_0 = D(0, T + \tau)\tau(L_0 N(d_1) - K N(d_2)),$$

where $d_1 = \frac{\log(\frac{L_0}{K}) + \frac{1}{2}\sigma^2 T}{\sigma\sqrt{T}}$ and $d_2 = d_1 - \sigma\sqrt{T}$ as per Section 1.2.4.

Whereas the Black formula is probably not accurate for modelling the Libor rate, it is much easier to visualise prices in the form of Black volatilities, so that it is a useful tool for quoting prices.

2.2.2 *Swaptions*

Swaptions are simply options on swaps. Consider the payer swaption (i.e. the option to enter into a swap where you pay the fixed rate and receive the floating rate). Specifically, say the strike is K, expiry is T, the underlying swap has a fixed leg with accrual periods $\{\tau_i\}_{i=1}^{N}$. Define the value of the swap rate at time T as R_T and the value of the annuity as $A_T = \sum_{i=1}^{N} \tau_i D(0, T_i)$. Then the value of the payer swaption is

$$P_0 = D(0, T) E^T [\max(R_T - K, 0) A_T]$$
$$= A_0 E^A [\max(R_T - K, 0)]$$

using a change of measure to that where the numeraire is the annuity. But $R_T = \frac{D(T,T) - D(T,T_N)}{A_T}$ (from Section 1.2.1) and so is a martingale under the measure with numeraire being the annuity. Thus, assuming lognormality of the swap rate, we obtain per Section 1.2.4, the Black formula for a swaption as

$$P_0 = A_0(R_0 N(d_1) - K N(d_2)),$$

where $d_1 = \frac{\log(\frac{R_0}{K}) + \frac{1}{2}\sigma^2 T}{\sigma\sqrt{T}}$ and $d_2 = d_1 - \sigma\sqrt{T}$.

Similarly, a receiver swaption is an option to enter into a swap to receive the fixed rate and pay the floating rate, and its value is given by

$$S_0 = A_0(K N(-d_2) - R_0 N(-d_1)).$$

The above payoff applies to physically settled swaptions. These are the norm in the US. However, in Europe and in the UK, cash-settled swaptions are the standard, and we do not mean a swaption settled in cash. Rather, it was felt to be more convenient for the settlement to be completely defined in terms of the swap rate (since only a fixing for the swap rate is required). As such, the cash annuity used for the settlement at time T is defined as

$$A_T^C = \sum_{i=1}^{N} \frac{1}{\left(1 + \frac{R_T}{n}\right)^{ni}} = \frac{1 - \frac{1}{\left(1 + \frac{R_T}{n}\right)^{nN}}}{\left(1 + \frac{R_T}{n}\right)^{n} - 1}.$$

Whereas market convention is to price a cash-settled swaption via Black's formula with annuity at time zero (today) valued at

$$A_0^C = D(0, T) \frac{1 - \frac{1}{\left(1 + \frac{R_0}{n}\right)^{nN}}}{\left(1 + \frac{R_0}{n}\right)^{n} - 1},$$

this is not strictly correct since the cash annuity is not a true numeraire as it is not an asset but some function of the swap rate. Whilst it generally gives pretty similar results to pricing of physically settled swaptions, the fact that we are not using a true numeraire means put-call parity (see Section 2.4.3) does not hold for cash-settled swaptions!

It is worth remarking that typically swaptions are quoted via implied volatilities from the normal model (see Section 1.2.4) and some strike interpolation methodology[8] which is used to obtain vols and prices of less liquid European swaptions.

2.3   Foreign Exchange

Foreign exchange (FX) essentially involves the rate of conversion from one currency to another. This is an important market in a globalised economy where companies operating internationally often have to consider costs in foreign locations as well as how to protect foreign profits earned. To this end, products to fix the rate of exchange in the future or to offer protection from currency moves have been popular.

---

[8]E.g. Stochastic Alpha Beta Rho (SABR) as covered in Chapter 6.

Most foreign exchange trading takes place in the OTC market rather than futures exchanges, due to its flexibility, and because the large number of combinations of currency pairs makes it difficult to come up with standardised contracts.

2.3.1 *Forwards and the Cross-Currency Swap*

An FX forward is an obligation to exchange a certain amount N_A of currency A for a predetermined amount N_B of currency B at a future time T. As discussed in Section 1.2.2, the fair forward FX rate can be determined from the spot FX rate and the discount curves of the two currencies.

As usual in the real world however, there is a complication in that it might be easier for financial institutions to fund in one currency as opposed to another. A case in mind is that of Japan. Japan has had ultra-low interest rates for over a decade. Coupled with the government policy of favouring a weak yen vis-à-vis the US dollar (with periodic interventions by selling yen as necessary), the environment has favoured borrowing in yen and investing in higher yielding currencies.[9] And there has been a ready supply of yen from domestic savers with few alternative avenues for investment. This excess supply of yen means that the forward FX rate may not be fully accounted for by the interest rate differential.

To better understand the implications, let us look at the cross-currency swap. Specifically, the details are as follows. On the settlement date T_0,[10] you pay your counterparty N_A of currency A (e.g. 1 US dollar) and receive $N_B = X_0 N_A$ (e.g. 85 yen) where X_0 is the spot FX rate. Then at periodic intervals T_i (e.g. every 6 months) with accrual fraction τ_i, you receive Libor in currency A and pay Libor plus a spread s in currency B. At the maturity date $T = T_M$ of the deal (e.g. 30 years later), you receive N_A of currency A from your counterparty and pay N_B of currency B.

---

[9]Primarily the US dollar but even the Australian dollar for the more adventurous.
[10]Usually two business days from the deal date.

Valuing everything in currency B, the deal has value today given by

$$X_0 N_A \left(-D^A(0, T_0) + \sum_{i=1}^{M} f_i^A \tau_i D^A(0, T_i) + D^A(0, T_N) \right)$$

$$-N_B \left(-D^B(0, T_0) + \sum_{i=1}^{M} \left(f_i^B + s \right) \tau_i D^B(0, T_i) + D^B(0, T_N) \right)$$

$$= X_0 N_A \left[\left(-D^A(0, T_0) + \sum_{i=1}^{M} f_i^A \tau_i D^A(0, T_i) + D^A(0, T_N) \right) \right.$$

$$\left. - \left(-D^B(0, T_0) + \sum_{i=1}^{M} \left(f_i^B + s \right) \tau_i D^B(0, T_i) + D^B(0, T_N) \right) \right],$$

where $f_i^A = (\frac{D^{A,F}(0, T_i)}{D^{A,F}(0, T_{i+1})} - 1)/\tau_i$ is the Libor rate for currency A from time T_i to time T_{i+1} as obtained from the forecasting curve $D^{A,F}(0, T)$ for currency A, and f_i^B is its counterpart for currency B.

In particular, the fair cross currency swap spread (to price the cross-currency swap at par) is given by

$$s = \left(-D^A(0, T_0) + \sum_{i=1}^{M} f_i^A \tau_i D^A(0, T_i) + D^A(0, T_M) \right.$$

$$\left. + D^B(0, T_0) - \sum_{i=1}^{M} f_i^B \tau_i D^B(0, T_i) - D^B(0, T_M) \right)$$

$$\left/ \sum_{i=1}^{M} \tau_i D^B(0, T_i). \right.$$

Typically, for curve building in FX, we need to solve for discount factors for the discounting curve and forecasting curve simultaneously. Specifically, the US dollar is taken as the base currency (where forecasting curve and discounting curve are the same). We can thus bootstrap the US dollar curve independently just from swap rates.

Then we solve for the spread in the other currency so that the cross-currency swap reprices to par (i.e. has fair value of zero today) and where plain swaps in the other currency are also repriced. In this sense, for each maturity T, we have two degrees of freedom $D^B(0, T)$ and $D^{B,F}(0, T)$, and two constraints (the par swap rate R and the cross currency spread s). So, this is a well posed problem.

Notice that if the forecasting curve for each currency is the same as its discounting curve, then the value of the spread is

$$
s = \left(-D^A(0, T_0) + \sum_{i=1}^{M} f_i^A \tau_i D^A(0, T_i) + D^A(0, T_M) \right.
$$
$$
\left. + D^B(0, T_0) - \sum_{i=1}^{M} f_i^B \tau_i D^B(0, T_i) - D^B(0, T_M) \right)
$$
$$
\bigg/ \sum_{i=1}^{M} \tau_i D^B(0, T_i)
$$

$$
= \left(-D^A(0, T_0) + \sum_{i=1}^{M} \left(\frac{D^A(0, T_{i-1})}{D^A(0, T_i)} - 1 \right) D^A(0, T_i) + D^A(0, T_M) \right.
$$
$$
\left. + D^B(0, T_0) - \sum_{i=1}^{M} \left(\frac{D^B(0, T_{i-1})}{D^B(0, T_i)} - 1 \right) D^B(0, T_i) - D^B(0, T_M) \right)
$$
$$
\bigg/ \sum_{i=1}^{M} \tau_i D^B(0, T_i)
$$

$$
= \left(-D^A(0, T_0) + \sum_{i=1}^{M} \left(D^A(0, T_{i-1}) - D^A(0, T_i) \right) + D^A(0, T_M) \right.
$$
$$
\left. + D^B(0, T_0) - \sum_{i=1}^{M} \left(D^B(0, T_{i-1}) - D^B(0, T_i) \right) - D^B(0, T_M) \right)
$$
$$
\bigg/ \sum_{i=1}^{M} \tau_i D^B(0, T_i)
$$

$$= \left(-D^A(0, T_0) + D^A(0, T_0) - D^A(0, T_M) + D^A(0, T_M)\right.$$
$$\left. +D^B(0, T_0) - D^B(0, T_0) + D^B(0, T_M) - D^B(0, T_M)\right)$$
$$\Big/ \sum_{i=1}^{M} \tau_i D^B(0, T_i)$$
$$= 0$$

So, if we really had no funding bias, the cross-currency swap spread should be zero. Note that the need to account for cross-currency funding bias was already widely recognised prior to the credit crunch, especially with regard to currency pairs involving the Japanese yen or an emerging market currency (albeit for different reasons). Since then, the spread has become even more pronounced.

Having flagged up the issue for your attention, it is beyond the scope of this book to pursue this discussion any further.

2.3.2   *Options, Strangles, and Risk Reversals*

The FX markets have developed a significant body of conventions over the years. Typically, options are not quoted via strikes but by deltas instead. The most liquid options tend to be at-the-money, 25-delta strangles and risk reversals and 10-delta strangles and risk reversals. We consider these below.

At-the-money options

These are not as innocent as they sound. Specifically, at-the-money typically means delta-neutral except for long expiries (e.g. over 10 years in USD/JPY) where it means the strike corresponds to the forward FX rate.

Delta-neutral refers to a call and put having the same delta. (Obviously, we mean call delta = −put delta.) Specifically, the Black–Scholes formula for a call is

$$C = Xe^{-r_f T} N(d_1) - Ke^{-rT} N(d_2)$$

with

$$d_1 = \frac{\log(\frac{X}{K}) + (r - r_f + \frac{1}{2}\sigma^2)T}{\sigma\sqrt{T}}, \quad d_2 = d_1 - \sigma\sqrt{T},$$

where X is spot FX, K is strike, T is expiry, r is domestic rate, r_f is foreign rate, and σ is vol.

Thus, the domestic spot delta of a call is given by

$$\Delta_C = \frac{\partial}{\partial X}\left(Xe^{-r_f T}N(d_1) - Ke^{-rT}N(d_2)\right)$$

$$= e^{-r_f T}N(d_1) + Xe^{-r_f T}n(d_1)\frac{1}{X\sigma\sqrt{T}} - Ke^{-rT}n(d_2)\frac{1}{X\sigma\sqrt{T}}$$

$$= e^{-r_f T}N(d_1) + Xe^{-r_f T}n(d_2)e^{-d_2\sigma\sqrt{T}-\frac{1}{2}\sigma^2 T}\frac{1}{X\sigma\sqrt{T}}$$

$$\quad - Ke^{-rT}n(d_2)\frac{1}{X\sigma\sqrt{T}}$$

$$= e^{-r_f T}N(d_1) + \frac{n(d_2)}{X\sigma\sqrt{T}}\left(Xe^{-r_f T}\frac{K}{X}e^{(-r+r_f)T} - Ke^{-rT}\right)$$

$$= e^{-r_f T}N(d_1)$$

with $n(x) = \frac{1}{\sqrt{2\pi}}e^{-\frac{1}{2}x^2}$, so that $n(d_1) = \frac{1}{\sqrt{2\pi}}e^{-\frac{1}{2}(d_2+\sigma\sqrt{T})^2} = n(d_2)e^{-d_2\sigma\sqrt{T}-\frac{1}{2}\sigma^2 T}$.

Similarly, we can show that the domestic spot delta for a put is $\Delta_P = e^{-r_f T}(N(d_1) - 1)$. So, delta neutrality requires $e^{-r_f T}N(d_1) = -e^{-r_f T}(N(d_1) - 1)$, i.e. we need to choose a strike such that $d_1 = N^{-1}(\frac{1}{2})$, i.e. $K = X\exp(-\sigma\sqrt{T}N^{-1}(\frac{1}{2}) + (r - r_f + \frac{1}{2}\sigma^2)T)$.

However, in FX, we can see the price of an option from either currency. Specifically, suppose we have an option to buy one unit of currency A (e.g. US dollar) for K units of currency B (e.g. yen). The Black–Scholes formula gives its price C in terms of currency B. But say the majority of market participants function in currency A,[11] then they would like to hedge in currency A. If they had sold an option and received currency B, then this option premium (which

---

[11]True in our example in that more financial institutions prefer to work in US dollars.

can be valued in currency A) serves as a natural hedge for the contract. This leads to the concept of a foreign delta, and some currency pairs have their at-the-money options quoted as being delta-neutral based on the foreign delta (in currency A)

$$\Delta_C^F = \frac{\partial}{\partial X}\left(\frac{C}{X}\right) = \frac{1}{X}\frac{\partial C}{\partial X} - \frac{C}{X^2}.$$

Notice that in currency B terms, the value is now

$$\Delta_C^F = \frac{\partial C}{\partial X} - \frac{C}{X} = \Delta_C - \frac{C}{X}.$$

On top of this, delta-neutral can be based on spot delta or forward delta. Forward delta is where the derivative of price is with respect to the forward rather than the spot. It is typically used for options whose expiries are not too short (e.g. over one year).

It is beyond the scope of this book to discuss all the conventions in FX. So it is better to conclude here, but it is certainly useful to make the reader aware that there are more complications than one would have initially guessed.

Strangles

Strangles are where you are long a call and a put both being out-of-the-money to a similar extent. It is thus a measure of volatility smile (i.e. how much higher out-of-the-money implied volatility is compared to at-the-money implied volatility). In FX, the market quotes market strangles. Specifically, the quotes are for 25-delta[12] and 10-delta strangles, and the strikes are chosen as follows:

Let $q_\Delta = \sigma_\Delta - \sigma_{Atm}$ be the quote of the Δ-delta strangle (e.g. where $\Delta = 25$). Then given the at-the-money volatility σ_{Atm}, we can determine the volatility of the strangle σ_Δ. The strikes of the strangle K_C and K_P are such that $\Delta_C = e^{-r_f T} N\left(d_1\left(K_C\right)\right)$ and $\Delta_P = e^{-r_f T}\left(1 - N\left(d_1\left(K_P\right)\right)\right)$. Notice that whilst this does not tell

---

[12]I.e. call delta is 0.25 and put delta is -0.25 based on the relevant delta convention — spot/forward, domestic/foreign.

us the volatilities at strikes K_C and K_P, it imposes the key constraint

$$C(K_C) + P(K_P) = C(K_C, \sigma_\Delta) + P(K_P, \sigma_\Delta),$$

i.e. the price of the strangle based on the true volatilities of call and put options agrees with the price of the strangle if both call and put options are priced with the volatility σ_Δ.

Risk reversals

A risk reversal can be described as being long a call and short a put with the same moneyness or vice versa. In this way, a risk reversal is a measure of skew (i.e. how much more out-of-the-money calls are worth vis-à-vis out-of-the-money puts). Typically, quotes are for 25-delta and 10-delta risk reversals. Specifically, the quote is of the form $Q_\Delta = \sigma_C - \sigma_P$, where σ_C and σ_P are implied volatilities for the strikes K_C and K_P for the appropriate delta.

The trouble is: What are these strikes? Since strikes for market strangles are not obtained from deltas computed from the true volatilities at those strikes, their strikes are different from those of risk reversals. As such, the problem is not uniquely determined in that some form of model dependent volatility interpolation over strikes, together with the quotes for market strangles is necessary, in order to obtain the strikes for the risk reversals since all we have is the constraint that the volatilities at this strike must satisfy.

2.3.3 Barriers and One-Touches

Many derivatives in foreign exchange have arisen out of hedging considerations. In the years between the introduction of the euro and the onset of the credit crunch, FX volatility has been remarkably low (at least in comparison with that of equities). Rightly or wrongly, barrier products have often been seen as a way to obtain an FX option at a lower cost. Barrier products and one-touches have thus been popular in FX.

For example, consider a down-and-out call option to buy EUR/USD at strike $K = 1.35$ with expiry $T = 1y$. If EUR/USD drops below $H = 1.28$ during the life of the option, then it will expire

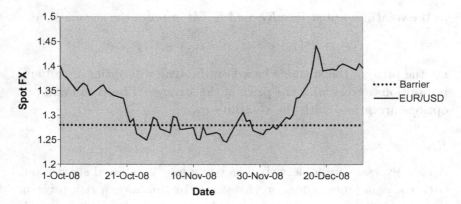

Figure 2.5:   We illustrate how at expiry, EUR/USD is above the strike of 1.35 but payoff for the knockout option is zero because EUR/USD has dropped below the barrier of 1.28 at some point prior to expiry.

worthless.[13] See Figure 2.5 for an illustration. Mathematically, the payoff at expiry is

$$\max\left(S_T - K, 0\right) 1_{\min_{0 < t \leq T} S_t > H}.$$

This option is clearly less valuable than an ordinary call option, since there is some probability that the option will expire worthless because of a temporary drop in EUR/USD. However, certain investors might be willing to take such a risk on the assumption that if the euro weakens even during its life, it should not recover too strongly for the option to be in-the-money at expiry.

We also have up-and-out calls where if the underlying rises above a certain level, the option expires worthless. For example, suppose we have a call option with strike 1.4 but it expires worthless if at any point in its life, EUR/USD goes above 1.5 (see Figure 2.6). This sounds like an odd product since the investor will find his protection from a rise in EUR/USD worthless if EUR/USD rises too much. But in practice, the idea is that this product would be packaged with other products, e.g. a one-touch to pay $1.5 - 1.4 = 0.1$, if EUR/USD hits 1.5; therefore, the package payoff is capped at 0.1 (as opposed to dropping to 0), if the barrier is breached.

---

[13]I.e. even if EUR/USD ends up above 1.35 at expiry, the payoff is zero.

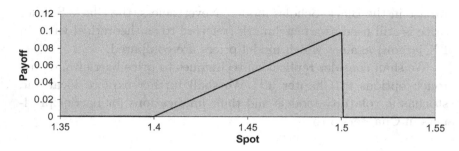

Figure 2.6:   Payoff of reverse knockout call (strike 1.4, barrier 1.5) increases as spot increases above strike but if spot exceeds barrier level, payoff is instead zero.

In a similar vein, we can have down-and-out puts, up-and-out puts and a whole variety of combinations, including double barrier options.

We now come to the one-touch option. An upside one-touch option pays 1 at expiry T, if the underlying breaches the barrier H (above current spot level) at some time not later than expiry. It is really the same as an American digital option. The payoff is given by

$$1_{\max_{0 < t \leq T} S_t > H}.$$

Similarly, the downside one-touch pays 1 at expiry T if the underlying breaches the barrier H (below current spot level) at some time not later than expiry. As discussed in Section 1.1.7, we can see from the Reflection Principle that a one-touch option is worth approximately twice the value of a (European) digital option of the same strike.

The Reflection Principle is indeed very useful in understanding barrier options. If we consider the Black–Scholes world, we can use it to derive the formulae for various barrier products. Haug [Hau07] gives a very detailed collection of formulae for different types of barrier products under a Black–Scholes model.

In reality, however, the Black–Scholes model cannot adequately capture the price of a barrier product. The reason is that we cannot choose a single implied volatility number (consistent with European options) to obtain the correct price, since barrier products clearly depend on the volatility smile at the point when the barrier is breached. If we had a volatility smile, then which volatility should we use in the Black–Scholes model? Nevertheless, the Black–Scholes price is still used as a benchmark (referred to as theoretical value in FX jargon) against which model prices are compared.

We shall consider replication techniques to price barrier and one-touch options in Chapter 3.[14] We shall further explore local and stochastic volatility models and their implications for barrier products in Chapters 5 to 7.

2.4   Equities

Stocks have traditionally been seen as the instruments by which an investor can seek higher yields if she is prepared to accept greater risks. Investing in equities has been popularised by the spectacular rises in the general stock market in the 1980s and 1990s (see Figure 2.7), in tandem with relatively stable economic growth in the developed economies in this period. With institutional investors playing an increasingly large role in the markets these days and with their quest for increasingly elusive yields in a low interest rate environment, they have become the biggest participants in the equity markets.

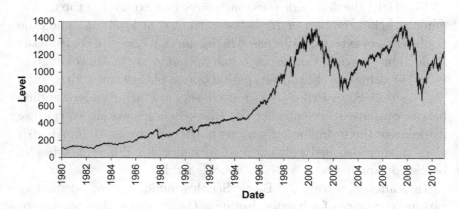

Figure 2.7:   S&P 500 index from 1980 to 2010. The index has seen spectacular rises until 2000 and then has struggled to surpass its highs since.
Source: Bloomberg data.

---

[14]Although these depend on assumptions regarding the volatility dynamics.

As with other assets, derivatives have played a meaningful role in tailoring the risk-reward profiles of various investment strategies.

2.4.1 *Forwards and Futures*

Forwards are OTC agreements to buy or sell certain quantities of stock in the future. This could be useful if for example a portfolio manager is due to receive a certain amount of money to invest say one month from now but wants to lock in the price of the stock purchase today.

A typical forward contract has payoff $S_T - K$, where S_T is the value of the stock at delivery time T and K is the strike. As discussed in Section 1.2.2, entering into a forward contract does not entitle you to dividends prior to maturity, so the fair value strike at a prior time t is

$$F_S(t, T) = \frac{1}{D(t, T)} \left(S_t - \sum_{i=1}^{N} a_i D(t, T_i) \right),$$

where dividends of amount a_i are due at times $\{T_i\}_{i=1}^{N}$ prior to the delivery time T and $D(t, T)$ is the discount factor for maturity T as seen at time t.

Futures are similar to forwards but are exchange traded. As such, they are marked to market at the end of each trading day, and the difference in value is settled daily (e.g. if you are long the future and its value has declined, then you are required to pay the difference to the exchange and vice versa). Furthermore, there is no discounting, so if you are long a future with strike $\hat{F}$ and delivery date T, its fair value at time t is really

$$V_t = E_t^B[S_T - \hat{F}],$$

where our numeraire is the money market account $B_t = e^{\int_0^t r_u du}$ which reflects accrued interest.

Hence, the fair value future price is given by setting

$$0 = E_t^B[S_T - \hat{F}],$$

so that we obtain

$$\hat{F}_S(t,T) = E_t^B[S_T]$$

$$= D(t,T)E_t^T\left[S_T\frac{B_T}{B_t}\right]$$

$$= D(t,T)E_t^T[S_Te^{\int_t^T r_u du}],$$

where the second equality is from a change to the T-forward measure.[15]

This means that if correlation between interest rates and the stock price is non-zero, there will be a convexity-style adjustment to the fair value future price. This is very much in line with the discussion of interest rates futures in Section 2.1.1 earlier.

Typically, futures are more common on indices (e.g. S&P 500, Euro Stoxx 50, Nikkei 225) and maybe a few big name stocks.[16] Forwards are instead more common for less liquid members of the universe of stocks.

2.4.2   *Exchange Traded Options*

As in FX, there is of course interest in protection from the movements of stock prices. Since most institutional investors are long stocks, there is a huge demand for protection in the event that stock prices decline, i.e. put options with strikes below the current stock price, especially for the major indices.

To this end, we have the following payoffs at expiry T:

$$C_T = \max(S_T - K, 0)$$

for a European call option,[17] and

$$P_T = \max(K - S_T, 0)$$

for a European put option.[18]

---

[15]I.e. whose numeraire is the discount bond with maturity T.
[16]Although they may be in the form of contracts for difference, i.e. cash settled.
[17]I.e. right to buy the stock for strike K.
[18]I.e. right to sell the stock at strike K.

And as discussed in Section 1.2.4, the values of these options is given under Black's model by

$$C_t = D(t, T)(F_S(t, T)N(d_1) - KN(d_2))$$

and

$$P_t = D(t, T)(KN(-d_2) - F_S(t, T)N(-d_1)),$$

where $d_1 = \frac{\log(\frac{F_S(t,T)}{K}) + \frac{1}{2}\sigma^2(T-t)}{\sigma\sqrt{T-t}}$, $d_2 = d_1 - \sigma\sqrt{T-t}$, and $F_S(t, T)$ is the forward price of a stock with delivery date T as seen at time t.

Whilst exchange traded options on indices are typically in European style (i.e. exercisable only at expiry) and hence can be treated via the above-mentioned approach, options on single name stocks tend to be in American style (i.e. they can be exercised at any time prior to expiry).

Valuing American options requires that we determine whether exercise is optimal. This can generally be done by solving the Black–Scholes partial differential equation (PDE)

$$\frac{\partial f_t}{\partial t} + r_t S_t \frac{\partial f_t}{\partial S_t} + \frac{1}{2}\frac{\partial^2 f_t}{\partial S_t^2}\sigma^2(S_t, t) = r_t f(S_t, t),$$

where at each node, we take the maximum of the value from early exercise versus continuation. In the example of a put option, we compute

$$f_{i,j} = \max\left(\max\left(K - S_{i,j}, 0\right), D\left(t_i, t_{i+1}\right) E\left[f\left(t_{i+1}\right) | f\left(t_i\right) = f_{i,j}\right]\right),$$

where i is the time index and j is the space (spot) index.

For call options, in the absence of dividends, it is never optimal to exercise early, so that the American option is worth the same as a European option. If there are dividends, then it could be optimal to exercise early since we are only entitled to the dividends after exercising the option.

2.4.3 Put-Call Parity

It is important to be aware that some relationships between products hold independently of the models used to price them. An important relationship is put-call parity, a discussion of which is a fitting conclusion to this chapter, and naturally leads us to the topic of static replication, covered in the next chapter.

A call option that entitles the holder to purchase at expiry T the underlying S_T at strike K has payoff $C_T = \max(S_T - K, 0)$. A put option with the same expiry and strike has payoff $P_T = \max(K - S_T, 0)$. It thus follows that being long a call option and short a put option with the same strike and expiry is equivalent to being long a forward position, i.e. $C_T - P_T = S_T - K$ (see Figure 2.8). Having obtained a portfolio with an equivalent payoff at time T, the value of being long a call and short a put option as seen today must be worth the same as this portfolio today, so $C_0 - P_0 = S_0 - KD(0, T)$. Notice that this combined portfolio has no optionality and hence its value is model independent.

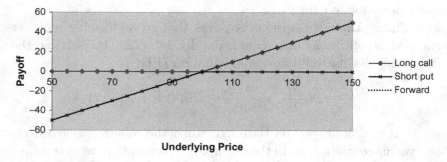

Figure 2.8:   Combining the payoff of being long a call option and short a put option of the same strike (100) simply gives us the payoff of a forward with that strike.

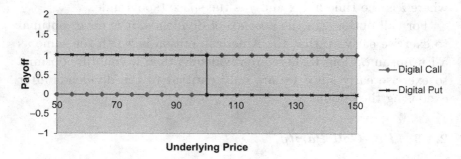

Figure 2.9:   Combining the payoff of a digital call option and digital put option of the same strike (100) will give a payoff of 1 regardless of the price of the underlying at expiry.

In a similar vein, a digital call option with expiry T based on underlying S_T at strike K has payoff $C_T^D = 1_{S_T > K}$ whilst a digital put option with the same strike and expiry has payoff $P_T^D = 1_{S_T \leq K}$. Thus, being long a digital call option and long a digital put option of the same strike will lead to a payoff of one at expiry T (see Figure 2.9). This gives the parity relationship $C_0^D + P_0^D = D(0, T)$.

2.5   Consolidation

2.5.1   *Summary*

In this chapter, we have discussed the most common market instruments in the various asset classes. This was useful to anchor the modelling framework, in that we need to be able to reprice linear instruments (i.e. where there is no optionality), and to have a good fit to vanilla options, in order to appropriately reflect the cost of hedging.

Starting with interest rates, the linear instruments include deposits (borrowing over a short fixed term), futures (to fix the rate of borrowing over a future period) and swaps (where you pay a fixed rate and receive a floating rate over several coupon periods or vice versa). Futures are exchange traded, whilst deposits and swaps are traded over-the-counter. We noted that there is a convexity adjustment for futures prices due to daily settlement of undiscounted P&L from traded prices, this adjustment growing with the maturity of the futures instrument. We discussed building a yield curve of discount factors for all maturities that reprices these instruments exactly, forming the basis for pricing all other interest rate products. Yield curve construction can be via bootstrap techniques (i.e. piecewise solving for discount factors to match prices of instruments with increasing maturity) or a global fit (which is smoother but where risk is not localised). Moving on, we injected a dose of present day realism by discussing overnight index swaps and basis swaps as a pre-taste of how after the 2008 crisis financial institutions can no longer fund at Libor but where borrowing for a shorter floating tenor is at preferential rates (versus a longer floating tenor).

Moving on to interest rate options, we considered caplets (options to pay/receive a Libor rate) and physically settled swaptions (options to enter into swaps). Here, we illustrated how a change of measure is useful in interest rates — for the caplet, the numeraire is the discount bond with maturity on the pay date of the Libor rate; for the swaption, it is the annuity. We also discussed the cash-settled swaption (the norm for sterling and euros), with a payoff totally dependent on the swap rate — and how the cash annuity is not a proper numeraire.

In FX, we have explored forwards (to fix an FX rate in the future) and cross-currency swaps (where you pay a floating rate in one currency and receive a floating rate in another plus a spread). The fair value spread of the cross-currency swap reflects again how theory (where the FX forward rate fully incorporates borrowing cost in both currencies so spread is zero) is not in keeping with the real world (where there is preference for borrowing in certain currencies). Moving on to FX options, we discussed how the market actually quotes for at-the-money options, strangles (long a call and a put) and risk reversals (long a call and short a put). Even at-the-money is subject to conventions (it is usually defined to be such that the delta of a call and a put are equal) and deltas also involve market conventions. In FX, barriers are liquid, as are one-touch options (i.e. where the payoff is 1 if a barrier is breached during the life of the instrument).

Coming to equities, there is much more use of exchange traded products than the other asset classes. We start with forwards and futures — the latter being exchange traded, and where again we must treat a convexity adjustment due to daily settlement of (undiscounted) P&L differences from movement in the price of the future. We next cover exchange traded options, with those on indices being European-style (exercise at expiry only) and those on single name stocks being American style (exercise any time prior to and including expiry) — the latter requiring valuation on a PDE. Finally, we considered put-call parity, which is a relation between call and put options that has to hold independent of the model used for valuation. We also considered the equivalent for digital options (i.e. payoff of 1, if underlying is above/below strike at expiry).

2.5.2 *Exercises*

(1) Suppose we have a curve built from swaps with annual coupons and spanning maturities $\{T_i = i\,y\}_{i=1}^{10}$. Suppose the swap rates $\{S_i\}_{i=1}^{10}$ are monotonically increasing (i.e. $S_i < S_j$ for $T_i < T_j$). Define annually compounded zero rates Z_i via $D(0, T_i) = \frac{1}{(1+Z_i)^i}$, where $D(0, T_i)$ is the discount factor up to time T_i. Also, define annually compounded forward rates F_i via $(1 + F_i(T_i - T_{i-1}))D(0, T_i) = D(0, T_{i-1})$. Determine which set of rates S_i, Z_i, or F_i is biggest.

(2) The Ho–Lee model assumes that the short rate has stochastic differential equation $dr_t = \theta(t)dt + \sigma dW_t$. Note that the money market account is defined via $B_T = e^{\int_0^T r_u du}$ and the discount bond is related to the short rate via $D(t, T) = E_t^B[e^{-\int_t^T r_s ds}]$. Further, let $f_{t,T}$ be the instantaneous forward rate applicable for time T as seen at time t, and defined via $D(t, T) = e^{-\int_t^T f_{t,s} ds}$. The instantaneous forward rate can be related to the short rate via $r_t = f_{t,t}$. Based on the formula in Section 2.1.1 and assuming the Libor rate L_T can be approximated via the instantaneous forward rate $f_{T,T}$ as seen at time T, determine the futures convexity adjustment based on the Ho–Lee model.

(We will discuss short rate models in Chapter 8. If you feel there is too much new material, it might be worth waiting until you have read Chapter 8 before attempting this. The reason for discussing it here is that the Ho–Lee model is a very popular model used for obtaining the futures convexity adjustment in practice.)

(3) Suppose you are given quotes on put options on interest rates of different strikes for a given maturity (i.e. payoffs are $\max(K - R_T, 0)$. For the 1% strike, the price is 0.002 and for the 2% strike, the price is 0.003. Can you construct an arbitrage based on put options of these 2 strikes? (Assume interest rates cannot go below zero.) Suppose rates can go below zero, how far below zero must rates be able to reach for an arbitrage not to exist?

(4) Compute the Black–Scholes delta and gamma for a call-option with payoff $\max(S_T - K, 0)$ at time T.

(5) Derive the formula for the Black–Scholes vega for a call option. What about a digital call option with payoff $1_{S_T > K}$ at time T?

3

Replication

"A bond is convex enough, so why do we need a convexity
adjustment?"

As discussed in Chapter 1, to hedge a derivative product, we seek to
set up a (possibly dynamic) hedging portfolio, so that the combined
value (of the derivative and the portfolio) is zero at future times,
regardless of market conditions. The value of the derivative must
therefore be worth that of the replicating portfolio.

Suppose the payoff of the derivative depends on the value of the
underlying on a fixed date (i.e. expiry), then surely it suffices for
us to have a replicating portfolio whose value agrees with the payoff of the derivative under all market conditions at expiry. If we
could set up this portfolio with available hedge instruments today
and not have to rebalance it before expiry, then we have just achieved
a static replication of our derivative. If we know the prices of all
market instruments involved, then this form of replication is model
independent.

In a more general context, suppose that in addition to its payoff
at expiry, the derivative can be subject to termination events based
on the value of the underlying at earlier times. Provided that we can
determine the required quantities of instruments needed to deal with
such termination, replication can be useful at least as a framework
to analyse pricing.

These two streams of replication will be considered in this
chapter.

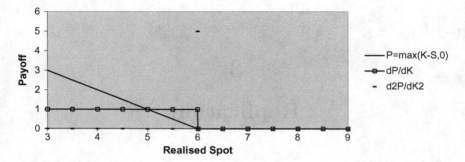

Figure 3.1:   We illustrate the payoff of a put option with strike $K = 6$ at expiry T together with its first derivative (Heaviside function) and second derivative (delta function) with respect to strike.

3.1   Static Replication

As discussed previously, the idea behind static replication is that we wish to obtain the value of a derivative whose payoff depends on the value of the underlying at expiry only. Suppose our market comprises the prices of call and put options across all strikes.

The payoff of a call option of strike K on underlying S_T at expiry T is $C_T = \max(S_T - K, 0)$ whilst that of a put option is $P_T = \max(K - S_T, 0)$.

It follows[1] that

$$\frac{\partial P_T}{\partial K} = 1_{S_T < K}.$$

Further,[2]

$$\frac{\partial^2 P_T}{\partial K^2} = \delta(S_T - K).$$

Similarly,

$$\frac{\partial C_T}{\partial K} = -1_{S_T > K} \quad \text{and} \quad \frac{\partial^2 C_T}{\partial K^2} = \delta(S_T - K).$$

---

[1] E.g. by considering the two linear segments making up the payoff $P_T = \max(K - S_T, 0)$ in Figure 3.1.

[2] Noting that $\frac{\partial P_T}{\partial K}$ comprises two constant segments with a discontinuity at $S_T = K$.

Thus,

$$\frac{\partial C_0}{\partial K} = -D(0,T)P(S_T > K),$$

$$\frac{\partial P_0}{\partial K} = D(0,T)P(S_T < K) \quad \text{and}$$

$$\frac{\partial^2 C_0}{\partial K^2} = \frac{\partial^2 P_0}{\partial K^2} = D(0,T)P(S_T = K),$$

where $D(0,T)$ is the value of a discount bond with maturity T and $P(S_T > K) = E^T\lfloor 1_{S_T > K}\rfloor$, i.e. we are taking expectations under the T-forward measure.[3]

(Note that we use $P(\bullet)$ to denote a probability and this should not be confused with the notation for the price of a put option.)

If we have a payoff $V_T = f(S_T)$ that depends on the underlying S_T at time T, its value can be obtained by integration via

$$V_0 = D(0,T) \int_{-\infty}^{\infty} f(z)P(S_T = z)dz,$$

where $P(S_T = z)$ can be obtained from the second derivative of call or put prices with respect to strike as above.

This is the main theoretical underpinning of static replication, i.e. we can obtain the implied probabilities of the underlying and integrate over them to get the value of the derivative. This is equivalent to constructing a replicating portfolio based on available market instruments.

The main drawback of static replication is that it potentially requires us to know the value of options across an infinite range of strikes. In particular, the prices of options that are very deep out-of-the-money can affect the price of the replicated product. However, typically, only options close-to-the-money are traded. In that sense, static replication is not truly model independent, as it is heavily dependent on smile extrapolation.

---

[3]I.e. with numeraire being the discount bond with maturity T.

3.1.1   *The Digital Option*

A digital call option pays 1, if the underlying S_T is above strike K at expiry T; whilst a digital put option pays 1, if the underlying is below K.

As seen earlier,

$$\frac{\partial C_T}{\partial K} = -1_{S_T > K}.$$

So, a digital call can be priced via a call spread, i.e. long $\frac{1}{2\delta}$ call options with strike $K - \delta$ and short $\frac{1}{2\delta}$ call options with strike $K + \delta$ (see Figure 3.2), with value

$$\frac{C_0(K - \delta) - C_0(K + \delta)}{2\delta} \to -\frac{\partial C_0}{\partial K} \quad \text{as } \delta \to 0.$$

We could construct the same payoff via put options as well.

Note that in the presence of volatility smile, it is not appropriate to price the digital option via the Black–Scholes formula with the same implied volatility as the standard call option. This is because we will ignore the substantial effect of smile. Specifically, our digital option should be worth

$$-\left\{ \frac{\partial C(\sigma(K), K)}{\partial K} + \frac{\partial C(\sigma(K), K)}{\partial \sigma} \frac{\partial \sigma(K)}{\partial K} \right\},$$

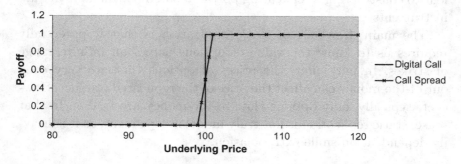

Figure 3.2:   Payoff of a digital call with strike 100, versus a call spread (i.e. long 0.5 call with strike 99, and short 0.5 call with strike 101). As the strikes of the call spread get increasingly close to 100, we approach the digital payoff.

where the first term is the Black–Scholes digital option price, whilst the second term comprises the Black–Scholes vega times the derivative of volatility with respect to strike. If smile is significant, then $\frac{\partial \sigma(K)}{\partial K}$ will have a large absolute value, so that the contribution from the second term will be substantial.

In a similar vein, a digital put option can be priced via a put spread, i.e. long $\frac{1}{2\delta}$ put options with strike $K + \delta$ and short $\frac{1}{2\delta}$ put options with strike $K - \delta$.

3.1.2   *The Libor-in-Arrears*

The typical floating leg has a coupon that is based on a Libor rate L_T set at the start of the period T and paid at the end of the period $T + \tau$. A Libor-in-arrears (LIA) product is where the set date and pay date of the Libor rate are the same (typically at the end of the period, but it makes no difference conceptually if they are at the start of the period, which we shall assume in the rest of this section for convenience). See Figure 3.3 for an illustration.

As discussed in Section 1.2.1,

$$L_T = \left(\frac{1}{D(T, T + \tau)} - 1 \right) \Big/ \tau,$$

where the Libor rate is a martingale under the $T+\tau$-forward measure with discount bond $D(t, T + \tau)$ as numeraire. Thus, the value of a floating leg payoff is

$$D(0, T + \tau)E^{T+\tau}[L_T] = D(0, T + \tau)L_0.$$

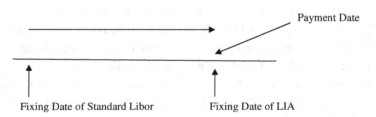

Figure 3.3:   The fixing date of a standard Libor is at the start of the period whilst the payment date is at the end. In contrast, the fixing date and payment date of an LIA are the same.

In contrast, the value of an LIA is

$$D(0,T)E^T[L_T] = D(0,T+\tau)E^{T+\tau}[L_T(1+L_T\tau)]$$
$$= D(0,T+\tau)\{L_0 + \tau E^{T+\tau}[L_T^2]\}$$
$$= D(0,T+\tau)L_0\left\{1 + \frac{E^{T+\tau}[L_T^2]}{L_0}\tau\right\},$$

where we have changed to the $T+\tau$-forward measure.

Notice this is more than the floating payoff grown at the prevailing Libor rate L_0 since $E^{T+\tau}[L_T^2] > L_0^2$, i.e. an LIA is worth more than a standard floating payoff. We refer to the difference as the convexity adjustment.

Conceptually, we expect the LIA to be more valuable, since as per our discussion in Section 2.1.1 about futures, in an LIA, we are in the fortunate situation of receiving a higher payoff earlier[4] when rates are high, and so are able to invest it at the higher rate.

From a pricing perspective, we can consider our earlier discussion on integrating over implied densities. However, it might be more instructive to demonstrate with an actual replication argument. We intend to obtain the fair LIA rate. To do this, we want to find the price C_0 of an LIA caplet with an arbitrary strike K and the price F_0 of an LIA floorlet with strike K. Then put-call parity can be used to find the fair LIA rate L_0^* via

$$C_0 - F_0 = D(0,T)(L_0^* - K).$$

Our LIA caplet has payoff $\max(L_T - K, 0)\tau$ at expiry T. We shall replicate our LIA caplet with standard market caplets with payoff $C_T^i = \frac{\max(L_T - K_i)\tau}{1+L_T\tau}$, where $K = K_0 < K_1 < K_2 < \cdots < K_N < \cdots$ Specifically, we wish to construct the replicating portfolio by determining the weight w_i for the option with strike K_i.

Suppose at expiry T, $L_T \leq K$. Then the LIA caplet is worthless and so is our replicating portfolio (since the lowest strike of the caplets is $K_0 = K$).

---

[4]I.e. at the start of the period.

Now, suppose $L_T = K_1$. Then our LIA caplet is worth $(K_1 - K_0)\tau$ whereas our replicating portfolio is worth $w_0 \frac{(K_1 - K_0)\tau}{1 + K_1\tau}$, giving $w_0 = 1 + K_1\tau$.

If instead $L_T = K_2$, our LIA caplet is worth $(K_2 - K_0)\tau$ whereas our replicating portfolio is worth $w_0 \frac{(K_2 - K_0)\tau}{1 + K_2\tau} + w_1 \frac{(K_2 - K_1)\tau}{1 + K_2\tau}$, giving

$$w_1 = \left[(K_2 - K_0) - w_0 \frac{(K_2 - K_0)}{1 + K_2\tau} \right] \frac{1 + K_2\tau}{(K_2 - K_1)}.$$

Similarly, we can obtain by considering the case $L_T = K_{i+1}$,

$$w_i = \left[(K_{i+1} - K_0) - \sum_{j=0}^{i-1} w_j \frac{(K_{i+1} - K_j)}{1 + K_{i+1}\tau} \right] \frac{1 + K_{i+1}\tau}{(K_{i+1} - K_i)}.$$

Continuing indefinitely for higher strikes and assuming the K_i's are infinitesimally close together, we get our replicating portfolio. Figure 3.4 gives a pictorial representation of how we construct the replicating portfolio. In practice, of course, we stop our replication at a sufficiently high strike (e.g. a few hundred percent).

We can replicate LIA floorlets via a portfolio of standard floorlets in the same way, and by combining the LIA caplet and LIA floorlet we obtain our fair LIA rate as desired.

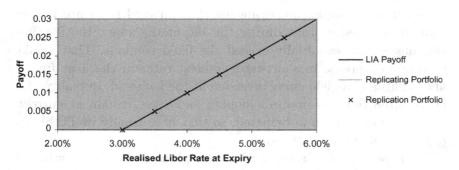

Figure 3.4: Illustration of replication of LIA caplet by constructing a portfolio of standard caplets, so that the payoffs match if the Libor rate at expiry is on the replication points indicated.

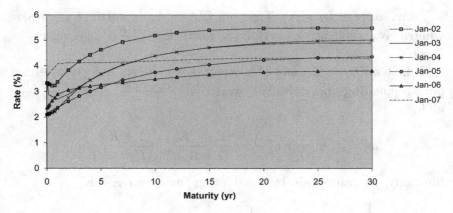

Figure 3.5:   Some euro swap curves from 2002 to 2007. Notice how the curves have been upward sloping much of the time until 2007.

Source: Bloomberg data.

3.1.3   *The Constant Maturity Swap*

The motivation for a constant maturity swap (CMS) comes from the observation that the yield curve tends to be upward sloping in the US and eurozone much of the time (see Figure 3.5 for some sample euro curves over the period). So, if you do a swap, floating coupons based on the 3-month Libor rate (in dollars) or 6-month Euribor rate (in euros) will at least initially be smaller than fixed coupons based on the comparable fixed rate for the maturity of the swap (e.g. 10-year swap rate).

An upward sloping curve means that forward rates are higher than spot rates, so that during the life of the swap, the floating coupons should eventually exceed the fixed coupons. That would require an increase in short-term interest rates in the near future and eventually a yield curve inversion at the long-end. In reality, the curve often remains upwards sloping and rates remain at current levels far longer than anticipated, so that it is usually profitable to pay 'float' and receive 'fixed'.

Perhaps, however, rates are low enough and you do not want to lock into a fixed rate over the life of the swap,[5] since there is a high probability of rates increasing (even if the curve remains upward

---

[5]E.g. for the next 10 years.

sloping). This brings us to the CMS, a product that pays a long-term swap rate (e.g. 10-year rate) which sets at the beginning of each coupon period. (For simplicity, let us assume in this section that the CMS rate is paid on the date it is set.)

Suppose the swap rate has increased. Whereas in a typical swap, the swap rate is to be received in regular intervals over the life of the swap, in the CMS, receiving the swap rate immediately allows you to invest at the same rate over the next 10 years. As discussed earlier in the context of the LIA, this is highly advantageous and so the CMS rate must be worth more than the swap rate, i.e. we have a convexity adjustment.

As discussed in Section 2.2.2, the market in euros and sterling (UK) involves cash-settled swaptions. A payer (right to pay the fixed leg) cash-settled swaption of strike K and based on the swap rate R_T at expiry T has payoff

$$\max(R_T - K, 0)A_C,$$

where the cash annuity is defined via

$$A_C(R_T) = \sum_{i=1}^{N} \frac{1}{\left(1 + \frac{R_T}{n}\right)^{ni}} = \frac{1 - \frac{1}{\left(1 + \frac{R_T}{n}\right)^{nN}}}{\left(1 + \frac{R_T}{n}\right)^{n} - 1}.$$

This means the payoff of a cash-settled swaption is fully specified as a function of the swap rate, and does not depend on any other rate.

If we consider the payoff of a CMS caplet, i.e. $\max(R_T - K, 0)$, we can see immediately that we can use a portfolio of cash-settled swaptions of strikes K_i to replicate this in a similar manner to our LIA as discussed in Section 3.1.2. Specifically, having obtained the weights $w_0, w_1, \ldots, w_{i-1}$, we need to choose w_i such that for $R_T = K_{i+1}$ we satisfy

$$K_{i+1} - K_0 = \sum_{j=0}^{i} w_j(K_{i+1} - K_j)A_C(K_{i+1}).$$

From the price of a CMS caplet and that of a CMS floorlet (obtainable by replication as well), we can obtain the fair value CMS rate by put-call parity as for our LIA.

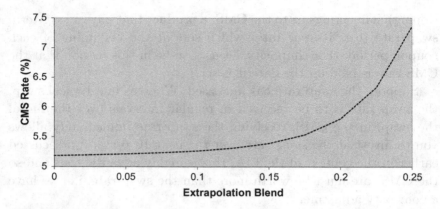

Figure 3.6:   We have fitted a SABR surface to the 10y by 10y swaption market representative of late 2010. Beyond a strike of 15%, we have assumed a flat vol. But what vol
should we extrapolate flat in, e.g. a normal vol (i.e. extrapolation blend 0), a lognormal
vol (i.e. 1) or in between? We see how the choice of extrapolation blend significantly
affects the replicated CMS rate. (Note that blend will be discussed in Section 5.3.3
whilst SABR will be discussed in Section 6.2. The message here is that the CMS rate
depends a lot on high strike vols.)

The convexity adjustment for the CMS rate is given by

$$R_0^* - R_0,$$

where R_0^* is the fair value CMS rate and R_0 is the fair value swap
rate. This convexity adjustment grows as expiry or tenor increases,
so that for a 30-year forward starting CMS rate on a 30-year tenor, a
convexity adjustment of 2% to 3% (in absolute rate levels) is possible
in contrast with a forward swap rate that might be also around 3%.
Furthermore, this convexity adjustment is the result of replicating
using swaptions with strikes going up to infinity in theory. Whereas
it is typical to obtain the volatilities from a surface like SABR,[6]
market quotes for swaptions tend to involve strikes of up to only
8%. So, assumptions regarding the extrapolation of volatility beyond
that represented by market prices have a very significant impact on
the CMS convexity adjustment (see Figure 3.6). In this sense, the
pricing of CMS products is not truly model-independent.

---

[6]See Chapter 6.

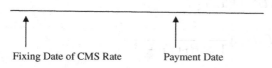

Reference Rate (e.g. 10-year)

Fixing Date of CMS Rate   Payment Date

Figure 3.7:   A CMS rate typically sets at the beginning of a period based on a reference swap rate (e.g. 10-year rate), and pays at the end of the period (e.g. 3 months later).

3.1.4   *Payment Delay*

We have slightly simplified the discussion in Section 3.1.3 assuming that our CMS rate was paid at the set date. In practice, it is more typical for a CMS rate to be set at the start of the period and paid at the end of the period (see Figure 3.7). From our earlier discussion about positive convexity from being paid early, we can anticipate that this payment delay of 3 or 6 months typically will lead to a negative convexity adjustment (vis-à-vis the CMS rate).

Let us consider the CMS payoff again based on the rate R_T set at time T. We are really evaluating the payoff

$$D(0, T)E^T[R_T].$$

If we have payment delay, so that payment is instead made at time $T_P > T$, then the new payoff is

$$D(0, T)E^T[R_T D(T, T_P)].$$

This is troublesome because we now have to take account of another interest rate (for discounting).

For replication, it is much more convenient to stick to the framework where we have a payoff solely dependent on R_T. So, it is natural to choose $D(T, T_P)$ to be a function of R_T. Perhaps a simple choice might be

$$D(T, T_P) = \frac{A}{1 + R_T(T_P - T)},$$

where the constant A is chosen to ensure no arbitrage by recovering the price of a discount bond with maturity T_P, i.e.

$$D(0, T_P) = D(0, T)E^T[D(T, T_P)]$$

$$= AD(0, T)E^T\left[\frac{1}{1 + R_T(T_P - T)}\right]$$

$$\Rightarrow A = \frac{D(0, T_P)}{D(0, T)}\bigg/ E^T\left[\frac{1}{1 + R_T(T_P - T)}\right].$$

3.1.5 *The Linear Swap Rate Model*

In the US, swaptions are physically settled with payoff at expiry

$$\max(R_T - K, 0)A_T.$$

This payoff is not fully determined by the swap rate R_T but further requires determination of the annuity

$$A_T = \sum_{i=1}^{N} \tau_i D(T, T_i).$$

In this sense, we cannot use physically settled swaptions to replicate CMS payoffs in the US.

For practical purposes, it is often adequate to simply assume that the same volatilities apply for fictitious cash-settled swaptions in the US, and replicate as before. This is not entirely satisfactory as the assumption is not really justifiable.

Furthermore, as discussed in Section 2.2.2, pricing cash-settled swaptions via Black's formula is not self consistent as the cash annuity is not a proper numeraire. This means that unless we adjust for the cash annuity price, we will not have an arbitrage-free replication for our CMS.

The above-mentioned leads to some interest in the use of physically settled swaptions to replicate CMS products by introducing a relation between the annuity-rebased discount bond price and the swap rate.

The idea behind this relation is attributed to Hunt and Kennedy [HK04]. Specifically, they posit that

$$\frac{D(T, T_P)}{A_T} = a_{T_P} + b_{T_P} R_T,$$

where T is the set date, $D(T, T_P)$ is the discount bond up to maturity $T_P \geq T$, and a_{T_P} and b_{T_P} are constants dependent on T_P.

Based on the above assumption, we now have a means of relating the physically settled swaption payoff

$$\max(R_T - K, 0) A_T$$

to the CMS payoff

$$\max(R_T - K, 0) = \max(R_T - K, 0)\frac{D(T, T)}{A_T} A_T \quad \text{since } D(T, T) = 1$$

$$= \max(R_T - K, 0)(a_T + b_T R_T) A_T$$

and can use replication in a similar vein as before.

Furthermore, if the market is comprised primarily of cash-settled swaptions (e.g. in the eurozone), we effectively would have to calibrate our physically settled swaption volatilities so as to recover the prices of cash-settled swaptions. This we are able to do since we can use physically settled swaptions to replicate cash-settled swaptions as well under the above framework. After all, the payoff for cash-settled swaptions is

$$\max(R_T - K, 0) A_C(R_T) = \max(R_T - K, 0) A_C(R_T)\frac{D(T, T)}{A_T} A_T$$

$$= \max(R_T - K, 0) A_C(R_T)(a_T + b_T R_T) A_T.$$

It is important to note that for no arbitrage the main constraints are

$$1 = \sum_{i=1}^{N} \frac{\tau_i D(T, T_i)}{A_T} = \sum_{i=1}^{N} \tau_i a_{T_i} + R_T \sum_{i=1}^{N} \tau_i b_{T_i},$$

giving

$$\sum_{i=1}^{N} \tau_i a_{T_i} = 1 \quad \text{and} \quad \sum_{i=1}^{N} \tau_i b_{T_i} = 0.$$

Also,

$$\frac{D(0, T_P)}{A_0} = E^A\left[\frac{D(T, T_P)}{A_T}\right] = a_{T_P} + b_{T_P} R_0,$$

giving

$$a_{T_P} = \frac{D(0, T_P)}{A_0} - b_{T_P} R_0.$$

3.1.6   *Auto-Quantoes*

Let us consider a typical foreign exchange (FX) option. The payoff at expiry T is $\max(S_T - K, 0)$ in domestic currency, where K is strike and S_T is the value of the underlying quoted as number of units of domestic currency per unit of foreign currency. For example, if the currency pair is GBP/USD, the domestic currency is the dollar, and the underlying is quoted as number of dollars per sterling (British pound).

What if the payoff is now defined to be numerically the same figure but payable in units of foreign currency (i.e. pounds here)? This is an auto-quanto (i.e. self-quanto).

The above is equivalent to a payoff of $\max(S_T - K, 0)S_T$ in dollars, since we can convert our sterling amount to dollars. So, we could price this payoff via replication,[7] where our replicating portfolio comprises standard FX options with payoff $\max(S_T - K_i, 0)$ payable in domestic currency (i.e. the dollar here). Here, we thus see another example of a product where static replication is applicable.

It should not be too hard to see that since we have a squared payoff (i.e. in S_T^2), the fair value strike for an auto-quanto has to be higher than S_0.

Conceptually, let us see how this is related to the martingale pricing equation. Specifically, recall that the martingale pricing equation

$$\frac{V_t}{A_t} = E_t^A\left[\frac{V_T}{A_T}\right]$$

requires that the asset V_t and the numeraire asset A_t are both domestic assets (i.e. valued in units of domestic currency).

---

[7]In the same vein as Sections 3.1.2 and 3.1.3.

In our example, $\max(S_T - K, 0)$ is in units of foreign currency (sterling), so we need to convert it to units of domestic currency (dollar) by multiplying by S_T.

3.1.7 *Variance Swaps*

Variance swaps are products that allow one to take a position on realised variance. Specifically, the payoff for a variance swap with strike K is typically defined as

$$V(\{T_i\}_{i=0}^N) - K,$$

where

$$V(\{T_i\}_{i=0}^N) = \frac{1}{T} \sum_{i=1}^N (\log S_{T_i} - \log S_{T_{i-1}})^2$$

is the realised variance over the period based on observations at $\{T_i\}_{i=1}^N$.

Typically, observations are on a daily basis, so that if the remaining period for observations is long enough (e.g. a few months), we can approximate the payoff via

$$\frac{1}{T} \sum_{i=1}^N (\log S_{T_i} - \log S_{T_{i-1}})^2 \to \frac{1}{T} \int_0^T (d\log S_t)^2 = V_T.$$

Consider a general diffusion process for the underlying asset

$$dS_t = \mu(S_t, \theta_t, t) S_t dt + \sigma(S_t, \theta_t, t) S_t dW_t,$$

where $\sigma(S_t, \theta_t, t)$ can be stochastic, so that

$$d\log S_t = \left(\mu(S_t, \theta_t, t) - \frac{1}{2}\sigma^2(S_t, \theta_t, t) \right) dt + \sigma(S_t, \theta_t, t) dW_t$$

from Ito's Lemma.

In addition, Ito's Lemma gives

$$d\log S_t = \frac{dS_t}{S_t} - \frac{1}{2} \frac{(dS_t)^2}{S_t^2} dt$$

$$= \frac{dS_t}{S_t} - \frac{1}{2}\sigma^2(S_t, \theta_t, t) dt.$$

Then,

$$V_T = \frac{1}{T} \int_0^T (d\log S_t)^2 = \frac{1}{T} \int_0^T \sigma^2(S_t, \theta_t, t) dt$$

$$= \frac{2}{T} \int_0^T \frac{dS_t}{S_t} - \frac{2}{T} \log \frac{S_T}{S_0}.$$

This means that to hedge a variance swap, we need to dynamically keep a position of $\frac{2}{TS_t}$ in the underlying, as well as set up a static position in the log-contract $r_T = \log S_T$. This log-contract can be priced by replication as per our earlier discussion.

It is instructive at this point to consider the formulation of the replication approach by Carr and Lee [CL05]. Specifically, we can write

$$f(S_T) = f(K) + \int_K^{S_T} f'(u) du$$

$$= f(K) + \int_K^{S_T} f'(K) du + \int_K^{S_T} (f'(u) - f'(K)) du$$

$$= f(K) + f'(K)(S_T - K) + \int_K^{S_T} \int_K^u f''(v) dv du$$

$$= f(K) + f'(K)(S_T - K) + \int_K^{S_T} \int_v^{S_T} du f''(v) dv$$

$$= f(K) + f'(K)(S_T - K) + \int_K^{S_T} f''(v)(S_T - v) dv$$

$$= f(K) + f'(K)(S_T - K) + \int_K^{S_T} f''(v)(S_T - v) 1_{S_T \geq K} dv$$

$$+ \int_{S_T}^K f''(v)(v - S_T) 1_{S_T < K} dv$$

$$= f(K) + f'(K)(S_T - K) + \int_K^\infty f''(v) \max(S_T - v, 0) dv$$

$$+ \int_0^K f''(v) \max(v - S_T, 0) dv,$$

where we have resorted to changing the order of integration amongst other things.

Notice that setting $K = S_0 = E[S_T]$ and taking expectations, we get

$$E[f(S_T)] = f(S_0) + \int_K^\infty f''(v)E[\max(S_T - v, 0)]dv$$

$$+ \int_0^K f''(v)E[\max(v - S_T, 0)]dv$$

$$\Rightarrow D(0,T)E[f(S_T)] = D(0,T)f(S_0)$$

$$+ \int_K^\infty f''(v)C(v,T)dv + \int_0^K f''(v)P(v,T)dv,$$

where $C(v,T)$ is the price of a call option with strike v and expiry T and $P(v,T)$ is the corresponding price of a put option.

So, the expected value of our payoff is a weighted sum of prices of calls and puts. This result ties in with our earlier discussion of how calls and puts give the implied probability of the underlying.[8]

In our variance swap, $f(S_T) = \log S_T$, so our weights are given by

$$f''(v) = -\frac{1}{v^2}.$$

It is worth mentioning that the variance swap is particularly sensitive to high strike volatilities, since we have to replicate over a theoretically infinite range of strikes. As discussed earlier, we do not always have reliable information on high strike volatilities, thus making the practical utility of replication more limited than otherwise appears. In particular, although the volatility swap with payoff $\sqrt{V(\{T_i\}_{i=0}^N)} - K$ has a model-dependent price, it is sometimes preferred by market participants to the variance swap, since it is less sensitive to high strike volatilities.[9]

A final remark is that static replication will not work for the variance swap in the presence of jumps, or discrete dividends

---

[8]This is yet another way of constructing a replicating portfolio. The discrete replication approach of Section 3.1.2 and 3.1.3 or the integration over an implied density approach of Section 3.1 will also work here.

[9]Chapter 7 discusses the volatility swap in more detail.

or stochastic interest rates, although in some cases, a reasonable approximation can be obtained.

3.2   Replication as a Framework

But alas, the list of products that could be treated via static replication is limited. Products whose payoffs depend on the value of an underlying at more than one point in time would generally not be amenable to static replication.

It should be remarked that it is difficult for an easy-to-calibrate model to have all the features desired of an underlying (e.g. proper forward volatility and skew evolution for all time points). To this end, a generalised replication framework can provide insights into what aspects of a model some products really depend on. We shall thus consider applying a replication framework to the treatment of barrier options in this section.

3.2.1   *Barriers Under Deterministic Volatility*

As discussed in Section 2.3.3, a barrier option has a payoff akin to a European option but would be extinguished if the underlying breaches a barrier prior to expiry. Let us consider the down-and-out European call with payoff

$$\max(S_T - K, 0)1_{\min_{0<t\leq T} S_t > H},$$

where S_t is the value of the underlying at time t, K is the strike, $H < S_0$ is the barrier level, and T is the expiry.

We intend to construct a replicating portfolio. Let us assume we have at our disposal European calls and puts and digitals with any strike and expiry.

Suppose our barrier option has survived until expiry T. Then its payoff is the same as a European call option, so we need to include a European call option in our replicating portfolio.

Let us now consider points in time $0 < T_0 < T_1 < \cdots < T_{N-1} < T_N = T$. We shall construct a replicating portfolio comprising the European call option and w_i of digital put options with strike H at expiry T. For the discussion below, we adopt the following notation:

At time t given spot S_t and implied volatility $\sigma(S_t, K, t)$ for strike K our European call option with strike K and expiry T has value $C(t, S_t, \sigma(S_t, t, K), K, T)$ whilst our digital put option with strike H and expiry T_i has value $P(t, S_t, \sigma(S_t, t, H), H, T_i)$.

Suppose at time T_{N-1}, the underlying is at the barrier level H. Then the barrier option is worth 0 since the barrier level is breached. So, our replicating portfolio should be worth zero as well. This gives

$$0 = C(T_{N-1}, H, \sigma(H, T_{N-1}, K), K, T)$$
$$+ w_{N-1} P(T_{N-1}, H, \sigma(H, T_{N-1}, H), H, T_{N-1})$$
$$= C(T_{N-1}, H, \sigma(H, T_{N-1}, K), K, T) + w_{N-1},$$

since $P(T_{N-1}, H, \sigma(H, T_{N-1}, H), H, T_{N-1}) = 1$ with spot being at the digital option's strike H, so that

$$w_{N-1} = -C(T_{N-1}, H, \sigma(H, T_{N-1}, K), K, T).$$

Suppose instead that at time T_{N-2}, the underlying is at the barrier level H, so that the barrier option is again worth zero. This requires our replicating portfolio to be worth zero, giving

$$0 = C(T_{N-2}, H, \sigma(H, T_{N-2}, K), K, T)$$
$$+ w_{N-1} P(T_{N-2}, H, \sigma(H, T_{N-2}, H), H, T_{N-1}) + w_{N-2},$$

from which we can obtain w_{N-2}.

Working backward in time, considering $S_{T_i} = H$, we obtain in general

$$0 = C(T_i, H, \sigma(H, T_i, K), K, T)$$
$$+ \sum_{j=i+1}^{N-1} w_j P(T_i, H, \sigma(H, T_i, H), H, T_j) + w_i,$$

and hence can determine each weight w_i. See Figure 3.8 for an illustration of the expiry points at which we construct our replicating portfolio.

Then replication gives the value of the barrier option today as

$$C(0, S_0, \sigma(S_0, 0, K), K, T) + \sum_{j=1}^{N-1} w_j P(0, S_0, \sigma(S_0, 0, H), H, T_j).$$

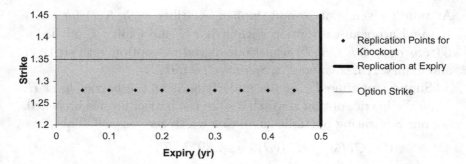

Figure 3.8:   When replicating a barrier option, we need a European call option to match the payoff at expiry, as well as digital put options with expiries at the points indicated to replicate the payoff upon knockout.

Notice that this approach is not really model-independent. After all, at future times, we need to evaluate the prices of unexpired options, which generally requires us to know the implied volatilities $\sigma(S_{T_i} = H, T_i, H)$ and $\sigma(S_{T_i} = H, T_i, K)$. If volatility is deterministic (e.g. in a Black–Scholes world), then replication would give the price of our barrier option. Otherwise, we still need a mechanism to determine $\sigma(S_t = H, t, K)$ in order to use replication.

It is worth mentioning that other barrier products can be treated by replication in a similar way. For example, the upside one-touch option with payoff

$$1_{\max_{0 < t \leq T} S_t > H}$$

can be treated by replicating with digital call options at the points indicated in Figure 3.9.

3.2.2   *Barriers Given Volatility Dynamics*

We have seen that replication is not really model-independent in the case of a barrier option. However, it still gives a useful framework to understand the pricing of barrier options. After all, for our down-and-out call option above, the price can be fully determined if we know the implied volatilities $\sigma(S_{T_i} = H, T_i, H)$ and $\sigma(S_{T_i} = H, T_i, K)$, i.e. if we know implied volatilities at future times conditional on spot being at the barrier level H. This

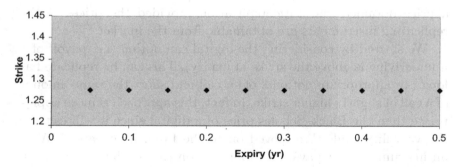

Figure 3.9: When replicating an upside one-touch option, we need digital options with expiries at the points shown to replicate the payoff when the barrier is breached.

is a considerably simpler requirement than knowing the implied volatilities for all values of spot at a future time.

In particular, if one has a good intuition as to how implied volatility behaves say if spot decreases from current levels (i.e. so that it hits the barrier), then a heuristic approach to approximate implied volatilities at the barrier level (based on current implied volatilities) can produce decent prices of barrier options. This approach has actually been used in some institutions.

Alternatively, even if we have a full term structure model of the underlying, it is only the behaviour of implied volatility when spot is at the barrier at a future time that affects the price of a barrier option. In this sense, when calibrating the model to fit the prices of barrier options, it is useful to bear in mind this particular aspect.[10]

3.3   Consolidation

3.3.1   *Summary*

Static replication involves constructing a portfolio today, which will have exactly the same payoff as the financial derivative of interest. The value of the portfolio must then be the value of the derivative. To the extent that there is no need for a model to determine how to rebalance the portfolio over time, one can be more confident of

---

[10]We shall discuss barrier products in detail in Chapter 7.

a price obtained via static replication provided the prices of the replicating instruments are obtainable from the market.

We started by considering the digital call option (i.e. payoff of 1 if underlying is above the strike at expiry). This can be replicated as long (an appropriate notional of) a call and short the same amount of a call of slightly higher strike. In fact, this approach is more appropriate than the Black–Scholes price of a digital since it will capture the volatility smile. We moved on to the Libor-in-arrears (LIA — an instrument that pays the Libor rate on the set date rather than at the end of the period), which attracts a convexity adjustment. We have presented this from the perspective of change of measure, an economic perspective (on how it is possible to invest a gain at the same rate or fund a loss at the same reduced rate) as well as via replication (constructing a portfolio of standard caplets to replicate an LIA caplet, and similarly for an LIA floorlet and then appealing to put-call parity for the par LIA rate). In this way, we have seen multiple explanations for the same phenomena of convexity and how squared (Libor) rates are actually not too bizarre.

We moved on to the constant maturity swap (CMS) (i.e. paying a long-term, say 10-year, rate applied to a shorter period of say 3 months), which was popular because the curve was upward sloping but rates seemed poised to rise. Here, since cash-settled swaptions depend on only the swap rate, we can naturally replicate a CMS caplet or floorlet via a portfolio of cash-settled swaptions. Again, put-call parity then determines the par CMS rate. Payment delay comes in because typically payment is at the end of the period (e.g. 3 months after the rate is set), and the solution is to treat discounting as a function of the swap rate and then apply replication as before. Problems with the cash annuity being not a proper numeraire have led some institutions to adopt the Linear Swap Rate approach (i.e. discount bond over physical annuity is taken as an affine function of the swap rate), so that physically settled swaptions can be used to replicate both cash-settled swaptions (to fit to the market) and CMS caplets (the end goal).

We wrapped up static replication proper by considering auto-quantoes (an FX product paid in the foreign currency instead) and also variance swaps. For the latter, we can show that if variance is observed continuously, hedging can be effected via a quantity of a log-contract in addition to a dynamic position in the underlying. For the log-contract, we can use replication. Here we have shown yet another variation of replication, via integrals (sums) over calls and puts (attributable to Carr and Lee).

Finally, we discussed replication as a general framework for the pricing of derivatives, even if the portfolio cannot be statically constructed. Here, barrier options and one-touch options are used for further illustration. The idea is that since a barrier option knocks out if the underlying breaches the barrier level prior to expiry but is otherwise a European vanilla option, the replicating portfolio will comprise a European vanilla option with the same expiry and strike and digital options for all prior expiries and strike being at the barrier level. The issue is how to value the surviving portfolio of options if knockout occurs before expiry. We showed that actually all we need is to know the dynamics of implied volatility if spot is at the barrier level (rather than for all levels of spot) at all future times prior to expiry. This is at least a simplification in the framework.

3.3.2 *Exercises*

(1) Consider the Black–Scholes model. What is the gamma of a digital option with payoff $1_{S_T > K}$ at time T? Why would you not want to delta-hedge such an option?

(2) Assume interest rates are lognormal. Compute the convexity adjustment for the fair value LIA rate. What would the convexity adjustment be if rates are normal? (In this question, assume semi-annual accrual, take the Libor rate to be 3% and normal vol to be 1.05%.) Compare the convexity adjustment for the LIA rate setting in 30 years' time under a lognormal versus normal model where lognormal vol is taken as 35%.

(3) For a cash-settled swaption, the cash-annuity is defined by $A_C(R_T) = \sum_{i=1}^{N} \frac{1}{(1+\frac{R_T}{n})^{ni}}$. This is just some function of R_T. Do a second order Taylor-expansion of $A_C(R_T)$ about R_0. Notice that under the T-forward measure, we get $E^T[A_C(R_T)] \approx$

$A_C(R_0)$. Further, assume that the swap rate follows a lognormal process, i.e. $dR_t = \sigma R_t dW_t$. Hence, show that $E^T[R_T] \approx R_0 - \frac{1}{2}R_0^2\sigma^2 T\frac{A_c''(R_0)}{A_c'(R_0)}$ gives the classical approximation for the CMS rate in the (skewless) lognormal world.

(4) For simplicity, assume the Ho–Lee dynamics $dr_t = \theta(t)dt + \sigma dW_t$. The forward rate is given via $f(t,T) = E_t^T[r_T]$. (All this will become clear when we discuss short rate models in Chapter 8.) Suppose the payment is not at T but at a much later time S (e.g. $S = T + 10y$). Derive a formula for the payment delay adjustment. Hence, see how little the impact of payment delay is when the underlying rate sets quickly (i.e. T is small).

4

Correlation Between Two Underlyings

"There is a very high correlation between the 10-year rate and the 9-year rate. There is no correlation between the 10-year rate and the 10-year rate."

In Chapter 3, we saw that if a derivative has a payoff that depends on the value of an underlying at only one point in time, then it might be possible to obtain its value from a model-independent replication. And it is preferable to make minimal model assumptions.

More generally, what if the derivative depends on the value of two or more underlyings observed at one future date? From replication, we know the marginal probability distributions of the two underlyings. Is there a way to come up with their joint distribution? This chapter explores copula techniques, which are commonly used in financial institutions to obtain the joint distribution for pricing such products.

It should be remarked that copula techniques have also been used in credit but the suitability of their application in some cases is more questionable, since such techniques do not capture the structural dependence of two underlyings.[1] We shall not cover credit in this book and so avoid such discussions in general.

---

[1] E.g. maybe a common driver is responsible for both processes.

4.1   Copulae

Suppose we know the marginal distributions $u = P(X_T < x)$ and $v = P(Y_T < y)$ of two underlyings X_T and Y_T at a future time T. To price a payoff that depends on the value of X_T and Y_T at time T, we need their joint distribution $P(X_T < x, Y_T < y)$.

A copula is a mapping $C(u, v) = C(P(X_T < x), P(Y_T < y)) = P(X_T < x, Y_T < y)$ from the marginal distributions to the joint distribution.

A copula needs to satisfy the following properties:

(1) $C(u, 0) = C(0, v) = 0$;
(2) $C(u, 1) = u = P(X_T < x)$, $C(1, v) = v = P(Y_T < y)$; and
(3) $0 \leq C(u_2, v_2) - C(u_1, v_2) - C(u_2, v_1) + C(u_1, v_1) \leq 1$ for $u_1 < u_2$, $v_1 < v_2$ (see Figure 4.1).

Notice that this mapping only applies to a specific time T and does not capture the co-dependence of X_T and Y_T over the time period $0 < t < T$. Further, we make no assumptions as to how X_t and Y_t behave vis-à-vis each other in general, so that a copula approach will be inadequate if there is a strong structural relation between X_t and Y_t, e.g. they are both driven by a common factor.

In products whose payoffs are heavily dependent on rare events (e.g. if loss is contingent on default of multiple tranches), this can lead to underestimation of tail probabilities since a common factor (e.g. prices of houses nationwide) could be the sole driver of extreme events (e.g. default of multiple tranches across diverse state geographies in the US). This is less likely to be a problem in interest rates

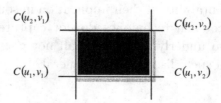

Figure 4.1:   Illustration of property 3 of a copula. This just means probability must be non-negative over any region.

(where copula techniques are used for spread options) or equities (where they are used for 'best-of' options), since the payoff is less influenced by extreme events.

4.1.1 *Marginal Distributions*

It follows that in order to use a copula technique, we first must obtain the marginal distributions of the underlyings. In Section 3.1, we explained how the prices of digital options give the implied probability distributions and densities of an underlying. Specifically, for a put option with strike K, expiry T, and payoff $P_T = \max(K - S_T, 0)$, we have

$$\frac{\partial P_0}{\partial K} = D(0, T) P(S_T < K),$$

and

$$\frac{\partial^2 P_0}{\partial K^2} = D(0, T) P(S_T = K).$$

Thus, if our underlying involves equity or foreign exchange (FX), we could obtain the implied marginal distributions from the prices of traded call and put options.

If our underlying were a constant maturity swap (CMS) rate instead, recall from Section 3.1.3 that replication (via cash-settled swaptions) can be used to obtain the prices of CMS caplets and floorlets across all strikes). Given these, we can use the above formulae to obtain the implied marginal distribution of a CMS rate. Alternatively (and more likely utilised in practice), we could use replication to obtain the price of a digital CMS put option (and hence the implied distribution) directly.

Since the above approach typically requires differentiating over prices of options with respect to strike, we need a smooth volatility surface.[2] This is not a problem as typically vol surfaces are built with smooth (i.e. twice differentiable) interpolation over strikes. However, another requirement is that we need to obtain probabilities over all strikes, which means our vol surface must be able to produce good

---

[2]E.g. a grid of volatilities by strikes with local interpolation, say linear as opposed to spline, in between is not likely to work.

prices for deep out-of-the-money options. This is not always the case as some volatility parameterisations commonly used in practice[3] are not arbitrage-free over all strikes.

Under such circumstances, it may be necessary to fit an arbitrage-free parametric distribution over market prices, and then obtain the implied marginal distribution from this distribution for purposes of using the copula technique.

4.1.2   *Gaussian Copulae*

A Gaussian copula is amongst the simplest class of copulae. It is naturally described by a correlation parameter. Specifically, we have

$$C(u, v) = N_2(N^{-1}(u), N^{-1}(v), \rho)$$
$$= N_2(N^{-1}(P(X_T < x)), N^{-1}(P(Y_T < y)), \rho),$$

where

$$N_2(x, y, \rho) = \frac{1}{2\pi\sqrt{1 - \rho^2}} \exp\left(-\frac{x^2 - 2\rho xy + y^2}{2(1 - \rho^2)}\right)$$

is the bivariate normal distribution, and $N^{-1}(x)$ is the inverse of the univariate normal distribution

$$N(x) = \frac{1}{\sqrt{2\pi}} \exp\left(-\frac{x^2}{2}\right).$$

It should be remarked that we are correlating the joint terminal distributions of the inverse marginals. Whereas this is a true correlation, it should not be interpreted as the correlation between the underlyings themselves. It also should be noted that the copula correlation is a terminal correlation rather than a local correlation, i.e. it should not be used to evolve the underlyings over time.

Whilst the Gaussian copula is simple and easily extendible to multiple underlyings, a significant drawback is that it is symmetric in the sense of the two underlyings (see Figure 4.2). This rarely corresponds to the historically observed joint distributions of any two underlyings in practice. It is possible to apply a transformation to

---

[3]E.g. the Stochastic Alpha Beta Rho (SABR) model discussed in Chapter 6.

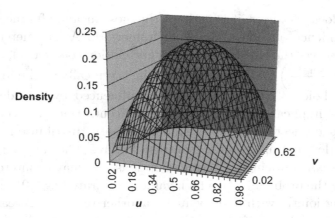

Figure 4.2:   Illustration of density of bivariate normal. Notice the symmetry in u and v. Correlation is 70% here.

skew the distribution towards one of the underlyings but the details are beyond the scope of this book.

4.1.3   *Archimedean Copulae*

Another popular class of copulae in use are Archimedean copulae. These are defined in terms of a generator function, i.e.

$$C(u, v) = \psi^{-1}(\psi(u) + \psi(v))$$

for some function $\psi(x)$ over $[0, 1]$.

Three particularly commonly used Archimedean copulae are the Clayton copula with generator function

$$\psi(x) = x^\theta - 1,$$

the Gumbel copula with generator function

$$\psi(x) = (-\log x)^\theta,$$

and the Frank copula with generator function

$$\psi(x) = -\log\left(\frac{e^{-\theta x} - 1}{e^{-\theta} - 1}\right).$$

Notice that we have a free parameter θ to capture correlation. This does not capture the correlation in the way a Gaussian copula does. However, it is perhaps the most meaningful measure of co-dependence outside a Gaussian framework. A parameterisation that preserves the Kendall tau (rank correlation coefficient), e.g. $\theta = 1 \big/ \left(1 - \frac{2\sin^{-1}\rho}{\pi}\right)$ for the Gumbel copula, is typically used in practice.

The choice of copulae is typically influenced by considerations as to the implications for probability concentration, i.e. whether it increases or decreases the likelihood of both distributions jointly yielding low or high values (contrast Figures 4.3a and 4.3b). For example, when pricing CMS spread options,[4] we may be interested in reducing the probability of a high value of one rate (e.g. 10-year rate) occurring jointly with a low value of another rate (e.g. 2-year rate).

For completeness, it is worth mentioning the three special cases below, where we end up with perfect postive correlation, zero correlation, and perfect negative correlation.

For perfect positive correlation, we have

$$C(u, v) = \min(u, v).$$

For zero correlation, we have

$$C(u, v) = uv.$$

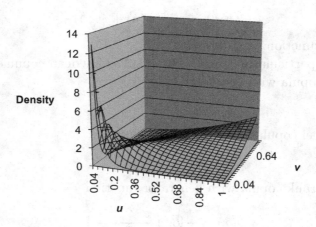

Figure 4.3a: Illustration of the density of the Clayton copula.

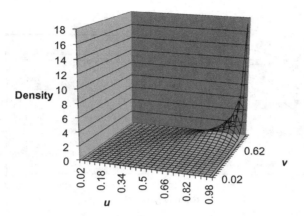

Figure 4.3b: Illustration of the density of the Gumbel copula. Notice the concentration of density is in different regions for the two copulae (compare with Figure 4.3a).

For perfect negative correlation, we have

$$C(u, v) = \max(u + v - 1).$$

4.2   Financial Products

It should be reiterated that copula techniques are generally only suitable if you have to price a payoff that depends on the value of two or more underlyings at a single point in time. In this section, we shall explore some of the more common payoffs in interest rates and equities that are amenable to such treatment.

4.2.1   *CMS Spread Options*

Recall our discussion in Section 3.1.3 about how an upward sloping yield curve coupled with a low interest rates environment in the 2000s provided an economic rationale for CMS products.[5] In a similar vein, an upward sloping curve which flattens at the long end provided the motivation for CMS spread products over the same period. Figure 4.4 shows typical shapes of the US yield curve over the 2000s.

---

[5]I.e. where the payoff is of a floating long-term rate of say 10 years but applied over a single shorter accrual period of say 3 months.

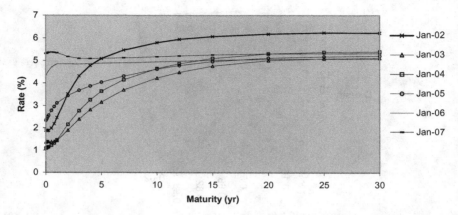

Figure 4.4: Sample US dollar yield curves from 2002 to 2007. Notice how the curves remained upward sloping until around 2006.
Source: Bloomberg data.

Basically, a CMS spread product involves the difference between two swap rates (e.g. 10-year rate and 2-year rate). Since the yield curve flattens at the long end, we expect the 10-year forward spread to be much closer to zero than the spread today. If however, the yield curve remains upward sloping and hence perpetuates its shape, the realised spread 10 years from now will be positive. So, there could be good reasons for betting against forward rates being realised — a familiar theme in the interest rates world.

A CMS spread is just a linear combination of two CMS rates. We could price each separately and hence obtain the combined value. However, to price a CMS spread option we would need the joint distribution of the two CMS rates at the set date.

Specifically, let us define the spread option to have payoff

$$\max(R_T^1 - R_T^2 - K, 0),$$

where R_T^1, R_T^2 are the values of the two swap rates (e.g. for 10-year and 2-year terms) at set date T and K is the strike.

We can use replication to obtain the implied marginal distributions of the two CMS rates. Then a single copula correlation/parameter specifies their joint distribution and hence fully determines the value of the CMS spread option.

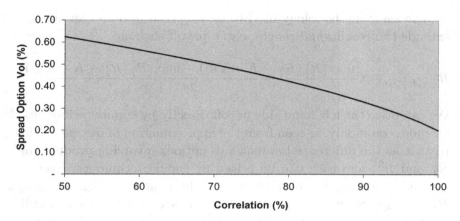

Figure 4.5: We illustrate how spread option vol decreases as correlation increases. We assume the underlying rates are normally distributed with vols of 0.5% and 0.7% for the 10-year and 2-year rates respectively.

Since replication is used to obtain the value of each CMS rate comprising the spread, the CMS convexity adjustment for each of the component rates has a significant impact on the price of a spread option. In particular, since the convexity adjustment is much higher for the swap rate of longer tenor (e.g. the 10-year rate versus the 2-year rate), this contributes significantly to the value of a CMS spread option when correlation is very close to 100%.

Nevertheless, a CMS spread option is very much a correlation product, with its value significantly dependent on the correlation between the two component rates (see Figure 4.5). From 2005 to 2008, when a liquid market existed for spread options of very long expiries (e.g. up to over 30 years), market participants often used strike-dependent correlations to fit the prices of quoted spread options.[6] Apart from its use in interpolating the price of a spread option with strike K in between two strikes K_1, K_2 for which quotes are available (i.e. $K_1 < K < K_2$), this is not necessarily a sound approach as it can produce negative joint densities.

---

[6]A bit akin to using strike-dependent implied volatilities to fit the prices of vanilla options.

The same methodology used to treat spread options can also be extended to conditional ranges, e.g. a payoff such as

$$R_T^1 1_{\{R_T^2 > K\}} \approx \frac{\max(R_T^1(R_T^2 - K - \delta, 0)) - \max(R_T^1(R_T^2 - K + \delta, 0))}{2\delta}.$$

We can price the left-hand side payoff directly by copula techniques. Or more commonly, as seen from the approximation above, we could treat it as the difference between two options involving products of R_T^1 and R_T^2, and each can be priced by copula techniques. Even if say the condition was observable at a different time, e.g. we have $R_T^1 1_{\{R_S^2 > K\}}$, where $S \neq T$ (but S and T are close), we could still treat the joint distribution via copula techniques provided we make assumptions about the impact of payment delay,[7] as well as the implications of different set dates on the copula correlation between the two underlyings.

Of course, copula techniques can also be used to treat more general payoffs dependent on two CMS rates observed at a single future time.

4.2.2   *Quantoes*

In Section 3.1.6, we considered the situation of an FX payoff in a non-natural currency. Let X_T be the value of an FX rate quoted as number of units of domestic currency per unit of foreign currency (e.g. GBP/USD is number of units of dollars per pound). Then a typical option has payoff $\max(X_T - K, 0)$ in domestic currency (i.e. in dollars here). If the payoff is in the foreign currency, then we have an auto-quanto, which is priced by converting it to the domestic currency.

This concept applies more generally. Specifically, consider the value of a domestic asset S_T. Suppose we have a contract $V_T = f(S_T)$ that pays based on the domestic asset S_T, but in units of foreign currency without conversion at the appropriate exchange rate. We note that the martingale equation works only in terms of domestic assets.

---

[7]As discussed in Section 3.1.4.

The value of our contract in terms of units of domestic currency is

$$V_T X_T.$$

Thus, we have

$$\frac{V_t X_t}{A_t} = E_t^A \left[\frac{V_T X_T}{A_T} \right],$$

where A_t is the value of any domestic asset chosen as numeraire.

We thus see that we now need to evaluate the payoff $f(S_T) X_T$ at time T. This can be done using the copula techniques discussed, given the marginal distributions of S_T and X_T at time T.

Note that our approach applies to all quantoes, in that S_T can be a stock,[8] a commodity product,[9] or even an FX rate.[10]

It should be remarked that a simple approach to treat quantoes is to add a term in the drift such as $-\rho \sigma_S \sigma_X dt$ to the log process. This effectively assumes that both underlyings are lognormally distributed. Specifically, consider for numeraire asset $A_t = B_t$ (i.e. money market account) the following:

$$dS_t / S_t = \mu_S dt + \sigma_S dW_t^S,$$
$$dX_t / X_t = (r_t - r_t^f) dt + \sigma_X dW_t^X,$$
$$dW_t^S dW_t^X = \rho dt, \quad \text{and} \quad dB_t = r_t B_t dt.$$

Then,

$$d\left(\frac{S_t X_t}{B_t} \right) \bigg/ \frac{S_t X_t}{B_t} = \frac{dS_t}{S_t} + \frac{dX_t}{X_t} + \frac{dS_t dX_t}{S_t X_t} - \frac{dB_t}{B_t}$$

$$= \mu_S dt + \sigma_S dW_t^S + (r_t - r_t^f) dt + \sigma_X dW_t^X + \rho \sigma_S \sigma_X dt - r_t dt$$

$$= 0 dt + \sigma_S dW_t^S + \sigma_X dW_t^X$$

from the martingale pricing equation, giving

$$\mu_S = r_t^f - \rho \sigma_S \sigma_X$$

as the drift of the foreign asset under the domestic risk-neutral measure.

---

[8]E.g. sterling (pound) stock payable in euros.
[9]E.g. dollar-denominated commodity, say oil, settled in yen.
[10]E.g. EUR/CHF payable in Swedish kroners.

For non-lognormal processes, such a simple quanto adjustment may not adequately capture the effect of volatility skew. Simple extensions may be possible though, e.g. the drift is $\mu_S(S_t, X_t, t) = r_t^f - \rho\sigma_S(S_t, t)\sigma_X(X_t, t)$ if both underlyings follow local vol processes, but that means modelling a quanto requires treatment of the FX process in addition to the underlying.[11]

4.2.3   'Best-of' Products

A 'best-of' product has payoff

$$\max(w_1 S_T^1 - K_1, w_2 S_T^2 - K_2)$$

based on the realised values of two assets S_T^1, S_T^2 at some future time T, where K_1, K_2 are strikes and w_1, w_2 are weights.

In equities, it is particularly common for one to be interested in payoffs involving returns of different assets over a period, e.g. the payoff could be

$$\max\left(\frac{S_T^1}{S_0^1} - 1, \frac{S_T^2}{S_0^2} - 1\right)$$

and of course it could be capped and floored.

Copula techniques can be readily used to capture the correlation of the two stocks at a future time, where their marginal distributions are given by the prices of vanilla equity options. If there is perfect correlation, such a product effectively pays based on the stock with the higher volatility over the period (assuming that the difference in drifts is not too pronounced). This product clearly benefits from lower correlation, since there is a greater likelihood of one of the underlyings paying off. Figures 4.6a and 4.6b should hopefully illustrate this point.

Naturally, there are also products that pay based on the 'worst-of' two returns, e.g.

$$\min\left(\frac{S_T^1}{S_0^1} - 1, \frac{S_T^2}{S_0^2} - 1\right).$$

---

[11] Essentially, we face the same situation when we apply copula techniques in that we also seek to utilise the FX marginal where the FX process is not necessarily lognormal.

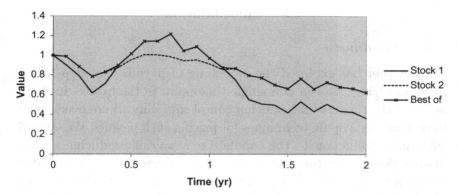

Figure 4.6a: We illustrate with two stocks with spot 1 at time zero, and vols 25% and 45% respectively. Here correlation is 80%. So, both stocks decline together.

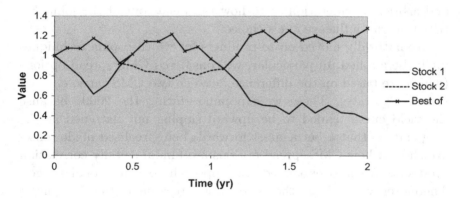

Figure 4.6b: We have the same two stocks as above but correlation is −80%. When stock 1 declines, stock 2 rises, so there is a higher probability of the 'best-of' product achieving a higher value.

These can also be treated in a similar way, but benefit from higher correlation between underlyings.

From the above discussion, it can be seen that copula techniques are particularly useful to treat products that are very sensitive to the correlation between two components, and there is a liquid market for the components. It is not difficult to extend the method to treat baskets involving multiple underlyings.

4.3 Consolidation

4.3.1 *Summary*

This chapter has explored the modelling of payoffs that depend on two underlyings as seen at a single time point in the future. In keeping with the theme of introducing complexity only where needed, we have discussed copula techniques for pricing such payoffs. We started with an introduction to the copula, i.e. a way of producing a joint distribution of two (or more) underlyings given their marginal distributions. We then showed that the marginal distributions can be obtained from the prices of digital options (which may require replication for pricing as in the case of CMS). We followed on with a mention of popular copula families, namely Gaussian and Archimedean (with three cases discussed further — Gumbel, Clayton, and Frank), and a brief consideration as to how tail behaviour of the joint distribution can influence one's choice.

We naturally moved on to products for which copula techniques might be applied. In particular, we considered CMS spread options (which are based on the difference between two CMS rates, e.g. 10y rate — 2y rate). These were popular during the 2000s because the yield curve tended to be upward sloping but flattened at the long end, so that a bet against forwards being realised made sense. We showed how CMS spread options are fundamentally correlation products. We also expanded the approach to conditional ranges. Thereafter, we explored the use of copula techniques to price quanto products (where we have an underlying paid in a different currency but with no FX rate applied). There is really no difference as to the fundamental ideas. Finally, we considered 'best-of' products, paying the maximum (or minimum) return amongst two underlyings to illustrate another application of copula techniques. We have avoided consideration of credit, but the use of copula techniques is somewhat different and perhaps more controversial.

4.3.2 *Exercises*

(1) Derive the density for the Gumbel and Clayton copulae.

(2) Suppose that two assets S_A and S_B have stochastic differential equations $dS_t^{A,B} = rS_t^{A,B} dt + \sigma_{A,B} S_t^{A,B} dW_t^{A,B}$, where $dW_t^A dW_t^B = \rho dt$. Derive the formula for the option that pays $\max(S_T^A - S_T^B, 0)$ at time T. Suppose $S_0^A = S_0^B$ and $\sigma_A = \sigma_B$. What happens to the value of the option as ρ goes to 100%?

(3) Consider a contract with payoff $\max(S_T^A, S_T^B)$ at time T. From your answer to Question 2, what is the value of such a payoff?

(4) Consider the simple convexity adjustment (Question 3 of Chapter 3) and apply it to the 10-year and 2-year CMS rates setting in 30 years' time. (Suppose for this example that both swap rates are currently at 4%, lognormal volatility is 15% and that swap rates are annually compounded.) Thus, explain how a spread option will have value even if correlation is 100%.

5

Local Volatility

"Our prices are from market instruments, so there
is no model risk."

Chapters 5 to 7 discuss local volatility and stochastic volatility, their
dynamics and implications for derivatives pricing. For simplicity,
we shall restrict ourselves to the consideration of equity or foreign
exchange (FX) in these chapters, whereas Chapters 8 and 9 will
extend our discussion into the realm of interest rates.

In Chapter 1, we saw how the implied volatility of an option
could vary depending on its expiry and strike. Implied volatility is
just a number which when used with the Black–Scholes formula gives
the observed price of an option and is therefore only a representation of price. Nevertheless, since implied volatility is not constant
over expiry and strike, clearly a lognormal model is not adequate to
describe the true dynamics of the underlying. See Figure 5.1 for an
example of volatility smiles in the FX markets.

In this chapter, we shall consider a process of the underlying that
can recover the prices of standard options for all expiries and strikes.
Going through the dynamics of such a process, we shall however
see why whilst fitting the prices of given spot starting options is
important, it is not an adequate criteria for modelling.

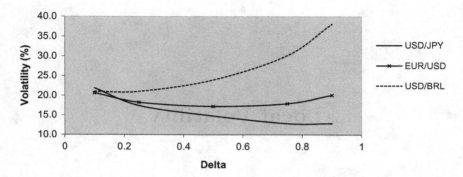

Figure 5.1:   The implied volatilities for FX options with expiry of 1 year are shown as
of 27 February 2009. Notice that different currency pairs have volatility smiles of very
different shapes.
Source: Bloomberg data.

5.1   The Theory

Notice that implied volatility $\Lambda(K, T)$ is specific to an expiry T and
strike K. However, if we were modelling an underlying, then its future
dynamics must be independent of the terms of a contract referring to it.
Instead, the only quantities its volatility can depend on would pertain
to the underlying value S_t and time t. Such a volatility $\sigma(S_t, t)$ that can
depend on S_t and t, is termed as a local volatility.

Suppose the underlying S_t follows the stochastic differential equation (SDE)

$$dS_t = \mu(t)S_t dt + \sigma(S_t, t)S_t dW_t,$$

where

the volatility $\sigma(S_t, t)$ is a function of the underlying S_t and
time t,
the drift $\mu(t) = r_t - q_t$ is as needed to ensure no arbitrage,
r_t is the domestic funding rate, and
q_t is a continuous dividend yield for equity or the foreign
funding rate for FX.

We could instead incorporate discrete dividends via the SDE

$$dS_t = (r_t S_t - D(t))dt + \sigma(S_t, t)S_t dW_t,$$

where $D(t)$ is a piecewise continuous function representing the effect
of the dividends.

We shall avoid discussing this further in the text as it just complicates the notation and also implementing this in practice can be more challenging numerically due to the discontinuous nature of the SDE.

Can $\sigma(S_t, t)$ be chosen so that the process is consistent with observed option prices on S_t for all expiries and strikes?

5.1.1   *Fokker–Planck Equation*

Today, at time zero, the value of the underlying is S_0. This is a point mass, since its probability density at time zero is $p(0, K) = \delta(S_0 - K)$. What is the probability density $p(t, K)$ of it being at K at a future time t?

Consider the familiar Ito's Lemma

$$df_t = \frac{\partial f_t}{\partial t}dt + \frac{\partial f_t}{\partial S_t}dS_t + \frac{1}{2}\frac{\partial^2 f_t}{\partial S_t^2}\sigma^2(S_t, t)S_t^2 dt$$

for a function $f(S_t, t)$ on a stochastic process S_t and time t.

$f(x, t)$ needs to be continuous and twice differentiable in x for Ito's Lemma to hold.

However, if we consider the theory of distributions, we can extend the definition of mathematical derivatives as follows[1]:

$$\frac{\partial}{\partial x}(x - K)^+ = 1_{\{x>K\}}$$

and

$$\frac{\partial}{\partial x}1_{\{x>K\}} = \delta_K(x),$$

where $1_{\{x>K\}}$ is the Heaviside step function, $\delta_K(x)$ is the Dirac delta function with point mass at K, and the n-th derivative $\delta_K^{(n)}(x)$ of the delta function is defined by

$$\int_{-\infty}^{\infty} f(x)\delta_K^{(n)}(x)dx = (-1)^n f^{(n)}(K)$$

for any arbitrary function $f(x)$. (Note that we shall also use $\delta'(x)$ and $\delta''(x)$ to refer to the first and second derivatives of $\delta(x)$.)

By extending Ito's Lemma in this way to non-differentiable $f(x, t)$, we get Tanaka's formula. For a reference with more details

---

[1] See Figure 3.1 for an illustration of similar derivatives.

of the above and its application to the rest of Section 5.1, the reader is referred to Savine [Sav00].

Our probability density $p(t, K)$ is actually the expectation over the Dirac mass $\delta_K(x)$ at time t. Let us apply Tanaka's formula to this Dirac mass to get

$$d\delta_K(S_t) = \left[\delta'_K(S_t, t)\mu(t)S_t + \frac{1}{2}\delta''_K(S_t, t)\sigma^2(S_t, t)S_t^2 \right] dt$$

$$+ \delta'_K(S_t, t)\sigma(S_t, t)S_t dW_t.$$

Taking expectations gives

$$dp(K, t) = \left[-\frac{\partial}{\partial K}\{p(K, t)\mu(t)K\} + \frac{1}{2}\frac{\partial^2}{\partial K^2}\{p(K, t)\sigma^2(K, t)K^2\} \right] dt$$

since $E[\bullet dW_t] = 0$,

$$E[\delta'_K(S_t, t)\mu(S_t, t)S_t] = \int_{-\infty}^{\infty} \delta'_K(S_t, t)\mu(S_t, t)S_t p(S_t, t) dS_t$$

$$= -\frac{\partial}{\partial K}(\mu(K, t)K p(K, t)),$$

and

$$E[\delta''_K(S_t, t)\sigma^2(S_t, t)S_t^2] = \int_{-\infty}^{\infty} \delta''_K(S_t, t)\sigma^2(S_t, t)S_t^2 p(S_t, t) dS_t$$

$$= \frac{\partial}{\partial K^2}(\sigma^2(K, t)K^2 p(K, t))$$

by applying $\int_{-\infty}^{\infty} f(x)\delta'_K(x)dx = -f'(K)$, $\int_{-\infty}^{\infty} f(x)\delta''_K(x)dx = (-1)^2 f''(K)$ and interchanging the order of integration (the expectation) and differentiation.

Dividing by dt gives the Fokker–Planck equation

$$\frac{\partial p}{\partial t}(K, t) = -\frac{\partial}{\partial K}\{p(K, t)\mu(t)K\} + \frac{1}{2}\frac{\partial^2}{\partial K^2}\{p(K, t)\sigma^2(K, t)K^2\},$$

which describes the evolution of a probability density over time, starting from a point mass at time zero.

The classical derivation of the Fokker–Planck equation, i.e. without employing Tanaka's formula, is a lot more involved and we shall not consider it in the text, although the reader is invited to attempt it in Question 1 of the exercises if he so wishes.

5.1.2 Dupire's Formula

More interesting is the question of how to recover $\sigma(S_t, t)$ to fit all given market prices.

Let us start with

$$f(S_t, t) = e^{-\int_0^t r_u du}(S_t - K)^+.$$

Applying Tanaka's formula, we get the equation (*):

$$d\left[e^{-\int_0^t r_u du}(S_t - K)^+\right]$$

$$= \left[-r_t e^{-\int_0^t r_u du}(S_t - K)^+ + e^{-\int_0^t r_u du}1_{\{S_t > K\}}\mu(t)S_t\right.$$

$$\left. + \frac{1}{2}e^{-\int_0^t r_u du}\delta_K(S_t)\sigma^2(S_t, t)S_t^2\right]dt$$

$$+ e^{-\int_0^t r_u du}1_{\{S_t > K\}}\sigma(S_t, t)S_t dW_t.$$

Taking expectations and noticing that the price of a call option with strike K and expiry t is given by $C(K, t) = E[e^{-\int_0^t r_u du}(S_t - K)^+]$, we get

$$dC(K, t) = \left\{E\left[-r_t e^{-\int_0^t r_u du}(S_t - K)^+ + e^{-\int_0^t r_u du}1_{\{S_t > K\}}\mu(t)S_t\right]\right.$$

$$\left. + \frac{1}{2}\frac{\partial^2 C}{\partial K^2}(K, t)\sigma^2(K, t)K^2\right\}dt$$

$$= E\left[-r_t e^{-\int_0^t r_u du}(S_t - K)^+\right.$$

$$\left. + e^{-\int_0^t r_u du}1_{\{S_t > K\}}\mu(t)\{(S_t - K)^+ + K\}\right]dt$$

$$+ \frac{1}{2}\frac{\partial^2 C}{\partial K^2}(K, t)\sigma^2(K, t)K^2 dt$$

$$= \left\{E\left[(\mu(t) - r_t)e^{-\int_0^t r_u du}(S_t - K)^+\right.\right.$$

$$\left.\left. + e^{-\int_0^t r_u du}1_{\{S_t > K\}}\mu(t)K\right] + \frac{1}{2}\frac{\partial^2 C}{\partial K^2}(K, t)\sigma^2(K, t)K^2\right\}dt$$

in a similar way as we obtained the Fokker–Planck equation above, and noting that $\int_{-\infty}^{\infty} f(x)\delta_K(x)dx = f(K)$ and $D(0,T)P(S_t = K) = \frac{\partial^2 C}{\partial K^2}(K,t)$ from Section 3.1.

In the presence of deterministic rates (including foreign rates and dividends), we do not have to worry about expectations of the product of rates and the underlying, and get[2] the much simpler

$$
dC(K,t)
$$

$$
= \left\{ (\mu(t) - r_t)C(K,t) - \frac{\partial C}{\partial K}(K,t)\mu(t)K \right.
$$

$$
\left. + \frac{1}{2}\frac{\partial^2 C}{\partial K^2}(K,t)\sigma^2(K,t)K^2 \right\} dt
$$

$$
\Rightarrow \frac{\partial C(K,t)}{\partial t} = (\mu(t) - r_t)C(K,t) - \frac{\partial C}{\partial K}(K,t)\mu(t)K
$$

$$
+ \frac{1}{2}\frac{\partial^2 C}{\partial K^2}(K,t)\sigma^2(K,t)K^2.
$$

Thus,

$$
\sigma^2(K,t) = 2\frac{\frac{\partial C}{\partial t}(K,t) - (\mu(t) - r_t)C(K,t) + \frac{\partial C}{\partial K}(K,t)\mu(t)K}{\frac{\partial^2 C}{\partial K^2}(K,t)K^2}.
$$

This is the familiar Dupire's equation for local volatility, which can be used to recover prices of options of all strikes and expiries observed in the market. We can also obtain an equation for local volatility from put prices, which should be obvious from put-call parity if not by a similar approach to the above.[3] Alternatively, we could formulate local volatility as a function of implied volatilities and their derivatives since the price of a call or put option is a monotonic function of implied volatility. We shall not pursue the last possibility here (as the algebra can be quite involved and little conceptual value is added from such an exercise).

---

[2]Using $D(0,T)P(S_t > K) = -\frac{\partial C}{\partial K}(K,t)$ from Section 3.1.
[3]The interested reader is referred to Question 2 of the exercises.

5.1.3   *Presence of Stochastic Interest Rates or Volatility*

If interest rates were stochastic in the equation above, we would not have been able to disentangle the product of rates and the underlying, so we would not have an equation based solely on the prices and mathematical derivatives of call options. Specifically, the formula for local volatility would be given by

$$\sigma^2(K,t) = 2\frac{\frac{\partial C}{\partial t}(K,t) - \varsigma}{\frac{\partial^2 C}{\partial K^2}(K,t)K^2}$$

with

$$\varsigma = E\left[(\mu(t) - r_t)e^{-\int_0^t r_u du}(S_t - K)^+ + e^{-\int_0^t r_u du}1_{\{S_t > K\}}\mu(t)K\right]$$

where evaluation of the terms in the expectation requires knowledge of the joint distribution of interest rates and the underlying.

   If we had stochastic volatility, then our earlier approach would give the conditional expectation of the stochastic variance, given a value of the underlying. Specifically, if our SDE were

$$dS_t = \mu(t)S_t dt + \sigma_t S_t dW_t,$$

where σ_t is stochastic, then our earlier equation (*) would become (on taking expectations):

$$dC(K,t) = E\left[-r_t e^{-\int_0^t r_u du}(S_t - K)^+ + e^{-\int_0^t r_u du}1_{\{S_t > K\}}\mu(t)S_t\right]dt$$

$$+ \frac{1}{2}\frac{\partial^2 C}{\partial K^2}(K,t)E[\sigma_t^2|S_t = K]K^2 dt$$

$$\Rightarrow \frac{\partial C(K,t)}{\partial t} = (\mu(t) - r_t)C(K,t) - \frac{\partial C}{\partial K}(K,t)\mu(t)K$$

$$+ \frac{1}{2}\frac{\partial^2 C}{\partial K^2}(K,t)E[\sigma_t^2|S_t = K]K^2$$

giving

$$E[\sigma_t^2|S_t = K] = 2\frac{\frac{\partial C}{\partial t}(K,t) - (\mu(t) - r_t)C(K,t) + \frac{\partial C}{\partial K}(K,t)\mu(t)K}{\frac{\partial^2 C}{\partial K^2}(K,t)K^2}$$

instead.

This equation will prove useful in developing a methodology to calibrate a local stochastic volatility model (i.e. one with a mixture of local and stochastic volatility). This is the province of Chapter 7.

5.2 Dynamics

Section 5.1 discusses how we can have a non-parametric local volatility function $\sigma(S_t, t)$ that can fit any non-arbitrageable set of implied volatilities for different expiries and strikes.[4] So far so good, why do we need any other model?

5.2.1 *Evolution of Smile Over Time*

The extent of the volatility skew in equities tends to decrease for longer expiries. In fact, even at-the-money volatility can sometimes drop sharply beyond very short expiries. Figure 5.2 shows representative volatility skews for two different expiries.

Implied volatility is just a representation of the price of a call or put (with price being a monotonic function of implied volatility). Since price is obtained by integrating over local volatility, the less pronounced skew for longer expiries suggests that the volatility skew

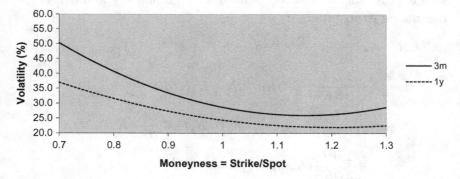

Figure 5.2:   We illustrate possible volatility skews in equities for 3-month options and 1-year options. The skew is more pronounced over short expiries.

---

[4]In practice, since we will inevitably have a finite set of options, we will need some assumptions on interpolation and extrapolation in order to construct our local volatility.

will flatten over time, whereas the lower volatility for longer expiries suggests that the at-the-money volatility will decrease over time.

For a simple mathematical illustration, consider the following SDE

$$dS_t = \mu(t)S_t dt + \sigma(t)S_t dW_t,$$

where we have suppressed any spot-dependence of volatility for simplicity.

The total variance up to period T is $\int_0^T \sigma^2(u)du$, so the implied volatility is

$$\Lambda(T) = \sqrt{\frac{\int_0^T \sigma^2(u)du}{T}}.$$

Suppose we have $\Lambda(T_2) < \Lambda(T_1)$ for $T_2 > T_1$. Then

$$\sqrt{\frac{\int_0^{T_2} \sigma^2(u)du}{T_2}} < \sqrt{\frac{\int_0^{T_1} \sigma^2(u)du}{T_1}}$$

$$\Rightarrow \int_0^{T_2} \sigma^2(u)du < \frac{T_2}{T_1} \int_0^{T_1} \sigma^2(u)du$$

$$\int_{T_1}^{T_2} \sigma^2(u)du < \frac{T_2}{T_1} \int_0^{T_1} \sigma^2(u)du - \int_0^{T_1} \sigma^2(u)du$$

$$= \frac{T_2 - T_1}{T_1} \int_0^{T_1} \sigma^2(u)du.$$

$$\therefore \sqrt{\frac{\int_{T_1}^{T_2} \sigma^2(u)du}{T_2 - T_1}} < \sqrt{\frac{\int_0^{T_1} \sigma^2(u)du}{T_1}}.$$

So the implied forward volatility of an option with expiry $T_2 - T_1$ as seen at time T_1 is less than that for an option with expiry T_1 as seen today. Take $T_2 = 2T_1$, and it is clear that the model requires future implied volatility to drop for an option with the same expiry.

However, in practice, excluding regime changes,[5] we tend to observe the same persistent pattern of pronounced skew and higher

---

[5]E.g. from stable markets to crisis periods or vice versa.

volatility at the short end. This suggests that there is something else that is perhaps responsible for the volatility smile.

The implications of the nature of forward volatility will be seen when we examine barrier products in Chapter 7 and when we examine cliquets in Chapter 11.

5.2.2   *Smile Dynamics With Respect to Underlying Moves*

Furthermore, the dynamics corresponding to a local volatility model may or may not be in accordance with what we observe. In particular, when the value of the underlying increases, the smile in a local volatility mode slides in the opposite direction. In some markets, this may reflect historical dynamics (e.g. some FX pairs) but in other markets (e.g. equities and other FX pairs), the smile usually slides in the direction of the underlying instead.

Hagan and Woodward [HW99] derive, via asymptotic methods for European call and put options, the following formula for implied volatility $\Lambda(K, F)$ as a function of current forward F and local volatility $\sigma(F)$:

$$\Lambda(K, F) = \sigma\left(\frac{1}{2}(F + K)\right)\left\{1 + \frac{1}{24}\frac{\sigma''\left(\frac{1}{2}(F + K)\right)}{\sigma\left(\frac{1}{2}(F + K)\right)}(F - K)^2 + \cdots\right\}.$$

To first order, we have

$$\Lambda(K, F) = \sigma\left(\frac{1}{2}(F + K)\right).$$

Suppose now that the forward increases from F to F^*. Then,

$$\Lambda(K, F^*) = \sigma\left(\frac{1}{2}(F^* + K)\right)$$

$$= \sigma\left(\frac{1}{2}(F + K + F^* - F)\right)$$

$$= \Lambda(K + F^* - F, F).$$

This means that as forward increases from F to F^*, the implied volatility for an option with strike K corresponds to one with a

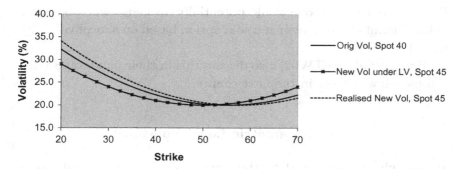

Figure 5.3:   Here, spot moves from 40 to 45. In this graph, as is more common for equities, we assume that the new implied vol surface moves in the direction of spot. The vol surface implied by a local vol model actually moves in the opposite direction.

higher strike $K + F^* - F$ on the original surface. Consider $K > F^*$ in Figure 5.3. We see that when forward increases, the option is actually picking up a more out-of-the-money volatility from the original surface as a consequence.

The effect of implied volatility sliding in the opposite direction to the movement of the underlying is reflected in the delta. Let the value of the call option be $C = C^{BS}(F, \Lambda(F))$, where C^{BS} is the Black–Scholes price, given a forward F and implied vol $\Lambda(F)$. Consider the delta

$$\Delta = \frac{\partial C}{\partial F}$$

$$= \frac{\partial C^{BS}}{\partial F} + \frac{\partial C^{BS}}{\partial \Lambda} \frac{\partial \Lambda}{\partial F}.$$

Since the implied volatility slides in the opposite direction from the movement of the underlying, the sign of $\frac{\partial \Lambda}{\partial F}$ will be opposite that in the case of implied vol moving in the same direction as the underlying. If this reflects the true market dynamics (e.g. for some FX pairs), then such treatment would indeed be appropriate. However, in markets where the smile should slide in the same direction as the underlying (e.g. equities and other FX pairs), the correction for delta due to implied volatility is incorrect, and an implied volatility model would give an even less accurate delta than the pure Black–Scholes delta for a European call or put option.

If that were the case, one would potentially mishedge when buying a delta amount of stock against a sold option based on a local volatility model.

Hagan *et al.* [HKLW02] also discuss this in their paper on SABR, a topic we will cover in the next chapter.

5.3   Parametric Local Volatility

Having given due regard to the characteristics and limitations of local volatility models, if we had to posit a simple form for local volatility, what would it be? Rather than have an idiosyncratic checkerboard of varying local volatilities over different regions, is there some unifying pattern we can discern and impose upon the volatility dynamics?

For this, we need to understand the origins of volatility smiles. Assuming that all (or at least part) of the volatility smile is due to our model not correctly describing volatility dynamics, what should the correct dynamics be?

5.3.1   *Normal*

In the interest rates world, it is said that at least when rates are in the region of 2% to 6%, absolute changes in volatility tend to be unaffected by the level of rates.[6] This suggests a model where the absolute volatility is constant, so that the absolute magnitude of shocks is independent from the current level of interest rates. For example, interest rates are as likely to move by 25 basis points (i.e. 0.25%) when they are at 2.5%, compared to when they are at 5.5%. When interest rates fall outside this region, we tend to be in to a period of instability, so that volatility is likely to rise dramatically at least in the short term.

In a lognormal world, absolute volatility is proportional to the level of the underlying. This usually makes sense for the typical

---

[6]See Rebonato and de Guillaume in [RdG10] or Karasinski in [Kar11], although the exact region referred to differs in the latter.

asset. For example, if you are considering a stock, apart from potential stock splits, how could its absolute price matter? It is merely a reference for transactions in the stock. And whether a stock is at $5 today or $200, its value is likely to move by a certain percentage (e.g. 10%) rather than an absolute amount.

The natural question is that if a normal model truly describes interest rates, whereas we are seeing them in a framework of lognormal volatilities, how would these volatilities look like?

In a normal model, the random term is λdW_t whereas it is $\sigma S_t dW_t$ in a lognormal model. So, approximately, the relation between a normal volatility and a lognormal volatility is given by $\lambda = \sigma S_0$ where we are interested in matching market prices of at-the-money options. Keeping λ constant, the smaller the initial value of the underlying S_0, the greater the required lognormal vol σ, and vice versa. Hence, we see that a normal model produces downward skewed lognormal volatilities (see Figure 5.4).

5.3.2   *Lognormal*

Much as we have tried to disabuse the notion of lognormal volatilities as a true reflection of market dynamics, they serve an extremely useful purpose nonetheless. As discussed in the previous sub-section

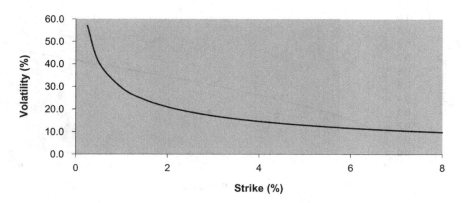

Figure 5.4:   We obtain prices for 20-year call options with varying strikes based on a normal model with forward rate of 3% and volatility of 0.5%. Then we find the implied lognormal volatility. This is seen to decrease with strike.

on normal volatilities, a proportional (i.e. lognormal) backbone to volatility makes sense for equities or foreign exchange where there is no particular attachment to the level of the underlying. In this way, even if we feel that a stochastic volatility model better describes our process, we might prefer to impose a stochastic multiplier on top of a lognormal backbone, e.g. we could have the SDE describing the underlying as below:

$$dS_t = \mu(t)S_t dt + z_t \sigma(t)S_t dW_t,$$

where z_t is a random process.

It is worth pointing out that in a lognormal model, the earlier discussion in the previous sub-section leads us to conclude that absolute (normal) volatilities will increase as the strike increases (see Figure 5.5).

5.3.3   *Blended*

It would be too much of a coincidence to expect either the normal or lognormal parameterisations of local volatility to capture the true dynamics of the underlying. So, why limit ourselves to these two possibilities? Can we have something that allows for dynamics somewhere between normal and lognormal?

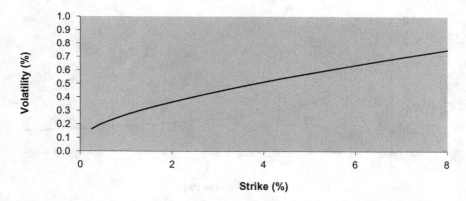

Figure 5.5:   We consider the same 20-year call options with forward rate 3% but this time apply a flat lognormal volatility of 15%. We then find the implied normal volatilities. These are clearly seen to increase with strike.

Let us consider the SDE[7]

$$dS_t = \sigma(bS_t + (1-b)S_0)dW_t,$$

where $0 \le b \le 1$.

Notice that if $b = 0$, we get the normal model (with absolute vol σS_0) and if $b = 1$, we get the lognormal model. For any other value of b, we get dynamics in between. Since this is a mixture of normal and lognormal, the underlying can attain any negative value (if $b < 1$).

What makes this process attractive is its analytic tractability. To see this, consider the substitution

$$x_t = bS_t + (1-b)S_0.$$

Then we have

$$dx_t = bdS_t = b\sigma(bS_t + (1-b)S_0)dW_t = b\sigma x_t dW_t.$$

Thus, x_t is a lognormal variate with volatility $b\sigma$, and we can easily obtain the price of a call option. Specifically, since

$$S_t = \frac{x_t - (1-b)S_0}{b},$$

the price of a call option is

$$D(0,T)E[(S_T - K)^+] = D(0,T)E\left[\left(\frac{x_T - (1-b)S_0}{b} - K\right)^+\right]$$

$$= \frac{D(0,T)}{b}E[(x_T - (1-b)S_0 - Kb)^+]$$

$$= \frac{D(0,T)}{b}E[(x_T - K^*)^+],$$

where $K^* = (1-b)S_0 + Kb$, and $D(0,T)$ is the price of a zero-coupon bond with maturity T.

Then we can use the same approach as we did before to price a call option in a lognormal world.

---

[7]We shall ignore the drift here, since that is easily obtained by no arbitrage. If we are modelling the forward process, then the drift is zero. Otherwise, we should add an appropriate drift.

5.3.4   *Constant Elasticity of Variance (CEV)*

But perhaps you do not believe that negative interest rates should be allowed, or maybe interest rates should not go below a certain negative level. Whereas Japan has had negative interest rates reaching minus a few basis points,[8] it does not make sense fundamentally for you to lend money if you are charged for it. On the equity/FX front, a negative value of the underlying is even more absurd because you cannot expect to be paid for the privilege to own a stock or a foreign currency. The CEV model partly solves this, albeit with the rather unpalatable feature of having absorption at zero.

Ignoring the specification of the drift term,[9] the SDE for the CEV model is

$$dS_t = \sigma S_t^{\beta} dW_t,$$

where typically $0 \leq \beta \leq 1$.

At the limit of $\beta = 1$, we recover the lognormal model (since the underlying will never go below zero). For values of β between 0 and 1, since we cannot take a fractional power of a negative number, we require $S_t \geq 0$. One possibility is to impose a reflecting boundary at zero. Another solution is to impose an absorbing boundary at zero. Specifically, if S_t reaches zero, it gets stuck there forever. For consistency with our treatment of other values of β, at $\beta = 0$, we have something akin to the normal model but with reflection or absorption at zero.

The consequence of an absorbing boundary is that given a sufficiently long expiry, the cumulative distribution function can show a significant probability of absorption at zero, e.g. in the case of 10-year rates seen 30 years from now (see Figure 5.6). Whilst this may be preferable to the situation where 10-year rates have a significant probability of reaching -5% in 30 years from now in a normal model (as per Figure 5.6), imagine the implications of either case on a CMS spread option that pays the difference between the 10-year CMS rate and 2-year CMS rate as seen 30 years from now.

---

[8]Since interest paid was zero and there were administrative charges.
[9]Since as per Section 5.3.3, our concern here is the vol parameterisation.

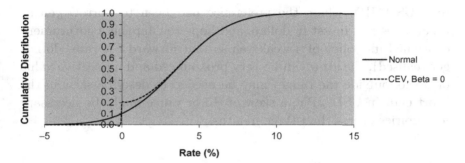

Figure 5.6: Here we consider a normal process versus a CEV process with beta zero. The underlying 10-year rate has forward value 3.5% and volatility 0.5%. The expiry is 30 years. You can see absorption of 20% of the cumulative distribution for the CEV process.

Notwithstanding the above, a reason for the popularity of the CEV model is the existence of a quasi-analytic formula for the price of a call option involving the non-central chi-squared distribution. In particular, for $0 < \beta < 1$, given the CEV process

$$dS_t = (r - q)S_t dt + \sigma S_t^\beta dW_t,$$

the price of a call option with strike K and expiry T is

$$C_0 = S_0 e^{-qT} \chi^2 \left(2y, 2 + \frac{1}{1 - \beta}, 2x \right)$$
$$- K e^{-rT} \left[1 - \chi^2 \left(2x, \frac{1}{1 - \beta}, 2y \right) \right],$$

where $\eta = \dfrac{r - q}{\sigma^2 S_0^{2(1-\beta)}(1-\beta)(e^{2(r-q)(1-\beta)T}-1)}$, $x = \eta S_0^{2(1-\beta)} e^{2(r-q)(1-\beta)T}$, $y = \eta K^{2(1-\beta)}$, and $\chi^2(z, \nu, \lambda) = 1 - P(Z < z)$ is the complementary distribution function of a non-central chi-squared variable Z with ν degrees of freedom and non-centrality parameter λ.

For the interested reader, Braumann *et al.* [BDL10] give a fairly interesting comparison of different numerical methods used for evaluating the non-central chi-squared complementary distribution function.

There is no reason why β needs to be restricted to $[0, 1]$ in practice. In particular, for certain FX rates with structural biases (e.g. USD/JPY where the preference had been to borrow yen at lower rates and invest in dollars and hope the Japanese government continued its policy of a weak yen so that forward FX rates do not get realised), the skew can be very pronounced and a negative value of β (i.e. outside the range) may be needed to describe skew in the short end. In USD/JPY, a skew of -3 or worse might be necessary for expiries of less than three months.

5.4   Consolidation

5.4.1   *Summary*

Local volatility (LV) is one approach to fitting the volatility smile. In this chapter, we have examined it in the context of equities and FX. The basic premise is to let the volatility of an underlying be a function of spot and time. A non-parametric LV model can fit self-consistent implied volatilities across all expiries and strikes.

We started with some machinery — the theory of distributions, where we considered an extension of the definition of a mathematical derivative to non-continuous functions, so that we can speak of derivatives of the Heaviside function (e.g. its first derivative is the Dirac delta function), the delta function itself and its derivatives. With this, Ito's Lemma on the SDE of a function of a stochastic variable extends naturally to Tanaka's formula. The Fokker–Planck equation on the evolution of the probability density of the underlying over time comes almost immediately from an application of Tanaka's formula (versus the much more laborious traditional approach). The celebrated Dupire's formula for obtaining local volatilities directly from the market prices of call options (and their numerical derivatives) is also derived using Tanaka's formula. We note that in the presence of stochastic volatility or stochastic interest rates, local volatilities are no longer obtainable straight from market option prices. However, Dupire's formula still gives the expected variance conditional on the value of spot under stochastic volatility. And under stochastic interest rates, correlation assumptions are in addition needed to obtain the local volatilities.

Notwithstanding that an LV model can fit the prices of options of all expiries and strikes, we next consider why such a model may not necessarily be suitable for all markets by exploring the dynamics of the model. Basically, we noted that if implied volatilities decrease as expiry increases, under an LV model, future volatilities will be less than current volatilities. This may not always be what we expect. Further, with reference to an asymptotic expansion by Hagan and Woodward, we showed that under an LV model, when spot moves, the smile moves in the opposite direction. Whilst this is the case in some markets (e.g. some FX pairs), it is contrary to what is observed in other markets (e.g. equities and other FX pairs). Thus, we provided the motivation for subsequent consideration of other models to fit the volatility smile.

We concluded this chapter by discussing various parametric forms of an LV model. Basically, a normal model and a lognormal model are special cases of an LV model. And if we have a normal model (popular in interest rates since it reflects the dynamics of volatility for long-term rates), the lognormal implied volatilities will display a downward sloping skew. Of course, the market is likely to be somewhere in between normal and lognormal in general, so we also considered a blended model (i.e. mixture between normal and lognormal) and derived the price of a call option under this model. We ended with the CEV model (where the volatility component is multiplied by the underlying raised to some power typically between 0 and 1) — this is popular due to the existence of a quasi-analytic solution for the prices of vanilla options, notwithstanding that there is a high probability of absorption of the distribution at zero over long expiries.

5.4.2 *Exercises*

(1) For a derivative $V(X_T)$ on an underlying X_T as seen at time T, its value is given by $V(X_t) = e^{-r(T-t)}E[V(X_T)] = e^{-r(T-t)}\int_{-\infty}^{\infty} V(x)p(x)dx$, where $p(\bullet)$ is the probability density function. By differentiating $V(X_t)$ with respect to t, applying Ito's Lemma on $V(X_T)$ and changing the order of integration,

derive the Fokker–Planck equation. (This is the more traditional approach that does not assume the theory of distributions.)

(2) Derive Dupire's formula in Section 5.1.2 in terms of put prices rather than call prices.

(3) Compute the forward delta of a call option based on the normal formula. (The price is given in Section 1.2.4.) Contrast this with the forward delta for an at-the-money (i.e. forward = strike) call option based on the lognormal formula (similar to Question 4 of Chapter 2 but the spot delta is referred to there).

(4) Consider the Taylor expansion of the integrand of the cumulative normal function for $x \approx 0$, i.e. $N(x) = 0.5 + \frac{1}{\sqrt{2\pi}} \int_0^x e^{-\frac{1}{2}z^2} dz = 0.5 + \frac{1}{\sqrt{2\pi}} \int_0^x (1 - \frac{1}{2}z^2 + \frac{1}{8}z^4 + \cdots) dz$. Thereby, find an approximation for the price of a lognormal option close-to-the-money. Attempt something similar for a normal option by doing a Taylor expansion for $n(x) = \frac{1}{\sqrt{2\pi}} e^{-\frac{1}{2}x^2}$, in addition. Hence obtain a normal vol in terms of a lognormal vol, by neglecting terms higher than $O(x)$ in the expansions for $N(x)$ and $n(x)$.

6

Stochastic Volatility

"You try to fit a small animal into a box. Its tail sticks out, so
you chop it off. Its ears stick out, so you chop them off.
Eventually the small animal fits into the box."

In Chapter 5, we explored how the implied volatility smile can be
completely captured by a local volatility (LV) model but the dynamics of such a model may not be appropriate for all markets. For
example, the volatility smiles that it generates at future times can
be much flatter than the current smile.

Consider a product which at time T_2 pays $\max(AS_{T_1} - S_{T_2}, 0)$,
where $T_1 < T_2$ are future times and $A > 0$ is a multiplier. This
product is very much dependent on the forward smile. Specifically,
at time T_1 it is just a put option with strike AS_{T_1} and time to
expiry $T_2 - T_1$. If current implied volatilities decrease sharply as
expiry increases, then a local volatility model may not be appropriate to price this product since future implied volatility will drop
significantly over time (under an LV model), which is not what we
expect.

Another natural way of generating smile is by introducing
stochastic volatility, covered in this chapter. Again our discussion
will be limited to the context of a single underlying, e.g. a stock or
a foreign exchange (FX) rate, with extensions to interest rates left
for Chapters 8 and 9.

6.1   General Dynamics of Stochastic Volatility

Consider an underlying described by the following stochastic differential equations (SDEs)

$$dS_t = \mu(S_t, t)S_t dt + \sigma_t S_t^{\beta} dW_t,$$
$$d\sigma_t = \phi(\sigma_t, t)dt + \eta(\sigma_t, t)dU_t, \quad \text{and}$$
$$dW_t dU_t = \rho dt.$$

[For equities and foreign exchange, it is typical for $\beta = 1$ but a more general framework is adopted here, as we would need it to discuss the important case of the Stochastic Alpha Beta Rho (SABR) model which is widely used in interest rates.]

To motivate our consideration of stochastic volatility, let us observe that there are periods of high volatility and periods of low volatility. Figures 6.1a and 6.1b should demonstrate this convincingly. This can roughly be interpreted as periods following a market shock and periods of calm markets. So, a model which incorporates random volatility is in keeping with empirical evidence. More importantly, however, stochastic volatility (SV) gives us dynamics that are somewhat in keeping with the observed behaviour of some assets (e.g. equities and some FX pairs).

We remark that in the presence of stochastic volatility, when selling a derivative, it is no longer possible to construct a risk-free

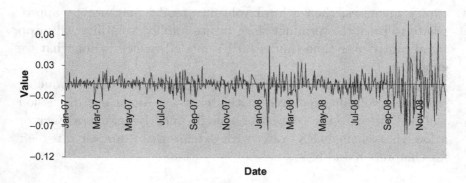

Figure 6.1a: Daily log-returns of Stoxx 50 index from 2007 to 2008. Notice the periods of low volatility and those of high volatility.
Source: Bloomberg data.

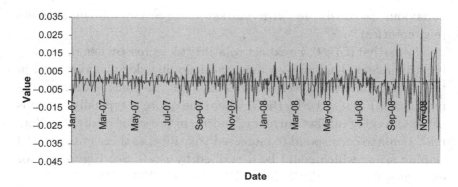

Figure 6.1b: Daily log-returns of spot GBP/USD from 2007 to 2008. Notice the periods of low volatility and those of high volatility.
Source: Bloomberg data.

portfolio[1] by maintaining a delta amount of an underlying. Consider again the SDEs

$$dS_t = \mu(S_t, t)S_t dt + \sigma_t S_t^\beta dW_t,$$
$$d\sigma_t = \phi(\sigma_t, t)dt + \eta(\sigma_t, t)dU_t, \quad \text{and}$$
$$dW_t dU_t = \rho dt.$$

There are two Wiener processes W_t and U_t, so in theory if you had sold a derivative, the hedge portfolio must comprise both the underlying and at least one option (to kill off the other Wiener component). In practice, dealers do not just delta hedge but also vega hedge, where vega $\nu = \frac{\partial V}{\partial \Lambda}$ is the sensitivity of a derivative's value V to the implied volatility Λ. And it is unrealistic to expect hedging to be perfect in any event, since no one really knows the true distribution of an underlying.

6.1.1 *Dynamics vis-à-vis Underlying Moves*

In the absence of the effect of correlation between the underlying and its volatility, as the underlying moves, we expect the volatility smile under an SV model to shift in the same direction.[2] This smile

---

[1]In the Black–Scholes spirit per Section 1.1.2.
[2]Contrast this with the dynamics of a local volatility model discussed in Section 5.2.2.

behaviour is consistent with market observation for some assets (e.g. equities).

Notice that if $\rho < 0$, we expect volatility to decrease when the underlying increases, leading to a downward sloping skew, as observed in the equity markets (as well as for USD/JPY). In contrast, for emerging market FX (say USD/BRL) where the quote is typically in terms of the emerging market currency,[3] a drop in the value of the Brazilian real[4] tends to correspond to increased volatility, so there is an upward sloping skew, which could be described by $\rho > 0$. See Figure 6.2 for examples of the volatilities for USD/JPY and USD/BRL.

Furthermore, since volatility is random, the probability of tail events is larger than if volatility is constant. This translates to higher implied volatility at the wings if volatility of volatility [i.e. the $\eta(\sigma_t, t)$ part] is higher. For example, the somewhat symmetric volatility smile of the EUR/USD FX rate (prior to 2010) can be explained by a meaningful volatility of volatility component (see Figure 6.3).

6.1.2   *Persistence of Smile*

Consider again the SDE for the volatility term. We note that since this is a diffusion process, the variance of the volatility process is expected to increase over time. This means that the effect of volatility

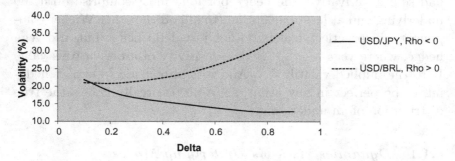

Figure 6.2:   We depict the USD/JPY and USD/BRL volatility smiles for 1y options as of 27 February 2009. The former corresponds to negative correlation between the underlying and the vol, whilst the latter corresponds to positive correlation.
Source: Bloomberg data.

---

[3]E.g. USD/BRL is quoted as the number of Brazilian reais per US dollar.
[4]I.e. higher value of USD/BRL.

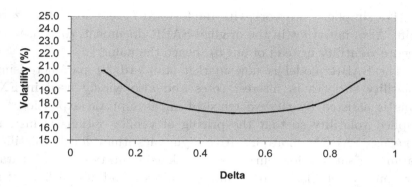

Figure 6.3:   We see here the EUR/USD 1-year volatility smile. The symmetric smile is generated by the volatility of volatility, which gives tail events a higher probability. *Source*: Bloomberg data.

randomness generating higher implied volatility at the wings will not disappear at future times, so we can expect the volatility smile observed today to persist over future times, notwithstanding that the spot volatility smile for long expiries tends to be less pronounced.

However, since we are relying on a diffusive process to explain smile (and skew), volatility of volatility (or correlation between the volatility and the underlying) needs time to make its effect felt. This means that a steep volatility smile in equities over short expiries cannot be properly explained by an SV model.[5] SV works much better to explain forward skew over mid to long expiries (whereas the effect of a jump on long expiries is minimal).

6.2   The Stochastic Alpha Beta Rho (SABR) Model

The SDEs for the SABR model (popularised by Hagan *et al.* in [HKLW02]) are

$$dF_t = \sigma_t F_t^{\beta} dW_t,$$
$$d\sigma_t = \nu \sigma_t dU_t, \quad \text{and}$$
$$dW_t dU_t = \rho dt,$$

where typically $0 \leq \beta \leq 1$.

---

[5]For this phenomenon, a jump diffusion model or an SV model with a jump component is more appropriate.

(For simplicity, we work with the forward F_t and hence have zero drift. Also, note that in the original SABR document, α_t is used to denote volatility instead of our σ_t, hence the name.)

The SABR model is now market standard for parameterising volatility surfaces in interest rates and also widely used in FX. This is assisted by the existence of an asymptotic expansion for implied volatility so that the pricing of vanilla options is instantaneous, SABR's more intuitive dynamics than local volatility parameterisations for purposes of risk computations (e.g. delta) for some asset classes (e.g. interest rates), and its rather intuitive parameterisation. We shall discuss the above further in this section.

For parameterising volatility surfaces, we have a grid of values of the initial volatility σ_0, the blend β, the correlation ρ, and the volatility of volatility ν corresponding to each expiry (for FX or equities), or each expiry and underlying maturity (for interest rate swaptions) — see Figure 6.4 for an example. In this sense, SABR is generally not used so much to describe the dynamics of an underlying but rather as a means of interpolating volatility across strikes.

SABR is actually a poor candidate for describing the evolution of an underlying over time. Notice that the SDE for the volatility process allows volatility to grow unchecked. In order to describe an appropriate amount of convexity at the wings, we therefore require very high volatilities of volatility for short expiries and much less extreme values for longer expiries. This is more properly controlled (in a single self-consistent model) via the existence of a mean reversion parameter, as in the Heston model, discussed in the next section.

6.2.1   *The Asymptotic Expansion*

A major reason for the popularity of SABR is the existence of an asymptotic expansion to find a good enough (for practical usage) approximation for the implied volatility of a European call or put.

Initial Volatility (%)

Expiry / Tenor	2y	5y	10y	20y
3m	6.1	5.4	4.6	3.7
1y	6.0	5.2	4.7	4.3
2y	5.7	4.9	4.4	4.1
5y	4.7	4.2	3.9	3.6
10y	3.9	3.7	3.8	3.4
20y	3.8	3.8	3.7	3.2

Volatility of Volatility (%)

Expiry / Tenor	2y	5y	10y	20y
3m	79	62	67	94
1y	49	40	40	45
2y	56	52	52	46
5y	63	60	64	59
10y	53	53	65	52
20y	30	28	26	23

Correlation (%)

Expiry / Tenor	2y	5y	10y	20y
3m	26	−1	−29	−71
1y	22	6	−12	−34
2y	1	−10	−24	−30
5y	−17	−23	−30	−32
10y	−21	−24	−26	−27
20y	−24	−17	−14	−15

Blend	0.5

Figure 6.4:   We show above some tables of SABR parameters (by expiry and tenor) that are representative of euro swaption vol surfaces.

Specifically, given the current forward level F, the implied volatility for an option with expiry T and strike K is

$$
\Lambda(K,T) = \frac{\sigma_0}{(FK)^{(1-\beta)/2}\left\{1 + \frac{(1-\beta)^2}{24}\log^2\frac{F}{K} + \frac{(1-\beta)^4}{1920}\log^4\frac{F}{K}\right\}}\left(\frac{z}{x(z)}\right)
$$

$$
\times \left\{1 + \left[\frac{(1-\beta)^2}{24}\frac{\sigma_0^2}{(FK)^{1-\beta}}\right.\right.
$$

$$
\left.\left. + \frac{1}{4}\frac{\rho\beta\nu\sigma_0}{(FK)^{(1-\beta)/2}} + \frac{2-3\rho^2}{24}\nu^2\right]T + \cdots\right\}
$$

where

$$z = \frac{v}{\sigma_0}(FK)^{(1-\beta)/2} \log \frac{F}{K}, \quad \text{and}$$

$$x(z) = \log \left\{ \frac{\sqrt{1 - 2\rho z + z^2} + z - \rho}{1 - \rho} \right\}.$$

For the case of an at-the-money option, this simplifies to

$$\Lambda(F, T) = \frac{\sigma_0}{F^{1-\beta}} \left\{ 1 + \left[\frac{(1-\beta)^2}{24} \frac{\sigma_0^2}{F^{2-2\beta}} \right. \right.$$

$$\left. \left. + \frac{1}{4} \frac{\rho\beta\nu\sigma_0}{F^{1-\beta}} + \frac{2 - 3\rho^2}{24}\nu^2 \right] T + \cdots \right\}.$$

Given the implied volatility, we can then use the Black–Scholes formula to price European call or put options.

For the interested reader, the details of the perturbation methods used to obtain the asymptotic expansion are best obtained from the papers by Hagan and Woodward [HW99] and by Hagan *et al.* [HKLW02]. The second paper also gives a very good intuition on the workings of SABR.

6.2.2   *SABR Dynamics*

Recall our equation for the delta in Section 5.2.2, specifically

$$\Delta = \frac{\partial C}{\partial F}$$

$$= \frac{\partial C^{BS}}{\partial F} + \frac{\partial C^{BS}}{\partial \Lambda} \frac{\partial \Lambda}{\partial F}.$$

First notice that the vega is $\frac{\partial C^{BS}}{\partial \Lambda} > 0$ for a standard call or put.

Since the volatility smile shifts in the same direction as the underlying moves, the contribution to delta from the $\frac{\partial \Lambda}{\partial F}$ multiplier is negative if correlation is positive (notice that our absolute strike has decreased relative to an increased forward) and vice versa if correlation is negative.

6.2.3   *Smile, Skew, and Backbone*

To better illustrate the effects of the various parameters of SABR, as per Hagan *et al.*, it is worth approximating the formula for implied volatility in Section 6.2.1 by

$$\Lambda(K,T) \approx \frac{\sigma_0}{F^{1-\beta}} \left\{ 1 - \frac{1}{2}(1 - \beta - \rho\lambda)\log\frac{K}{F} \right.$$
$$\left. + \frac{1}{12}\left[(1 - \beta)^2 + (2 - 3\rho^2)\lambda^2\right]\log^2\frac{K}{F} + \cdots \right\},$$

where

$$\lambda = \frac{\nu}{\sigma_0}F^{1-\beta}.$$

The above holds, provided the strike K is not too far from the forward F and expiry T is small.[6]

Notice that for the at-the-money volatility, we have approximately

$$\Lambda(F,T) \approx \frac{\sigma_0}{F^{1-\beta}}.$$

Furthermore, since the equation is mainly in terms of $\frac{K}{F}$, at least locally the smile shape[7] remains unchanged as the forward moves. This means the volatility smile slides along the backbone as controlled by β, so we really have a CEV local volatility parameterisation (for at-the-money volatilities) as discussed in Section 5.3.4 (with $\beta = 1$ corresponding to the lognormal case and $\beta = 0$ like the normal case but with absorption at zero). See Figure 6.5 for an illustration.

Further, notice from the first order term in $\log\frac{K}{F}$, that the component $\frac{1}{2}\rho\lambda$ in the multiplier means a positive ρ corresponds to higher volatility for higher strikes (i.e. an upward sloping volatility skew).

---

[6]Note that the above approximation is very rough (e.g. it does not even account for how the vol of vol and correlation effects change with expiry) and should not be used for pricing.

[7]I.e. relation between at-the-money and out-of-the-money vols.

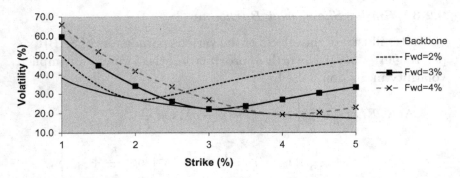

Figure 6.5: We depict the new implied volatility surfaces as the forward moves. Here we are using a blend of 0.5, initial vol of 2.5%, correlation of 0%, vol of vol of 80%, and an option expiry of 10 years. Notice how the at-the-money volatilities slide down the backbone corresponding to a CEV process with beta of 0.5.

On the other hand, from the second order term in $\log \frac{K}{F}$, the multiplier $(2 - 3\rho^2)\lambda^2$ means that provided $\rho < \sqrt{\frac{2}{3}}$, a larger ν corresponds to higher implied volatility as strikes move further away from the forward (i.e. for both high and low strikes).

Thus, in the SABR model, σ_0 controls the level of the at-the-money volatility, β affects the delta dynamics, ν controls the convexity/smile, and ρ controls the skew.[8]

In the markets, typically at-the-money options are very liquid. Furthermore, strangles[9] and risk reversals[10] are also popular (e.g. for strikes corresponding to 25 delta and possibly 10 delta for FX). The prices of these three instruments correspond to the parameters σ_0, ν, and ρ. For FX, typically, β is taken as 1. In interest rates, historical analysis of past returns may be used to determine β. This is typically closer to 1 for short expiries and closer to zero for long expiries.

---

[8]The delta dynamics refer to how the at-the-money volatility moves with respect to changes in the underlying. Convexity/smile refers to the relation between out-of-the-money versus at-the-money vols. Skew refers to the relation between high strikes versus low strikes vols.

[9]I.e. long both a call with strike $F + \kappa$ and long a put with strike $F - \kappa$ for some $\kappa > 0$, or where strikes are defined based on delta.

[10]I.e. long a call with strike $F + \kappa$ and short a put with strike $F - \kappa$, or with strikes defined based on delta.

Since σ_0, ν, and ρ capture distinct features, calibrating these parameters to any given smile for an expiry (and tenor) by best fit (optimisation) tends to produce stable results over day-to-day market moves. This is again another reason for the popularity of SABR. However, both β and ρ can describe skew (the first from a local volatility perspective and the second from a stochastic volatility perspective). As such, it is usually not a good idea to simultaneously calibrate β and ρ, as the parameters (calibrated together) may not be stable when calibrating over day-to-day market moves. If the user prefers, then ρ can be fixed and σ_0, ν, and β can be calibrated instead.

6.2.4 *Issues with SABR*

One of the main reasons for SABR's popularity is the asymptotic expansion, which allows for fast pricing of vanilla European options. This is necessary due to the huge volume of vanilla options traded and the need to be able to respond quickly to market changes.

However, the asymptotic expansion was developed based on the assumption of small $\nu^2 T$ (i.e. small volatility of volatility and expiry). This does not hold in practice since volatility of volatility is of order $O(1)$ (e.g. in Figure 6.4, the 5-year by 10-year vol of vol is 0.64), and SABR has been used to parameterise interest rate volatilities of expiries up to 30 years even. Whilst the formula has proven remarkably robust, it is too much to expect it to work well when stretched so far beyond the assumptions for which its use was justifiable.

For one, the implied volatility for strikes very close to zero (say under 1%) can be non-arbitrage free, in that implied densities obtained via prices of butterflies,[11] with payoff $\frac{C(K+\delta)+C(K-\delta)-2C(K)}{\delta^2}$, can be negative (see Figure 6.6). (Note that butterflies always have a non-negative payoff as per Figure 6.7.) This is especially so if volatility of volatility is high and forwards are low. This is a problem that is very real in the interest rates environment especially post 2008 where short

---

[11] A butterfly is constructed by being long δ^2 call with strikes $K + \delta$ and $K - \delta$, and short $2\delta^2$ calls with strike K.

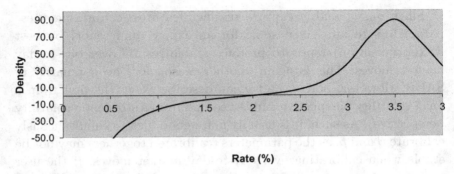

Figure 6.6:   Consider the implied density of the same forward rate (as specified by the parameters) in Figure 6.5 based on 10-year expiry options. We see that it goes negative when interest rates go below 2%, which is highly undesirable.

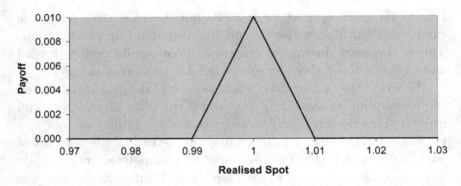

Figure 6.7:   Here we show the payoff of a butterfly. We are long a call option with strike 0.99, short two call options with strike 1 and long another call option with strike 1.01. The payoff is always above zero and peaks at 0.01 if realised spot is 1.

term forward rates (e.g. 1-year swap rate starting in 3 months' time) can be under 1% and long-term forward rates (e.g. 10-year swap rate starting in 30 years) can be as low as 3%. This is in contrast to long-term rates generally not falling below 4% to 5%, prior to this period.

Another remark is that the SABR expansion underestimates the concavity of positive rates for long expiries, so that the effect of SV is underestimated. This means that the calibrated volatility of volatility may be artificially inflated to compensate for this.

Furthermore, SABR has explosive growth of volatility at the wings. In interest rates, constant maturity swap (CMS) products tend to be priced by replication,[12] so that volatilities for very high strikes (e.g. 50%) are relevant to the convexity adjustment. Clearly, a method to control the growth of SABR volatility for high strikes is needed to avoid unrealistic prices for CMS products.

In FX, a problem faced is the theoretical possibility of infinite variance. This is because the choice of $\beta = 1$ coupled with stochastic volatility, means that moments can explode in a finite amount of time (e.g. 20 years), which gets shorter if correlation is positive, quite possible in emerging markets.[13]

Furthermore, there is a minimum amount of smiliness that SABR produces, and the steepness of the skew for certain emerging markets currencies (e.g. USD/RUB) in late 2008 and 2009 meant at times that SABR could not fit the volatilities in these markets.

6.3   Heston Model

In the earlier section, we suggested that to prevent the variance of volatility from exploding over time, we need a mechanism for dampening its growth. We now consider the Heston model specified by the SDEs:

$$dF_t = \sqrt{V_t}F_t dW_t,$$
$$dV_t = \kappa(\theta(t) - V_t)dt + \eta\sqrt{V_t}dU_t, \quad \text{and}$$
$$dW_t dU_t = \rho dt,$$

where κ is the mean reversion speed and $\theta(t)$ is the long-run mean of variance.

Note that the choice of a square root process for variance is motivated by the existence of a Fourier transform technique for pricing European call and put options under this formulation, so that calibration to market prices is efficient. We will explore this in Section 6.3.3.

---

[12] As discussed in Section 3.1.3.
[13] We will discuss moments explosion further in Section 6.5.

In practice, analysis of time-series of various markets (e.g. in FX and equities) tends to suggest a lognormal process for volatility, so that the SDEs

$$dF_t = \sigma_t F_t dW_t,$$

$$\sigma_t = \min(e^{y_t}, M) \quad \text{(where } M \text{ is some cap to}$$

$$\text{prevent vol growing too fast),}$$

$$dy_t = \left(\kappa(\theta(t) - y_t) - \frac{1}{2}\eta^2\right)dt + \eta dU_t, \quad \text{and}$$

$$dW_t dU_t = \rho dt$$

would give a better reflection of market dynamics. However, the lack of quasi-analytic formulae for pricing European options under the above model means calibration of model parameters often has to be by forward induction on a PDE, which is considerably slower.

6.3.1   *The Effect of Mean Reversion*

For ease of illustration, consider the process

$$dy_t = \kappa(\theta(t) - y_t)dt + \eta dU_t.$$

This is the Ornstein–Uhlenbeck (OU) process.[14]
We have

$$dy_t + \kappa y_t dt = \kappa\theta(t)dt + \eta dU_t$$

$$\Rightarrow d(y_t e^{\kappa t}) = e^{\kappa t}(\kappa\theta(t)dt + \eta dU_t)$$

$$\Rightarrow y_t e^{\kappa t} - y_0 = \kappa\int_0^t \theta(s)e^{\kappa s}ds + \eta\int_0^t e^{\kappa s}dU_s$$

$$\Rightarrow y_t = y_0 e^{-\kappa t} + \kappa\int_0^t \theta(s)e^{\kappa(s-t)}ds + \eta\int_0^t e^{\kappa(s-t)}dU_s.$$

---

[14]The calculations are a lot easier since the process is Gaussian but the conclusions regarding the effect of mean reversion do not change if volatility/variance follows other processes, e.g. CEV or lognormal.

Then

$$E[y_t] = y_0 e^{-\kappa t} + \kappa \int_0^t \theta(s) e^{\kappa(s-t)} ds,$$

and

$$\text{var}[y_t] = \eta^2 \int_0^t e^{2\kappa(s-t)} ds = \frac{\eta^2}{2\kappa}(1 - e^{-2\kappa t}).$$

Note that

$$\frac{\eta^2}{2\kappa}(1 - e^{-2\kappa t}) < \eta^2 t \quad \text{for all } \kappa > 0,\ t > 0$$

with $\frac{\eta^2}{2\kappa}(1 - e^{-2\kappa t}) \to \eta^2 t$ as $\kappa \to 0$.

In this way, we see that mean reversion sharply (i.e. exponentially) reduces the growth of variance for long expiries. It should follow that if we are interested in matching the variance of volatility over a horizon T, the higher the mean reversion speed κ the greater the vol of volatility η must be. Now, given another horizon $\tau < T$, it should follow that the variance over the interval $[0, \tau]$ must be greater (than in the absence of mean reversion), since there is less time for the effect of the higher vol of volatility to be counteracted by decay (see Figure 6.8).

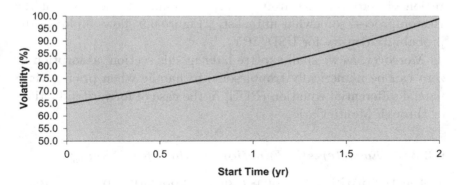

Figure 6.8: We calibrate an OU process with mean rev 50% based on a normal vol of 65% for a term of two years. If our start time increases (and end time remains unchanged), then the period, for which the volatility applies, decreases (being zero when start time is two years), so there is less time for vol decay. This leads to higher effective forward volatility over short periods.

The prices of strangles in the FX market suggest very large volatilities of volatility in the Heston model, counteracted by very large mean reversion speeds as well (e.g. $\eta = 0.4$, $\kappa = 2.5$ are typical orders of magnitude for EUR/USD).

6.3.2   *Heston Dynamics*

Looking at the SDE for the variance process

$$dV_t = \kappa(\theta(t) - V_t)dt + \eta\sqrt{V_t}dU_t,$$

the square root term in the volatility part is particularly unpleasant.

Specifically, there is the possibility of absorption at zero (i.e. if variance reaches zero, it gets stuck there forever). We have seen before in Section 5.3.4 that absorption at zero can occur in the CEV process. Since volatility of variance is typically very large in the Heston model, although counteracted by a somewhat large mean reversion speed, we should be aware that the amount of absorption is very substantial. In theory, absorption at zero will only occur if $\kappa\theta < \frac{\eta^2}{2}$ (referred to as the Feller condition) but in practice we may have to treat absorption due to numerical effects as well. As a rough guide to the amount of absorbed density, the larger the value of η versus κ and $\theta(t)$, the greater the amount of absorption. A large region of zero variance from absorption makes the density of the Heston process somewhat unrealistic. Figure 6.9 shows a plot of the probability density for USD/JPY.

Moreover, as we shall explore later in this section, absorption at zero can be numerically troublesome to handle when pricing via a partial differential equation (PDE) in the case of forward induction, or through Monte Carlo.

6.3.3   *Characteristic Function Method for Pricing*

Just as the SABR method has acquired popularity to the existence of an asymptotic expansion to allow efficient pricing of European options, a major reason for the popularity of the Heston model is

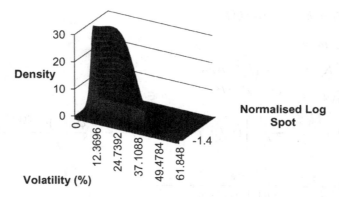

Figure 6.9: We show here the probability density of USD/JPY under the Heston model after a horizon of two years. Notice how much mass is centred around variance of zero, due to the effect of absorption. We have generated the above with representative parameters for mid 2008 (domestic rate of 2%, foreign rate of 5%, initial variance and long-run variance of 0.02, mean reversion speed of 75%, vol of variance of 46% and correlation of −70%), and we have dealt with the problem of absorption via zero-flux boundary conditions to be discussed in Section 7.2.3.

the existence of a Fourier transform method to price European call and put options efficiently.

Let us rewrite the equations in a way more amenable to interest rates, i.e. with a displaced diffusion process for the forward (as lognormal is not ideal for interest rates) and a stochastic volatility multiplier so that we can renormalise the parameters of the SDE:

$$dF_t = \sqrt{z_t}\sigma(bF_t + (1 - b)F_0)dW_t,$$

$$dz_t = \kappa(1 - z_t)dt + \eta\sqrt{z_t}dU_t, \quad \text{and}$$

$$dW_t dU_t = \rho dt.$$

Specifically, in the Heston model, the price of a European call option with strike K and expiry T is given by

$$D(0,T)E^T[(F_T - K)^+] = D(0,T)\left\{\xi_0 - \frac{K'}{2\pi}\right.$$

$$\left. \times \int_{-\infty}^{\infty} \frac{e^{(-iu+1/2)\log(\xi_0/K')}}{u^2 + 1/4}\hat{q}(u)du\right\},$$

where $\xi_t = bF_t + (1 - b)F_0$,

$$\nu_t = b^2\sigma^2 z_t,$$

$$K' = bK + (1 - b)F_0,$$

$$\hat{q}(u) = e^{A(u) - (u^2 + 1/4)B(u)\nu_0}, u \in R,$$

$$A(u) = -\frac{\kappa\alpha'}{(\eta')^2}\left[\psi_+(u)T + 2\log\frac{\psi_-(u) + \psi_+(u)e^{-\zeta(u)T}}{2\zeta(u)}\right],$$

$$B(u) = \frac{1 - e^{-\zeta(u)T}}{\psi_-(u) + \psi_+(u)e^{-\zeta(u)T}},$$

$$\psi_\pm(u) = \mp(iu\rho'\eta' + \hat{\kappa}) + \zeta(u),$$

$$\zeta(u) = \sqrt{u^2(\eta')^2(1 - (\rho')^2) + 2iu\eta'\rho'\hat{\kappa} + \hat{\kappa}^2 + \frac{(\eta')^2}{4}},$$

$$\hat{\kappa} = \kappa - \frac{1}{2}\rho'\eta',$$

$$\alpha' = b^2\sigma^2,$$

$$\eta' = |b|\sigma\eta, \quad \text{and}$$

$$\rho' = |b|\rho.$$

This formula is attributed to Lipton [Lip02]. To avoid disrupting the flow of the text, we shall hive off the derivation into a separate appendix at the end of this chapter. (Note that unlike the asymptotic expansion for the implied vol of a European option under the SABR model, the Fourier transform method gives an exact price for a European option under the Heston model.)

At this stage, however, it is worth remarking that the transformations $\xi_t = bF_t + (1 - b)F_0$ and $\nu_t = b^2\sigma^2 z_t$ (from the original F_t and z_t) in the formula give

$$d\xi_t = \sqrt{\nu_t}\xi_t dW_t,$$

$$d\nu_t = \kappa(\alpha' - \nu_t)dt + \eta'\sqrt{\nu_t}dU'_t, \quad \text{and}$$

$$dW_t dU'_t = \rho'dt$$

using the definitions of α', η', and ρ' above.

Notice that this transformed set of SDEs gives the more typical formulation of the Heston model in an FX or equity setting, so our earlier definition is a generalisation.

It is worth pointing out that we can extend the Heston model to include time-dependent parameters $\kappa(t)$, $\eta(t)$, and $\rho(t)$ to get the system of SDEs

$$dF_t = \sqrt{V_t}F_t dW_t,$$
$$dV_t = \kappa(t)(\theta(t) - V_t)dt + \eta(t)\sqrt{V_t}dU_t, \quad \text{and}$$
$$dW_t dU_t = \rho(t)dt.$$

Elices [Eli07] has shown that we can also price European options efficiently in this setup via Fourier transform methods. Arguably the time-dependent parameters give the necessary degrees of freedom to fit the prices of vanilla options across all expiries and for multiple strikes. However, it is not clear that bootstrapping these parameters from the prices of vanilla options will be stable, and in the interests of brevity, we shall not discuss this approach here.

6.3.4 *The Heston Partial Differential Equation (PDE)*

The Heston model has the right features to describe the dynamics of an equity or FX process and variants of it are popular for pricing options dependent on forward smile. To price a general derivative, it is necessary to utilise either PDE or Monte Carlo techniques as there is no analytic or Fourier transform solution.

Under the Heston model, the PDE for the price of a derivative P_t is

$$\frac{\partial P_t}{\partial t} + \frac{1}{2}V_t F_t^2 \frac{\partial^2 P_t}{\partial F_t^2} + \kappa(\theta(t) - V_t)\frac{\partial P_t}{\partial V_t}$$

$$+ \frac{1}{2}\eta^2 V_t \frac{\partial^2 P_t}{\partial V_t^2} + \rho\eta V_t F_t \frac{\partial^2 P_t}{\partial F_t \partial V_t} = r_t P_t.$$

This presents no particular difficulties.

If however we need to calibrate to prices by forward induction, the Fokker–Planck equation in the probability density p_t is

$$\frac{\partial p_t}{\partial t} = \frac{1}{2} \frac{\partial^2}{\partial F_t^2} (V_t F_t^2 p_t) - \kappa \frac{\partial}{\partial V_t} ((\theta(t) - V_t) p_t)$$

$$+ \frac{1}{2} \eta^2 \frac{\partial^2}{\partial V_t^2} (V_t p_t) + \rho \eta \frac{\partial^2}{\partial F_t \partial V_t} (V_t F_t p_t).$$

The main difficulty here is that we need a good approach for treating absorption of the density when variance is at zero. We will discuss this in Chapter 7, where we will show how to calibrate the local volatility part of a local stochastic volatility (LSV) model by forward induction.

6.3.5 *Simulating the Heston Process*

Absorption at zero also causes problems when doing a Monte Carlo simulation. Consider the standard Euler discretisation

$$V_{t+\Delta} = V_t + \kappa(\theta(t) - V_t)\Delta + \eta\sqrt{V_t \Delta} z_1,$$

$$x_{t+\Delta} = x_t - \frac{1}{2} V_t \Delta + \sqrt{V_t \Delta}(\rho z_1 + \sqrt{1 - \rho^2} z_2), \quad \text{and}$$

$$F_t = \exp(x_t),$$

where Δ is a small time interval and z_1, z_2 are independent and identically distributed $N(0, 1)$ variates. (Note that $corr(dx_t, dV_t) = E((\rho z_1 + \sqrt{1 - \rho^2} z_2) z_1) dt = \rho dt$ as required since $E[z_1] = E[z_2] = E[z_1 z_2] = 0$.)

This will not work since we cannot take the square root of a negative number, whereas there is no constraint on $V_{t+\Delta}$ going below zero in a simulation. Whilst the simplest modification would involve flooring $V_{t+\Delta}$ by zero at each point in time, convergence can be very slow and we will need to use very small time steps if the volatility of volatility η is large (as is typically the case).

Andersen [And07] proposes a scheme for much more efficient simulation of the Heston process. This chapter outlines briefly how it works.

The main idea is that for large enough realised variance, we have an approximately squared Gaussian process, whereas for small variance, we have approximately an exponential process with a probability p of absorption at zero.

Given the value of the variance process V_t at time t, we generate $V_{t+\Delta}$ using

$$V_{t+\Delta} = \begin{cases} a(b + Z_V)^2 & \text{if } \psi \leq \psi_C \quad \text{for some} \\ & \qquad \psi_C \in [1,2] \text{ of our choice} \\ \Psi^{-1}(U_V, p, \beta) & \text{otherwise,} \end{cases}$$

where Z_V is a normal $N(0,1)$ variate,
    U_V is a uniform $U(0,1)$ variate,

$$\Psi(x) = P(V_{t+\Delta} \leq x) = p + (1-p)(1 - e^{-\beta x}) \text{ so that}$$

$$\Psi^{-1}(u) = \Psi^{-1}(u; P, \beta) = \begin{cases} 0 & \text{if } 0 \leq u \leq p \\ \dfrac{1}{\beta} \log\left(\dfrac{1-p}{1-u}\right) & \text{if } p < u \leq 1 \end{cases}$$

$$m = E[V_{t+\Delta}] = \theta(t) + (V_t - \theta(t))e^{-\kappa\Delta},$$

$$s^2 = \text{var}[V_{t+\Delta}] = \frac{V_t \eta^2 e^{-\kappa\Delta}}{\kappa}(1 - e^{-\kappa\Delta}) + \frac{\theta(t)\eta^2}{2\kappa}(1 - e^{-\kappa\Delta})^2,$$

$$\psi = \frac{m^2}{s^2},$$

$$b^2 = \frac{2}{\psi} - 1 + \sqrt{\frac{2}{\psi}\left(\frac{2}{\psi} - 1\right)} \geq 0,$$

$$a = \frac{m}{1 + b^2},$$

$$p = \frac{\psi - 1}{\psi + 1} \in [0,1], \quad \text{and}$$

$$\beta = \frac{1-p}{m} = \frac{2}{m(\psi + 1)} > 0.$$

Now, to properly capture the correlation between the underlying and the variance process, we should discretise the process for the underlying as follows:

$$\log F_{t+\Delta} = \log F_t + \frac{\rho}{\eta}(V_{t+\Delta} - V_t - \kappa\theta(t)\Delta) + \left(\frac{\kappa\rho}{\eta} - \frac{1}{2}\right)$$

$$\times \int_t^{t+\Delta} V_u du + \sqrt{1-\rho^2} \int_t^{t+\Delta} \sqrt{V_u} dW_u$$

(This can be seen since $V_{t+\Delta} = V_t + \int_t^{t+\Delta} \kappa(\theta(u) - V_u)du + \eta\int_t^{t+\Delta}\sqrt{V_u}dU_u$ gives $\int_t^{t+\Delta}\sqrt{V_u}dU_u = \frac{1}{\eta}\{V_{t+\Delta} - V_t - \int_t^{t+\Delta}\kappa(\theta(u) - V_u)du\}$ which we can substitute in place of the $\rho\sqrt{V_t}dU_t$ term in the SDE $d\log F_t = -\frac{1}{2}V_t dt + \rho\sqrt{V_t}dU_t + \sqrt{1-\rho^2}\sqrt{V_t}dW_t$.)

Using the approximation

$$\int_t^{t+\Delta} V_u du \approx \frac{1}{2}\Delta(V_t + V_{t+\Delta}),$$

and observing that the integral

$$\int_t^{t+\Delta} \sqrt{V_u} dW_u$$

is Gaussian with mean zero and variance $\int_t^{t+\Delta} V_u du$, we obtain

$$\log F_{t+\Delta} = \log F_t + \frac{\rho}{\eta}(V_{t+\Delta} - V_t - \kappa\theta(t)\Delta)$$

$$+ \frac{1}{2}\Delta\left(\frac{\kappa\rho}{\eta} - \frac{1}{2}\right)(V_t + V_{t+\Delta})$$

$$+ \sqrt{\frac{1}{2}\Delta(1-\rho^2)(V_t + V_{t+\Delta})} Z,$$

where Z is a normal $N(0,1)$ variate.

6.4   Approximating Stochastic Volatility

Introducing stochastic volatility is not without its costs. For one, we have an additional factor and introducing an additional factor on a PDE increases computational time exponentially. Furthermore, the most efficient-to-calibrate (and still realistic) of SV models (i.e. the Heston model) has the rather unsatisfying property of absorption of

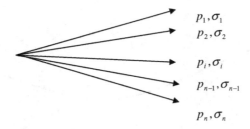

Figure 6.10: The n states of volatility σ_i, each with a corresponding probability p_i.

variance at zero. Can we avoid the hassle with some approximation that works adequately for simple products?

It turns out the solution is the discrete multi-state volatility, whose simplicity has made it popular in many banks.

6.4.1 *Discrete Multi-State Volatility*

The idea is to have a discrete approximation to stochastic volatility. Specifically, suppose that volatility at time zero is σ_0 and at infinitesimal time $(t > 0)$, volatility jumps to one of n states with probabilities p_i (see Figure 6.10). For example, taking $n = 3$ with arbitrary probabilities $p^+ = \frac{1}{6}$, $1 - p^+ - p^- = \frac{2}{3}$, $p^- = \frac{1}{6}$ and states of volatility $\sigma^+ > \sigma_0 > \sigma^-$ (calibrated so that prices of at-the-money options and strangles are matched) might be enough for common developed economy FX pairs. See Figure 6.11 for an example of the generated vol smile.

The idea is that on a PDE, we will price the underlying backward on each of the 3 states of volatility and combine the prices to get the price of the derivative.

By definition, we have assumed correlation between the variance process and the underlying is zero so that we will not be able to reflect market skew.[15] In practice, this is dealt with by introducing local volatility, i.e. we have 3 local volatility processes with different initial vols as per our states above. This goes into the realm of LSV models, which will be discussed in Chapter 7. Comparing the price of one-touch options in some typical developed economy currency

---

[15]I.e. differences in vols for high versus low strikes.

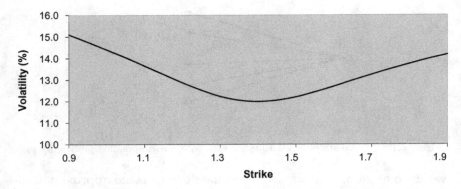

Figure 6.11: Here we illustrate how the multi-state vol model generates a smile. We have initial spot of 1.4, and 3 states of vol (6%, 12%, and 18%) each with probability of 1/3. We price call options of different strikes with expiry of 2 years. The resultant lognormal implied vols are clearly higher at the wings.

pairs shows surprisingly good agreement between a local stochastic volatility model and a multi-state local volatility model.

6.4.2 *Limitations of Multi-State Volatility*

However, since volatility jumps to one of n states just after time zero and then stays constant, the multi-state volatility model is not suitable for valuing products that depend heavily on forward smile. Consider a forward starting option which at time T_2 pays $\max(AS_{T_1} - S_{T_2}, 0)$, where $T_1 < T_2$ are future times (as in the introduction to this chapter). It is clear that we need the smile at time T_1 of an option with time to expiry $T_2 - T_1$ and strike AS_{T_1}.

Consider for illustration the extreme case when there are two states of volatility, i.e. 100% and 2%. Suppose also that the underlying is 1.5 at time zero. Now, if we had a scenario where the underlying's value is really large, e.g. 4.2 after 1 year, then it almost certainly has come from the state with 100% volatility, whereas if the underlying's value is close to 1.5, e.g. 1.44, it most likely has come from the state with 2% volatility. It is thus clear that given a state of the underlying at a future time, the prevailing volatility has a significant probability of being at 100% or at 2%, and a somewhat smaller probability of being distributed across the two scenarios. This means forward smile has become flat in some scenarios!

Of course, in practice, the states of volatility will not be so extreme and we can use many more states to give a more satisfying approximation to a continuous volatility process, however the above illustration should make clear why the multi-state volatility model may not be suitable for products heavily dependent on forward smile. And of course, there are theoretical objections (regarding inconsistencies) to using a mixture model as elegantly presented by Piterbarg [Pit03a]. However, it is worth pointing out that the non-arbitrage free nature of implied volatilities under the SABR model did not prevent SABR from becoming the industry standard for parameterising interest rate volatilities. Ultimately, the question is always one regarding materiality of the inconsistencies for the matter at hand.

6.5   Moments Explosion

As strange as it sounds, SV models can come with the very real possibility of having infinite higher order moments within finite time. This is especially so in the realms of FX and equities where we tend to want the underlying to follow a lognormal process.

Consider a generalisation of the Heston model:

$$dF_t = \sqrt{V_t} F_t dW_t,$$
$$dV_t = \kappa(\theta(t) - V_t)dt + \eta V_t^p dU_t, \quad \text{and}$$
$$dW_t dU_t = \rho dt.$$

Andersen and Piterbarg discuss in [AP07] how typical SV models can lead to infinite values of variance within finite time for some values of p. Basically, the larger the value of p, the faster moments explosion occurs. Whereas for $0 < p < \frac{1}{2}$, moments will always remain finite; for the popular Heston case (i.e. $p = \frac{1}{2}$), variance can be infinite within time scales typical for long-dated trades.[16] In

---

[16]E.g. 30-year PRDCs are common — more on this product in Chapter 10.

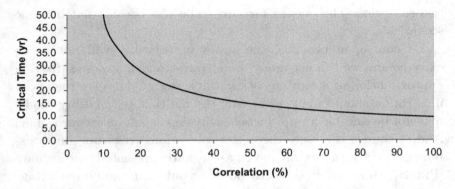

Figure 6.12:   Here we illustrate the critical time beyond which the second moment explodes. We have assumed mean reversion of 30%, initial vol of 20%, and vol of variance of 100%, which are not unusual parameters for the interest rates or FX markets. Note that 30 years is not an uncommon expiry for rates products or the Power Reverse Dual Currency (PRDC) market. So, the second moment can become infinite within the period for which the model has to be utilised!

particular, the higher the correlation between the stochastic volatility and the underlying, the faster it is before we get infinite variance (see Figure 6.12).

This can be a real problem since we may want to value products that depend on the second moment of the underlying. For example, convexity products like the CMS[17] are typical in interest rates whilst auto-quantoes[18] exist in FX, and moments explosion will lead to a theoretically infinite price.

For SABR, we have $p = 1$ which is the worst possible case, unless the SABR blend is less than 1, in which case surprisingly moments explosion will not occur at all. In interest rates, we tend to be more willing to use a CEV process with a blend less than 1, so we should be fine after all. However, the practical implication of a blend close to 1 is that we could have very large moments. In the sense of CMS, this means our convexity adjustment can be huge (e.g. a 2% CMS convexity adjustment for a 30-year CMS rate starting 40-year forward is not that unusual, that on top of the rather tiny swap rate of about 3% — much like a small animal with a massive tail).

---

[17]See Section 3.1.3.
[18]See Section 3.1.6.

In any event, notwithstanding the theoretical possibility of infinite moments, practical implementation will avoid this. For instance, on a PDE, we will always artificially restrict our boundaries (as we can only work within a finite domain). The theoretical possibility of infinite moments means however that increasing the region within our boundaries will not give convergence in price, however slow the increase in price may be.

6.5.1 *An Illustration of Moments Explosion*

Perhaps it is best to illustrate with a very simple case of infinite moments, so the reader may be convinced that this is a very real phenomenon.

Consider now the process

$$dF_t = \sigma_t F_t dW_t,$$

where $\sigma_0 = \hat{\sigma}$ and at an infinitesimal time $t > 0$, σ_t jumps so that $\log \sigma_t$ has distribution $N(\log \hat{\sigma} - \frac{1}{2}\nu^2, \nu^2)$ and σ_t then remains constant thereafter.

Suppose now we are interested in the second moment $E[F_t^2]$. We see that

$$E[F_t^2] = \int_0^\infty \int_0^\infty \frac{1}{2\pi F \sigma^2 \nu \sqrt{t}} F^2 e^{-\frac{(\log F - \log F_0 + \frac{1}{2}\sigma^2 t)^2}{2\sigma^2 t}}$$

$$\times e^{-\frac{(\log \sigma - \log \hat{\sigma} + \frac{1}{2}\nu^2)^2}{2\nu^2}} d\sigma dF$$

$$= \int_{-\infty}^\infty \int_0^\infty \frac{1}{2\pi \sigma^2 \nu \sqrt{t}} e^{2y} e^{-\frac{\left(y - \log F_0 + \frac{1}{2}\sigma^2 t\right)^2}{2\sigma^2 t}}$$

$$\times e^{-\frac{\left(\log \sigma - \log \hat{\sigma} + \frac{1}{2}\nu^2\right)^2}{2\nu^2}} d\sigma dy$$

$$= \int_{-\infty}^\infty \int_0^\infty \frac{1}{2\pi \sigma^2 \nu \sqrt{t}} e^{-\frac{(y - \log F_0 - \frac{3}{2}\sigma^2 t)^2}{2\sigma^2 t}} F_0^2$$

$$\times e^{\sigma^2 t} e^{-\frac{\left(\log \sigma - \log \hat{\sigma} + \frac{1}{2}\nu^2\right)^2}{2\nu^2}} d\sigma dy$$

$$= F_0^2 \int_0^\infty \frac{1}{\sqrt{2\pi}\sigma\nu} e^{\sigma^2 t} e^{-\frac{\left(\log\sigma - \log\hat\sigma + \frac{1}{2}\nu^2\right)^2}{2\nu^2}} d\sigma$$

$$= F_0^2 \int_{-\infty}^\infty \frac{1}{\sqrt{2\pi}\nu} e^{e^{2x}t} e^{-\frac{\left(x - \log\hat\sigma + \frac{1}{2}\nu^2\right)^2}{2\nu^2}} dx$$

$$= \infty,$$

where we have changed to the variables $y_t = \log F_t$ and $x_t = \log \sigma_t$, and also utilised the technique of completion of squares.

And of course it gets worse for higher order moments.

6.6   Consolidation

6.6.1   *Summary*

This chapter concerns itself with stochastic volatility (SV) models. Starting with some empirical evidence of volatility clustering as backdrop, we moved on to consider how correlation between the underlying and the stochastic volatility generates skew, whereas the volatility of volatility term accounts for smile which persists over time since variance of volatility grows with time. Furthermore, when spot moves, implied volatility moves in the same direction under an SV model.

We moved on to consider various SV models, starting with SABR. This model is popular due to the existence of an asymptotic expansion (due to Hagan *et al.*) for the implied volatility, so that fast pricing of European options is possible, leading to it being market standard for vanilla interest rates options and also extensively used in FX options. We explored how the various parameters of SABR (initial volatility, correlation, and volatility of volatility) correspond to specific features of the volatility surface (overall level, skew, and smile respectively), so that calibrating SABR parameters to market option prices tends to be stable (i.e. the problem tends not to have multiple local minima). On the other hand, the SABR blend describes the backbone (i.e. how overall volatility moves with changes in interest rates), and thus significantly affects the delta of a derivative. The intuition attached to the various SABR parameters helps promote the acceptance of the model. However, there are various issues with SABR: It is not arbitrage-free (for low strikes, density can be negative); volatilities for high strikes tend to be explosive (leading to over-pricing of CMS products); and the effect of stochastic volatility is underestimated. Furthermore, SABR is not really used to model the evolution of an underlying over time, since the absence of mean reversion leads to unrealistic growth of variance of volatility; instead, it is used for smile interpolation for a given expiry (and tenor in the case of interest rates).

In light of the above, we proceeded to another popular SV model — the Heston model. Unlike SABR, the volatility process is subject to mean reversion. This dampens the growth of the variance of volatility over time, so that the smile does not become too pronounced for long expiries vis-à-vis shorter expiries, in keeping with what is observed in the market. We considered how calibrating to variance for a fixed term, leads to higher forward volatility (over a shorter period) in the presence of mean reversion. This enables us to cope with pronounced smiles and skew at short expiries in conjunction with realistic smiles at longer expiries. The Heston model with variance that follows a square root process with huge volatility of variance (balanced by a large mean reversion speed) in practice suffers from high amount of absorption of variance at zero, which is not really realistic. Nevertheless, it is popular in industry, since there is a Fourier transform approach for the pricing of European options, so that calibration to vanilla options can be quickly effected. This compensates for its less realistic dynamics versus a lognormal model of stochastic volatility (more in keeping with observed market dynamics) for which no quasi-analytic pricing of European options exist. We then discussed the pricing PDE for the Heston model and wrapped up our discussion on the Heston model by considering how to efficiently simulate this via Monte Carlo, using an approach suggested by Andersen.

Stochastic volatility models have one additional factor (versus the local volatility equivalent), which makes them much (exponentially) slower to treat on PDEs. Further, the huge volatility scenarios that can result from evolving the volatility process can contribute to slow convergence in pricing and instability of risk calculations. We considered an approximation of stochastic volatility by a model which assumes that at time zero, volatility can jump to a discrete set of states (with given probability) and remains constant thereafter. This reduces the pricing problem to a sum of Black–Scholes pricing prices and so is extremely fast and hence popular in industry. We explored though the limitations as to when such a model will fail. We ended our discussion by considering the phenomenon of moments explosion expounded by Andersen and Piterbarg — within finite time, various SV models have infinite moments, including the second moment, which is of particular concern in interest rates, since this is key for the prices of CMS products.

6.6.2   *Exercises*

(1) Risk reversals and strangles are described in Section 2.3.2 as packages of calls and puts with strikes on either side of the forward. Using the approximation to the SABR formula per Section 6.2.3, compute the implied vols for strikes $0.8F$, F, and $1.25F$, where $F = 1$ is the initial value of the forward. Take $\sigma_0 = 15\%$, $\beta = 1$, $\rho = -30\%$, and $\nu = 50\%$ initially. Try varying each of σ_0, ρ, and ν one at a time and see how the smile changes. Hence, convince yourself that a mapping between σ_0, ρ, ν, and atm option prices, risk reversal prices, strangle prices is meaningful and stable.

(2) Take the actual SABR formula per Section 6.2.1 with $\sigma_0 = 0.5\%$, $\beta = 0$, $\rho = -25\%$, $\nu = 30\%$, and $F = 4\%$. By considering an expiry of 20 years and strikes at 10 basis points increments from 1% to 2% inclusive, try and construct an arbitrage involving butterflies (i.e. long a call at strike $K - \delta$, short two calls at strike K and long a call at strike $K + \delta$ where $\delta > 0$). This is an illustration of the problem of negative densities under the SABR model for very low strikes and long enough expiry.

(3) Consider a very steep skew. Would SABR always be able to fit this?

(4) For a Heston model, take mean reversion of 15%. Calibrate η, ρ, $\theta(t)$ to the prices of strangles and risk reversals over 5 years (using the characteristic function method for pricing European options in Section 6.3.3.). What does the implied vol smile look like for 5 years versus 1 month? Repeat this for mean reversion of 200%.

Appendix: Derivation of the Fourier Transform Approach to Price a European Option

Following on from Section 6.3.3, we begin with the system of SDEs:

$$dF_t = \sqrt{z_t}\sigma(bF_t + (1-b)F_0)dW_t,$$
$$dz_t = \kappa(1 - z_t)dt + \eta\sqrt{z_t}dU_t, \quad \text{and}$$
$$dW_t dU_t = \rho dt,$$

or equivalently in terms of the transformed variables ξ_t and ν_t:

$$d\xi_t = \sqrt{\nu_t}\xi_t dW_t,$$
$$d\nu_t = \kappa(\alpha' - \nu_t)dt + \eta'\sqrt{\nu_t}dU_t', \quad \text{and}$$
$$dW_t dU_t' = \rho' dt,$$

where we adopt the notation as per Section 6.3.3 in this appendix. We shall follow the approach as per Andreasen [Andr02] below. The value of a call option under the T-forward measure is

$$D(0,T)E^T[(F_T - K)^+] = D(0,T)E^T\left[\left(\frac{\xi_T}{b} - \frac{1-b}{b}F_0 - K\right)^+\right]$$

$$= \frac{D(0,T)}{|b|}E^T[\text{sgn}(b)(\xi_T - K')^+]$$

$$= \frac{D(0,T)}{|b|}E^T[\text{sgn}(b)(e^{x_T} - K')^+]$$

with K' defined above and $e^{x_t} = \xi_t$.

Note that

$$E^T[(e^{x_T} - K')^+] = e^{x_0} - E^T[\min(e^{x_T}, K')]$$

$$= e^{x_0} - \int_{-\infty}^{\infty} \min(e^x, K')p(x_0 - x)dx$$

$$= e^{x_0} - (g * p)(x_0),$$

where $p(\bullet)$ is the density of $x_0 - x_T$, $g(x) = \min(e^x, K')$ and $*$ is the convolution operator.

Define the Fourier transform as

$$\hat{\phi}(u) = \int_{-\infty}^{\infty} e^{iux}\phi(x)dx, \quad u \in R,$$

so that our function can be recovered as

$$\phi(x) = \frac{1}{2\pi} \int_{-\infty}^{\infty} e^{-iux}\hat{\phi}(u)du.$$

Then the standard convolution result gives for $\Pi = \varphi * \phi$,

$$\hat{\Pi} = \hat{\varphi}\hat{\phi}.$$

In our case, since g is not integrable but $G(x) = e^{-\frac{x}{2}}g(x)$ is integrable with

$$\hat{G}(u) = \int_{-\infty}^{\infty} e^{iux}e^{-\frac{x}{2}}\min(e^x, K')dx$$

$$= \int_{-\infty}^{\log K'} e^{(iu+\frac{1}{2})x}dx + K' \int_{\log K'}^{\infty} e^{(iu-\frac{1}{2})x}dx$$

$$= \frac{1}{iu + \frac{1}{2}}[e^{(iu+\frac{1}{2})x}]_{-\infty}^{\log K'} + \frac{K'}{iu - \frac{1}{2}}[e^{(iu-\frac{1}{2})x}]_{\log K'}^{\infty}$$

$$= \frac{(K')^{iu+\frac{1}{2}}}{iu + \frac{1}{2}} - \frac{(K')^{iu+\frac{1}{2}}}{iu - \frac{1}{2}}$$

$$
= \frac{(K')^{iu+\frac{1}{2}} \left(\left(iu - \frac{1}{2} \right) - \left(iu + \frac{1}{2} \right) \right)}{-u^2 - \frac{1}{4}}
$$

$$
= \frac{(K')^{iu+\frac{1}{2}}}{u^2 + \frac{1}{4}}
$$

$$
= \frac{K' e^{-(-iu+1/2) \log K'}}{u^2 + 1/4},
$$

we have

$$
(g * p)(x_0) = \int_{-\infty}^{\infty} g(x) p(x_0 - x) dx
$$

$$
= e^{\frac{x_0}{2}} \int_{-\infty}^{\infty} G(x) \{ e^{-(x_0 - x)/2} p(x_0 - x) \} dx
$$

$$
= e^{\frac{x_0}{2}} (G * q)(x_0),
$$

where $q(x) = e^{-\frac{x}{2}} p(x)$.

Then for $h(x) = e^{-\frac{x}{2}} (g * p)(x) = (G * q)(x)$, $\hat{h}(u) = \hat{G}(u) \hat{q}(u)$ so that

$$
(g * p)(x) = \frac{e^{\frac{x}{2}}}{2\pi} \int_{-\infty}^{\infty} e^{-iux} \hat{h}(u) dx = \frac{e^{\frac{x}{2}}}{2\pi} \int_{-\infty}^{\infty} e^{-iux} \hat{G}(u) \hat{q}(u) dx.
$$

Thus, it remains to find $\hat{q}(u)$. For this, notice that if $H(t, s) = E_t^T [e^{s(x_T - x_t)}], s \in C$, then

$$
\hat{q}(u) = H\left(0, -\frac{1}{2} + iu \right).
$$

But

$$
H(t, s) = E_t^T \left[e^{-\frac{1}{2} s \int_t^T \nu_u du + s \int_t^T \sqrt{\nu_u} dW_u} \right]
$$

$$
= E_t^T \left[e^{-\frac{1}{2}(s - s^2) \int_t^T \nu_u du - \frac{1}{2} s^2 \int_t^T \nu_u du + s \int_t^T \sqrt{\nu_u} dW_u} \right]
$$

$$= \tilde{E}_t \left[e^{-\frac{1}{2}(s-s^2) \int_t^T \nu_u du} \right]$$

$$= \tilde{E}_t \left[e^{-\int_t^T r_u du} \right],$$

where we have used a complex version of Girsanov's Theorem to change to the new measure $\tilde{Q}$, under which

$$d\tilde{U}_t = dU_t' - \rho' s \sqrt{\nu_t} dt,$$

giving

$$d\nu_t = (\kappa \alpha' - (\kappa - \rho' \eta' s) \nu_t) dt + \eta' \sqrt{\nu_t} d\tilde{U}_t,$$

and $r_t = \frac{s-s^2}{2} \nu_t$, so that we obtain

$$dr_t = (\theta - a r_t) dt + \Omega \sqrt{r_t} d\tilde{Z}_t,$$

with $\theta = \frac{s-s^2}{2} \kappa \alpha'$,

$$a = \kappa - \rho' \eta' s, \quad \text{and}$$

$$\Omega = \sqrt{\frac{s-s^2}{2}} \eta'.$$

$H(t, s)$ can now be obtained as the solution to the CIR model for the price of a discount bond, which is widely available. This will yield the formula given in Section 6.3.3.

7

Local Stochastic Volatility

"A cow is a cow, a horse is a horse."

In Chapters 5 and 6, we have explored local volatility (LV) and stochastic volatility (SV) models as means of explaining the observed market smile of European options. Notwithstanding their differing qualities of fit, we have seen how the two approaches are fundamentally different, in terms of their assumptions regarding the behaviour of the underlying. This is reflected in the different types of forward smile generated over future times.[1] Furthermore, these differences lead to different attributes of risk sensitivities generated.

However, why should we assume that the smile dynamics of a market underlying can nicely be categorised into being either due to LV or SV? Perhaps, the smile is attributable to features of both. To this end, we shall explore the local stochastic volatility (LSV) model in this chapter.

To motivate our discussion, we shall begin the chapter by considering the prices of certain relatively typical products under a local versus stochastic volatility model, as well as discuss where the market prices are. We then continue with exploring how to treat an LSV model on a partial differential equation (PDE) framework, especially as regards to the calibration of the local volatility component.

---

[1] E.g. the LV smile evolves as per the forward smile whereas SV preserves the smile.

7.1   Forward-Volatility Sensitive Products

How we capture volatility smile is important because of its implications for the dynamics of smile evolution. This is best seen by considering some popular products that depend on forward volatility.

7.1.1   *Prices of One-Touch Under Local Volatility Versus Stochastic Volatility*

We have briefly encountered barrier options in Chapter 3. Barrier features are popular in foreign exchange (FX). This could be because there is greater demand in FX for products to hedge future commitments, and adding barrier features makes such products cheaper. Whereas we have discussed replication as a means of pricing these products, barrier replication is not model-independent in that we need a methodology to generate the forward smile when spot breaches the barrier. Let us now examine a particular barrier product in more detail.

Recall that an upside one-touch pays 1 at expiry T if at any time t with $0 < t \leq T$, the value of the underlying breaches a barrier H above the current spot level S_0. Similarly, a downside one-touch pays 1 if the underlying breaches a barrier H^* below the current spot level.

Ignoring discounting, the value of an upside one touch is $P(\max_{0<t\leq T} S_t \geq H)$. Notice that if S_t follows a normal process $S_t = S_0 + rt + \sigma W_t$, we can apply the Reflection Principle,[2] namely $P(\max_{0<t\leq T} W_t \geq y, W_T < x) = P(W_T \geq 2y - x)$, so that

$$P\left(\max_{0<t\leq T} W_t \geq y\right) = P\left(\max_{0<t\leq T} W_t \geq y, W_T < y\right)$$

$$+ P\left(\max_{0<t\leq T} W_t \geq y, W_T \geq y\right)$$

$$= P(W_T \geq y) + P(W_T \geq y)$$

$$= 2P(W_T \geq y).$$

(To determine $P(\max_{0<t\leq T} S_t \geq H)$ itself, in light of the drift rt in the spot process, we would need to apply a change of measure.

---

[2]Per Section 1.1.7.

Specifically,

$$P\left(\max_{0<t\leq T} S_t \geq H\right) = P\left(\max_{0<t\leq T}(S_0 + rt + \sigma W_t) \geq H\right)$$

$$= P\left(\max_{0<t\leq T}(rt + \sigma W_t) \geq H - S_0\right)$$

$$= \tilde{P}\left(\max_{0<t\leq T}(\sigma\tilde{W}_t) \geq H - S_0\right)$$

$$= \tilde{P}\left(\max_{0<t\leq T}\tilde{W}_t \geq \frac{H - S_0}{\sigma}\right)$$

$$= 2\tilde{P}\left(\tilde{W}_T \geq \frac{H - S_0}{\sigma}\right),$$

where we have changed to the measure $\tilde{Q}$ defined by the Wiener process $d\tilde{W}_t = dW_t + \frac{r}{\sigma}dt$. But such details do not affect the key ideas.)

A digital call with expiry T pays 1 if the underlying is above the barrier H at expiry. So, very approximately, an upside one-touch is worth two digital calls with the same expiry.

Similarly, we could apply the Reflection Principle to obtain the price if the underlying follows a lognormal process. In FX, the lognormal price of barrier products is referred to as the theoretical value (TV), and this is used as a benchmark to compare the effect of smile.

Figure 7.1a shows a plot of the prices of upside and downside one-touches versus the TV for a currency pair with a symmetric smile (e.g. EUR/USD), whilst Figure 7.1b shows a plot where there is a pronounced skew (e.g. USD/JPY). We immediately observe that the price under LV is much higher than that under SV. The market price happens to be somewhere in between. As such, we posit that a model where volatility smile is explained partially by stochastic volatility and partially by local volatility best reflects the market. Specifically, we can define such a process via

$$dS_t = (r_t - q_t)S_t dt + A(S_t, t)\sqrt{V_t}dW_t,$$

where $A(S_t, t)$ is a local volatility multiplier, and V_t is a stochastic process for the variance (e.g. $dV_t = \kappa(\theta_t - V_t)\,dt + \eta\sqrt{V_t}dU_t$, $dW_t dU_t = \rho dt$ gives the LSV extension to the Heston model).

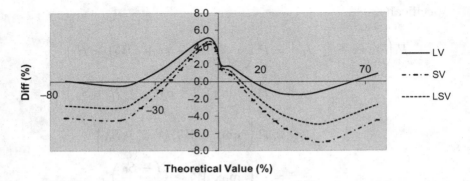

Figure 7.1a: We show here the price difference of EUR/USD 1-year one-touch options versus the theoretical value. We have represented downside one-touches with negative TV so that they can be plotted on the same graph. Basically, the more out-of-the-money a one-touch is, the smaller its TV. Notice how the LV model produces much higher prices than the SV model. FX spot and vols used are representative of May to June 2008.

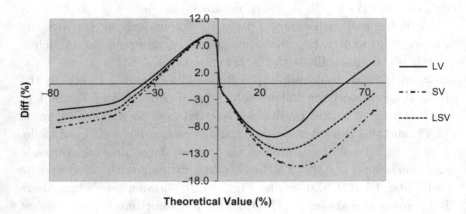

Figure 7.1b: We show here a plot similar to that in Figure 7.1a but for USD/JPY — a currency pair with downward sloping vol skew. Again, notice that LV produces higher prices than SV, and LSV produces a price in between. FX spot and vols used are representative of May to June 2008.

How do we explain the prices of one-touch options under an LV or SV model?

For an LV model, the smile corresponds to higher volatility as the spot moves further away from current values. This accentuates any excursion so that the probability of hitting far away barriers is increased, which is reflected in an increase in the prices of out-of-the-money one-touch options.

Now, let us consider the stochastic volatility case. The following is due to Hull and White [HW87]. Suppose volatility is stochastic and the process driving it is uncorrelated to spot. Then the price of a call option with strike K and expiry T is

$$C(K,T) = D(0,T)E^T[E^T[(F_T - K)^+|V]]$$
$$= \int_0^\infty BS(F_0, K, T, \sqrt{V})\phi(V)dV,$$

where $BS(F_0, K, T, \sigma)$ is the value of a Black–Scholes call given implied volatility σ, $V = \frac{1}{T}\int_0^T \sigma_u^2 du$ is the average variance over the interval $[0, T]$, and $\phi(V)$ is the density of V under the T-forward measure.

Notice further that

$$BS(F_0, F_0, T, \sigma) = D(0,T)\left[F_0 N\left(\frac{1}{2}\sigma\sqrt{T}\right) - F_0 N\left(-\frac{1}{2}\sigma\sqrt{T}\right)\right]$$

$$= D(0,T)F_0\left[2N\left(\frac{1}{2}\sigma\sqrt{T}\right) - 1\right]$$

$$\approx D(0,T)F_0\left[2\left(\frac{1}{2} + \frac{\sigma}{2}\sqrt{\frac{T}{2\pi}}\right) - 1\right]$$

$$= D(0,T)\sigma F_0\sqrt{\frac{T}{2\pi}},$$

where we have used the equation for an option on an at-the-money forward in Section 1.2.4 and the following properties:

$$N(-x) = 1 - N(x) \quad \text{for all } x, \quad \text{and}$$

$$N(x) = N(0) + \frac{1}{\sqrt{2\pi}}\int_0^x e^{-\frac{1}{2}z^2}dz$$

$$= \frac{1}{2} + \frac{1}{\sqrt{2\pi}}\int_0^x\left(1 - \frac{1}{2}z^2 + \cdots\right)dz \approx \frac{1}{2} + \frac{x}{\sqrt{2\pi}} \quad \text{for small } x.$$

Thus, we have

$$C(F_0, T) = \int_0^\infty BS(F_0, F_0, T, \sqrt{V})\phi(V)dV$$

$$\approx D(0,T)F_0\sqrt{\frac{T}{2\pi}}\int_0^\infty \sqrt{V}\phi(V)dV$$

$$= D(0,T)F_0\sqrt{\frac{T}{2\pi}}E[\sqrt{V}].$$

Suppose we now keep constant $E[V] = \Lambda^2$, where Λ is the implied volatility of an at-the-money option. Since the square root function is concave, we see from above that a higher volatility of volatility leads to a decrease in the prices of at-the-money call options.

Since it is clear that in the wings of the distribution,[3] option prices grow more than linearly with respect to $\sqrt{V}$, we therefore get higher values of a one touch under an SV model than the TV price in the wings.

However, the decrease in effective volatility of at-the-money options (in an SV model) reduces the probability of the underlying moving far away from current levels, hence leading to lower prices of one touch options vis-à-vis an LV model.

7.1.2   *Effect of Local Volatility Versus Stochastic Volatility on Volatility Swap*

We considered the variance swap in Chapter 3. This is a product whose payoff is

$$V - K,$$

where $V = \frac{1}{N-1}\sum_{i=1}^{N} R_i^2$ is the realised variance (with some deals adjusting for the mean), $R_i = \log \frac{S_{i+1}}{S_i}$ or $R_i = S_{i+1} - S_i$ are log-returns (more typical) or returns, and K is some strike.

If the intervals for the returns are frequent enough (e.g. daily) and the period is long enough (e.g. three months or more), then

---

[3]I.e. close to the centre of the TV axis in Figures 7.1a and 7.1b since TV is smaller at the centre.

we could approximate this discrete variance by $V \approx \frac{1}{T} \int_0^T (dR)^2$. If we assume that the underlying is continuous[4] and we do not have stochastic interest rates, then we can replicate this payoff statically[5] and hence do not need a model.

However, what if we now have a product that pays $\sqrt{V} - K^*$? This is a volatility swap, and unfortunately it is not amenable to replication. This is where our choice of an LV versus SV model matters: We get the same price for a variance swap but different prices for a volatility swap. (For simplicity, let us ignore discounting, which is a second order effect.)

Consider the definition of variance, i.e. for a random variable X, we have

$$\mathrm{var}(X) = E[X^2] - E^2[X].$$

Take $X^2 = V$ (i.e. the realised variance). We can rewrite our above equation to get

$$E^2[\sqrt{V}] = E[V] - \mathrm{var}(\sqrt{V}).$$

Note that replication gives the value of a variance swap, i.e. $E[V]$.

For a local volatility model, $\mathrm{var}(\sqrt{V}) \approx 0$, so

$$E[\sqrt{V}] \approx \sqrt{E[V]}.$$

Thus, the fair value strike for a volatility swap under an LV model is approximately the square root of the fair value strike for a variance swap, i.e. there is almost no negative convexity of a volatility swap with respect to a variance swap.

On the contrary, from the definition of an SV model, $\mathrm{var}(\sqrt{V}) > 0$. This means

$$E[\sqrt{V}] = \sqrt{E[V] - \mathrm{var}(\sqrt{V})}$$
$$< \sqrt{E[V]}.$$

This illustrates the familiar result that a volatility swap has a negative convexity with respect to a variance swap under an SV model.

---

[4]I.e. stochastic volatility is fine but not jumps or discrete dividends.
[5]Per Section 3.1.7.

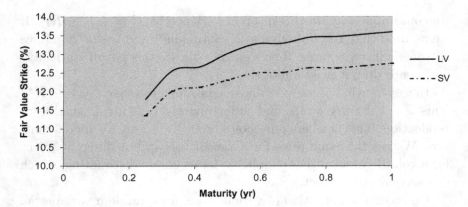

Figure 7.2: We show here the fair value strike of a volatility swap for EUR/USD under the LV and SV model across different maturities. (This is based on a representative stochastic volatility as of May 2011.) Notice how the fair value strike of the vol swap is lower under the SV model than under the LV model, representing negative convexity.

Figure 7.2 shows how the fair value strike of a vol swap compares under an LV versus SV model.

To understand this phenomenon better, let us consider the approximate equation for the price of an at-the-money option given a stochastic volatility process which is uncorrelated with the underlying process. From Section 7.1.1, we have

$$C(F_0, T) \approx D(0, T) F_0 \sqrt{\frac{T}{2\pi}} E[\sqrt{V}].$$

But we know from the same approximation that

$$C(F_0, T) \approx D(0, T) F_0 \sqrt{\frac{T}{2\pi}} \Lambda,$$

where Λ is the implied volatility of the at-the-money option.

Thus, we obtain

$$E[\sqrt{V}] \approx \Lambda.$$

This means that if we have a stochastic volatility process that is uncorrelated to the underlying process, then the fair value strike of the volatility swap is approximately given by the at-the-money volatility.

Note that this does not contradict our earlier finding that under SV, there is negative convexity of a volatility swap with respect to a variance swap. After all, the fair value strike of a variance swap is higher than the at-the-money volatility since a variance swap is a positive convexity product, whose price is obtained by static replication.[6]

Of course, in practice, market prices are somewhere between those from LV and SV models. So, once again, the natural question to ask is: Do we need an LSV model to properly capture the negative convexity of a volatility swap with respect to a variance swap?

For the interested reader, we will examine other products sensitive to forward volatility in Chapter 11.

7.2 Implementing a Local Stochastic Volatility Model

The stochastic differential equation (SDE) for a local stochastic volatility model is given by

$$dS_t = (r(t) - q(t))S_t dt + A(S_t, t)\sqrt{V_t}dW_t,$$

where typically

$$dV_t = \kappa(\theta(t) - V_t)dt + \eta\sqrt{V_t}dU_t$$

or

$$V_t = \min(e^{2z_t}, M^2), dz_t = \left(\kappa(\theta(t) - z_t) - \frac{1}{2}\eta^2\right)dt + \eta dU_t$$

with

$$dW_t dU_t = \rho dt.$$

We could easily treat this via Monte Carlo[7] or a standard PDE approach. However, it is more tricky to calibrate this model.

It is typical to first calibrate the SV parameters, i.e. κ, η, ρ, and $\theta(t)$. This we do assuming no LV but with only part of the smile and skew explained by SV. For example, if we think $\alpha = 65\%$ of the smile and skew is explained by SV, we can multiply targets for risk reversal and strangle prices by α. If the Heston base is used, Chapter 6 explains how the existence of a Fourier transform

---

[6]E.g. involving log-contracts if variance is defined via log-returns.
[7]With Andersen's approach to treat the square root process covered in Chapter 6.

solution to the prices of European call and put options makes calibration particularly convenient. However, it should be noted that a lognormal process for the underlying volatility corresponds much more with the observed market, with a high (but still plausible) cap, e.g. $M = 1000\%$ chosen to avoid moments explosion.[8]

The mean reversion speed κ controls how volatility of variance, and hence the prices of strangles over different expiries relate. $\theta(t)$ could be used to fit the prices of at-the-money options. The other parameters should be seen more with reference to a point in time (e.g. expiry of 5 years), with η affecting prices of strangles, and ρ determining prices of risk reversals. It is possible to have time-dependent versions of η and ρ, so that we could hit market prices over varying expiries. As mentioned in Section 6.3.3, Elices [Eli07] presents a comprehensive approach to the calibration of an SV model with time-dependent parameters . However, using a bootstrap procedure may not always lead to stability of these parameters, when calibrated to day-to-day fluctuations in the prices of market instruments.

Having calibrated the SV parameters, how do we determine the LV multiplier $A(S_t, t)$?

This topic is particularly well treated by Clark [Cla11], who gives detailed guidance for a user interested in implementing the methodology. In the remainder of this chapter, we shall attempt to give a more succinct presentation of the material covered by Clark, illustrating mainly based on the choice of a Heston-style stochastic volatility.

7.2.1   *Dupire's Equation for Local Stochastic Volatility*

Consider Dupire's equation from Section 5.1.3. In the presence of stochastic volatility, we have

$$E[\sigma_t^2 | S_t = K] = 2 \frac{\frac{\partial C}{\partial t}(K, t) - (\mu(t) - r(t))C(K, t) + \frac{\partial C}{\partial K}(K, t)\mu(t)K}{\frac{\partial^2 C}{\partial K^2}(K, t)K^2},$$

where $\mu(t) = r(t) - q(t)$ and $\sigma_t^2 = A^2(S_t, t)V_t$ in our LSV case.

---

[8]Discussed in Chapter 6.

Notice that

$$E[\sigma_t^2|S_t = K] = A^2(K,t)E[V_t|S_t = K].$$

Thus, we obtain the local volatility multiplier

$$A(K,t) = \sqrt{\frac{E[\sigma_t^2|S_t = K]}{E[V_t|S_t = K]}},$$

where

$$E[V_t|S_t = K] = \frac{E[V_t 1_{S_t=K}]}{E[1_{S_t=K}]}.$$

Notice that whilst Dupire's formula gives $E[\sigma_t^2|S_t = K]$, we need to obtain $E[V_t 1_{S_t=K}]$ and $E[1_{S_t=K}]$ by forward induction on the Fokker–Planck equation for the LSV model, integrating numerically where necessary.

7.2.2 *Craig–Sneyd Approach for Numerical Solution of Partial Differential Equations*

Following our discussion in Chapter 5, the Fokker–Planck equation under the LSV model (with Heston style SV) for the transition probability $p(x_t, V_t, t)$ is

$$\frac{\partial p}{\partial t} = -\frac{\partial}{\partial x}\left(\left(r(t) - q(t) - \frac{1}{2}A^2(x,t)V\right)p\right)$$

$$+\frac{1}{2}\frac{\partial^2}{\partial x^2}(A^2(x,t)Vp) - \frac{\partial}{\partial V}(\kappa(\theta(t) - V)p)$$

$$+\frac{1}{2}\frac{\partial^2}{\partial V^2}(\eta^2 Vp) + \rho\frac{\partial^2}{\partial V \partial x}(A(x,t)\eta Vp),$$

where $x_t = \log S_t$.

This can be shown to be equivalent to

$$\frac{\partial p}{\partial t} = \left(-r(t)+q(t)+\frac{1}{2}A^2(x,t)V+2A(x,t)V\frac{\partial A(x,t)}{\partial x}+\rho\eta A(x,t)\right)\frac{\partial p}{\partial x}$$

$$+\frac{1}{2}A^2(x,t)V\frac{\partial^2 p}{\partial x^2}$$

$$+ \left(-\kappa\theta(t) + \kappa V + \eta^2 + \rho\eta\frac{\partial A(x,t)}{\partial x}V \right)\frac{\partial p}{\partial V}$$

$$+ \frac{1}{2}\eta^2 V \frac{\partial^2 p}{\partial V^2} + \rho\eta V A(x,t)\frac{\partial^2 p}{\partial V \partial x}$$

$$+ \left(A(x,t)\frac{\partial A(x,t)}{\partial x}V + V\left(\frac{\partial A(x,t)}{\partial x}\right)^2 \right.$$

$$\left. + V A(x,t)\frac{\partial^2 A(x,t)}{\partial x^2} + \kappa + \rho\eta\frac{\partial A(x,t)}{\partial x} \right) p.$$

If volatility is lognormal, then we get a somewhat similar equation.

A common approach to solve such an equation is by the Craig–Sneyd method [CS88]. The idea is that for a general diffusive PDE with number of factors $N \leq 6$ and implicitness parameter $\theta(0 \leq \theta \leq 1)$, where we are time-stepping the variable P, we have

$$AP^{n+1} = (A + B)P^n,$$

where

$$A = \prod_{i=1}^{N}(1 - \theta\Delta t(q_{ii}\delta_{x_i}^2 + r_i\delta_{x_i})) \quad \text{and}$$

$$B = \Delta t \sum_{i=1}^{N}(q_{ii}\delta_{x_t}^2 + r_i\delta_{x_i}) + \Delta t \sum_{i=1}^{N}\sum_{j=1}^{i-1}q_{ij}\delta_{x_i x_j} - f\Delta t$$

with δ_{x_i} and $\delta_{x_i}^2$ being the first and second order centred differences, $\delta_{x_i x_j}$ being the cross difference, r_i being the convection coefficient, q_{ij} being the diffusion coefficients and $-f$ being the forcing term.

Specifically, the scheme involves solving a sequence of N tridiagonal equations:

$$(1 - \theta\Delta t(q_{11}\delta_{x_1}^2 + r_1\delta_{x_1}))u^{(n+1,1)}$$

$$= \left[1 + \Delta t(1 - \theta)(q_{11}\delta_{x_1}^2 + r_1\delta_{x_1}) + \Delta t \sum_{i=2}^{N}(q_{ii}\delta_{x_i}^2 + r_i\delta_{x_i}) \right.$$

$$\left. + \Delta t \sum_{i=1}^{N}\sum_{j=1}^{i-1}q_{ij}\delta_{x_i}\delta_{x_j} - f\Delta t \right]u^n,$$

$$(1 - \theta \Delta t (q_{22} \delta_{x_2}^2 + r_2 \delta_{x_2})) u^{(n+1,2)}$$
$$= u^{(n+1,1)} - \theta \Delta t (q_{22} \delta_{x_2}^2 + r_2 \delta_{x_2}) u^n,$$

$$\dots$$

$$\dots$$

$$(1 - \theta \Delta t (q_{NN} \delta_{x_N}^2 + r_N \delta_{x_N})) u^{n+1}$$
$$= u^{(n+1,N-1)} - \theta \Delta t (q_{NN} \delta_{x_N}^2 + r_N \delta_{x_N}) u^n.$$

to sequentially obtain $u^{(n+1,1)}$, $u^{(n+1,2)}$, ..., $u^{(n+1,N-1)}$ and u^{n+1}, so we can avoid any expensive matrix inversions.

In the absence of cross terms, this scheme is unconditionally stable for $N \leq 3$ when $\theta \geq \frac{1}{2}$. This covers really most practical cases of interest, since it is too computationally inefficient to work on PDEs with dimension higher than three. $\theta = \frac{1}{2}$ covers the important case which yields higher order accuracy for equally spaced discretisations of the PDE grid — an extension of the well-known Crank--Nicolson method in one dimension. Furthermore, boundary conditions are preserved as we are solving the exact equation at each stage, as opposed to some versions of locally-one-dimensional schemes.

We are effectively applying implicitness to the diffusion and convection terms, the latter being particularly prone to numerical instability if not treated with care.

7.2.3 *Forward Induction to Calibrate Local Volatility Component of Heston*

Whilst the Craig–Sneyd scheme presents a very effective means of solving most PDEs of interest, forward induction on the Heston model can be particularly challenging. The reason is that under the Heston model, there is a substantial probability of the process being absorbed at zero. This means that there is a Dirac delta mass of the probability density at zero. This seriously complicates the boundary conditions that we have to treat. (Note that this problem does not appear if we choose a lognormal stochastic volatility component instead.)

In the absence of an absorbing mass at zero, it is typically an acceptable (if sometimes inaccurate) assumption to impose a condition of zero second derivatives at the boundary. This allows at most linear growth of the underlying at the boundary, which is somewhat more general than imposing a Dirichlet or Neumann condition at the boundary.

To treat the absorbing probability mass at zero, a method involving application of a zero-flux boundary condition as proposed by Lucic in [Luc08], which is discussed below, is very interesting.

Lucic bases his ideas on the work of Feller who studied what corresponds to the CIR equation in finance, i.e. the SDE

$$dr_t = \kappa(\theta - r_t)dt + \sigma\sqrt{r_t}dW_t.$$

Specifically, this has a Fokker–Planck equation for the probability mass p_t of

$$\frac{\partial p}{\partial t} = \frac{1}{2}\sigma^2\frac{\partial^2}{\partial r^2}(rp) - \frac{\partial}{\partial r}(\kappa(\theta - r)p).$$

Consider $\int_0^\infty p(t,r)dr = 1$. Taking the time derivative (and changing the order of integration and differentiation), we get

$$\int_0^\infty \left(\frac{1}{2}\sigma^2\frac{\partial^2}{\partial r^2}(rp) - \frac{\partial}{\partial r}(\kappa(\theta - r)p)\right)dr = 0.$$

This gives the boundary condition at $r = 0$ as

$$\frac{1}{2}\sigma^2\frac{\partial}{\partial r}(rp) - \kappa(\theta - r)p = 0$$

(since the left-hand side of the above clearly has value 0 at $r = \infty$ with $p = \frac{\partial p}{\partial r} = 0$).

By analogy, we could extend this reasoning to obtain the following zero-flux boundary condition for the LSV model:

$$\frac{1}{2}\eta^2\frac{\partial}{\partial V}(Vp) - \kappa p(\theta(t) - V) + V\rho\eta\frac{\partial}{\partial x}(A(x,t)p) = 0$$

at $p(x,V,t)|_{V=0}$.

7.3   Consolidation

7.3.1   *Summary*

Following on from Chapters 5 and 6, this chapter considers the local stochastic volatility (LSV) model — i.e. a model with local volatility (LV) and stochastic volatility (SV) components. We motivate the discussion by considering some products sensitive to forward smile rather than just the vanilla options smile. First, we showed how an LV model produces a higher price for a one-touch option (paying 1 if the underlying breaches a barrier at any time prior to expiry) than an SV model. The market price happens to lie somewhere in between. We considered preserving the variance in an SV model and showed how it leads to expected volatility and hence the price of at-the-money options decreasing. We next considered the volatility swap (which again is heavily affected by assumptions of whether we have an LV versus SV model, unlike its cousin the variance swap). Here, the LV model produces a higher fair value strike because the variance of the volatility is zero, whereas the SV model produces a fair value strike closer to the at-the-money volatility.

Next, we naturally moved on to discussing the implementation of the LSV model. The first consideration is how to obtain LV multipliers in the presence of SV. We showed how this could be done using the expected variance conditional on spot obtainable from Dupire's formula, together with forward induction on the Fokker–Planck equation to obtain the distribution of spot and variance at a future time. We explored the Craig–Sneyd PDE which provides an efficient method for solving the two- dimensional Fokker–Planck PDE for the LSV model. We noted that due to huge absorption at the boundary of zero variance, traditional choices of boundary conditions may not work well. We concluded by presenting the approach suggested by Lucic involving a zero-flux boundary condition (which ensures the integral of probabilities is 100%).

7.3.2   *Exercises*

(1) Show how the Black–Scholes PDE $\frac{\partial V}{\partial t} + rS\frac{\partial V}{\partial S} + \frac{1}{2}\frac{\partial^2 V}{\partial S^2}\sigma^2 S^2 = rV$ with final condition $V(S,T) = V_T(S)$ can be transformed into

a typical diffusion equation $\frac{\partial u}{\partial \tau} = \alpha \frac{\partial^2 u}{\partial x^2}$ with initial condition $u(x,0) = u_0(x)$, where $u(x,\tau) = u(\log S, T - t)$. It would help to make the substitution $V = ue^{\alpha x + \beta \tau}$. (Do not bother finding the initial condition. The exercise is more to convince you that the Black–Scholes PDE is a standard diffusion.)

(2) Consider the diffusion equation $\frac{\partial u}{\partial t} = \alpha \frac{\partial^2 u}{\partial x^2}$. Let $u_i^n = u(j\Delta x, n\Delta t)$. The explicit scheme for discretisation uses $\frac{u_j^{n+1} - u_j^n}{\Delta t} = \alpha \frac{u_{j+1}^n - 2u_j^n + u_{j-1}^n}{(\Delta x)^2}$ whereas the implicit scheme uses $\frac{u_j^{n+1} - u_j^n}{\Delta t} = \alpha \frac{u_{j+1}^{n+1} - 2u_j^{n+1} + u_{j-1}^{n+1}}{(\Delta x)^2}$. Consider the Fourier node $\hat{u}_j^n(k) = \lambda^n e^{ik(j\Delta x)}$, where i is the imaginary root of -1 (note that the solution can be expressed as an integral over Fourier nodes, i.e. $u_j^n = \frac{1}{2\pi} \int_{-\infty}^{\infty} \hat{u}_j^n(k) e^{-ik(j\Delta x)} dk$). By substituting this Fourier node into the explicit scheme, find a condition on $\frac{\Delta t}{(\Delta x)^2}$ such that the scheme is stable. Show also that the implicit scheme is unconditionally stable.

(3) Consider the Craig–Sneyd discretisation for three space variables. By performing the steps sequentially, show that the scheme is consistent (i.e. we do indeed recover a discretised form of the original PDE when we ignore higher order terms).

(4) Find a self-similarity solution, i.e. $f(z) = \frac{1}{\sqrt{t}} u(x,t)$ where $z = \frac{x}{\sqrt{t}}$ to the diffusion equation $\frac{\partial u}{\partial t} = \frac{1}{2}\alpha \frac{\partial^2 u}{\partial x^2}$ with initial condition $u(x,0) = \delta(x)$ and subject to the additional condition $\int_{-\infty}^{\infty} u(x,t)dx = 1$. (Note that like the Black–Scholes equation, the Fokker–Planck equation can be transformed into a standard diffusion, so solving the above diffusion equation with the given initial and boundary conditions, is a key step towards solving the actual Fokker–Planck equation.)

(5) Build a simple Monte Carlo framework based on stochastic vol. Convince yourself that the fair value strike of a vol swap is not very different from the at-the-money vol.

8

Short Rate Models

"A short rate does not exist, so how can it cross a barrier?"

In Chapters 3 and 4, we have considered typical approaches to pricing interest rate products that relate to observables determined at one point in time (e.g. a constant maturity swap (CMS) product pays based on say the 10-year swap rate on 15 March 2016).

However, various products have payoffs which depend on the relation between observables at different points in time. For example, suppose you have a Bermudan swaption which entitles you to enter into a swap maturing on 20 June 2015, exercisable on 20 June each year from 2010 onwards. You would really be considering how a 5-year swap rate on 20 June 2010 compares with a 4-year swap rate on 20 June 2011, a 3-year swap rate on 20 June 2012, a 2-year swap rate on 20 June 2013, and a 1-year swap rate on 20 June 2014.

You can already observe a key difference vis-à-vis products in equities or foreign exchange (FX), where at each date, you typically consider the same quantity, namely the price of the underlying (i.e. a stock or FX rate). This situation lends itself to the modelling of the underlying directly.

But in interest rates, even if you had to consider the same variable at each future date (e.g. the 10-year swap rate in a CMS product), it is not amenable to direct modelling. First, the 10-year swap rate as of 20 June 2010 is a function of discount factors over the period 20 June 2010 to 20 June 2020, whereas the 10-year swap rate as of 20 June 2011 is a function of discount factors over the period 20 June

2011 to 20 June 2021. So, clearly there is a need to consider how the discount factors for future cashflows might be correlated with the swap rate. Furthermore, the 10-year swap rate as of 20 June 2010 is not a distinct entity rolled over into another 10-year swap rate as of 20 June 2011. Rather, it is a combination of discount factors.

The above discussion should hopefully persuade you that in general it does not make sense to model a distinct quantity such as the 10-year swap rate and how it evolves over time, but rather you would need to model the evolution of the entire yield curve together (i.e. a term structure model). It is actually sufficient if we could come up with a model, which at a future point in time, can give us the value of a discount bond to any maturity. We can then construct Libor rates and swap rates as combinations of these discount factors.

This is a much more complex task than modelling one underlying. The most popular classes of term structure models are the short rate, Libor Market and Markov functional models. In this chapter, we shall explore short rate models, whereas in Chapter 9, we shall explore the Libor Market Model. This book will not discuss Markov functional models in the interest of brevity, since they are the least popular of the three main classes of term structure models, but an interested reader is referred to the excellent work by Pelsser [Pel00].

Our discussion is based on the classical assumption that we can borrow and lend at some risk-free rate. Since the credit crunch, this is no longer true: Libor is typically the reference rate for floating legs; market participants who are party to a CSA-arrangement (i.e. some form of collateral agreement where both parties agree to settle the changes in the mark-to-market of their positions vis-à-vis each other at the end of each day, as more fully described in Section 12.1.3) can fund at the overnight index swap rate; for others, funding is more punitive. Many of the ideas in this chapter and the next can extend to this new world order, to which we shall briefly acquaint ourselves in Chapter 12. But it is beyond the scope of this book to incorporate funding considerations into our term structure modelling setup.

8.1   The Setup

A short rate model is a model which attempts to capture the dynamics of the entire yield curve at a future point in time via the short rate r_t (i.e. the fictitious risk-free rate of interest for investing a unit amount for an instantaneous point in time). This is possible since the value of a discount bond with expiry T as seen at a future time t is given by the no-arbitrage equation

$$\frac{D(t,T)}{B(t)} = E_t^Q \left[\frac{D(T,T)}{B(T)} \right],$$

where $B(t) = e^{\int_0^t r_s ds}$ is the money-market account[1] and $D(t,T)$ is the value of a discount bond of maturity T as seen at time t, so that $D(T,T) = 1$, and we get

$$D(t,T) = E_t^Q \left[e^{-\int_t^T r_s ds} \right].$$

It would be nice for $D(t,T)$ to be a simple function of the short rate r_t, for otherwise evaluating the value of a discount bond given the state of the short rate r_t at a future time t can be computationally expensive.[2]

If we consider time zero (i.e. today), then we get

$$D(0,T) = E_0^Q \left[e^{-\int_0^T r_s ds} \right],$$

which gives the condition that any short rate model must satisfy if it is to recover the prices of discount bonds (and hence be of any use for pricing derivatives).

In this chapter, $D(t,T)$ is a quantity dependent on the values of state variables at a future time t, whereas $D(0,T)$ is the current yield curve today[3] and should be seen as an input to any interest rate model.

---

[1] I.e. the value of continuously investing and rolling over a unit notional at the risk-free rate until time t.

[2] Specifically, it might involve evaluating an expectation on a partial differential equation (PDE).

[3] Obtained from the prices of deposits, futures, and swaps.

The term short rate model is often used in a more generic sense to refer to any model that gives a simple form for the short rate but it may sometimes be more convenient to parameterise differently. For example, the Heath–Jarrow–Morton (HJM) model (discussed in Section 8.1.2) is based on instantaneous forward rates. However, Baxter [Bax97] shows that any HJM model adapted to a finite-dimensional Brownian motion filtration (i.e. with a finite number of factors) is equivalent to a short rate model. In practice, this covers all useful variants of the HJM model. Going forward, we shall use the term short rate model to include any HJM model as well.

One should not worry too much about whether the short rate is an instantaneous interest rate or not. Indeed, the shortest time interval for borrowing is typically one day. However, the short rate can sometimes be used as a proxy for an interest rate of a short tenor (e.g. a Libor rate with tenor of 3 months or 6 months). The main appeal of the more popular short rate models, though, is that the value of a discount bond can be expressed as a (preferably parametric) function of the realised value of the short rate. To that extent, the main requirement is that we can express the prices of discount bonds as Markovian in a small number of state variables. (In comparison, the Markov functional model simply posits state variables and requires that discount bonds be expressed as Markovian in a small number of these state variables. In this sense, a short rate model is a special case of a Markov functional model.) It is worth mentioning that we thus are not restricting a short rate model to the dynamics of the short-end of the yield curve. And as such, it does not make sense to ask if we should consider a 'long rate model' for long-term interest rates.

8.1.1   *The Short Rate Framework*

The above discussion suggests that a short rate model is usually expressed by an explicit SDE for the short rate, e.g.

$$dr_t = \kappa(t)(\theta(t) - r_t)dt + \sigma(t)dW_t,$$

gives the Hull–White model which we shall encounter shortly after this.

Alternatively, an SDE for a state variable and an expression for the short rate in the form of the state variable will also do. For example, the Black–Karasinski model can be described via

$$dy_t = \kappa(t)(\theta(t) - y_t)dt + \sigma(t)dW_t, \quad \text{and} \quad r_t = e^{y_t}.$$

8.1.2 The Heath–Jarrow–Morton (HJM) Parameterisation

The HJM model, from Heath *et al.* [HJM92], posits the following dynamics for instantaneous forward rates $f_{t,T}$ (i.e. as seen at time t and applicable to an infinitesimal point in time starting from T). This is defined from the value of a discount bond $D(t,T)$ via

$$D(t,T) = e^{-\int_t^T f_{t,s}ds}.$$

We posit the process of the instantaneous forward rate to be

$$df_{t,T} = \mu(t,T,\{\theta\})dt + \sigma(t,T,\{\theta\})dW_t,$$

where $\{\theta\}$ represents state variables which can include values of the forward rates, and for simplicity we restrict ourselves to a single Wiener process W_t.

Then Ito's Lemma gives

$$
\begin{aligned}
dD(t,T) &= D(t,T)\left[f_{t,t}dt - \int_t^T \frac{\partial f_{t,s}}{\partial t}dsdt - \int_t^T \frac{\partial f_{t,s}}{\partial W_t}dsdW_t \right. \\
&\quad \left. + \frac{1}{2}\left(\int_t^T \frac{\partial f_{t,s}}{\partial W_t}ds \right)^2 dt \right] \\
&= D(t,T)\left[\left[r_t - \int_t^T \mu(t,s,\{\theta\})ds \right. \right. \\
&\quad \left. \left. + \frac{1}{2}\left(\int_t^T \sigma(t,s,\{\theta\})ds \right)^2 \right] dt - \int_t^T \sigma(t,s,\{\theta\})dsdW_t \right] \\
&= D(t,T)\left[r_t dt - \int_t^T \sigma(t,s,\{\theta\})dsdW_t \right],
\end{aligned}
$$

where the last equality is from no arbitrage,[4] and we note that $r_t = f_{t,t}$ (i.e. the short rate is a special case of an instantaneous forward rate).

This gives

$$\int_t^T \mu(t, s, \{\theta\})ds = \frac{1}{2}\left(\int_t^T \sigma(t, s, \{\theta\})ds\right)^2,$$

and differentiating with respect to T then yields the following condition for the drift

$$\mu(t, T, \{\theta\}) = \sigma(t, T, \{\theta\})\int_t^T \sigma(t, s, \{\theta\})ds.$$

It is also useful to relate the instantaneous forward rate with the short rate. In particular, notice that

$$D(t, T) = e^{-\int_t^T f_{t,s}ds} = E_t^Q\left[e^{-\int_t^T r_s ds}\right].$$

So, differentiating with respect to T gives

$$-f_{t,T}D(t, T) = -E_t^Q\left[r_T e^{-\int_t^T r_s ds}\right]$$
$$= -D(t, T)E_t^T[r_T],$$

where the last equation is obtained by changing form the risk-neutral measure[5] to the T-forward measure,[6] giving rise to the Radon–Nikodym derivative $\frac{dQ^T}{dQ^*} = \frac{D(T,T)B(t)}{B(T)D(t,T)} = \frac{e^{-\int_t^T r_s ds}}{D(t,T)}$.

Thus, we have

$$f_{t,T} = E_t^T[r_T].$$

Converting from a short rate to a forward rate process can be helpful to visualise the relation with discount bonds without the expectations.

---

[4]Since under the risk-neutral measure any asset should have drift r_t.

[5]With money market account $B(t) = e^{\int_0^t r_s ds}$ as numeraire.

[6]With discount bond $D(t, T)$ of maturity T as numeraire.

8.1.3 *Pricing a Discount Bond Given the Model's State*

It would be very useful if we are able to express the prices of discount bonds for any maturity T as seen at any time t as a simple function of the short rate r_t or a small number of state variables. This is because evaluating the expression $D(t,T) = E_t^Q[e^{-\int_t^T r_s ds}]$ can otherwise be very expensive.

8.2 The Hull–White Model

A parameterisation of the Hull–White model (due to Hull and White [HW90]) closer to its original form is

$$dr_t = \kappa(t)(\theta(t) - r_t)dt + \sigma(t)dW_t,$$

where

$\kappa(t)$ is the mean reversion speed,
$\sigma(t)$ is volatility, and
$\theta(t)$ is the long-run mean of the short rate.

Intuitively, the idea is that the further the short rate drifts away from the long-run mean, the stronger the pull back towards the long-run mean.

Since we shall never need $\theta(t)$ directly, but rather just a means of obtaining the price of discount bonds as a function of a state variable, it is more convenient to parameterise in the form

$$dx_t = -\kappa(t)x_t dt + \sigma(t)dW_t, \quad \text{and} \quad r_t = \varphi(t) + x_t,$$

where $x_0 = 0$ and $\varphi(t)$ is chosen so that prices of all discount bonds today are recovered (i.e. $D(0,T) = E_0^Q[e^{-\int_0^T r_s ds}]$).

The above SDE gives

$$dx_t + \kappa(t)x_t dt = \sigma(t)dW_t$$

$$\Rightarrow e^{-\int_0^t \kappa(s)ds} d\left(e^{\int_0^t \kappa(s)ds} x_t\right) = \sigma(t)dW_t$$

$$\Rightarrow d\left(e^{\int_0^t \kappa(s)ds}x_t\right) = e^{\int_0^t \kappa(s)ds}\sigma(t)dW_t$$

$$\Rightarrow e^{\int_0^t \kappa(s)ds}x_t - e^{\int_0^\tau \kappa(s)ds}x_\tau = \int_\tau^t e^{\int_0^s \kappa(u)du}\sigma(s)\,dW_s \quad \text{for } \tau < t$$

$$\Rightarrow x_t = x_\tau \frac{\phi(\tau)}{\phi(t)} + \int_\tau^t \frac{\phi(s)}{\phi(t)}\sigma(s)dW_s,$$

where we have defined $\phi(t) = e^{\int_0^t \kappa(u)du}$.

Now, consider the price of a discount bond at a future time given by

$$D(t,T) = E_t^Q\left[e^{-\int_t^T r_s ds}\right]$$

$$= E_t^Q\left[\exp\left(-\int_t^T \left\{\varphi(u) + x_t\frac{\phi(t)}{\phi(u)}\right.\right.\right.$$

$$\left.\left.\left. + \int_t^u \frac{\phi(s)}{\phi(u)}\sigma(s)dW_s\right\}du\right)\right]$$

$$= \exp\left(-\int_t^T \varphi(u)du - x_t\phi(t)\int_t^T \frac{du}{\phi(u)}du\right)$$

$$\times E_0^Q\left[\exp\left(-\int_t^T \int_s^T \frac{du}{\phi(u)}\phi(s)\sigma(s)dW_s\right)\right]$$

$$= \exp\left(-\int_t^T \varphi(u)du - x_t\phi(t)(\Phi(T) - \Phi(t))\right.$$

$$\left. + \frac{1}{2}\int_t^T (\Phi(T) - \Phi(s))^2\phi^2(s)\sigma^2(s)ds\right)$$

$$= \exp(-A(t,T) - B(t,T)x_t),$$

where we have defined

$$\Phi(t) = \int_0^t \frac{du}{\phi(u)},$$

$$B(t,T) = \phi(t)(\Phi(T) - \Phi(t)), \quad \text{and}$$

$$A(t,T) = \int_t^T \varphi(u)du - \frac{1}{2}\int_t^T (\Phi(T) - \Phi(s))^2\phi^2(s)\sigma^2(s)ds.$$

(The above derivation involved changing the order of integration to get the third equality and observing that $E[e^X] = e^{\frac{1}{2}\Sigma}$, where $X \sim N(0, \Sigma)$ to get the fourth equality.)

Given that $A(t, T)$ and $B(t, T)$ are deterministic, we have just established that discount bonds with any maturity T at any future time t are a simple function of the state variable x_t.

In Section 8.1.1, we described the Black–Karasinski model via

$$dy_t = \kappa(t)(\theta(t) - y_t)dt + \sigma(t)dW_t, \quad \text{and} \quad r_t = e^{y_t}.$$

More generally, we can consider the form

$$r_t = F(t, y_t),$$

where $F(t, y_t)$ is some transformation of the state variable y_t.

Pelsser [Pel00] shows that the only transformation (other than the identity $F(t, y_t) = y_t$ as per the Hull–White model) which admits a simple functional form for the prices of discount bonds in terms of state variables is where $F(t, y_t)$ is quadratic in y_t. This leads to some interest in quadratic Gaussian models which we shall discuss later in Section 8.5.

Coming back to the Hull–White model, if we consider $t = 0$, we get (noting that $x_0 = 0$):

$$D(0, T) = \exp(-A(0, T))$$

$$= \exp\left(-\int_0^T \varphi(u)du + \frac{1}{2}\int_0^T (\Phi(T) - \Phi(s))^2 \phi^2(s)\sigma^2(s)ds\right).$$

This gives

$$\int_0^T \varphi(u)du = -\log D(0, T) + \frac{1}{2}\int_0^T (\Phi(T) - \Phi(s))^2 \phi^2(s)\sigma^2(s)ds$$

as the condition required to match the prices of all zero-coupon bonds today.

(Notice that for practical purposes, we do not need to obtain $\varphi(t)$ itself.)

8.2.1   *Mean Reversion*

Mean reversion, in the context of derivatives pricing, is often mis-understood as it does not affect the mean of the prices of market instruments — the mean price[7] of a market instrument must be its forward price due to no-arbitrage arguments. Therefore, mean rever-sion does not affect the drift of an asset, e.g. the drift of a discount bond must be $r_t D(t, T) dt$ under the risk-neutral measure. After all, notice that calibration to market requires choosing $\varphi(t)$ or $\theta(t)$ above and hence the long-run mean which takes account of the speed of mean reversion.

However, mean reversion does imply that the further we deviate from the mean, the stronger the pull on the variable in the direction towards the mean. This would appear to constrain the variance of the process. Thus, mean reversion can be said to lead to vol dampening. We have seen an argument in Section 6.3.1 illustrating how mean reversion reduces variance growth over time. However, the impor-tance of this concept makes it worth revisiting below.

Consider for illustration a simplified process

$$dx_t = -\kappa x_t dt + \sigma dW_t,$$

where mean reversion speed is constant. Its solution[8] is given by

$$x_t = x_\tau e^{\kappa(\tau-t)} + \sigma \int_\tau^t e^{\kappa(s-t)} dW_s \quad (\text{for } \tau < t)$$

with variance given by

$$\text{var}(x_t | x_\tau) = \sigma^2 \int_\tau^t e^{2\kappa(s-t)} ds$$

$$= \frac{\sigma^2}{2\kappa}(1 - e^{2\kappa(\tau-t)}).$$

Notice that $\frac{\sigma^2}{2\kappa}(1 - e^{-2\kappa t}) < \sigma^2 t$ for $t > 0$, $\kappa > 0$. So, if we calibrated our process to ensure that variance at time t is constant, then we require a larger σ to counter the effect of a higher value of mean reversion κ.

---

[7]I.e. expectation under the relevant measure.
[8]As per Section 6.3.1.

However, as can be seen, the variance of x_t given a prior state $\tau > 0$ involves less dampening over the shorter period $[\tau, t]$, whereas we had calibrated based on dampening over the period $[0, t]$. This means the forward variance over the period $[\tau, t]$ will be larger if mean reversion is larger.

Since we calibrate to match terminal vols, it follows that the larger the mean reversion in the model, the higher the forward vols. This will have implications for the pricing of caplets versus swaptions, which we will consider later in this section.

8.2.2   *Term Volatility and Caplet Pricing*

Consider now a caplet which pays $\max(L_T(T, T+\tau) - K, 0)\tau$ at time $T + \tau$, where $L_t(T, T + \tau)$ is the Libor rate applicable to the period $[T, T + \tau]$ as seen at time t.

Its value is given by

$$
\frac{V_0}{D(0, T+\tau)} = E^{T+\tau}\left[\frac{\max(L_T(T, T+\tau) - K, 0)\tau D(T, T+\tau)}{D(T, T+\tau)}\right]
$$

$$
= E^{T+\tau}\left[\max\left(\left(\frac{D(T, T)}{D(T, T+\tau)} - 1\right)/\tau - K, 0\right)\tau\right]
$$

$$
= E^{T+\tau}\left[\max\left(\frac{D(T, T)}{D(T, T+\tau)} - (1 + K\tau), 0\right)\right].
$$

At the beginning of Section 8.2, we have seen that the value of a discount bond of maturity T at future time t is given by

$$
D(t, T) = \exp(-A(t, T) - B(t, T)x_t)
$$

for deterministic $A(t, T)$ and $B(t, T) = \phi(t)(\Phi(T) - \Phi(t))$. Thus,

$$
\frac{dD(t, T)}{D(t, T)} = r_t dt - B(t, T)\sigma(t)dW_t
$$

under the risk-neutral measure.

Let $F_t = \frac{D(t,T)}{D(t,T+\tau)}$. Then since (by definition) this is a martingale under the $T + \tau$-forward measure with numeraire being the discount bond maturing at $T + \tau$, we obtain

$$\frac{dF_t}{F_t} = (B(t, T + \tau) - B(t, T))\sigma(t)dW_t$$

$$= (\Phi(T + \tau) - \Phi(T))\phi(t)\sigma(t)dW_t$$

using $B(t, T) = \phi(t)(\Phi(T) - \Phi(t))$ to get the last equality.

Notice that F_t is lognormal. It follows that the price of a caplet can be obtained via Black's formula as

$$V_0 = D(0, T + \tau)\left[F_0 N(d_1) - (1 + K\tau)N(d_2)\right]$$

$$= D(0, T + \tau)\left[\frac{D(0, T)}{D(0, T + \tau)}N(d_1) - (1 + K\tau)N(d_2)\right]$$

$$= D(0, T)N(d_1) - D(0, T + \tau)(1 + K\tau)N(d_2),$$

where

$$d_1 = \frac{\log\left(\frac{F_0}{1+K\tau}\right)}{\Sigma\sqrt{T}} + \frac{1}{2}\Sigma\sqrt{T} = \frac{\log\left(\frac{D(0,T)}{D(0,T+\tau)(1+K\tau)}\right)}{\Sigma\sqrt{T}} + \frac{1}{2}\Sigma\sqrt{T},$$

$$d_2 = d_1 - \Sigma\sqrt{T}, \quad \text{and}$$

$$\Sigma^2 T = (\Phi(T + \tau) - \Phi(T))^2 \int_0^T \phi^2(s)\sigma^2(s)ds$$

per Section 1.2.4.

Notice how mean reversion is reflected in the $\Phi(t)$ and $\phi(t)$ terms. The forward volatility appears to increase with increasing mean reversion due to the $\phi(t) = e^{\int_0^t \kappa(u)du}$ multiplier, but this is counteracted by the greater volatility decay due to the $\Phi(t) = \int_0^t \frac{du}{\phi(u)}$ terms up to time $T + \tau$. For a caplet, this decay happens over a shorter period than for a swaption, so that mean reversion raises caplet volatilities relative to swaption volatilities.

8.2.3   *Swaption Pricing*

A physically settled payer (i.e. paying the fixed rate and receiving the floating leg) swaption has value at expiry T of

$$\max(R_T - K, 0)A_T,$$

where K is strike, $A_t = \sum_{i=1}^{N} \tau_i D(t, T_i)$ is the value of an annuity (i.e. series of cashflows at future dates T_i with accrual fraction τ_i as seen at time t, and (from Section 1.2.1) $R_t = \frac{D(t,T_0)-D(t,T_N)}{A_t} = \frac{\sum_{i=1}^{N} L_t(T_{i-1},T_i)\tau_i D(t,T_i)}{A_t}$ is the forward swap rate as of time t applicable to a swap starting at T_0 and ending at T_N with fixed cash flows at dates T_i.

Jamshidian [Jam89] shows how this payoff can be decomposed into a portfolio of options on discount bonds. For simplicity, take $T_0 = T$ (i.e. the typical case where the swaption exercises into a spot-starting swap). Then it can be observed that the value of the payer swaption is higher if the prices of discount bonds at time T are lower. But discount bond prices are a monotonically decreasing function of the short rate. So, let us consider

$$\frac{V_0}{D(0,T)} = E^T[\max(R_T - K, 0)A_T]$$

$$= E^T\left[\max\left(\sum_{i=1}^{N}(L_T(T_{i-1},T_i) - K)\tau_i D(t,T_i), 0\right)\right]$$

$$= E^T\left[\sum_{i=1}^{N}(L_T(T_{i-1},T_i) - K)\tau_i D(t,T_i)1_{x_T > x^*}\right]$$

for some critical x^* obtained by root-finding so that the forward swap rate equals the strike.

Now, let us obtain the strike K_i^* for each of the i-th caplet such that it corresponds to the forward Libor rate where $x_T = x^*$. This gives us

$$\frac{V_0}{D(0,T)} = E^T\left[\sum_{i=1}^{N}\max(L_T(T_{i-1},T_i) - K_i^*, 0)\tau_i D(t,T_i)\right]$$

$$= \sum_{i=1}^{N} E^T[\max(L_T(T_{i-1},T_i) - K_i^*, 0)\tau_i D(t,T_i)].$$

Thus, we have effectively converted the problem to one of pricing a portfolio of caplets of different strikes.

Another common approach is to assume that swap rates are normal/lognormal and then come up with some approximation so that a quasi-analytic form for the variance is obtainable. We shall discuss this further in the case of the multi-factor Hull–White model.

Notice that our specification of the Hull–White model, i.e.

$$dr_t = \kappa(t)(\theta(t) - r_t)dt + \sigma(t)dW_t$$

has time-dependent mean-reversion speed $\kappa(t)$ and volatility $\sigma(t)$. This allows us to simultaneously calibrate to a strip of caplets together with co-terminal swaptions. (Co-terminal swaptions are part of a collection, where the exercise dates are different but the end date is the same. For example, we can have a set of co-terminal swaptions to exercise into a swap with end date on 20 June 2015, exercisable on 20 June in each of 2010, 2011, 2012, 2013, and 2014.) See Figure 8.1 for an illustration of the regions of the swaption grid whose volatilities we seek to calibrate to.

The reason for calibrating to co-terminal swaptions is that term structure models are typically used to price Bermudan swaptions, or other structures with early exercise features. In this sense, the final maturity of the structure tends to remain the same. And it makes sense to thus hedge these structures with instruments (e.g. physically settled swaptions) where the final maturity is the same.

As suggested at the last paragraph of Section 8.2.1, if we had only calibrated the volatility $\sigma(t)$ to the prices of co-terminal swaptions, then the higher the mean reversion speed assumed, the higher the prices our model will give for caplets (see Figure 8.2).

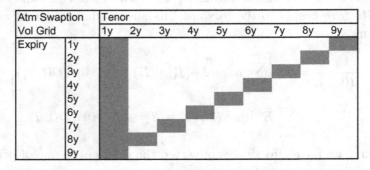

Figure 8.1:   Calibration is often to co-terminals (i.e. expiry + maturity = end date of deal) to match instrument cash flows, and to short tenor instruments (e.g. caplets or 1y tenor swaptions) to control forward vol. Targets are shaded above.

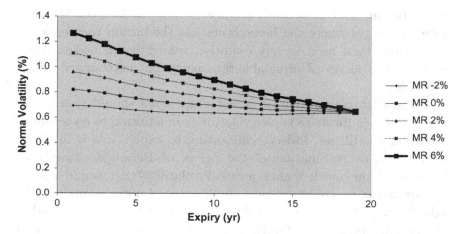

Figure 8.2:   Here we have calibrated the Hull–White model with piecewise constant volatilities at annual time points and different mean reversion assumptions to representative prices of 20-year co-terminal swaptions (i.e. expiry + tenor = 20 years) as of late 2010. Notice how caplet vols increase sharply especially for short expiries as mean reversion increases.

Calibration to caplets is relevant in that it controls forward volatility, which affects the value of early exercise features. Alternatively, forward volatility reflects the probability of transitioning from a state of interest rates at a point in time into another state at a future time, hence affecting the prices of path dependent products (e.g. tarns where the deal terminates if total coupons paid exceed a certain level). Further discussion of forward volatility is to be found in Chapter 11.

However, it is not always ideal to calibrate to both caplets and co-terminal swaptions, because the economics behind these markets can lead to inconsistent prices. Specifically, swaption volatilities tend to be depressed because there are lots of issuers selling callable bonds and swapping these with banks, so that banks tend to be net long swaption volatilities and would sell swaption vols to hedge. On the other hand, corporates tend to want protection from potential rises in short-term interest rates and hence buy caplets from banks, which are then short caplet volatilities and need to buy caplet vols to hedge. This leads to caplet volatilities being typically higher than swaption volatilities. This discrepancy used to be somewhat structurally mitigated in the US, because of huge issuance of long-dated fixed-rate mortgages where the homeowner has the option to prepay, so that banks then need to buy swaption volatilities to hedge. However, the prevalence of adjustable rate mortgages has changed things somewhat.

From that perspective, it is not clear if we should necessarily aim to fully calibrate to caplet volatilities in addition to co-terminal swaption volatilities. Indeed, calibrating to caplet vols is likely to lead to an overestimation of the prices of Bermudan swaptions because of the much higher forward volatility that would result. Alternatively, we could choose a single value of mean reversion κ to reflect our views on forward volatility or to hit the prices of traded Bermudan swaptions. A further remark is that jointly calibrating to caplet and co-terminal swaption volatilities can lead to more instability. Actually, when using a one-factor model for pricing Bermudan swaptions, we might have to depress mean reversion slightly. This is to account for having ignored the effect of decorrelation and hence obtaining higher prices of forward starting swaptions than in a multi-factor model.

Incidentally, some authors suggest restricting ourselves to a single volatility parameter σ, as time-dependent volatility does not reflect typical observed market behaviour (e.g. we do not expect volatility to increase or decrease deterministically over time). However, the realities of calibration requirements (i.e. to hit co-terminal swaptions at a minimum) often mean that time-dependent volatility is a necessary compromise for the Hull–White model to be usable.

8.2.4   *Multi-factor Hull–White*

To price an instrument primarily dependent on the overall level of interest rates, the one-factor model is adequate. However, if we are interested in an instrument that depends on the behaviour of rates (of two or more tenors) vis-à-vis each other (e.g. a CMS spread option), then at least two factors are necessary.

Historical time series analysis of interest rates data suggests that the most common mode of yield curve moves is a parallel shift,

Correlation (%)	3m	6m	1y	2y	3y	5y	7y	10y	12y	15y	20y	30y
3m	100	87	65	42	32	27	25	23	21	19	18	16
6m	87	100	91	70	58	51	47	42	40	37	35	32
1y	65	91	100	91	82	74	69	62	60	57	55	52
2y	42	70	91	100	96	90	86	80	77	75	72	69
3y	32	58	82	96	100	97	94	89	87	84	82	78
5y	27	51	74	90	96	100	99	96	94	92	90	87
7y	25	47	69	86	94	99	100	99	98	96	94	92
10y	23	42	62	80	89	96	99	100	100	98	97	96
12y	21	40	60	77	87	94	98	100	100	99	98	97
15y	19	37	57	75	84	92	96	98	99	100	99	98
20y	18	35	55	72	82	90	94	97	98	99	100	99
30y	16	32	52	69	78	87	92	96	97	98	99	100

Figure 8.3a: We show here the correlations between the daily returns of rates of different tenors. Clearly, rates at the very short end have low correlations with long tenor rates, but even the 5-year rate is very highly correlated to the 30-year rate, suggesting certain modes of yield curve movements. Data is from October 2006 to April 2011. *Source*: Bloomberg data.

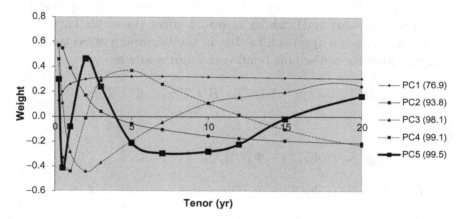

Figure 8.3b: We show the key principal components of US yield curve moves. The total accumulated explained variance is shown in brackets after the relevant principal component. We see that the first principal component (which is roughly a parallel shift with less pronounced effects on the short end) accounts for 76.9% of variance. And the first five principal components together account for 99.5% of yield curve variance. Data is from October 2006 to April 2011.
Source: Bloomberg data.

followed by a steepening/flattening and then a twist (see Figures 8.3a and 8.3b). So, these are potential scenarios we might want to incorporate if we are pricing products that are sensitive to such movements of the yield curve.

Let us consider the following two-factor extension to the Hull–White model.[9] The process is given by the SDEs

$$dx_t = -\kappa_x(t)x_t dt + \sigma_x(t)dW_t^x,$$
$$dy_t = -\kappa_y(t)y_t dt + \sigma_y(t)dW_t^y,$$
$$r_t = \varphi(t) + x_t + y_t, \quad \text{and}$$
$$dW_t^x dW_t^y = \rho(t)dt.$$

If we wanted to use it to model steepening of the yield curve, then an appropriate choice of parameters would involve a large mean reversion speed for one of the factors [e.g $\kappa_y(t) = 20\%$], whereas we would need a meaningfully negative correlation so that the factors move in different directions [e.g. $\rho(t) = -50\%$]. In this way, the factor y_t would represent a shock that decays quickly (i.e. primarily affecting the short end), whilst x_t would affect the whole curve.

Using the same approach as that in the beginning of Section 8.2, the equation for a discount bond comes out easily as

$$D(t,T) = \exp(-A(t,T) - B(t,T)x_t - C(t,T)y_t),$$

where

$$B(t,T) = \phi_x(t)(\Phi_x(T) - \Phi_x(t)),$$

$$C(t,T) = \phi_y(t)(\Phi_y(T) - \Phi_y(t)), \quad \text{and}$$

$$A(t,T) = \int_t^T \varphi(u)du - \frac{1}{2}\int_t^T (\Phi_x(T) - \Phi_x(s))^2 \phi_x^2(s)\sigma_x^2(s)ds$$
$$- \frac{1}{2}\int_t^T (\Phi_y(T) - \Phi_y(s))^2 \phi_y^2(s)\sigma_y^2(s)ds$$
$$- \int_t^T \rho(s)(\Phi_x(T) - \Phi_x(s))(\Phi_y(T)$$
$$- \Phi_y(s))\phi_x(s)\phi_y(s)\sigma_x(s)\sigma_y(s)ds.$$

---

[9]Note that the original two-factor Hull–White model is very different.

In order to calibrate to swaption volatilities, consider the swap rate

$$R_t = \frac{D(t, T_0) - D(t, T_N)}{A_t}.$$

(A_t is the annuity and should not be confused with $A(t, T)$ above.)

We are interested in the volatility part of the SDE

$$dR_t = \frac{1}{A_t} \left[dD(t, T_0) - dD(t, T_N) - R_t \sum_{i=1}^{N} \tau_i dD(t, T_i) \right] + (\cdots) dt$$

$$= \frac{1}{A_t} \left[-D(t, T_0)(B(t, T_0)\sigma_x(t)dW_t^x + C(t, T_0)\sigma_y(t)dW_t^y) \right.$$

$$+ D(t, T_N)(B(t, T_N)\sigma_x(t)dW_t^x + C(t, T_N)\sigma_y(t)dW_t^y)$$

$$\left. + R_t \sum_{i=1}^{N} \tau_i D(t, T_i)(B(t, T_i)\sigma_x(t)dW_t^x + C(t, T_i)\sigma_y(t)dW_t^y) \right]$$

$$+ (\cdots) dt.$$

If we now make the 'drift-freeze' approximation $D(t, T) \approx \frac{D(0,T)}{D(0,t)}$ and do the same for the annuity and swap rate in the SDE, we could find an equivalent normal vol Λ^N that satisfies $dR_t = \Lambda^N dW_t$, or lognormal vol Λ^{LN} that satisfies $dR_t = \Lambda^{LN} R_t dW_t$. In this way, we can plug this into the normal or Black formula to get an approximation for the price of a swaption. (This approximation is not too bad for at-the-money swaptions, giving a route to calibration or perhaps a pre-calibration step.)

In a similar vein, we could extend to multiple risk factors, i.e.

$$dx_t^i = -\kappa_i(t)x_t^i dt + \sigma_i(t)dW_t^i,$$

$$r_t = \varphi(t) + \sum_{i=1}^{N} x_t^i, \quad \text{and}$$

$$dW_t^i dW_t^j = \rho_{ij}(t)dt.$$

But it is more common for the Libor Market Model[10] to be used in these circumstances.

---

[10]To be discussed in Chapter 9.

8.3 Blend Model

The Hull–White model posits a normal process for the short rate. This leads to the very desirable feature of analytic tractability. However, it does come at the price of a significant probability of negative interest rates. See Figure 8.4 for an illustration.

In contrast, the Black–Karasinski model posits the short rate as the exponential of a Gaussian variate. This clearly avoids the possibility of negative interest rates. However, apart from the lack of analytic tractability for the discount bond, there is another issue of potential explosion of bond prices. After all, a discount bond is based on the exponential of a short rate, and interest rates involve ratios of discount bonds. Taking the exponential of an exponential is thus not really ideal (at least from a stability perspective). Nevertheless, during the 1990s, a lognormal representation of rates seemed to give a decent fit to markets, hence this model was popular then.

Another approach involves the Cox–Ingersoll–Ross model [CIR85]

$$dr_t = \kappa(t)(\theta(t) - r_t)dt + \sigma(t)\sqrt{r_t}dW_t.$$

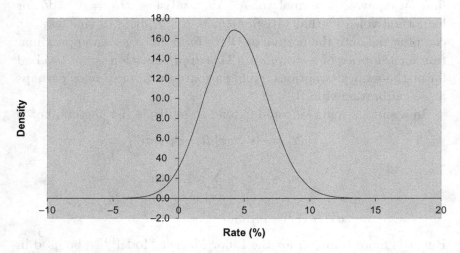

Figure 8.4:   We show here the probability density of the 20-year forward 10-year sterling swap rate under the Hull–White model. This is based on representative data as of late 2010. Notice there is a non-negligible probability of negative rates being realised.

This model has the advantage of avoiding negative interest rates,[11] and also has a quasi-analytic formula for the price of a discount bond. However, the set of possibilities admissible to this model is not sufficiently rich to capture some of the observed shapes of curves and volatilities.

The decade of low interest rates since 2000 has led to new challenges in capturing the dynamics of interest rates, as it became clear that lognormality did not hold whilst normality gave too high a probability of negative rates. And so it is natural to ask if we could have a model where the user can choose from a continuous spectrum of interest rate dynamics, between normal and lognormal.

What about mixing a normal with a lognormal representation of the short rate?

8.3.1   *Mixing Normal and Lognormal Short Rates*

Consider the following model defined via

$$dx_t = \kappa(t)(\theta(t) - x_t)dt + \sigma(t)dW_t, \quad \text{and}$$

$$r_t = \left(1 + \frac{e^{\alpha x_t} - 1}{\alpha}\right) r_0.$$

We see that $\alpha = 0$ corresponds to our Hull–White model, whilst $\alpha = 1$ corresponds to the Black–Karasinski model. Thus, α is a blend parameter that determines how close the short rate dynamics are to the normal versus lognormal distributions. It is best to consider this in light of our discussion in Chapter 5 on the difference in dynamics of normal and lognormal variates.

The introduction of this blend model should not be seen as a panacea for capturing skew in a short rate world. Indeed, since the lognormal parameterisation admits no analytic solution for the price of discount bonds, the above blend model also does not. So, it is computationally inefficient. Furthermore, the explosive features in a lognormal short rate model are not mitigated by the blend, as the

---

[11]Negative interest rates should be avoided in theory provided mean reversion speed is sufficiently large. In practice, the numerical implementation will lead to negative rates which must be handled appropriately.

exponential term is still there. Further, the most appropriate blend may be different for long and short expiries, so that a constant blend model may not be rich enough to capture skew.

To this extent, the blend model is not the most popular of models in use. For speed, Gaussian short rate models are preferred. And where skew is to be treated, it is also common to either consider the much more flexible Cheyette parameterisation (described in Section 8.4) or the quadratic Gaussian parameterisation (described in Section 8.5).

8.3.2   *Constructing the Pricing Grid*

As alluded to earlier, if we cannot get a closed form for the price of a discount bond, then given a state of the short rate at future time t, we require evaluation of the following formula for the price of a discount bond

$$D(t, T) = E_t^Q \left[e^{- \int_t^T r_s ds} \right]$$

via numerical means.

Suppose we are pricing on a PDE grid, then if at a node we require a swap rate or Libor rate, we need to obtain the prices of discount bonds for any maturity of interest. If we do not have this as a function of a small number of state variables, then we instead have to evaluate this expectation by constructing a PDE grid up to the relevant maturity T. To be specific, under the blend model, if we were interested in an option on a discount bond with strike K maturing in 22 years and expiry 2 years from today, we would need to construct a grid in x_t for up to 22 years (see Figure 8.5). The price of the discount bond at each node is then based on solving the PDE back from 22 years to 2 years.

In contrast, if we were using a model with analytic discount bonds (e.g. Hull–White), then the grid needs only to be constructed for up to 2 years. To this extent, we would require a lot more computational time for the blend model than the Hull–White model. Furthermore, evaluating the price of discount bonds numerically on a PDE is obviously less stable than resorting to an analytic formula.

Figure 8.5:   The grid for a blend model has to be built up to maturity of instrument (22y) rather than expiry (2y).

Similar complications arise in a Monte Carlo valuation in the absence of a simple function to determine the price of a discount bond.

8.4   Cheyette Model

One of the more desirable features of a short rate model is the existence of an analytic formula for the prices of discount bonds as a function of a small number of state variables. To this end, the Cheyette model [Che92] is particularly interesting.

Consider the HJM parameterisation with one Brownian driver

$$df_{t,T} = \mu(t, T, \{\theta\})dt + \sigma(t, T, \{\theta\})dW_t.$$

We restrict ourselves to

$$\sigma(t, T, \{\theta\}) = g(T)h(t, \{\theta\}),$$

where $g(T)$ is a function of maturity and $h(t, \{\theta\})$ is a function of time and state variables.

Define the terms

$$\eta(t, \{\theta\}) = g(t)h(t, \{\theta\}), \quad \text{and}$$

$$\kappa(t) = -\frac{g'(t)}{g(t)} \quad \left(\Rightarrow g(t) = e^{-\int_0^t \kappa(s)ds}\right)$$

with $g'(t)$ being the derivative of $g(t)$ with respect to t. Notice that $\kappa(t)$ is effectively the mean reversion speed whilst $\eta(t, \{\theta\})$ is effectively the local volatility.

Then the one-factor Cheyette model is given by the pair of SDEs

$$dx_t = (-\kappa(t)x_t + y_t)dt + \eta(t, x_t, y_t)dW_t, \quad \text{and}$$
$$dy_t = (\eta^2(t, x_t, y_t) - 2\kappa(t)y_t)dt,$$

where we have defined $x_0 = y_0 = 0$.

8.4.1   *The Cheyette Framework*

Under the Cheyette model, the instantaneous forward rate is given by

$$f(t, T) = f(0, T) + \frac{g(T)}{g(t)}\left[x_t + \frac{y_t}{g(t)}\int_t^T g(s)ds\right].$$

In the interest of brevity, the derivation of the above is to be found in the appendix to this chapter.

In the Cheyette model, the value of a discount bond with maturity T as seen at a future time t is a simple function of the state variables x_t and y_t, namely

$$D(t, T) = \frac{D(0, T)}{D(0, t)}e^{-G(t,T)x_t - \frac{1}{2}G^2(t,T)y_t},$$

where

$$G(t, T) = \int_t^T e^{-\int_t^u \kappa(s)ds}du.$$

This makes the Cheyette model computationally efficient for valuing derivatives once we have evolved the appropriate state variables x_t and y_t, and hence contributes to its popularity.

As for the derivation of the price of a discount bond, we have

$$-\log D(t, T) = \int_t^T f(t, s)ds$$
$$= \int_t^T f(0, s)ds + \int_t^T \frac{g(s)}{g(t)}\left[x_t + \frac{y_t}{g(t)}\int_t^s g(u)du\right]ds$$

$$= -\log \frac{D(0,T)}{D(0,t)}$$

$$+ \int_t^T e^{-\int_t^s \kappa(u)du} \left[x_t + y_t e^{\int_0^t \kappa(u)du} \int_t^s e^{-\int_0^u \kappa(v)dv} du \right] ds$$

$$= -\log \frac{D(0,T)}{D(0,t)} + G(t,T)x_t + y_t \int_t^T \frac{\partial G}{\partial T}(t,s)G(t,s)ds$$

$$= -\log \frac{D(0,T)}{D(0,t)} + G(t,T)x_t + \frac{1}{2}G^2(t,T)y_t$$

using $g(t) = e^{-\int_0^t \kappa(s)ds}$ in the third equality and the definition of $G(t,T)$ in the fourth equality.

In the Cheyette model,

$$\eta(t, x_t, y_t) = g(t)h(t, x_t, y_t) \quad \text{whilst}$$

$$\sigma(t, T, \{\theta\}) = g(T)h(t, x_t, y_t) = \frac{g(T)\eta(t, x_t, y_t)}{g(t)},$$

so $\eta(t, x_t, y_t)$ gives a parameterisation of the dependence of volatility on the level of rates, i.e. we can use it to control whether the model is closer to normal, lognormal, or some other parameterisation.

Andreasen [Andr00] suggests making $\eta(t, x_t, y_t)$ a function of the swap rates for better capturing the dynamics of co-terminal swaptions when pricing Bermudan swaptions. This is possible since swap rates are fully determined from discount bonds, which are functions of the state variables x_t and y_t.

It is the ability of the Cheyette model to cope with a range of volatility skew, whilst still producing analytic prices for discount bonds as a function of a few state variables, that makes this model particularly popular with practitioners.

8.4.2 State Variables of Cheyette

It is worth pointing out that a one-factor Cheyette model is Markovian in two state variables. This is not fatal for use on a PDE, since two-dimensional PDEs are still much more efficient than Monte

Carlo techniques. The PDE for the Cheyette model is

$$\frac{\partial V_t}{\partial t} + (-\kappa(t)x_t + y_t)\frac{\partial V_t}{\partial x_t} + \frac{1}{2}\eta^2(t, x_t, y_t)\frac{\partial^2 V_t}{\partial x_t^2}$$

$$+ (\eta^2(t, x_t, y_t) - 2\kappa(t)y_t)\frac{\partial V_t}{\partial y_t} = r_t V_t.$$

We can consider an N-dimensional Cheyette model specified via

$$dx_t^i = \left(-\kappa_i(t)x_t^i + \sum_{j=1}^{N} y_t^{ij}\right) dt + \eta_i(t, \{\theta\})dW_t^i,$$

$$dy_t^{ij} = (\eta_i(t, \{\theta\})\eta_j(t, \{\theta\}) - (\kappa_i(t) + \kappa_j(t))y_t^{ij})dt, \quad \text{and}$$

$$dW_t^i dW_t^j = \rho_{ij}(t)dt$$

for $i = 1, \ldots, N$, $j = 1, \ldots, N$.

As before, we can show that the value of a discount bond is an analytic function of the state variables, specifically

$$D(t, T) = \frac{D(0, T)}{D(0, t)}e^{-G(t,T)\cdot x - \frac{1}{2}G^T(t,T)yG(t,T)},$$

where

$G(t, T)$ is the vector whose N elements are $G_i(t, T) = \int_t^T e^{-\int_t^s \kappa_i(u)du}ds$,
x is the vector whose N elements are x_t^i, and
y is the matrix whose $N \times N$ elements are y_t^{ij}.

An N-factor Cheyette model is Markovian in $\frac{N(N+3)}{2}$ state variables. So, we rapidly have an explosion of state variables. In fact, even if $N = 2$, then we will end up with five state variables. This is too many for efficient pricing on a PDE. So, it appears it would be unrealistic to use the Cheyette model on a PDE to price CMS spread products where we need at least two factors.

8.4.3 The Convection Terms in the Cheyette Partial Differential Equation (PDE)

If we look again at the PDE for the one-factor Cheyette model

$$\frac{\partial V_t}{\partial t} + (-\kappa(t)x_t + y_t)\frac{\partial V_t}{\partial x_t} + \frac{1}{2}\eta^2(t, x_t, y_t)\frac{\partial^2 V_t}{\partial x_t^2}$$

$$+ \left(\eta^2(t, x_t, y_t) - 2\kappa(t)y_t\right)\frac{\partial V_t}{\partial y_t} = r_t V_t,$$

we will see that there are only convection terms in the state variable y_t.

Whilst elliptic PDEs are stable with steady state solutions, convection terms are particularly unpleasant as they imply a growth of the domain of dependence over time. It would be best to extend the implicitness of any PDE treatment to the convection terms. Specifically, if stability is of concern, Andreasen [Andr00] suggests the following scheme (as an adaptation of the Craig–Sneyd algorithm) for V_t given $V_{t+\Delta t}$ [only accurate to order $O(\Delta y^2)$]:

$$\left[\frac{1}{\Delta t} - \frac{1}{2}D_x\right]U_t = \left[\frac{1}{\Delta t} + \frac{1}{2}D_x + D_y\right]V_{t+\Delta t} \quad \text{and}$$

$$\left[\frac{1}{\Delta t} - \frac{1}{2}D_y\right]V_t = \frac{1}{\Delta t}U_t - \frac{1}{2}D_y V_{t+\Delta t},$$

where

$$D_x = (\kappa(t)x_t - y_t)\frac{\partial}{\partial x_t} + \frac{1}{2}\eta(t, x_t, y_t)\frac{\partial^2}{\partial x_t^2},$$

$$D_y = (\eta^2(t, x_t, y_t) - 2\kappa(t)y_t)\frac{\partial}{\partial y_t}, \quad \text{and}$$

U_t is an intermediate stage solution.

To eliminate spurious oscillations, we can use the upwinding operators, i.e.

$$\mu\frac{\partial V}{\partial y} = \begin{cases} \mu\dfrac{V(y) - V(y - \Delta y)}{\Delta y} & \text{if } \mu < 0 \\[2ex] \mu\dfrac{V(y + \Delta y) - V(y)}{\Delta y} & \text{if } \mu > 0, \end{cases}$$

but this will mean accuracy is reduced to order $O(\Delta y)$ only.

Notice that y_t is a peripheral state variable in that it does not correspond directly to an observable that affects the payoff (e.g. the level of rates). Indeed, if we have no skew (i.e. $\eta(t)$ is independent of x_t and y_t),[12] then y_t is deterministic and can be incorporated into x_t, so that the model is reduced to being fully specified by one state variable x_t.

Andreasen claims that it is possible to get away with a small number of points in the y_t grid (e.g. 10). However, it is worth noting that depending on the shape of local volatility, we may still require a fairly refined grid in y_t to get decent accuracy for pricing and risk computations.

8.4.4   *Extending with Stochastic Volatility*

Chapters 5 and 6 compared the different dynamics of local versus stochastic volatility models in the context of equities and FX. The same arguments would lead us to consider incorporating some degree of stochastic volatility in the interest rates case. For the Cheyette model, incorporating stochastic volatility is not difficult. The new SDEs are

$$dx_t = (-\kappa(t)x_t + y_t)dt + \eta(t, x_t, y_t)\sqrt{z_t}dW_t,$$

$$dy_t = (\eta^2(t, x_t, y_t) - 2\kappa(t)y_t)dt,$$

$$dz_t = \beta(t)(1 - z_t)dt + \lambda(t)\sqrt{z_t}dU_t, \quad \text{and}$$

$$dW_t dU_t = 0,$$

if we are considering a Heston-style volatility multiplier. We can of course use another process for volatility instead, e.g. lognormal. (The choice of zero correlation between the Wiener processes for the short rate and the stochastic vol is a compromise for convenience, to avoid the nasty drift terms that would otherwise appear from change of measure. This of course means that our stochastic volatility will only explain smile whilst skew has to be explained by local volatility.)

---

[12]E.g. in the Hull–White case.

The price of a discount bond is still given by

$$D(t,T) = \frac{D(0,T)}{D(0,t)} e^{-G(t,T)x_t - \frac{1}{2}G^2(t,T)y_t},$$

so there are no particular difficulties in this case.

Of course, there is one more state variable z_t to evolve, and a PDE approach would involve dealing with the three-factor PDE

$$\frac{\partial V_t}{\partial t} + (-\kappa(t)x_t + y_t)\frac{\partial V_t}{\partial x_t} + \frac{1}{2}\eta^2(t, x_t, y_t)z_t\frac{\partial^2 V_t}{\partial x_t^2} + (\eta^2(t, x_t, y_t)$$

$$- 2\kappa(t)y_t)\frac{\partial V_t}{\partial y_t} + \beta(t)(1 - z_t)\frac{\partial V_t}{\partial z_t} + \frac{1}{2}\lambda^2(t)z_t\frac{\partial^2 V_t}{\partial z_t^2} = r_t V_t$$

This is at the limit of feasibility for treatment on a PDE, and computational expense will be comparable to pricing on a Monte Carlo framework.

8.5 The Quadratic Gaussian Model

Recall from our earlier discussion that a desirable feature for a short rate model is that discount bonds are analytic functions of a few state variables. This leads to the Hull–White and Cheyette models being popular. However, if we were interested in using PDE techniques (which tend to be better for treating early exercise features), then keeping the number of state variables at a minimum is essential. To this end, the Cheyette model is not ideal, since a one-factor Cheyette model is Markovian in two state variables (rather than one). And it is not feasible to use a PDE for a two-factor Cheyette model (necessary for products that depend on the difference between two swap rates, e.g. 10-year rate minus 2-year rate in a spread option) since it is only Markovian in five state variables. As for the Hull–White model, it does not have a local volatility parameterisation to describe volatility skew.

An alternative way of describing skew is the Quadratic Gaussian Model (QGM). This posits the short rate as a quadratic function of a Gaussian state variable.

8.5.1   *The Setup*

The following parameterisation is from Tezier [Tez05]. This is a more general version of the Squared Gaussian Model described by Pelsser [Pel00].

Define the short rate r_t as follows:

$$dZ_t = \sigma(t)dW_t \quad \text{and}$$

$$r_t = \gamma(t)Z_t^2 + b(t)Z_t + a(t),$$

where $\sigma(t)$ is volatility, $\gamma(t)$ describes skew (see next paragraph on its interpretation), $b(t)$ represents a deterministic drift to vol, $a(t)$ is used to fit the prices of discount bonds at time zero, and W_t is a Wiener process under the risk-neutral measure.

Notice that if $\sigma(t) = \sigma$ (constant), we can write our equations as

$$r_t = \lambda_t W_t + a(t) \quad \text{and}$$

$$\lambda_t = \gamma(t)\sigma^2 W_t + b(t)\sigma,$$

where λ_t can be interpreted as a stochastic volatility multiplier, and we effectively have a stochastic volatility model for the short rate where correlation is 100% if $\gamma(t) > 0$ and -100% if $\gamma(t) < 0$. Such an extreme correlation between the short rate and volatility might make sense for describing rates for currencies with very skewed volatilities (e.g. the Japanese yen).

The main reason for interest in such a model is the availability of the following analytic form for the prices of discount bonds at a future time t:

$$D(t,T) = \frac{D(0,T)}{D(0,t)}e^{-\{\Gamma(t,T)Z_t^2 + B(t,T)Z_t + A(t,T)\}},$$

where $\Gamma(t,T)$, $B(t,T)$ satisfy the two PDEs below (which are Riccati's equations with closed form solutions):

$$\frac{\partial \Gamma(t,T)}{\partial t} - 2\Gamma^2(t,T)\sigma^2(t) + \gamma(t) = 0 \quad \text{and}$$

$$\frac{\partial B(t,T)}{\partial t} - 2\Gamma(t,T)B(t,T)\sigma^2(t) + b(t) = 0$$

with terminal conditions $\Gamma(T,T) = B(T,T) = 0$.

We can see this by substituting the equation for the discount bond into the pricing PDE

$$\frac{\partial D(t,T)}{\partial t} + \frac{1}{2}\sigma^2(t)\frac{\partial^2 D(t,T)}{\partial Z_t^2} = r_t D(t,T) \quad \text{to get}$$

$$- D(t,T)\left(\frac{1}{D(0,t)}\frac{\partial D(0,t)}{\partial t} + \frac{\partial \Gamma(t,T)}{\partial t}Z_t^2 + \frac{\partial B(t,T)}{\partial t}Z_t + \frac{\partial A(t,T)}{\partial t}\right)$$

$$+ \frac{1}{2}\sigma^2(t)((2\Gamma(t,T)Z_t + B(t,T))^2 - 2\Gamma(t,T))D(t,T)$$

$$= (\gamma(t)Z_t^2 + b(t)Z_t + a(t))D(t,T)$$

and then equating terms in Z_t^2, Z_t, and constants.

We obtain $A(t,T)$ from the no-arbitrage condition $D(0,T) = D(0,t)E_0^t[D(t,T)]$, i.e.

$$A(t,T) = \log E_0^t \lfloor e^{-\{\Gamma(t,T)Z_t^2 + B(t,T)Z_t\}} \rfloor.$$

To compute $A(t,T)$, we need the distribution of Z_t under the t-forward measure (with numeraire being the discount bond with maturity t). The SDE for a discount bond under the risk-neutral measure (with numeraire being the money market account) is

$$\frac{dD(t,T)}{D(t,T)} = r_t dt - (2\Gamma(t,T)Z_t + B(t,T))\,\sigma(t)dW_t.$$

Under a change of measure to the t-forward measure, we therefore get

$$dZ_t = -(2\Gamma(t,T)Z_t + B(t,T))\,\sigma^2(t)dt + \sigma(t)dW_t^*.$$

Since the drift is linear in Z_t, this is an Ornstein–Uhlenbeck process and Z_t is still Gaussian.

To ensure no arbitrage, we need

$$f(0,t) = E_0^t[r_t]$$
$$= E_0^t[\gamma(t)Z_t^2 + b(t)Z_t + a(t)],$$

giving

$$a(t) = f(0,t) - \gamma(t)E_0^t\lfloor Z_t^2 \rfloor - b(t)E_0^t[Z_t].$$

The above framework can be easily extended to Quadratic Gaussian Models of multiple factors. Specifically, the short rate r_t is given by

$$dZ_t = \Sigma dW_t \quad \text{and}$$
$$r_t = Z_t^T \eta Z_t + \beta^T Z_t + \alpha,$$

where Σ is the $N \times N$ matrix equivalent of $\sigma(t)$, η is the $N \times N$ matrix equivalent of $\gamma(t)$, β is the N-dimensional vector equivalent of $b(t)$, α is the N-dimensional vector equivalent of $a(t)$, and W_t is the N-dimensional vector of independent Brownian variates.

8.5.2   *Pricing of Caplets/Swaptions*

As per Section 8.2.2, the price of a caplet is given by

$$\frac{V_0}{D(0, T+\tau)} = E^{T+\tau}\left[\max\left(\frac{D(T,T)}{D(T,T+\tau)} - (1+K\tau), 0\right)\right],$$

where $D(T, T+\tau)$ is an exponential over a quadratic function of Z_T.

This works out to be

$$V_0 = \frac{1}{\sqrt{2\pi V(T)}} \int_{-\infty}^{\infty} \{(D(0,T)e^{-(\Gamma(T,T+\tau)z^2 + B(T,T+\tau)z + A(T,T+\tau))}$$
$$- D(0,T+\tau)(1+K\tau))^+ e^{-\frac{(z-m(T)^2)}{2V(T)}}\}dz,$$

where

$$m(T) = E_0^T[Z_T] \quad \text{and}$$
$$V(T) = E_0^T[Z_T^2] - m^2(T).$$

As for swaptions, a similar approach to the drift-freeze method described in Section 8.2.4 can produce a closed form approximation that is decent at least for at-the-money swaptions.

The set of term structures admissible to the QGM is unfortunately not quite as rich as that for the Hull–White model. In particular, the extremely low interest rates environment (under 50 basis points for expiries less than 1-year for 2009), coupled with higher absolute volatility (around 0.7% to 1% normal volatility) has proved extremely difficult for Quadratic Gaussian Models to cope, leading to some market participants temporarily seeking other alternatives.

8.6 Consolidation

8.6.1 *Summary*

In interest rates, unlike equities or FX, we cannot model one underlying (after all, what is the 10-year swap rate in 15 years' time and what is it in 20 years' time?) but need to model the evolution of the entire yield curve simultaneously. In Chapter 1, we have discussed how it is sufficient for an interest rate model to produce discount factors for all maturities at any given time.

In this chapter, we considered short rate models — one of the three main classes of interest rate models. We set up the framework by establishing that a discount bond at a future time is the expected value (under the risk-neutral measure) of the exponent of minus the integral of the short rate up to maturity. Whereas it may be intuitive to think of a short rate as an instantaneous interest rate, a short rate model really is just a process Markovian in a small number of state variables that can give the value of a discount bond at a future time. We next discussed the Heath–Jarrow–Morton (HJM) framework of instantaneous forward rates, defining it via the equation for a discount bond. Since a discount bond is an asset and hence its drift must be the risk-free rate under the risk-neutral measure, we established the drift of the instantaneous forward rate (necessary for no arbitrage) under the HJM model. We further related the instantaneous forward rate to the short rate via an expectation under the T-forward measure. This hopefully should convince the reader of their inter-relatedness.

Moving on, we considered the Hull–White model — a very popular short rate model. We started with the SDE for the Hull–White model and established the SDE for the discount bond at a future time, noting that this depends only on the value of a single state variable (particularly convenient for pricing derivatives on a PDE), and deriving the drift necessary to recover all discount factors today.

We discussed mean reversion and considered how it leads to volatility dampening, so that calibrating to variance over a fixed period means that forward volatility (over a shorter period) will be increased in the presence of mean reversion. We moved on to derive the formula for pricing a caplet, noting that it can be obtained via something similar to Black's formula based on a suitable volatility. We further derived the swaption pricing formula by observing that swaption prices are monotonic in the short rate and using Jamshidian's trick to decompose a swaption into a portfolio of caplets with varying strikes. We then discussed how calibration to swaptions having chosen a (positive) mean reversion speed leads to higher caplet volatilities because there is greater time for volatility decay from mean reversion in swaptions. This means that for Bermudan swaptions, the higher forward volatility from increasing mean reversion will increase their prices. We finished the discussion by considering a multi-factor Hull–White model, which can be used to capture non-parallel yield curve moves important for some products (e.g. spread options that depend on rates of different tenors moving in different directions), and discussed a 'drift-freeze' approximation for swaption pricing, which works well for at-the-money swaptions.

Proceeding to a generalisation since rates need not be normal or lognormal, we explored the SDE for the Cox–Ingersoll–Ross model and a blend model (which captures rate dependence in between normal and lognormal). We noted that for the blend model there is no analytic form for the discount bond given the value of a state variable, so that the expectation in the discount bond formula must actually be evaluated numerically. Thus, a pricing grid must be constructed up to the maturity of the rates involved, rather than the expiry of the option (e.g. we need a grid up to 22 years for an option on a 20-year swap expiring in 2 years' time).

Naturally, we then explored the Cheyette model, which is very popular in industry. The idea is basically to posit two state variables (in the one-factor case), which together describe the instantaneous forward rate. The real attraction of this model is that discount bonds are Markovian in these two state variables, and there is still the freedom to specify the local volatility process, hence allowing a lot more flexibility to fit smile and skew. That we do not need to price discount bonds as expectations also leads to greater stability for sensitivities calculations. Whereas two state variables can still be treated via PDE methods, we noted that the n-factor Cheyette model is only Markovian in $\frac{n(n+3)}{2}$ state variables, so that even a two-factor Cheyette model is not amenable to PDE techniques. We also presented Andreasen's algorithm for dealing with the convection terms in the Cheyette PDE. We wrapped up by extending the Cheyette model in the face of stochastic volatility, noting that this is not difficult if there is zero correlation between the state variables and the stochastic volatility multiplier.

Finally, we touched upon the QGM, where the short rate is a quadratic function of a Gaussian state variable. The one-factor case can be interpreted as a short rate model which has stochastic volatility with correlation $\pm 100\%$ vis-à-vis the short rate. The main attraction of QGM is that the discount bond under a two-factor model is Markovian in two state variables, so that derivatives can be priced via PDE techniques. We derived the formula for the discount bond given the state variable, which is quite involved. And we conclude by presenting the formula for a caplet under QGM.

8.6.2   *Exercises*

(1) Consider the Hull–White model with SDE $dr_t = \kappa(t)(\theta(t) - r_t)dt + \sigma(t)dW_t$. Following the same logic as we did in the text, determine $\theta(t)$. Can you see why in practice calculating $\theta(t)$ directly is not the best approach when implementing the Hull–White model?

(2) Consider again the Hull–White model. Using $f_{t,T} = E_t^T[r_T]$, obtain the volatility of the SDE of the discount bond $D(t,T) = e^{-\int_t^T f_{t,s}ds}$.

(3) Consider a two-factor short rate model described by $dx_t = -\kappa_x(t)x_tdt + \sigma_x(t)dW_t^x$, $dy_t = -\kappa_y(t)y_tdt + \sigma_y(t)dW_t^y$, $r_t = \varphi(t) + x_t + y_t$ and $dW_t^x dW_t^y = \rho(t)dt$. Find $corr(df_{t,T_1}, df_{t,T_2})$ where $f_{t,T}$ is the HJM instantaneous forward rate.

(4) Consider the construction of a trinomial tree for the general short rate model of form $dy_t = \kappa(\theta(t) - y_t)dt + \sigma dW_t, r_t = g(y_t)$. The approach typically involves constructing the tree for

$dx_t = -\kappa x_t dt + \sigma dW_t$, then on each node of the tree, solving for $\alpha(t)$, where $y_t = x_t + \alpha(t)$ so that the prices of discount bonds are recovered. Assuming we have already built the tree for x_t, describe the procedure for finding $\alpha(t)$ on the tree, making use of Arrow–Debreu prices (i.e. prices A_j^n of securities that pay 1 if and only if $x_t = x_j^n$, where x_j^n is spatial node j on the tree corresponding to time index n) which can be calculated from the tree. Note that we solve for $\alpha(t)$ on the tree, rather than calculate this analytically because otherwise we will not match discount bond prices due to discretisation errors. (Hull [Hul11] describes the building of the trinomial tree in much greater detail.)

(5) Consider again the Hull–White model with constant mean reversion $\kappa = 1\%$. Suppose also interest rates are flat at 4% so that discount bond prices are given by $D(0,T) = e^{-0.04T}$ First find the SDE for the instantaneous forward rate $f_{t,T} = E_t^T[r_T]$. Take the forward rate as a proxy for the Libor rate. Suppose we choose $\sigma(t)$ such that the term vol of the forward rate (i.e. Λ where $\Lambda^2 T = var(f_{0,T})$) is constant at 0.7% for annual expiries 1y, 2y, ..., 15y. Find the prices of swaptions with expiry 1y and tenors 2y, 5y, and 10y. Also, find the prices of swaptions with expiries 2y and 5y and the same combination of tenors. Hence, determine their implied vols. What happens if mean reversion increases to $\kappa = 10\%$?

Appendix: Derivation of the Instantaneous Forward Rate under the Cheyette Model

This appendix follows naturally from Section 8.4.1.

As per Section 8.4, the one-factor Cheyette model is parameterised by

$$dx_t = (-\kappa(t)x_t + y_t)dt + \eta(t, x_t, y_t)dW_t, \quad \text{and}$$
$$dy_t = (\eta^2(t, x_t, y_t) - 2\kappa(t)y_t)dt,$$

where $\eta(t, x_t, y_t) = g(t)h(t, x_t, y_t)$ and $\kappa(t) = -\frac{g'(t)}{g(t)}$, with $g(t)$ and $h(t, x_t, y_t)$ defined via the volatility of the instantaneous forward rate, i.e. $\sigma(t, T, x_t, y_t) = g(T)h(t, x_t, y_t)$, where $df_{t,T} = \mu(t, T, x_t, y_t)dt + \sigma(t, T, x_t, y_t)dW_t$. (Also, we define $x_0 = y_0 = 0$.)

We seek to show that under the Cheyette model, the instantaneous forward rate is

$$f(t, T) = f(0, T) + \frac{g(T)}{g(t)}\left[x_t + \frac{y_t}{g(t)}\int_t^T g(s)ds\right].$$

The derivation is as follows:

Starting with the relation of the instantaneous forward rate to the discount bond price

$$D(t, T) = e^{-\int_t^T f_{t,s}ds}$$

in Section 8.1.2 and the derivation that

$$\mu(t, T, \{\theta\}) = \sigma(t, T, \{\theta\})\int_t^T \sigma(t, s, \{\theta\})ds,$$

we get the following equation for the instantaneous forward rate:

$$\begin{aligned}
f(t, T) &= f(0, T) + \int_0^t \sigma(u, T, x_u, y_u)\int_u^T \sigma(u, s, x_u, y_u)dsdu \\
&\quad + \int_0^t \sigma(u, T, x_u, y_u)dW_u \\
&= f(0, T) + g(T)\int_0^t h^2(u, x_u, y_u)\int_u^T g(s)dsdu \\
&\quad + g(T)\int_0^t h(u, x_u, y_u)dW_u.
\end{aligned}$$

But

$$dy_t = (\eta^2(t, x_t, y_t) - 2\kappa(t)y_t)dt$$

$$\Rightarrow dy_t - 2\frac{g'(t)}{g(t)}y_t dt = g^2(t)h^2(t, x_t, y_t)dt$$

by substituting for $\eta(t, x_t, y_t)$ and $\kappa(t)$

$$\Rightarrow g^2(t)d\left(\frac{y_t}{g^2(t)}\right) = g^2(t)h^2(t, x_t, y_t)dt$$

$$\Rightarrow d\left(\frac{y_t}{g^2(t)}\right) = h^2(t, x_t, y_t)dt$$

$$\Rightarrow y_t = g^2(t)\int_0^t h^2(s, x_s, y_s)ds \quad \text{(since } y_0 = 0)$$

and

$$dx_t = (-\kappa(t)x_t + y_t)dt + \eta(t, x_t, y_t)dW_t$$

$$\Rightarrow dx_t - \frac{g'(t)}{g(t)}x_t dt = y_t dt + g(t)h(t, x_t, y_t)dW_t$$

$$\Rightarrow d\left(\frac{x_t}{g(t)}\right) = \frac{y_t}{g(t)}dt + h(t, x_t, y_t)dW_t$$

$$x_t = g(t)\int_0^t \frac{y_u}{g(u)}du + g(t)\int_0^t h(u, x_u, y_u)dW_u$$

$$= g(t)\int_0^t g(u)\int_0^u h^2(s, x_s, y_s)dsdu \qquad \text{(since } x_0)$$

$$+ g(t)\int_0^t h(u, x_u, y_u)dW_u.$$

Thus, we obtain

$$\frac{g(T)}{g(t)}\left[x_t + \frac{y_t}{g(t)}\int_t^T g(s)ds\right]$$

$$= g(T)\int_0^t g(u)\int_0^u h^2(s, x_s, y_s)dsdu + g(T)\int_0^t h(u, x_u, y_u)dW_u$$

$$+ g(T)\int_0^t h^2(s, x_s, y_s)ds\int_t^T g(s)ds$$

$$= g(T)\int_0^t h^2(u, x_u, y_u)\int_u^T g(s)dsdu + g(T)\int_0^t h(u, x_u, y_u)dW_u$$

using

$$\int_0^t h^2(u, x_u, y_u)\int_u^T g(s)dsdu$$

$$= \int_0^t h^2(u, x_u, y_u)du\int_t^T g(s)ds + \int_0^t h^2(u, x_u, y_u)\int_u^t g(s)dsdu$$

$$= \int_0^t h^2(u, x_u, y_u)du\int_t^T g(s)ds + \int_0^t g(s)\int_0^s h^2(u, x_u, y_u)duds.$$

This verifies the equation in Section 8.4.1 above.

9

The Libor Market Model

"I forgot my calculus whilst learning algebra."

Chapter 8 introduces an approach to modelling the term structure of interest rates. Basically, since all interest rate quantities (e.g. swap rates or Libor rates) can be described as functions of discount factors, it is sufficient that any such model gives us the value of discount bonds for all maturities T as seen at any future time t of interest. Short rate models were the first, and have generally proven adequate for describing the dynamics of flow exotics.

However, such models are not intuitive: For instance what exactly is a short rate? And how do we relate the volatility of this rather abstract quantity to market observables (e.g. Libor rates and swap rates)?

Brace, Gatarek and Musiela [BGM97] described a framework whereby we could model Libor rates directly — the Libor Market Model (LMM). From these, we could obtain the values of discount bonds at future times, and hence all relevant interest rate quantities. Jamshidian [Jam97] then suggested an alternative involving modelling swap rates directly — the Swap Market Model, but the equations are more involved and it has proven harder to choose parameters such that this model achieves some consistency with Libor volatilities or with a wide spectrum of swaption volatilities, so the Swap Market Model has not caught on.

In this chapter, we shall explore the LMM. Apart from being able to think of volatilities as applying intuitively to given Libor rates, it gives a huge amount of flexibility, since we can control the volatility of each Libor rate independently, and the correlations between each of the Libor rates. This is extremely useful for strongly path dependent products (e.g. accumulators like snowballs, where a coupon is affected by previous Libor rates as well), or where a short rate model does not provide adequate decorrelation for longer expiries (e.g. long-dated CMS spread options). However, the LMM is only Markovian in a large number of state variables, so that it is extremely time consuming to simulate. Further, it cannot be treated on partial differential equations (PDEs), so that it is not ideal to use on products with early exercise features (e.g. Bermudan swaptions) since some form of regression is needed to estimate a (suboptimal) exercise boundary. As such, the LMM has not turned out to be as popular as its initial promise.

9.1   The Setup

Consider a set of N Libor rates $\{L_i(t)\}_{i=1}^{N}$, where $L_i(t)$ applies to the interval $[T_{i-1}, T_i]$ with $T_{i-1} < T_i$. We require that T_N is the longest maturity of interest, and set $T_0 = t$. See Figure 9.1 for an illustration. (In practice, we may not get $T_0 = t$ since for example futures dates are fixed, so some special treatment of the first stub and interpolation of sorts may be required. However, for the purpose of our discussion, such a level of detail is not useful.)

Define also $\tau_i = T_i - T_{i-1}$ as the accrual fraction for the relevant period. (Typically, the periods are spaced 3 months apart in US dollar swaps and 6 months apart for euro and sterling swaps.) From these Libor rates, we can obtain the discount factor for any expiry

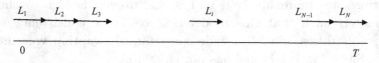

Figure 9.1: In the LMM, the setup involves consecutive Libor rates that span the period $[0, T]$.

of interest, via

$$D(t, T_i) = \prod_{j=1}^{i} \frac{1}{1 + L_j \tau_j}$$

or by interpolation between $D(t, T_{i-1})$ and $D(t, T_i)$ for maturity T such that $T_{i-1} < T < T_i$.

To define a general LMM, posit the following set of stochastic differential equations (SDEs) for the Libor rates

$$dL_i(t) = \mu(\{L_i(t)\}_{i=1}^{N}, t)dt + \sum_{j=1}^{M} \sigma_{i,j}(L_i(t), t)dW_t^j,$$

i.e. there can be up to M correlated Wiener processes driving each Libor rate.

As a practical consideration, Figure 8.3b in the previous chapter shows that five principal components typically captures about 99.5% of the variance of yield curve moves historically. Whilst we can in theory have a separate Wiener process driving each Libor rate and then apply some correlations (derived historically or otherwise) between these processes, doing so will generally yield little benefit; on the contrary, it will just introduce significant numerical noise in our valuation. So, an approach to pick out the most relevant principal components is usually applied.

Let us now consider the simpler case where we have a single Wiener process driving all the Libor rates

$$dL_i(t) = \mu(\{L_i(t)\}_{i=1}^{N}, t)dt + \sigma_i(L_i(t), t)dW_t.$$

Notice that if we choose the T_i-forward measure with numeraire being the discount bond with maturity T_i, then $L_i(t)$ is a martingale,[1] i.e. $\mu(\{L_i(t)\}_{i=1}^{N}, t) = 0$ under this measure.

However, each $L_i(t)$ is only a martingale under the choice of a different T_i-forward measure, whereas we need a single measure to evaluate a payoff depending on $\{L_i(t)\}_{i=1}^{N}$. Thus, we cannot avoid a change of measure that will introduce a drift to the SDEs for the majority of the Libor rates. We shall see this next.

---

[1]Per arguments given in Section 2.2.1.

9.1.1   *The Drift Under the Terminal Measure*

In the analysis below, we shall consider a single Wiener process W_t driving all Libor rates. The ideas can be extended to the general case of multiple Wiener drivers above, but the notation becomes more involved and it does not add any explanatory value, so we will not pursue this here.

Consider the Libor rate $L_i(t)$ under the T_i-forward measure (i.e. a martingale) with SDE

$$dL_i(t) = \sigma_i(L_i(t), t)dW_t^i.$$

Consider a change of measure from the T_i-forward measure to the T_{i+1}-forward measure with Radon–Nikodym derivative given by

$$
\begin{aligned}
R(t) &= \frac{dQ^{T_{i+1}}}{dQ^{T_i}}(t) \\
&= \frac{D(t, T_{i+1})D(0, T_i)}{D(t, T_i)D(0, T_{i+1})} \\
&= \frac{D(0, T_i)}{(1 + L_{i+1}(t)\tau_{i+1})D(0, T_{i+1})}.
\end{aligned}
$$

Notice that

$$
\begin{aligned}
dR(t) &= -\frac{D(0, T_i)\tau_{i+1}dL_{i+1}(t)}{(1 + L_{i+1}(t)\tau_{i+1})^2 D(0, T_{i+1})} \\
&= -\frac{\tau_{i+1}\sigma_{i+1}(L_{i+1}(t), t)}{1 + L_{i+1}(t)\tau_{i+1}}R(t)dW_t^{i+1}.
\end{aligned}
$$

Thus, Girsanov's Theorem gives

$$dW_t^i = -\frac{\tau_{i+1}\sigma_{i+1}(L_{i+1}(t), t)}{1 + L_{i+1}(t)\tau_{i+1}}dt + dW_t^{i+1},$$

so that

$$
\begin{aligned}
dL_i(t) &= \sigma_i(L_i(t), t)\left[-\frac{\tau_{i+1}\sigma_{i+1}(L_{i+1}(t), t)}{1 + L_{i+1}(t)\tau_{i+1}}dt + dW_t^{i+1}\right] \\
&= -\frac{\tau_{i+1}\sigma_{i+1}(L_{i+1}(t), t)\sigma_i(L_i(t), t)}{1 + L_{i+1}(t)\tau_{i+1}}dt + \sigma_i(L_i(t), t)dW_t^{i+1}.
\end{aligned}
$$

Working inductively,[2] we see that

$$dL_i(t) = -\frac{\tau_{i+1}\sigma_{i+1}(L_{i+1}(t), t)\sigma_i(L_i(t), t)}{1 + L_{i+1}(t)\tau_{i+1}} dt$$

$$+ \sigma_i(L_i(t), t) \left[-\frac{\tau_{i+2}\sigma_{i+2}(L_{i+2}(t), t)}{1 + L_{i+2}(t)\tau_{i+2}} dt + dW_t^{i+2} \right]$$

$$= \dots$$

$$= -\sigma_i(L_i(t), t) \sum_{j=i+1}^{N} \frac{\tau_j\sigma_j(L_j(t), t)}{1 + L_j(t)\tau_j} dt + \sigma_i(L_i(t), t) dW_t^N.$$

Thus, we have the drift of each Libor rate $L_i(t)$ under the measure where the discount bond with the longest maturity T_N is numeraire (i.e. the terminal measure).

From the above equation, it is clear that under the terminal measure, the drift of $L_i(t)$ depends on $\{L_j(t)\}_{j=i+1}^{N}$. Further, since $D(t, T_i) = \prod_{j=1}^{i} \frac{1}{1+L_j\tau_j}$, to get discount factors for any expiry T, we require $L_1(t)$. Hence, even a one-factor LMM is Markovian in only N state variables $\{L_j(t)\}_{j=1}^{N}$, if it is described by N Libor rates.

This is a major drawback of the LMM. First, a fairly large number of state variables is involved. For example, if we are interested in a 30-year swap in US dollars, since Libor rates are quarterly, we have a total of 120 state variables. This means computation time would be about 120 times that if we only needed one state variable.

Furthermore, there is no chance to put the LMM on a PDE (which can realistically handle only up to three state variables). (There are some approaches that involve freezing the drift and hence making this a one-factor model, e.g. the simplest involves using

$$dL_i(t) \approx -\sigma_i(L_i(t), t) \sum_{j=i+1}^{N} \frac{\tau_j\sigma_j(L_j(0), t)}{(1 + L_j(0)\tau_j)} dt + \sigma_i(L_i(t), t) dW_t^N,$$

and other approaches involving predictor–corrector or Brownian bridge techniques exist. But these approaches tend not to be able to give sufficiently accurate forward swap rates for long expiries, e.g. of

---

[2]I.e. changing measure to the T_{i+2}-forward measure and proceeding to change measure in the same way until we are in the T_N-forward measure.

10 years or more. So, they are not much utilised in practice.) This means we need to somehow figure out how to deal with early exercise on a Monte Carlo, where we do not know the conditional expectation of the continuation value at a future point in time. We will discuss this further in Section 9.4.

9.1.2   *The Drift Under the Spot Libor Measure*

Given

$$dW_t^i = -\frac{\tau_{i+1}\sigma_{i+1}(L_{i+1}(t),t)}{(1 + L_{i+1}(t)\tau_{i+1})}dt + dW_t^{i+1}$$

from the previous section, we can instead obtain (by changing from the T_i-forward measure to the T_{i-1}-forward measure):

$$dL_i(t) = \sigma_i(L_i(t),t)\left[\frac{\tau_i\sigma_i(L_i(t),t)}{(1 + L_i(t)\tau_i)}dt + dW_t^{i-1}\right]$$

$$= \frac{\tau_i\sigma_i^2(L_i(t),t)}{(1 + L_i(t)\tau_i)}dt + \sigma_i(L_i(t),t)dW_t^{i-1}.$$

Inductively, we obtain[3]:

$$dL_i(t) = \frac{\tau_i\sigma_i^2(L_i(t),t)}{(1 + L_i(t)\tau_i)}dt$$

$$+ \sigma_i(L_i(t),t)\left[\frac{\tau_{i-1}\sigma_{i-1}(L_{i-1}(t),t)}{(1 + L_{i-1}(t)\tau_{i-1})}dt + dW_t^{i-2}\right]$$

$$= \ldots$$

$$= \sigma_i(L_i(t),t)\sum_{j=1}^{i}\frac{\tau_j\sigma_j(L_j(t),t)}{(1 + L_j(t)\tau_j)}dt + \sigma_i(L_i(t),t)dW_t^0.$$

But what is the measure Q^0 that gives us the corresponding Wiener process W_t^0?

Consider now the discrete analogue to the money market account. Specifically, money is to be invested as follows:

(1) At time zero, given \$1, we purchase a quantity $\frac{1}{D(0,T_1)}$ of zero-coupon bonds maturing at time T_1;

---

[3]By changing to the T_{i-2}-forward measure and so on.

(2) At time T_1, since our initial investment is worth $\frac{1}{D(0,T_1)}$, we purchase a quantity $\frac{1}{D(0,T_1)D(T_1,T_2)}$ of zero-coupon bonds with maturity T_2;

(3) At time T_2, since our initial investment is worth $\frac{1}{D(0,T_1)D(T_1,T_2)}$, we purchase a quantity $\frac{1}{D(0,T_1)D(T_1,T_2)D(T_2,T_3)}$ of zero-coupon bonds with maturity T_3; and

(4) We continue indefinitely.

Its value at time t for $T_i < t \leq T_{i+1}$ is given by

$$B(t) = \frac{D(t, T_{i+1})}{\prod_{j=1}^{i+1} D(T_{j-1}, T_j)}.$$

(Note that this satisfies $B(0) = 1$.)

$B(t)$ is well-defined for all t, and as such is a proper numeraire. It is actually the numeraire corresponding to our above measure Q^0, and is popularly known as the spot Libor measure.

Under the spot Libor measure, the drift of $L_i(t)$ depends on $\{L_j(t)\}_{j=1}^{i}$. This is slightly more pleasant in that if we are only interested in discount factors up to maturity T_i, then there is no need to simulate any Libor rates with a greater maturity, hence lowering computational expense. This is particularly useful if we wish to bootstrap volatilities of standard market instruments (e.g. caplets and swaptions), since when pricing them, we do not need to simulate Libor rates beyond the maturity (end dates) of the underlying instruments. In Section 9.2.1, we shall see that vols of these standard instruments also depend only on those of Libor rates up to the end dates of the underlying instruments.

However, notice that in contrast to the terminal measure, the drift for $L_i(t)$ is positive, being

$$\sigma_i(L_i(t), t) \sum_{j=1}^{i} \frac{\tau_j \sigma_j(L_j(t), t)}{(1 + L_j(t)\tau_j)}.$$

This is not ideal as we could potentially end up with an explosive contribution to the growth of Libor rates from this drift, given some parameterisation of $\sigma_j(L_j(t), t)$, e.g. a simple lognormal form such as $\sigma_j(L_j(t), t) = \sigma_j L_j$. This is less stable numerically and can lead to worse convergence qualities for pricing and risk computations.

9.1.3   Caplet Volatilities

In the LMM, each SDE represents a Libor rate. This lends to an intuitive understanding of the model. Consider now the specific choice of $\sigma_i(L_i(t), t) = \sigma_i L_i(t)$, i.e. lognormal time-homogeneous volatilities for each Libor rate. This gives

$$dL_i(t) = \mu(\{L_i(t)\}_{i=1}^{N}, t)dt + \sigma_i L_i(t)dW_t.$$

Since change of measure does not affect volatility, this σ_i is just the lognormal volatility of a caplet (say we can take the at-the-money caplet volatility observed from the market). In this way, model volatility is actually just market volatility — hence the name Libor Market Model. This was especially convenient in the late 1990s when the LMM first came about, as a lognormal model for caplet volatilities was somewhat plausible then, with volatility skew far less pronounced.

Even in the presence of volatility skew however, we see that a time-independent volatility parameterisation for the LMM corresponds to the equivalent parameterisation of caplet volatility.

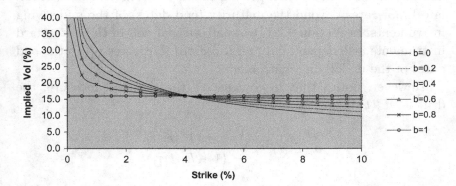

Figure 9.2:   We illustrate how different values of blend b lead to very different profiles for implied lognormal caplet vols for an expiry of 10 years based on a time-independent vol $\sigma_i = 16\%$ and initial Libor rate of 4%.

And certain parameterisations of volatility correspond to cases where analytic formulae for caplets exist, e.g. $\sigma_i(L_i(t), t) = \sigma_i(bL_i + (1 - b)L_0)$ gives the blend model (see Figure 9.2 for the effect of different choices of blend), whereas $\sigma_i(L_i(t), t) = \sigma_j L_i^\beta$ gives the CEV model (both covered in Chapter 5).

In the same way, time-dependent LMM volatilities are more intuitive, since they apply to concrete Libor rates, rather than to some abstract quantity like a short rate.

9.2 Swaption Pricing

As discussed in Chapter 2, a swaption is an option on a swap.

Consider a swap starting at T_S, ending at T_E, with fixed cash flow dates $\{T_i\}_{i=S+1}^E$ and accrual periods τ_i between T_{i-1} and T_i. The value of the par swap rate is given by

$$R(t) = \frac{D(t, T_S) - D(t, T_E)}{A(t)},$$

where

$$A(t) = \sum_{i=S+1}^E \tau_i D(t, T_i)$$

is the value of an annuity (i.e. stream of cashflows paying τ_i at time T_i), and the payoff of a payer swaption (i.e. paying the fixed rate and receiving the floating rate) at expiry T_S is given by

$$\max(R(T) - K, 0) \sum_{i=S+1}^E \tau_i D(T, T_i).$$

Swaptions are amongst the most liquid of interest rate options (even more so than caps), so it is necessary for any interest rate model to be able to calibrate to prices of relevant swaptions.[4]

Whereas the Libor Market Model is defined via consecutive spanning Libor rates and so almost immediately gives us caplet volatilities, it takes somewhat more effort to obtain swaption volatilities.

---

[4]We will discuss more on what are relevant swaptions later in this chapter.

9.2.1   *The Swap Rate Under Libor Market Model*

To price a swaption under the LMM, one can simulate the collection of Libor rates via Monte Carlo, and compute the relevant discount factors $\{D(T, T_i)\}_{i=S}^{E}$ at time T and hence the swap rate and the value of the swaption payoff. However, for calibration purposes, it is usually not satisfactory[5] to be required to perform root-finding or optimisation over the prices obtained via Monte Carlo. Let us now examine the SDE for the swap rate further below.

Libor rates are the fundamentals of the LMM, and any swap rate is a function of Libor rates. So, focusing on the volatility part of the swap rate, we can see that

$$dR(t) = \sum_{i=1}^{E} \frac{\partial R}{\partial L_i}(t)dL_i(t) + (\cdots)dt$$

$$= \sum_{i=1}^{E} \frac{\partial R}{\partial L_i}(t)\sigma_i(L_i(t), t)dW_t + (\cdots)dt.$$

It may be useful to specify concretely $\frac{\partial R}{\partial L_i}(t)$, and this we shall do next.

Since the equation for a discount bond in terms of Libor rates is

$$D(t, T_i) = \prod_{j=1}^{i} \frac{1}{1 + L_j(t)\tau_j},$$

its SDE (focusing on the volatility part with $m(\{\theta\}, t)$ or $m^*(\{\theta\}, t)$ representing the drift parts, $\{\theta\}$ being state variables) is given by

$$dD(t, T_i) = m(\{\theta\}, t)dt - D(t, T_i)\sum_{j=1}^{i} \frac{\tau_j dL_j}{1 + L_j(t)\tau_j}$$

$$= m^*(\{\theta\}, t)dt - D(t, T_i)\sum_{j=1}^{i} \frac{\tau_j \sigma_j(L_j(t), t)}{1 + L_j(t)\tau_j}dW_t.$$

---

[5] Being too slow and numerically unstable.

Given the equation for the swap rate, its SDE (again focusing on the volatility part) is

$$dR(t) = \mu(\{\theta\}, t)dt + \frac{1}{A(t)}\left[dD(t, T_S) - dD(t, T_E) \right.$$

$$\left. - R(t) \sum_{i=S+1}^{E} \tau_i dD(t, T_i) \right]$$

$$= \mu^*(\{\theta\}, t)dt + \frac{1}{A(t)}\left[-D(t, T_S) \sum_{j=1}^{S} \frac{\tau_j \sigma_j(L_j(t), t)}{1 + L_j(t)\tau_j} \right.$$

$$+ D(t, T_E) \sum_{j=1}^{E} \frac{\tau_j \sigma_j(L_j(t), t)}{1 + L_j(t)\tau_j}$$

$$\left. + R(t) \sum_{i=S+1}^{E} D(t, T_i) \sum_{j=1}^{i} \frac{\tau_j \sigma_j(L_j(t), t)}{1 + L_j(t)\tau_j} \right] dW_t.$$

We thus see that the volatility for a swaption based on a swap starting at T_S and ending at T_E depends on the volatility of Libor rates $\{L_i\}_{i=1}^{E}$. We shall consider how volatilities of Libor rates relate to swaption volatilities by exploring the volatility triangle next.

9.2.2   *The Volatility Triangle*

For convenience, let $T_i = i\Delta$, i.e. the set times of our Libor rates are equally spaced apart.

Let us consider the following parameterisation of volatilities

$$\sigma_i(L_i, t) = \sigma_{i,j} \quad \text{for } T_{j-1} \leq t < T_j \ (j = 1, 2, \ldots, i-1),$$

i.e. each Libor rate has piecewise constant volatility over the interval $[T_{j-1}, T_j)$. (Note that it is not meaningful to discuss the volatility of the Libor rate $L_i(t)$ after $t = T_{i-1}$ since T_{i-1} is the time when that particular Libor rate sets.) This parameterisation can be visualised via a triangle of Libor volatilities as in Figure 9.3.

Consider now at-the-money swaption volatilites. Notice that the underlying swaps are characterised by expiry and tenor. Given a discrete universe of N Libor rates, we have the ingredients to cover

Libor Volatilities Vol Grid		Time					
		T_1	T_2	T_{i-1}		T_{N-2}	T_{N-1}
Rate	L_1						
	L_2	$\sigma_{2,1}$					
	L_3	$\sigma_{3,1}$	$\sigma_{3,2}$				
	L_i	$\sigma_{i,1}$	$\sigma_{i,2}$	$\sigma_{i,i-1}$			
	L_{N-1}	$\sigma_{N-1,1}$	$\sigma_{N-1,2}$			$\sigma_{N-1,N-2}$	
	L_N	$\sigma_{N,1}$	$\sigma_{N,2}$			$\sigma_{N,N-2}$	$\sigma_{N,N-1}$

Figure 9.3:   We display the grid of Libor rate volatilities and the periods for which they are relevant.

Swaption Vols (spanned by LMM)		Tenor						
		T_1	T_2	T_3	T_{N-i}	T_{N-3}	T_{N-2}	T_{N-1}
Expiry	T_1	$\Lambda_{1,1}$	$\Lambda_{1,2}$	$\Lambda_{1,3}$	$\Lambda_{1,N-i}$	$\Lambda_{1,N-3}$	$\Lambda_{1,N-2}$	$\Lambda_{1,N-1}$
	T_2	$\Lambda_{2,1}$	$\Lambda_{2,2}$	$\Lambda_{2,3}$	$\Lambda_{2,N-i}$	$\Lambda_{2,N-3}$	$\Lambda_{2,N-2}$	
	T_3	$\Lambda_{3,1}$	$\Lambda_{3,2}$	$\Lambda_{3,3}$	$\Lambda_{3,N-i}$	$\Lambda_{3,N-3}$		
	T_i	$\Lambda_{i,1}$	$\Lambda_{i,2}$	$\Lambda_{i,3}$	$\Lambda_{i,N-i}$			
	T_{N-2}	$\Lambda_{N-2,1}$	$\Lambda_{N-2,2}$					
	T_{N-1}	$\Lambda_{N-1,1}$						

Figure 9.4:   We display the range of swaptions that could be priced by the LMM constructed up to end date T_N.

swaps of a fixed maturity (end date), i.e. up to T_N, so the universe of swaps (explainable by our model) with increasing expiries have gradually more limited tenors. Let us denote the swaption volatility with expiry T_i and tenor T_j by $\Lambda_{i,j}$ as depicted in Figure 9.4. (Note that the maturity/end date of the underlying swap is thus $T_i + T_j$.)

Naturally, the question is to ask how we can relate these swaption volatilities to our Libor volatilities.

Let us start by observing that a swaption with expiry T_i and tenor $T_1 = \Delta$ is really like a caplet. (In practice, there are complications since caplets in US dollars are quarterly and those in euros are semi-annual, whereas swaption tenors tend to be in units of years. Thus, in a strict sense, the shortest tenor swaption is not a caplet.

We ignore these complications in that they do not affect the key ideas discussed. In any case, the above is a coherent framework that relates caplet volatilities to our swaption vol matrix.)

As we have seen in Section 9.2.1, the price of a swaption with expiry T_i and tenor T_j depends on the volatility of Libor rates $\{L_k(t)\}_{k=1}^{i+j}$ up to time $T_i + T_j$. So, we have the following procedure to bootstrap our piecewise constant Libor rates from at-the-money swaption volatilities.

Specifically, start with swaptions of expiry T_1 and tenors T_1, $T_2, \ldots, T_{N-1}$. We solve for this sequentially to get $\sigma_{2,1}, \sigma_{3,1}, \ldots, \sigma_{N,1}$.

Now, proceed to swaptions of expiry T_2 and tenors T_1, $T_2, \ldots, T_{N-2}$. We solve for this sequentially to get $\sigma_{3,2}, \ldots, \sigma_{N,2}$.

We continue bootstrapping in this way until we get to a swaption of expiry T_{N-1} and tenor T_1. We solve for this to get $\sigma_{N,N-1}$.

Thus, we have obtained the volatilities $\sigma_i(L_i, t)$ of all Libor rates $\{L_i(t)\}_{i=1}^{N}$ for all times of interest $t \leq T_{N-1}$, fitting all at-the-money swaption volatilities in the process.

In practice, this bootstrap methodology is not too popular. The reason is mainly because the swaption matrix involving a large number of combinations of expiries and tenors is not always in sync. In particular, liquid points (e.g. 5-year expiry into 10-year tenor) are updated very frequently whilst less liquid points (e.g. 13-year expiry into 16-year tenor) can contain stale data. Bootstrapping will cause volatilities for later time points and more distant Libor rates to be heavily dependent on their predecessors, and hence fluctuate wildly if earlier data is unreliable. Indeed, it may not be possible to fit all available data, since negative forward variance might be implied.

Another good reason for not considering a bootstrap to all volatilities is that a certain amount of time-homogeneity of Libor volatilities is desirable, and it is clearly not going to happen with such a bootstrap. The argument is that any mechanism that leads to Libor rate volatilities varying with expiry tends to preserve itself over time, rather than evolve in the manner implied by forwards (e.g. decrease over time). So, using time-dependent volatilities to capture this may not be particularly appropriate. This is a more relevant argument in stable times. In times of market crisis, the current shape of volatilities over expiries is unlikely to be perpetuated.

A further reason to not overly concern ourselves with fitting swaption volatilities is that the above approach fails to account for volatility skew, whereas clearly volatilities for different strikes are not the same (whether in a normal, lognormal, or blended sense.). It may thus be more important to treat skew, dependent on our product, and it may be too complicated to treat skew with such a bulky specification of volatility.

In practice, it is common to instead focus on caplet and co-terminal swaption volatilities[6] when pricing Bermudan swaptions. (See Figure 8.1 in Section 8.2.3 for a diagrammatic illustration.) If we are instead interested in pricing Constant Maturity Swap products, e.g. paying the 10-year CMS rate, then we calibrate to the relevant tenor independent of expiry (e.g. 1-year expiry into 10-year tenor, 2-year expiry into 10-year tenor, ..., 19-year expiry into 10-year tenor).

9.2.3 *Approximation for At-the-money Swaptions*

In Section 9.2.1, we have seen that the SDE for the volatility part of the swap rate under the LMM is given by

$$dR(t) = \mu^*(\{\theta\}, t)dt + \frac{1}{A(t)} \left[-D(t, T_S) \sum_{j=1}^{S} \frac{\tau_j \sigma_j(L_j(t), t)}{1 + L_j(t)\tau_j} \right.$$

$$+ D(t, T_E) \sum_{j=1}^{E} \frac{\tau_j \sigma_j(L_j(t), t)}{1 + L_j(t)\tau_j}$$

$$\left. + R(t) \sum_{i=S+1}^{E} D(t, T_i) \sum_{j=1}^{i} \frac{\tau_j \sigma_j(L_j(t), t)}{1 + L_j(t)\tau_j} \right] dW_t .$$

The main unpleasantness of this SDE is that the volatility at time t depends on the values of multiple quantities (e.g. discount factors and annuities) that are the result of simulation up to time t. Thus, in its full generality, there is no simple formula for the price of a swaption.

---

[6]I.e. volatilities of swaptions where maturity (= expiry + tenor) is constant, e.g. 1-year expiry into 19-year tenor, 2-year expiry into 18-year tenor, ..., 19-year expiry into 1-year tenor.

However, an at-the-money normal volatility is approximately related to an at-the-money lognormal volatility via

$$\sigma_N \approx \sigma_{LN} R(0),$$

where $R(0)$ is the prevailing par swap rate.

This can be seen since per Section 1.2.4, the price of an at-the-money normal option is $\sigma_N \sqrt{\frac{T}{2\pi}}$, whereas that for an at-the-money lognormal option is

$$R(0)(N(d_1) - N(d_1 - \sigma_{LN}\sqrt{T}))$$

$$= R(0) \int_{d_1 - \sigma_{LN}\sqrt{T}}^{d_1} \frac{1}{\sqrt{2\pi}} e^{-\frac{1}{2}z^2} dz$$

$$= \frac{R(0)}{\sqrt{2\pi}} \int_{d_1 - \sigma_{LN}\sqrt{T}}^{d_1} (1 + O(z^2)) dz \quad \text{using a Taylor expansion}$$

$$\approx \frac{R(0)}{\sqrt{2\pi}} \sigma_{LN}\sqrt{T}.$$

Similarly, we can treat the volatility of an at-the-money swaption by assuming normality (or lognormality) and freezing the drift — approximating all stochastic quantities with their forward values as seen today, i.e.

$$R(t) \approx R(0), \quad D(t,T) \approx \frac{D(0,T)}{D(0,t)}, \quad A(t) \approx \frac{A(0)}{D(0,t)}, \quad L(t) \approx L(0).$$

This leads to the following approximation for the normal volatility Λ_N of an at-the-money swaption under the LMM model:

$$\Lambda_N^2 T = \int_0^T \frac{1}{A^2(0)} \left[-D(0,T_S) \sum_{j=1}^S \frac{\tau_j \sigma_j(L_j(0), t)}{1 + L_j(0)\tau_j} \right.$$

$$+ D(0, T_E) \sum_{j=1}^E \frac{\tau_j \sigma_j(L_j(0), t)}{1 + L_j(0)\tau_j}$$

$$+ R(0) \sum_{i=S+1}^E D(0, T_i) \sum_{j=1}^i \left. \frac{\tau_j \sigma_j(L_j(0), t)}{1 + L_j(0)\tau_j} \right]^2 dt.$$

with similar formulae if we wish to treat the swap rate as lognormal or a blend between lognormal and normal. And the above readily extends to multiple Wiener processes driving the system of Libor rates. The above argument relies on the drifts of the swap rate, annuity and discount factors being small relative to volatilities (an acceptable compromise), so that they could be ignored in a first order approximation.

But this approach really works only for an at-the-money option. We will explore approximate terminal processes for the swap rate in the presence of skew in Section 9.3.1, which will prove useful in pricing swaptions of other strikes.

9.2.4   *Effect of Correlations*

Consider now the case where we have multiple Brownian drivers. Specifically, our system of SDEs is

$$dL_i(t) = \mu(\{L_i(t)\}_{i=1}^N, t)dt + \sum_{j=1}^M \sigma_{i,j}(L_i(t), t)dW_t^j.$$

It may be convenient to consider $M = N$, $\sigma_{i,j}(L_i(t), t) = \delta_{ij}\sigma_i(L_i(t), t)$ and $dW_t^i dW_t^j = \rho_{i,j}(t)dt$, i.e. each Libor rate is driven by its own Brownian motion and $\rho_{i,j}(t)$ is the correlation between Libor rates i and j.

Consider now the following approximation (as per Section 9.2.3) for the normal volatility of an at-the-money swaption with expiry T:

$$\Lambda_N^2 T = \int_0^T \frac{1}{A^2(0)} \left\{ \sum_{j=1}^E C_j(t)dW_t^j \right\}^2$$

$$= \frac{1}{A^2(0)} \int_0^T \left\{ \sum_{j=1}^E C_j^2(t) + 2\sum_{j=1}^E \sum_{i=1}^{j-1} \rho_{i,j}(t)C_i(t)C_j(t) \right\} dt,$$

for $1 \leq j \leq S$:

$$C_j(t) = -D(0, T_S) \frac{\tau_j \sigma_j(L_j(0), t)}{1 + L_j(0)\tau_j} + D(0, T_E) \frac{\tau_j \sigma_j(L_j(0), t)}{1 + L_j(0)\tau_j}$$

$$+ R(0) \frac{\tau_j \sigma_j(L_j(0), t)}{1 + L_j(0)\tau_j} \sum_{i=S+1}^{E} D(0, T_i);$$

for $S + 1 \leq j \leq E$:

$$C_j(t) = D(0, T_E) \frac{\tau_j \sigma_j(L_j(0), t)}{1 + L_j(0)\tau_j} + R(0) \frac{\tau_j \sigma_j(L_j(0), t)}{1 + L_j(0)\tau_j} \sum_{i=j}^{E} D(0, T_i).$$

Suppose that X and Y are random variates with identical marginal distributions, then

$$\text{var}(X + Y) = \text{var}(X) + \text{var}(Y) + 2\text{cov}(X, Y)$$
$$= 2\text{var}(X)[1 + \text{corr}(X, Y)].$$

Notice that

$$\text{var}(2X) = 4\text{var}(X),$$

so $\text{var}(X + Y) < \text{var}(2X)$ unless $\text{corr}(X, Y) = 1$ (in which equality holds).

This suggests any value of $\rho_{i,j}(t) < 1$ requires higher $C_i(t)$, $C_j(t)$ to match the same implied at-the-money swaption volatility.

We have seen in Section 9.2.2 that it is possible to match the prices of all at-the-money swaptions via a single correlation driver. However, what should be clear from this section is that forward volatilities of the Libor rates will be higher if correlation is lower, when we calibrate only to co-terminal swaptions. This makes sense intuitively as well, since a swap rate being an average over Libor rates typically tends to be less volatile than the constituent Libor rates which do not always move together. Hence, we need higher forward Libor volatilities to match a given swaption volatility as correlation decreases.

Correlation is particularly important for certain products. For example, consider the CMS spread option that pays the 10-year swap rate minus the 2-year swap rate observed on a future set date T.

If rates were highly correlated, then we expect both swap rates to move in unison, so that the spread is unlikely to change much, and so this product would not be worth much (unless it is in-the-money). On the other hand, low correlation implies a higher likelihood of a high 10-year rate versus a low 2-year rate and vice versa, so that spread volatility is higher and the CMS spread option is worth a lot more (see Figure 9.5). This is quite an important matter, since spread options were extremely popular prior to the crisis of 2008 due to significant interest in betting on an upward sloping yield curve persisting, and lots of legacy trades remain.

On the same topic, it is worth highlighting that there are products that are very sensitive to the behaviour of individual forward rates, and that of forward rates vis-à-vis each other. Consider for instance, the snowball with payoff as follows:

In period 1, the coupon is $C_1 = 5\%$.

In period i $(i > 1)$, the coupon is $C_i = \max(C_{i-1}+3\%-L_i(T_{i-1}), 0)$, where $L_i(T_{i-1})$ is the Libor rate that sets at the beginning of the period.

Such a product does not depend so much on the total variance of interest rates in the period, but rather the behaviour of Libor in each period (relative to the 3% barrier) as well as the correlation of Libor

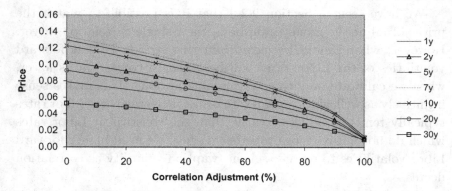

Figure 9.5:   We display the prices of spread options under the LMM based on different correlation assumptions. We start with a calibrated LMM model, and then impose a correlation shift from 0% to 100% across the board. As expected, we see that spread option prices decrease as correlation increases.

rates vis-à-vis each other (since any decline in coupon for a period is reflected in lower coupons for all future periods). The snowball is an example of a product where the LMM is a particularly appropriate choice, given its provision for extensive control over the dynamics of the underlying Libor rates, which heavily influence the price of such an esoteric product.

9.3 Beyond a Lognormal Libor Market Model

As mentioned in Section 9.1.3, the original LMM was based on lognormal Libor rates but subsequent innovations and increasing awareness of features of the model in relation to standard products in the interest rates markets (e.g. swaptions and caplets) since then has meant that treatment of skew is now common. The typical approach is to come up with some local volatility parameterisation, as well as to have an extension that incorporates stochastic volatility. We have explored the concepts of local and stochastic volatility in Chapters 5 to 7 and the implications for forward volatility and risk sensitivities of the underlying in the context of foreign exchange (FX) and equities. Similar conclusions can be reached for interest rates, so we shall not repeat the discussion. In the following subsections, we shall consider some possible extensions as well as approaches to calibrate the model based on such parameterisations.

9.3.1 *Extending With Local Volatility*

A parameterisation favoured by Andersen, Andreasen [AA00] and Piterbarg [Pit03c] involves

$$\sigma_{i,j}(L_i(t), t) = \sigma_{i,j}(t)\{b_i(t)L_i(t) + (1 - b_i(t))L_i(0)\},$$

so that the SDEs for the Libor rates are

$$dL_i(t) = \mu(\{L_i(t)\}_{i=1}^{N}, t)dt + \{b_i(t)L_i(t)$$

$$+ (1 - b_i(t))L_i(0)\} \sum_{j=1}^{M} \sigma_{i,j}(t)dW_t^j.$$

(Whereas this parameterisation has the non-desirable feature of allowing for a non-negligible probability of negative interest rates, it is otherwise quite intuitive in its description of skew as a mixture between normal and lognormal components. In any case, it illustrates some useful ideas for calibrating the LMM, so we shall adopt this parameterisation for the rest of the section.)

Rather than approximate the SDE for the swap rate as normal, it makes sense to approximate it based on a blended distribution. But what is the blend for the swap rate?

According to Piterbarg [Pit03c], the process for the swap rate can be related to that for the Libor rates by matching both the value 'along the forward path' (i.e. the drift-freeze approach discussed earlier), and the slope. Details are as follows:

As per our discussion in Section 9.2.1, the SDE for the swap rate is

$$dR(t) = M(t)dt + \sum_{i=1}^{E} \frac{\partial R}{\partial L_i}(t) \sum_{j=1}^{M} \sigma_{i,j}(L_i(t), t)dW_t^j$$

$$= M(t)dt + \sum_{i=1}^{E} \frac{\partial R}{\partial L_i}(t)\{b_i(t)L_i(t)$$

$$+ (1 - b_i(t))L_i(0)\} \sum_{j=1}^{M} \sigma_{i,j}(t)dW_t^j.$$

We wish to write it as a blended SDE for the swap rate as follows:

$$dR(t) \approx M(t)dt + \{B(t)R(t) + (1 - B(t))R(0)\} \sum_{j=1}^{M} s_j(t)dW_t^j.$$

Agreement 'along the forward path' requires that

$$\sum_{i=1}^{E} \frac{\partial R}{\partial L_i}(0)L_i(0) \sum_{j=1}^{M} \sigma_{i,j}(t)dW_t^j = R(0) \sum_{j=1}^{M} s_j(t)dW_t^j.$$

If we define $w_i = \frac{\partial R}{\partial L_i}(0)\frac{L_i(0)}{R(0)}$, then we see that

$$s_j(t) = \sum_{i=1}^{E} w_i \sigma_{i,j}(t),$$

giving the expected result as per a drift freeze.

Substituting this into the blended SDE for the swap rate gives

$$dR(t) = M(t)dt + \{B(t)R(t) + (1 - B(t))R(0)\} \sum_{i=1}^{E} w_i \sum_{j=1}^{M} \sigma_{i,j}(t)dW_t^j.$$

Now considering the condition involving matching the slope, we differentiate the vol part of both equations with respect to each Libor rate $L_k(t)$. This gives

$$\frac{\partial}{\partial L_k} \left[\{B(t)R(t) + (1 - B(t))R(0)\} \sum_{i=1}^{E} w_i \sum_{j=1}^{M} \sigma_{i,j}(t)dW_t^j \right]$$

$$= B(t)\frac{\partial R}{\partial L_k}(t) \sum_{i=1}^{E} w_i \sum_{j=1}^{M} \sigma_{i,j}(t)dW_t^j$$

and

$$\frac{\partial}{\partial L_k} \left[\sum_{i=1}^{E} \frac{\partial R}{\partial L_i}(t)\{b_i(t)L_i(t) + (1 - b_i(t))L_i(0)\} \sum_{j=1}^{M} \sigma_{i,j}(L_i(t), t)dW_t^j \right]$$

$$= \sum_{i=1}^{E} \frac{\partial^2 R}{\partial L_k \partial L_i}(t)\{b_i(t)L_i(t) + (1 - b_i(t))L_i(0)\} \sum_{j=1}^{M} \sigma_{i,j}(t)dW_t^j$$

$$+ \frac{\partial R}{\partial L_k}(t)b_k(t) \sum_{j=1}^{M} \sigma_{k,j}(t)dW_t^j.$$

Equating the above 'along the forward path' and ignoring second order terms (i.e. second derivatives of $R(t)$) gives

$$B(t)\frac{\partial R}{\partial L_k}(0) \sum_{i=1}^{E} w_i \sum_{j=1}^{M} \sigma_{i,j}(t)dW_t^j = \frac{\partial R}{\partial L_k}(0)b_k(t) \sum_{j=1}^{M} \sigma_{k,j}(t)dW_t^j,$$

simplifying to

$$B(t) \sum_{i=1}^{E} w_i \sigma_{i,j}(t) = b_k(t)\sigma_{k,j}(t)$$

for $j = 1, \ldots, M$ and $k = 1, \ldots, E$.

We can then find $B(t)$ (i.e. the equivalent blend for the swap rate) via a least-squares minimisation of

$$\sum_{j=1}^{M}\sum_{k=1}^{E}\left\{B(t)\sum_{i=1}^{E}w_i\sigma_{i,j}(t) - b_k(t)\sigma_{k,j}(t)\right\}^2$$

to obtain

$$B(t) \approx \sum_{k=1}^{E}\left\{b_k(t)\frac{\sum_{j=1}^{M}\sigma_{k,j}(t)s_j(t)}{\sum_{j=1}^{M}s_j(t)}\right\}.$$

The above SDE for the swap rate has time-dependent blend and volatility. As such, we cannot obtain analytic formulae for the prices of swaptions. As it stands it is an improvement on a brute force calibration of the LMM parameterised by Libor rates, since we can price swaptions of any strike by solving a one-dimensional PDE, which is very efficient. However, an analytic approximation could be obtained via the idea of parameter averaging (to find time-independent parameters of an SDE which give a reasonable approximation to the terminal distribution at expiry time T under the given SDE) as discussed by Piterbarg [Pit03c]. We shall consider this after the next sub-section on stochastic volatility, as the same treatment can be utilised in the stochastic volatility case.

9.3.2   *Extending With Stochastic Volatility*

We can easily extend the LMM to incorporate stochastic volatility by the addition of the stochastic variance multiplier z_t as described by the SDEs

$$dz_t = \kappa(\theta - z_t)dt + \eta\sqrt{z_t}dU_t \quad \text{and}$$

$$dL_i(t) = \mu(\{L_i(t)\}_{i=1}^{N}, z_t, t)dt + \sqrt{z_t}\sum_{j=1}^{M}\sigma_{i,j}(L_i(t), t)dW_t^j,$$

where $dU_t dW_t^j = 0$ for all j (the choice of a driver for the variance that is uncorrelated with the other Wiener processes being motivated by the desire not to complicate the drift under a change of measure as discussed in Section 8.4.4), and $\theta = 1$ is often an appropriate choice since z_t can be seen as a scaling factor.

(We can also have a lognormal parameterisation of the stochastic variance multiplier, e.g.

$$dy_t = \left(\kappa(\theta - z_t) - \frac{1}{2}\eta^2 \right) dt + \eta dU_t \quad \text{and}$$

$$z_t = \min(e^{2y_t}, M^2)$$

but there could be implications as to how easy it is to come up with approximations to swaption prices for purposes of calibration.)

The parameterisation where a blend parameter describes skew can be complemented with stochastic volatility to capture smile. In particular, since we are using a mean reverting stochastic volatility process, it is quite possible to capture a rich set of smiles across different maturities without having to use time-dependent volatility of variance η. After all, the mean reversion accounts for dampening of forward volatility over expiry (as discussed in Chapter 6).

9.3.3 *Parameter-averaging to Approximate the Average Skew*

Going back to the square root process for the stochastic variance multiplier, Andersen and Brotherton-Radcliffe [ABR05] suggested an asymptotic expansion approach to obtain the prices of caplets and swaptions under this model, thus making calibration particularly convenient.

Piterbarg [Pit03c] also described a parameter-averaging technique to obtain an SDE with time-independent parameters, whose terminal distribution is approximately that of the swap rate. We shall give an outline of its application below. (A proof is beyond the scope of this book.)

Let us start with the system of SDEs

$$dz_t = \kappa(\theta - z_t)dt + \eta\sqrt{z_t}dU_t, \quad \text{and}$$

$$dL_i(t) = \mu(\{L_i(t)\}_{i=1}^N, z_t, t)dt + \sqrt{z_t}\{b_i(t)L_i(t)$$

$$+ (1 - b_i(t))L_i(0)\} \sum_{j=1}^M \sigma_{i,j}(t)dW_t^j.$$

We wish to approximate the swap rate via the following SDEs:

$$dz_t = \kappa(\theta - z_t)dt + \eta\sqrt{z_t}dU_t, \quad \text{and}$$

$$dR(t) \approx M(t)dt + \sqrt{z_t}\{B(t)R(t) + (1 - B(t))R(0)\}\sum_{j=1}^{M}s_j(t)dW_t^j.$$

An approach involving matching the volatility and its derivative 'along the forward path' as per Section 9.3.1 gives

$$s_j(t) = \sum_{i=1}^{E}w_i\sigma_{i,j}(t)$$

and

$$B(t) = \sum_{k=1}^{E}\left\{b_k(t)\frac{\sum_{j=1}^{M}\sigma_{k,j}(t)s_j(t)}{\sum_{j=1}^{M}s_j(t)}\right\} \quad \text{as before.}$$

Whereas in the absence of stochastic volatility, swaption pricing involves solving a one-factor PDE, it now involves solving a two-factor PDE, which is much more computationally expensive. This motivates the search for an approximation that yields to swaption pricing via quasi-analytic means.

We now wish to find Λ, β such that

$$dR(t) \approx \sqrt{z_t}\Lambda(\beta R(t) + (1 - \beta)R(0))dW_t \quad \text{and}$$

$$dz_t = \kappa(\theta - z_t)dt + \eta\sqrt{z_t}dU_t$$

under the measure where the numeraire is the annuity (hence zero drift).[7]

Piterbarg [Pit03c] establishes the following parameter-averaging theorem:

Let $f(t,x)$ be a local volatility function and $f_\varepsilon(t,x) = f(t\varepsilon^2, x_0 + (x - x_0)\varepsilon)$ be a rescaling of this function. Further, let

$$dX_t^\varepsilon = f_\varepsilon(t, X_t^\varepsilon)\sqrt{z_t}\sigma(t)dW_t, \quad X_0^\varepsilon = x_0.$$

---

[7]Notice per Section 6.3.3 that this is a modification of the Heston equation and Fourier transform techniques can be applied to obtain the prices of European swaptions.

Then if

$$dY_t^\varepsilon = \bar{f}_\varepsilon(Y_t^\varepsilon)\sqrt{z_t}\sigma(t)dW_t, \quad Y_0^\varepsilon = x_0,$$

where

$$\bar{f}_\varepsilon^2(x) = \int_0^T f_\varepsilon^2 w(t)dt, \quad w(t) = \frac{v^2(t)\sigma^2(t)}{\int_0^T v^2(t)\sigma^2(t)dt}, \quad \text{and}$$

$$v^2(t) = E[z_t(X_\varepsilon(t) - x_0)^2],$$

we have

$$\int_{-\infty}^\infty (E[(Y_T^\varepsilon - K)^+] - E[(X_T^\varepsilon - K)^+])dK = o(\varepsilon^2), \quad \varepsilon \to 0.$$

From this theorem, the effective skew is given by

$$\beta = \int_0^T b(t)w(t)dt,$$

where

$$w(t) = \frac{v^2(t)\sigma^2(t)}{\int_0^T v^2(t)\sigma^2(t)dt}, \quad \text{and} \quad v^2(t) = \theta^2 \int_0^t \sigma^2(s)ds$$

$$+ \theta\eta^2 e^{-\kappa t} \int_0^t \sigma^2(s)\frac{e^{\kappa s} - e^{-\kappa s}}{2\kappa}ds.$$

To see this, let

$$f(t,x) = \frac{1}{x_0}(b(t)x + (1 - b(t)x_0)), \quad x_0 = R_0.$$

Further,

$$f_1(t,x) = f(t,x),$$

giving

$$\bar{f}_1^2(x) = \frac{1}{x_0^2} \int_0^T (b(t)x + (1 - b(t)x_0))^2 w(t)dt.$$

Let us now approximate $\bar{f}_1(x)$ by a function with the same value and slope at $x = x_0$.

Then

$$\bar{f}_1(x_0) = 1, \quad \text{and}$$

$$\frac{d\bar{f}_1}{dx}(x_0) = \frac{\int_0^T b(t)(b(t)x + (1 - b(t)x_0))w(t)dt}{x_0 \left[\int_0^T (b(t)x + (1 - b(t)x_0))^2 w(t)dt\right]^{\frac{1}{2}}} \Bigg|_{x=x_0}$$

$$= \frac{1}{x_0} \int_0^T b(t)w(t)dt.$$

Notice that $\bar{f}_1(x) = \frac{1}{x_0}(\beta x + (1 - \beta)x_0)$ satisfies the above, so $\bar{f}_1(x_0)$ gives the time-independent local volatility, and we obtain $\beta = \int_0^T b(t)w(t)dt$ above.

9.4 Pricing Early Exercise Products

Early exercise features provide for termination of a product prior to its maturity. For example, the callable feature gives a party the right to terminate the product early as per his discretion. Specifically, consider a swap where you receive floating Euribor coupons and pay 4% annual coupons on 1 June of each year from 2010 to 2040. Suppose your counterpart has the right to terminate the swap on each coupon date, starting from 1 June 2011. If interest rates rise, then he would terminate the swap (and hence end any future cashflows) as he can receive a higher fixed rate for a new swap for the remaining term. In this way, callability is valuable to the party given the discretion and disadvantageous to the other party, and tends to be compensated in the product's coupons (e.g. you might have paid 4.5% fixed instead if the swap were non-callable). Callability has been popular due to its facility to engineer payoffs with higher yields under certain circumstances.

But in order to decide whether to exercise the right to terminate the swap, your counterpart would need to know the value of continuation.[8] Only if the continuation value is less than the value from immediate exercise, will it be optimal to exercise.

---

[8]I.e. the conditional expectation of discounted future cashflows, including future exercise opportunities.

On a PDE, there is no complication, since we can determine the conditional expectation of continuation at each node by backward induction from the last cashflow date of the product. So, we have enough information to determine if early exercise is worthwhile on each exercise date. If pricing via Monte Carlo, this can be problematic however, since for a given realised path, we do not have an easy way to determine the continuation value. What we need is an algorithm (even if marginally suboptimal) to determine whether to exercise on a given date based on the values of state variables on each simulated path.

Andersen has come out with a regression-based approach to determine whether early exercise is worthwhile. Longstaff and Schwartz have developed another regression-based approach. We explore these below.

9.4.1 *The Andersen Algorithm*

Andersen set out his approach in [And00]. The idea is that given state variables $\{X_t\}$, we could choose a function $f(\{X_t\})$. We will

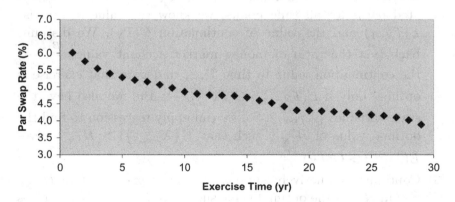

Figure 9.6: Above, we display the optimal exercise boundary for a 30-year Non-Call 1-year (i.e. exercisable after 1-year with maturity in 30 years) euro Bermudan swaption for each of the exercise dates. The level at which the par swap rate needs to be at the exercise dates for exercise to be worthwhile decreases as we get closer to maturity of the Bermudan swaption, as the value of holding (i.e. potential future exercise) decreases. This is based on representative euro data as of early 2011.

then decide to exercise early if $f(\{X_t\}) > H_t$, where H_t is a time-dependent early exercise boundary to be estimated by regression.

As a simple example, suppose we wanted to determine whether our counterpart would exercise the Bermudan option to cancel the swap above. As discussed, it is worth exercising the option only if rates rise. So, a suitable choice of function on coupon dates T_i might be

$$f(\{X_{T_i}\}) = R(T_i, T_N),$$

where $R(T_i, T_N)$ is the par rate for a swap with start date T_i and maturity T_N. (Notice that since our counterpart cannot exercise on non-coupon dates, the function would have to have infinite value on non-coupon dates.) See Figure 9.6 for an example of an estimated optimal exercise boundary for a Bermudan swaption.

The procedure works as follows:

(1) Generate a set of paths via (relatively few, e.g. 1,000) Monte Carlo simulations for all time points of interest, i.e. the exercise dates $T_1, T_2, \ldots, T_{N-1}, T_N$.

(2) Suppose we are at exercise date T_{N-1}. We want to know if it is worth exercising or holding until time T_N. Since we have generated paths for all time points, we know the value of exercise $E(T_{N-1})$ and the value of continuation $C(T_N)$. We discount back (via the ratio of money market account values $\frac{B_{T_{N-1}}}{B_{T_N}}$) the continuation value to time T_{N-1} and note that exercise is optimal only if $E(T_{N-1}) > C(T_N)\frac{B_{T_{N-1}}}{B_{T_N}}$. But we also have the state variables $\{X_{T_{N-1}}\}$. So, we can apply regression to find the optimal value of $H_{T_{N-1}}$ such that $f(\{X_{T_{N-1}}\}) > H_{T_{N-1}}$ gives $E(T_{N-1}) > C(T_N)\frac{B_{T_{N-1}}}{B_{T_N}}$.

(3) Continuing inductively, suppose we are at exercise date T_i, we obtain H_{T_i} as the optimal value such that $f(\{X_{T_i}\}) > H_{T_i}$ gives $E(T_i) > C(T_{i+1})\frac{B_{T_i}}{B_{T_{i+1}}}$.

(4) Having found the exercise boundaries $H_{T_1}, H_{T_2}, \ldots, H_{T_{N-1}}$ in this way, we now generate a set of paths via our usual Monte Carlo approach (using different random variables). On any given

Monte Carlo path, for an exercise date T_i, we simply apply the function $f(\{X_{T_i}\})$ to the state variables X_{T_i} and exercise if and only if the condition $f(\{X_{T_i}\}) > H_{T_i}$ is satisfied.

(5) Finally, we average the values of our payoff across all paths, as per the typical Monte Carlo procedure.

The main disadvantage of the Andersen method is the need for one to choose an appropriate function $f(\{X_t\})$ of the state variables. This is very payoff-dependent, so one must have an intimate understanding of what affects the value of a particular payoff. Further, this approach is hard to apply generically across products in a pricing library, since the function has to be specially tailored to individual payoffs. Nevertheless, an inspired choice can lead to very good convergence properties for the given payoff.

9.4.2 *The Longstaff–Schwartz Algorithm*

Another algorithm for determining whether early exercise is suitable in a Monte Carlo valuation is due to Longstaff and Schwartz [LS01]. The main idea is that we wish to estimate the value of continuation as a simple function of the state variables. So, along each path, we could compare the estimated continuation value with the exercise value, and determine if exercise is optimal. The question in this instance is how to obtain this function of state variables. Longstaff and Schwartz suggest choosing some basis functions and then doing a linear least squares regression to estimate the dependency relation. We describe the algorithm below.

The algorithm:

(1) As in Section 9.4.1, let us start by generating via Monte Carlo a small set of (say 1,000) paths for time points $T_1, T_2, \ldots, T_{N-1}, T_N$.

(2) Suppose we are at time point T_{N-1}. We know the values of state variables $\{X_{T_{N-1}}\}$. We need to choose basis functions $\{f_\alpha\}$, so that $\{f_\alpha(\{X_{T_{N-1}}\})\}$ form the explanatory variables to predict the value of continuation. For example, suppose we have an American option to purchase a stock for strike K on

any date prior to expiry T. Then a relevant state variable $\{X_{T_{N-1}}\} = S_{T_{N-1}}$ could be the value of the stock at time T_{N-1}, and a possible choice of basis functions might be polynomial powers of S_t, i.e. $\{S_t, S_t^2, S_t^3, \ldots\}$ up to the degree of the polynomial desired. (For a Bermudan swaption, a suitable state variable might be the swap rate.)

(3) Based on our paths, we know the value of continuation as seen at time T_{N-1}, namely $C(T_N)\frac{B_{T_{N-1}}}{B_{T_N}}$. So, we regress the values $C(T_N)\frac{B_{T_{N-1}}}{B_{T_N}}$ against the values of the explanatory variables $\{f_\alpha(\{X_{T_{N-1}}\})\}$ to get the coefficients $\beta_{T_{N-1}}^\alpha$ such that $y_{T_{N-1}} = \sum_{\alpha=1}^N \beta_{T_{N-1}}^\alpha f_\alpha(\{X_{T_{N-1}}\})$ gives the best fit (in a linear least-squares sense) to $C(T_N)\frac{B_{T_{N-1}}}{B_{T_N}}$.

(4) We can continue in this way inductively for earlier time points T_i, and hence estimate[9] $\beta_{T_i}^\alpha$ such that $y_{T_i} = \sum_{\alpha=1}^N \beta_{T_i}^\alpha f_\alpha(\{X_{T_i}\})$ gives the best fit to $C(T_{i+1})\frac{B_{T_i}}{B_{T_{i+1}}}$.

(5) Now, armed with our algorithm to predict the value of continuation, we generate a new set of paths via Monte Carlo, and apply $y_{T_i} = \sum_{\alpha=1}^N \beta_{T_i}^\alpha f_\alpha(\{X_{T_i}\})$ along each path to predict the continuation value. Comparing this with the exercise value, we can decide whether to exercise the option along the given path, and hence value the payoff with early exercise features.

Our discussion was extremely rudimentary in merely outlining the ideas involved in the Longstaff–Schwartz algorithm. Of course, in practice, there are more complications. Firstly, the exercise value may not be known from the state variables but may require estimation via the same regression technique above. For example, if exercise leads you to acquire a portfolio of options with a given strike, then it is necessary to compute the value of the options given the state variables. (Typically for many interest rate models, prices of discount bonds at a future time are analytic functions of state variables. However, for some models, analytic formulae for simple options, e.g. swaptions may not exist.)

---

[9]Via linear least squares regression.

Further, the choice of state variables can have a huge bearing on the accuracy of the algorithm, and how suboptimal it would otherwise be. Specifically, when pricing interest rates instruments, it is typical to choose state variables to capture relevant features of the product. For example, a swap rate would capture the overall level of rates up to a certain maturity, whereas having both a long-term rate and a short-term rate would capture the effect of steepening of the curve (particulary relevant to CMS spread products). Sometimes, it might be helpful to have state variables being options, e.g. when pricing a callable Power Reverse Dual Currency (PRDC) (whose underlying is a strip of FX options), using these FX options as state variables could assist convergence. This has however to be balanced with the desire for a sufficiently generic framework which could handle a variety of products, rather than to be required to find an individual set of state variables for each product, which can be extremely inefficient in a production setting.

Finally, it is worth remarking that since we are relying on regression in both the Andersen and Longstaff–Schwartz methods to determine the algorithms for early exercise, these algorithms will always be suboptimal. More worrying is that optimisations tend to be less stable than exact root-finding or analytic approaches. This is particularly true with regard to sensitivities computations, where the typical approach is to bump the market observable, re-price and compute the sensitivity as a numerical derivative. For example, delta is computed via $\frac{F(S+\delta)-F(S)}{\delta}$, where δ is a small perturbation to the underlying S. Since δ is small, dividing by it tends to magnify any numerical errors, which can be particularly troublesome where pricing involves an optimisation. (This is so even if we use the same set of random variables to generate the original scenarios and the bumped scenarios in pricing.)

To this end, a common approach to achieve stable risk is to 'freeze' the exercise boundary when computing sensitivities. So, we do not rerun the regression but use the same exercise boundary in the Andersen approach or the same predicted exercise points (for each path) in the Longstaff–Schwartz approach, and merely apply the above to the paths generated from the bumped market variables.

The following justification for 'freezing' the exercise boundary is attributable to Piterbarg [Pit03c]. Let $V(S) = F(S, B(S))$ be the value of the derivative with underlying S and optimal exercise boundary $B(S)$. Then

$$\frac{\partial V}{\partial S} = \frac{\partial F}{\partial S} + \frac{\partial F}{\partial B}\frac{\partial B}{\partial S}.$$

But since $B(S)$ is an optimal exercise boundary, $\frac{\partial B}{\partial S} = 0$ locally. Thus, we get

$$\frac{\partial V(S)}{\partial S} = \frac{\partial F(S, B(S))}{\partial S}.$$

This means it is alright to 'freeze' the exercise boundary when computing sensitivities, provided it is truly an optimal exercise boundary (or close enough to one in practice).

9.5   Consolidation

9.5.1   *Summary*

This chapter is about the Libor Market Model (LMM), which originated from Brace, Gatarek and Musiela. The main idea is to directly model consecutive Libor rates which span the time period of interest for pricing the financial derivative. From these, we can obtain discount factors for all maturities at any future time. We showed that whereas each Libor rate is a martingale under the measure whose numeraire is the discount bond with maturity being the pay date of that Libor rate, drift terms will be unavoidable if we want to evaluate all Libor rates simultaneously under a single measure. This is necessary for pricing products that depend on the value of cashflows as seen across different time points (e.g. callable products). We then derived the drift for the LMM under the terminal measure (i.e. numeraire is discount bond with maturity being the pay date of the last Libor rate) and the spot Libor measure (the discrete analogue to the money market account). The former gives better convergence since the drift is negative, whilst the latter is better suited to bootstrapping volatilities of market instruments (e.g. caplets, swaptions), since the drift depends only on earlier Libor rates. We next considered how market caplet volatilities can directly be used in the LMM since change of measure does not affect volatilities.

As swaptions are the main options in rates and fast calibration is highly desirable, we proceeded to discuss swaption pricing under the LMM, starting by deriving the volatility part of the SDE for the swap rate. We next considered piecewise-constant (over time) Libor volatilities, and related these to the grid of swaption implied volatilities, showing how we can theoretically recover the entire grid of at-the-money swaption volatilities (provided they are self-consistent) via piecewise-constant Libor volatilities. We further considered an approximation for the at-the-money swaption volatility under the LMM using a 'drift-freeze' approach. We then discussed using multiple Wiener drivers and the sensitivity to correlations of certain products.

Naturally, the next step was to consider extending the LMM to cover skew. We illustrated this with a blended (mix of normal and lognormal) parameterisation of the volatility of each Libor rate, and then showed Piterbarg's derivation of the approximate blend and volatility of the swap rate, by matching the value and slope along the forward path. Thereby, we have reduced the swaption pricing problem to a one-dimensional problem involving the SDE for the swap rate, which admits far more efficient solutions. We then explored an extension to treat stochastic volatility, with the caveat that correlations between the stochastic volatility multiplier and the Wiener components of the Libor rates are zero, to avoid nasty terms appearing in the drift (from change of measure). This presents a framework for both smile and skew. We wrapped up this part by discussing the parameter averaging approach by Piterbarg, which approximates the swap rate process with one involving time-homogeneous parameters for the swap rate. In this way, swaptions can be priced analytically via the blended formula, or via Fourier transform techniques in the presence of a Heston-style stochastic volatility.

Since the LMM is only Markovian in a large number of state variables (basically the number of Libor rates), it is not amenable to

PDE techniques and only Monte Carlo pricing is feasible. We took this opportunity to consider the treatment of early exercise via Monte Carlo. We started with the Andersen algorithm, which involves positing a functional form where early exercise is optimal if a boundary is breached (e.g. if the 10-year swap rate is above some level). The method then involves doing a pre-simulation and using these paths to estimate the boundary. We proceeded to the Longstaff–Schwartz approach which involves coming up with basis functions to predict the value of early exercise and that of continuation. Again, a pre-simulation is done with the generated paths used for regression to determine the coefficients of the value functions for early exercise and for continuation given the choice of basis functions. We finally discussed how freezing the early exercise boundary when running sensitivities calculations is useful for stability, as the Monte Carlo noise in estimating the exercise boundary could swamp the calculations otherwise.

9.5.2   *Exercises*

(1) Suppose that each Libor rate is driven by a separate Wiener process $dL_i(t) = \sigma_i(L_i(t), t)dW_t^i$ (under the measure with numeraire being the discount bond maturing at the pay date of the Libor rate) with correlation structure given by $dW_t^i dW_t^j = \rho_{ij}(t)dt$. Using the same approach as in Section 9.1.1, find the drift of each Libor rate under the terminal measure.

(2) Consider the correlation matrix Ω. We can perform an eigenvector decomposition so that $\Omega = S\Lambda S^T$, where Λ is a diagonal matrix of eigenvalues and S is the eigenvector matrix whose determinant is 1. Suppose now that z is a vector of independent and identically distributed $N(0,1)$ random variates. Show that $x = S\sqrt{D}z$ is a vector whose correlation structure corresponds to Ω.

(3) Consider a lognormal Libor Market Model. For simplicity, assume that Libor rates apply over 1y periods. Take current Libor rates to be flat at 3%. Using the discussion on the volatility triangle in Section 9.2.2 and the swaption approximation in

Section 9.2.3, obtain the forward vol structure given the following grid of lognormal swaption vols.

Expiry/Tenor	1y	2y	3y
1y	20%	18%	15%
2y	16%	14%	
3y	12%		

(4) Consider a two-factor lognormal Libor Market Model. Ignore the drift, so that we can write $dL_t^i = \cdots dt + \sigma_i L_t^i(a_{i1}dW_t^1 + a_{i2}dW_t^2)$, where $a_{i1}^2 + a_{i2}^2 = 1$ and $dW_t^1 dW_t^2 = 0$. Now, let us suppose $a_{i1} = \sin\theta_i$. Find $\mathrm{corr}(dL_i, dL_j)$. What advantage does this representation have if we wish to calibrate correlations?

(5) The Longstaff–Schwartz algorithm involves a choice of basis functions. Suppose we have $n + 1$ dependent variables $\{y_i\}_{i=0}^n$ to fit corresponding to the explanatory variables $\{x_i\}_{i=0}^n$. Show that a polynomial of degree n can pass through all these points. However, by considering the behaviour of such a polynomial, discuss how there is a danger of over-fitting when we use the Longstaff–Schwartz algorithm with polynomial powers that are too high.

10

Long-Dated Foreign Exchange

"Job for life."

Typically, foreign exchange rates, and even more so stock prices, display much higher volatility than interest rates products (e.g. bonds) of short expiry. For ease of modelling, it has thus been convenient to ignore stochastic interest rates for foreign exchange (FX) and equity options of short expiry. More precisely, we can choose a measure with the discount bond of maturity T as numeraire asset, so that the forward price of the asset is a martingale under this measure. In this way, we could model the process for the forward price directly (with the volatility of the forward process already incorporating interest rates volatility).

However, economic conditions have led to the popularity of very long-dated products at least prior to the financial crisis of 2008. For example, US interest rates have tended to be much higher than Japanese interest rates (see Figure 10.1a), implying that USD/JPY[1] forward FX rates should be much lower than spot by no-arbitrage arguments. It is easy to see this: Suppose that you could either deposit \$1 at an annual rate of $r_U = 4\%$ for the next 30 years to get $(1 + r_U)^{30}$, or convert it to $X = ¥90$ and deposit it at an annual rate of $r_J = 2\%$ to obtain $X(1 + r_J)^{30}$. Then since you can agree to a forward FX rate F to convert $\$(1 + r_U)^{30}$ into yen 30 years for now, no arbitrage requires that the forward FX rate for delivery in 30 years' time must be worth $F = X(\frac{1+r_J}{1+r_U})^{30} = ¥50.26$ per dollar.

---

[1]I.e. number of yen per dollar.

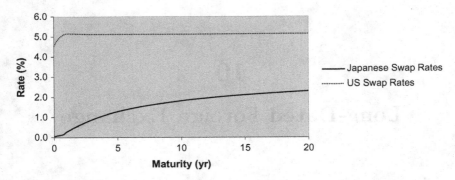

Figure 10.1a: We see here that US dollar rates are much higher than Japanese yen rates even for long maturities. Interest Rates are as of 28 February 2006.
Source: Bloomberg data.

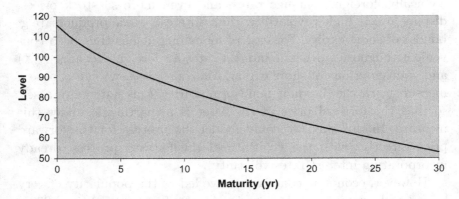

Figure 10.1b: The interest rate differential in Figure 10.1a translates to a steeply downward sloping curve for the USD/JPY forward FX rate as maturity increases. This is still true after the 2008 financial crisis although the difference is less pronounced.
Source: Bloomberg data.

This represents a significant appreciation (increase in value) of the yen as implied by the forward.[2] See Figure 10.1b for an illustration.

But Japanese and international investors find it hard to believe that future USD/JPY FX rates will be at levels implied by the forward FX rate, and are prepared to bet against the realisation of

---

[2] A lower value of USD/JPY corresponds to a stronger yen, since $1 is worth fewer yen.

the forward FX rate. This leads to the prevalence of long-dated FX options benefiting from a weaker yen than implied by the forward, with expiry of 30 years. The product that has evolved as a result is the Power Reverse Dual Currency (PRDC), which comprises a strip of coupons, with payoff at time T (i.e. a coupon date) given by $M \max(X_T - K, 0)$, based on the FX rate X_T, multiplier M and strike K. In addition, these products tend to have embedded early termination features as investors seek higher yields and are prepared to sell optionality to achieve this. For example, callable PRDCs where the issuer can terminate the deal at her discretion are popular, as are PRDC tarns (target redemption notes) where if the total coupons paid reach some level, the deal terminates automatically and the investor is repaid his notional.

On the equities front, confidence in long-term market growth and also the demand of investors with long time horizons,[3] have led to interest in relatively long-dated products, e.g. with maturities of up to 15 years.

In this chapter, we shall see why for long-dated products, it is not appropriate to ignore the stochastic nature of interest rates. In so far as hedging involves considering interest rate risk, interest rates volatilities are a lot more important for very long expiries (than for shorter expiries), and stochastic interest rates affect both forward volatility and terminal correlations of forwards and hence the value of early termination features embedded in long-dated products. The elevated volatilities in interest rates (amongst other assets) following the 2008 financial crisis make it more essential that we do not ignore the modelling of stochastic interest rates.

Whereas this chapter is mainly concerned with long-dated FX, the same concepts apply to long-dated equity products. The two main differences are: (1) Equity volatility tends to be higher than FX volatility and FX is subject to the interest rates of both currencies, so the effect of stochastic interest rates in FX tends to be more

---

[3]E.g. pension funds who have to concern themselves with liabilities when employees retire decades in the future.

significant than in equities. (2) Equity often requires a treatment of discrete dividends, especially in the short end, which can pose a numerical challenge at times. Still, with the similarities, it is not really meaningful to have a separate discussion on long-dated equity products.

10.1   Growth of Interest Rates Volatility With Time

The reason why stochastic interest rates is of particular importance for long-dated FX options is that whereas spot FX volatility grows proportional to the square root of time, interest rate volatility grows much faster with time.

The forward FX rate is defined by

$$F(t,T) = S_t \frac{D^f(t,T)}{D(t,T)},$$

giving (where we are only interested in the vol part):

$$\frac{dF(t,T)}{F(t,T)} = \cdots dt + \frac{dS_t}{S_t} + \frac{dD^f(t,T)}{D^f(t,T)} - \frac{dD(t,T)}{D(t,T)}.$$

Notice how the volatility of the FX forward up to time T comprises the volatility of the spot FX rate, and the volatility of the domestic and foreign discount bonds with maturity T.

Consider the following stochastic differential equation (SDE) for an FX process

$$dS_t = \left(r_t - r_t^f\right) S_t dt + \sigma S_t dW_t.$$

Its solution is

$$S_t = S_0 \exp\left[\left(\int_0^t \left(r_u - r_u^f - \frac{1}{2}\sigma^2\right) du + \sigma W_t\right)\right],$$

so the purely spot FX contribution to log-variance up to time T is $\sigma^2 T$.

Now, consider the following short rate process given by

$$dx_t = -\kappa x_t dt + \lambda dW_t \quad \text{and}$$
$$r_t = \varphi(t) + x_t.$$

From Section 8.2, we know that the value of a discount bond with maturity T as seen at time t is given by

$$D(t, T) = \exp(-A(t, T) - B(t, T)x_t),$$

where $\phi(t) = e^{\int_0^t \kappa(u)du} = e^{\kappa t}$, $\Phi(t) = \int_0^t \frac{du}{\phi(u)} = \int_0^t e^{-\kappa u}du = \frac{1}{\kappa}(1 - e^{-\kappa t})$, so

$$B(t, T) = \phi(t)(\Phi(T) - \Phi(t)) = \frac{1}{\kappa}(1 - e^{-\kappa(T-t)}),$$

giving

$$\frac{dD(t, T)}{D(t, T)} = r_t dt - B(t, T)\lambda dW_t.$$

Then the log-variance up to time T of a discount bond with maturity T is given by

$$\lambda^2 \int_0^T B^2(u, T)du = \frac{\lambda^2}{\kappa^2} \int_0^T (1 - e^{-\kappa(T-u)})^2 du.$$

If we consider the simpler case of zero mean reversion, then we obtain (applying a Taylor expansion):

$$\lim_{\kappa \to 0} \frac{\lambda^2}{\kappa^2} \int_0^T (1 - e^{-\kappa(T-u)})^2 du$$

$$= \lim_{\kappa \to 0} \frac{\lambda^2}{\kappa^2} \int_0^T (1 - 1 + \kappa(T - u) + \cdots)^2 du$$

$$= \lambda^2 \int_0^T (T - u)^2 du$$

$$= \frac{\lambda^2}{3}T^3$$

Notice that as expiry T increases, log-variance for the domestic discount bond grows, proportional to T^3, much faster than for spot FX which grows proportional to T. The same applies for the foreign discount bond. This means that for a long enough expiry, interest rates volatility is likely to be comparable to spot FX volatility. This is notwithstanding interest rates volatility being typically much lower than spot FX volatility (e.g. $\sigma \sim 15\%$ whereas $\lambda \sim 0.75\%$, so that the interest rates variance contribution only gets significant when expiry is over 10 years).

10.1.1   *Effect of Interest Rates on Forward Foreign Exchange Volatility*

Consider again the forward FX rate $F(t,T) = S_t \frac{D^f(t,T)}{D(t,T)}$. As discussed earlier, as expiry increases, the contribution of the stochastic interest rates part becomes ever larger as a proportion of the total forward FX volatility. See Figure 10.2 for an illustration of the volatility from the interest rate and spot components versus the forward FX volatility.

To examine the effect of stochastic interest rates on forward FX volatility, it is useful to consider a specific example of Gaussian rates and a log-normal spot FX process, i.e. the system of SDEs given by the Heath–Jarrow–Morton (HJM) parameterisation

$$dS_t = (r_t - r_t^f)S_t dt + \sigma_S(t)S_t dW_t^S,$$

$$df_d(t,T) = \mu_d(t,T)dt + \sigma_d(t,T)dW_t^d, \quad \text{and}$$

$$df_f(t,T) = \mu_f(t,T)dt + \sigma_f(t,T)dW_t^f,$$

where $dW_t^d dW_t^f = \rho_{df}(t)dt$, $dW_t^d dW_t^S = \rho_{dS}(t)dt$, and $dW_t^f dW_t^S = \rho_{fS}(t)dt$.

Since the domestic discount bond is defined by

$$D(t,T) = e^{-\int_t^T f(t,u)du},$$

its process is given by

$$\frac{dD(t,T)}{D(t,T)} = r_t dt - \int_t^T \sigma_d(t,u)du\, dW_t^d.$$

(Recall that $D(t,T)$ is an asset under the risk-neutral measure.)

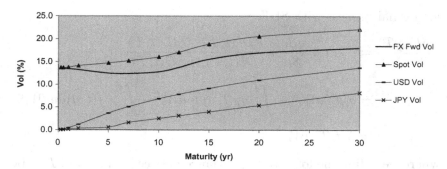

Figure 10.2:   We display here an example of the forward FX vol for USD/JPY across different maturities, together with the spot FX vol and the vol of the US dollar and Japanese yen discount bonds. (This is based on data typical of late 2009.) It should be clear that the forward FX vol is heavily affected by the interest rates vol components as maturity increases. (The spot and rates components do not appear to sum up to the forward FX variance because we have not displayed the correlation components between rates or across rates and spot FX.)

Similarly, we can find the volatility part of the foreign discount bond to be

$$\frac{dD^f(t,T)}{D^f(t,T)} = \cdots dt - \int_t^T \sigma_f(t,u)du dW_t^f.$$

The drift of the foreign discount bond (under the risk-neutral measure) would involve a quanto term (involving the correlation between the foreign rate and spot FX), since it is the product of the foreign discount bond and spot FX (i.e. $D^f(t,T)S_t$) that is actually a domestic asset and hence it is this product that grows at r_t. (An example of how to calculate this quanto term is given in Question 1 of the exercises, where we established that

$$\mu_f(t,T) = \sigma_f(t,T)\left(\int_t^T \sigma_f(t,s)ds - \rho_{fS}(t)\sigma_S(t)\right).$$

The forward FX rate is a martingale under the T-forward measure.[4] Further, as shown earlier in Section 10.1, it follows a

---

[4]With numeraire being the discount bond with maturity T.

lognormal process with SDE

$$\frac{dF(t,T)}{F(t,T)} = \cdots dt + \frac{dS_t}{S_t} + \frac{dD^f(t,T)}{D^f(t,T)} - \frac{dD(t,T)}{D(t,T)}$$

$$= \sigma_S(t)dW_t^S + \int_t^T \sigma_d(t,u)dudW_t^d - \int_t^T \sigma_f(t,u)dudW_t^d$$

$$= \Lambda(t,T)dW_t,$$

where we define the forward log-variance between time t and T to be

$$\int_t^T \Lambda^2(u,T)du = \int_t^T \left\{ \sigma_S^2(u) + \left(\int_u^T \sigma_d(u,v)dv \right)^2 \right.$$

$$+ \left(\int_u^T \sigma_f(u,v)dv \right)^2 \Bigg\} du$$

$$- \int_t^T \left\{ 2\rho_{df}(u) \int_u^T \sigma_d(u,v)dv \int_u^T \sigma_f(u,v)dv \right\} du$$

$$+ \int_t^T \left\{ 2\rho_{dS}(u)\sigma_S(u) \int_u^T \sigma_d(u,v)dv \right.$$

$$- 2\rho_{fS}(u)\sigma_S(u) \int_u^T \sigma_f(u,v)dv \Bigg\} du.$$

This is the case as we are simply summing up the contributions from spot FX, the interest rates components, and correlations between rates as well as across rates and spot FX.

To analyse this further, consider two points in time T_1 and T_2. We shall take the interest rates volatilities as given.[5] We wish to calibrate the implied spot FX volatility $\sigma_S(t)$ to match the implied volatilities Λ_1 and Λ_2 of at-the-money FX options with expiries at T_1 and T_2. Suppose further we make $\sigma_S(t)$ piecewise constant so that

$$\sigma_S(t) = \begin{cases} \sigma_1 & \text{if} \quad 0 < t \leq T_1 \\ \sigma_2 & \text{if} \quad T_1 < t \leq T_2. \end{cases}$$

---

[5]E.g. the result of calibration to swaption prices in their respective currencies.

Consider the forward FX variance from time T_1 to T_2. From above, this is

$$\Sigma_1 = \sigma_2^2(T_2 - T_1) + \int_{T_1}^{T_2} \left\{ \left(\int_u^{T_2} \sigma_d(u,v) dv \right)^2 \right.$$

$$+ \left. \left(\int_u^{T_2} \sigma_f(u,v) dv \right)^2 \right\} du$$

$$-2 \int_{T_1}^{T_2} \rho_{df}(u) \int_u^{T_2} \sigma_d(u,v) dv \int_u^{T_2} \sigma_f(u,v) dv du$$

$$+2\sigma_2 \int_{T_1}^{T_2} \left\{ \rho_{dS}(u) \int_u^{T_2} \sigma_d(u,v) dv - \rho_{fS}(u) \int_u^{T_2} \sigma_f(u,v) dv \right\} du.$$

Calibrating to at-the-money options with expiries T_1 and T_2 gives

$$\Lambda_1^2 T_1 = \sigma_1^2 T_1 + \int_0^{T_1} \left\{ \left(\int_u^{T_1} \sigma_d(u,v) dv \right)^2 + \left(\int_u^{T_1} \sigma_f(u,v) dv \right)^2 \right\} du$$

$$-2 \int_0^{T_1} \rho_{df}(u) \int_u^{T_1} \sigma_d(u,v) dv \int_u^{T_1} \sigma_f(u,v) dv du$$

$$+2\sigma_1 \int_0^{T_1} \left\{ \rho_{dS}(u) \int_u^{T_1} \sigma_d(u,v) dv \right.$$

$$\left. - \rho_{fS}(u) \int_u^{T_1} \sigma_f(u,v) dv \right\} du \qquad (*)$$

and

$$\Lambda^2 T_2 = \sigma_1^2 T_1 + \sigma_2^2(T_2 - T_1) + \int_0^{T_2} \left\{ \left(\int_u^{T_2} \sigma_d(u,v) dv \right)^2 \right.$$

$$+ \left. \left(\int_u^{T_2} \sigma_f(u,v) dv \right)^2 \right\} du$$

$$-2 \int_0^{T_2} \rho_{df}(u) \int_u^{T_2} \sigma_d(u,v) dv \int_u^{T_2} \sigma_f(u,v) dv du$$

$$+ 2\sigma_1 \int_0^{T_1} \left\{ \rho_{dS}(u) \int_u^{T_2} \sigma_d(u,v)dv \right.$$

$$\left. - \rho_{fS}(u) \int_u^{T_2} \sigma_f(u,v)dv \right\} du$$

$$+ 2\sigma_2 \int_{T_1}^{T_2} \left\{ \rho_{dS}(u) \int_u^{T_2} \sigma_d(u,v)dv \right.$$

$$\left. - \rho_{fS}(u) \int_u^{T_2} \sigma_f(u,v)dv \right\} du.$$

Thus, if instead we had no stochastic interest rates, the forward variance from time T_1 to T_2 is

$$\Sigma_2 = \Lambda_2^2 T_2 - \Lambda_1^2 T_1$$

$$= \sigma_2^2 (T_2 - T_1) + \int_0^{T_2} \left\{ \left(\int_u^{T_2} \sigma_d(u,v)dv \right)^2 + \left(\int_u^{T_2} \sigma_f(u,v)dv \right)^2 \right.$$

$$\left. - 2\rho_{df}(u) \int_u^{T_2} \sigma_d(u,v)dv \int_u^{T_2} \sigma_f(u,v)dv \right\} du$$

$$- \int_0^{T_1} \left\{ \left(\int_u^{T_1} \sigma_d(u,v)dv \right)^2 + \left(\int_u^{T_1} \sigma_f(u,v)dv \right)^2 \right.$$

$$\left. - 2\rho_{df}(u) \int_u^{T_1} \sigma_d(u,v)dv \int_u^{T_1} \sigma_f(u,v)dv \right\} du$$

$$+ 2\sigma_1 \int_0^{T_1} \left\{ \rho_{dS}(u) \int_{T_1}^{T_2} \sigma_d(u,v)dv - \rho_{fS}(u) \int_{T_1}^{T_2} \sigma_f(u,v)dv \right\} du$$

$$+ 2\sigma_2 \int_{T_1}^{T_2} \left\{ \rho_{dS}(u) \int_u^{T_2} \sigma_d(u,v)dv - \rho_{fS}(u) \int_u^{T_2} \sigma_f(u,v)dv \right\} du$$

being a simple difference of the two variances for expiries T_1 and T_2.

We see then that the presence of stochastic interest rates will lead to higher forward variance if the following condition applies:

$$\Sigma_1 - \Sigma_2 = - \int_0^{T_1} \left\{ \left(\int_u^{T_2} \sigma_d(u,v)dv \right)^2 + \left(\int_u^{T_2} \sigma_f(u,v)dv \right)^2 \right.$$

$$- 2\rho_{df}(u) \int_u^{T_2} \sigma_d(u,v)dv \int_u^{T_2} \sigma_f(u,v)dv \Bigg\} du$$

$$+ \int_0^{T_1} \left\{ \left(\int_u^{T_1} \sigma_d(u,v)dv \right)^2 + \left(\int_u^{T_1} \sigma_f(u,v)dv \right)^2 \right.$$

$$- 2\rho_{df}(u) \int_u^{T_1} \sigma_d(u,v)dv \int_u^{T_1} \sigma_f(u,v)dv \Bigg\} du$$

$$- 2\sigma_1 \int_0^{T_1} \left\{ \rho_{dS}(u) \int_{T_1}^{T_2} \sigma_d(u,v)dv \right.$$

$$- \rho_{fS}(u) \int_{T_1}^{T_2} \sigma_f(u,v)dv \Bigg\} du$$

$$> 0.$$

Further, we see that equation (*) above is a quadratic equation in σ_1. Thus, we have

$$\sigma_1 = \frac{-b + \sqrt{b^2 + T_1 c}}{T_1}$$

where

$$b = \int_0^{T_1} \left\{ \rho_{dS}(u) \int_u^{T_1} \sigma_d(u,v)dv - \rho_{fS}(u) \int_u^{T_1} \sigma_f(u,v)dv \right\} du, \quad \text{and}$$

$$c = \left(\Lambda_1^2 T_1 - \int_0^{T_1} \left\{ \left(\int_u^{T_1} \sigma_d(u,v)dv \right)^2 + \left(\int_u^{T_1} \sigma_f(u,v)dv \right)^2 \right. \right.$$

$$- 2\rho_{df}(u) \int_u^{T_1} \sigma_d(u,v)dv \int_u^{T_1} \sigma_f(u,v)dv \Bigg\} du \Bigg).$$

Notice that if $\rho_{dS}(u) = 0$ and $\rho_{fS}(u) > 0$, then $b < 0$, so σ_1 increases as $\rho_{fS}(u)$ increases; whereas if $\rho_{fS}(u) = 0$ and $\rho_{dS}(u) < 0$, then $b < 0$, so σ_1 increases as $\rho_{dS}(u)$ decreases. So, typically, a higher correlation between the foreign rate and spot FX processes increases forward volatility, whilst a more negative correlation between the domestic rate and spot FX processes increases forward volatility.

The effect of the domestic/spot and foreign/spot correlations on forward volatilities has significant implications for the prices of callable products in long-dated FX, since it means if we increase correlation between the foreign rate and spot FX process, the values of options at future times will increase and the value of the feature to terminate the product will correspondingly increase.

10.1.2 *Stochastic Interest Rates and Terminal Foreign Exchange Correlation*

Let us now examine the correlation between the spot FX S_t and forward FX rate $F(t, T) = S_t \frac{D^f(t,T)}{D(t,T)}$. We have

$$\text{cov}(S_t, F(t,T)) = E\left[S_t^2 \frac{D^f(t,T)}{D(t,T)}\right] - E[S_t]E\left[S_t \frac{D^f(t,T)}{D(t,T)}\right],$$

$$\text{var}(F(t,T)) = E\left[S_t^2 \left(\frac{D^f(t,T)}{D(t,T)}\right)^2\right] - E^2\left[S_t \frac{D^f(t,T)}{D(t,T)}\right], \quad \text{and}$$

$$\text{corr}(S_t, F(t,T)) = \frac{\text{cov}(S_t, F(t,T))}{\sqrt{\text{var}(S_t)\text{var}(F(t,T))}}.$$

If interest rates were not correlated to spot, then we get

$$\text{cov}(S_t, F(t,T)) = (E[S_t^2] - E^2[S_t])E\left[\frac{D^f(t,T)}{D(t,T)}\right]$$

$$= \text{var}(S_t)E\left[\frac{D^f(t,T)}{D(t,T)}\right]$$

and

$$\text{corr}(S_t, F(t,T)) = \sqrt{\frac{\text{var}(S_t)}{\text{var}(F(t,T))}} E\left[\frac{D^f(t,T)}{D(t,T)}\right].$$

Of course if further interest rates were not stochastic, we obtain

$$\text{var}(F(t,T)) = (E[S_t^2] - E^2[S_t]) \left(\frac{D^f(t,T)}{D(t,T)}\right)^2$$

$$= \text{var}(S_t) \left(\frac{D^f(t,T)}{D(t,T)}\right)^2 \quad \text{and}$$

$$\text{cov}(S_t, F(t,T)) = \text{var}(S_t) \frac{D^f(t,T)}{D(t,T)},$$

simplifying to $\text{corr}(S_t, F(t,T)) = 100\%$ as expected.

But otherwise, the terminal correlation between the spot FX and FX forward will decrease as a result of stochastic interest rates. This has implications for the prices of long-dated FX products with path-dependant early termination features. For example, consider a trigger PRDC which terminates (i.e. redeems) if spot FX is above some level (e.g. USD/JPY spot of 100) as seen at yearly intervals starting 3 years in the future. Notice that the value of continuation is for a strip of FX options, and it is dependent on forward FX instead. So, effectively, we need to evaluate the effect of termination by a trigger in light of the values of forward FX rates vis-à-vis spot FX. Similarly, for a tarn,[6] we need to evaluate the effect of the current coupon (from spot FX) being large enough to reach the target and hence terminate the deal, versus the value of future coupons (dependent on forward FX).

10.2 Effect of Interest Rates on Forward Foreign Exchange Skew

Stochastic interest rates form a significant part of the volatility of the forward FX process, especially for long maturities. Not surprisingly, the choice of the processes for interest rates affects the skew of the forward FX process, in conjunction with the process for spot FX.

As discussed in Chapter 8, analytical tractability is a very important consideration for the choice of the process for interest rates.

---

[6]Described in the introduction to this chapter.

Specifically, it is very useful to be able to obtain the prices of discount bonds at a future date as a (quasi-)analytic function of state variables at that date. To this end, Gaussian interest rates models are popular. Whereas it is also possible to posit a Cheyette framework for interest rates, that comes at the expense of one additional state variable. This is not the preferred choice in long-dated FX modelling because an additional state variable increases computation time and takes us out of the realm of PDEs (which can cope with only up to three factors).

Furthermore, Gaussian interest rates are justifiable in the context of long-dated FX modelling, since typically the main reason for introducing stochastic interest rates is its implications for forward FX volatility and terminal correlation of FX forwards vis-à-vis the FX spot. The intricacies of interest rates modelling would probably only unnecessarily complicate things, since we have to finally calibrate spot FX vols, so that the observed forward FX skew is recovered. Given this preference for Gaussian interest rates processes in long-dated FX modelling, we shall investigate its implications for forward FX skew below.

10.2.1　*Gaussian Interest Rates and Forward Foreign Exchange Skew*

As can be seen in Section 10.1.1, Gaussian interest rates lead to the process for discount bonds being lognormal. Specifically, if we posit the following HJM parameterisation

$$df_d(t, T) = \mu_d(t, T)dt + \sigma_d(t, T)dW_t^d$$

for the domestic forward rate, we get the following SDE for the process for the domestic discount bond

$$\frac{dD(t, T)}{D(t, T)} = r_t dt - \int_t^T \sigma_d(t, u)du dW_t^d,$$

and something similar for the vol part of the SDE for the foreign discount bond.

Now, consider the following system of SDEs defining the spot FX rate:

$$dS_t = (r_t - r_t^f)S_t dt + \sigma_S(S_t, t)S_t dW_t^S,$$

$$df_d(t, T) = \mu_d(t, T)dt + \sigma_d(t, T)dW_t^d, \quad \text{and}$$

$$df_f(t, T) = \mu_f(t, T)dt + \sigma_f(t, T)dW_t^f,$$

where $dW_t^d dW_t^f = \rho_{df}(t)dt$, $dW_t^d dW_t^S = \rho_{dS}(t)dt$, and $dW_t^f dW_t^S = \rho_{fS}(t)dt$.

The forward FX rate is defined by

$$F(t, T) = S_t \frac{D^f(t, T)}{D(t, T)},$$

so

$$\frac{dF(t, T)}{F(t, T)} = \cdots dt + \frac{dS_t}{S_t} + \frac{dD^f(t, T)}{D^f(t, T)} - \frac{dD(t, T)}{D(t, T)}.$$

We have seen in Section 10.1.1 that if spot FX follows a lognormal process (i.e. $\sigma_S(S_t, t) = \sigma_S(t)$), then the forward FX rate also follows a lognormal process.

We have further seen in Section 5.3.4 that we could induce skew on spot FX by positing the following CEV parametric form

$$\sigma_S(S_t, t) = \sigma_S(t)S_t^{\beta(t)-1},$$

where $\beta(t) = 1$ corresponds to a lognormal model whereas $\beta(t) = 0$ corresponds to a normal model, so that the lower the value of $\beta(t)$ the more pronounced the skew (i.e. higher lognormal volatility of spot FX for lower strikes versus higher strikes).

What are the implications of this for the skew of the forward FX rate?

Since Gaussian interest rates imply a lognormal contribution to the forward FX rate, it follows that typically they would dilute the skew contribution from spot FX, i.e. if we posit a similar parametric form of the volatility for forward FX[7]

$$\sigma_F(F_t, t) = \sigma_F(t) F_t^{b(t)-1},$$

then skew dilution will imply $b(t)$ is closer to 1 than $\beta(t)$.

Since typically, we observe a downward sloping vol skew in USD/JPY and AUD/JPY (the currency pairs for which long-dated FX products are most popular), i.e. $b(t) < 1$, to fit the markets we require $\beta(t) < b(t)$. For emerging market pairs however (e.g. USD/BRL), an upward sloping vol skew is more common, i.e. $b(t) > 1$ and we will require $\beta(t) > b(t)$. Figure 10.3 illustrates how stochastic rates dilute the effective skew of the forward FX.

For the interested reader, Piterbarg [Pit05b] has a rather interesting approach to skew averaging to calibrate spot FX skew given forward FX skew and Gaussian interest rates.

10.2.2   *Calibration of Local Foreign Exchange Volatility With Stochastic Interest Rates*

Given our discussion in the beginning of Section 10.2, when modelling long-dated FX products, it is typical to go for Gaussian

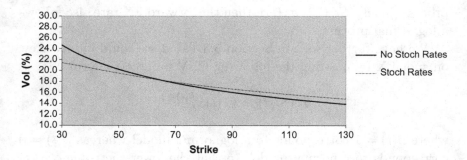

Figure 10.3:   Above we illustrate the dilution of the 20y vol skew in the presence of stochastic interest rates. We have chosen volatilities such that the at-the-money forward vol (at strike 65) is the same, and assume that spot FX follows a CEV process with beta of 0.3 in both cases. Representative parameters (yen rates of 2%, dollar rates of 4%, yen mean rev of 0.5%, yen vol of 0.5%, dollar mean rev of 2.5%, dollar vol of 1%, dollar-yen rates corr of 25%, yen-spot corr of 0%, and dollar-spot corr of 15%) are used.

---

[7]Obtained via a moments matching approach to recover the prices of FX options from our stochastic interest rates and FX model.

interest rates. Whereas the CEV framework for spot FX was useful in Section 10.2.1 to illustrate how Gaussian interest rates affect forward FX skew, it is not really ideal for long-dated FX. In particular, absorption of spot FX at zero has non-zero probability. This is clearly problematic (since currencies should not be worth zero) and the best practical example demonstrating the issue is a product which depends on 1/FX. (Such products actually exist: There used to be interest in some USD/JPY products that involve paying say ¥100 for \$1 if spot USD/JPY S_T is above 100 at time T, and paying ¥100 per dollar applied to a notional of \$$\frac{100}{S_T}$ otherwise.)

We have specified a system of SDEs involving Gaussian interest rates and non-parametric local volatility for spot FX in its full generality in Section 10.2.1. Some form of local volatility for spot FX used to be popular because the dependence on three state variables allows for pricing on a PDE (until subsequent interest in the implications of stochastic volatility for forward FX took hold).

But how can we calibrate our local volatility model for spot FX in order to match the observed smile of forward FX as implied by the options markets? It turns out that Bloch and Nakashima [BN08] have presented a rather neat solution if we posit that local volatility is piecewise constant. We consider this below.

Let us start with Tanaka's formula and we note from Section 5.1.2 that applying it to the price of a call option $C(K,T) = E[e^{-\int_0^t r_u du}(S_t - K)^+]$, we obtain

$$
\begin{aligned}
dC(K,t) = E\,\Big[&-r_t^f e^{-\int_0^t r_u du}(S_t - K)^+ \\
&+ e^{-\int_0^t r_u du} 1_{\{S_t > K\}}\big(r_t - r_t^f\big)K \Big]\, dt \\
&+ \frac{1}{2}\frac{\partial^2 C}{\partial K^2}(K,t)\sigma^2(K,t)K^2 dt.
\end{aligned}
$$

Thus, we get

$$
\sigma^2(K,t) = 2\frac{\dfrac{\partial C(K,t)}{\partial t} - \zeta}{\dfrac{\partial^2 C}{\partial K^2}(K,t)K^2}
$$

where

$$\zeta = E\left[-r_t^f e^{-\int_0^t r_u du}(S_t - K)^+ - e^{-\int_0^t r_u du}1_{\{S_t > K\}}(r_t - r_t^f)K\right].$$

If interest rates are deterministic, Dupire's formula simplifies to

$$\sigma^2(K,t) = 2\frac{\frac{\partial C}{\partial t}(K,t) + r_t^f C(K,t) + \frac{\partial C}{\partial K}(K,t)\left(r_t - r_t^f\right)K}{\frac{\partial^2 C}{\partial K^2}(K,t)K^2},$$

which is easily computed from prices of traded options.

We want to relate the FX local volatility under stochastic interest rates $\sigma_S(S_t, t)$ to the FX local volatility under deterministic rates $\sigma_D(S_t, t)$, since the latter is easily obtained from Dupire's formula above. Bloch and Nakashima show that if we evaluate $\frac{\partial}{\partial t}\text{var}(\log \frac{S_t}{S_0})$, some manipulation of terms yields the relationship

$$\sigma_S^2(K,t) = \sigma_D^2(K,t) + 2\,\text{cov}\left(r_t^f, \log F(t,t)|S_t = K\right)$$
$$- 2\text{cov}(r_t, \log F(t,t)|S_t = K).$$

where $F(t,T)$ is the *FX* forward with maturity T as seen at time t.

Let us now define $\sigma_S(S_t, t)$ as piecewise constant over time intervals $(T_{i-1}, T_i]$, $i = 1, \ldots, N$. Then we obtain for maturity T_i:

$$\sigma_S^2(K,T_i) = \sigma_D^2(K,T_i) + 2\sum_{j=1}^{i}\sigma_S(K,T_i)\int_{T_{j-1}}^{T_j}\rho_{fS}(u)\gamma_f(u,T_i)du$$

$$- 2\int_0^{T_i}\gamma_f(u,T_i)\Gamma_f(u,T_i)du$$

$$- 2\sum_{j=1}^{i}\sigma_S(K,T_i)\int_{T_{j-1}}^{T_j}\rho_{dS}(u)\gamma_d(u,T_i)du$$

$$- 2\int_0^{T_i}\gamma_d(u,T_i)\Gamma_d(u,T_i)du$$

$$+ 2\int_0^{T_i}\rho_{df}(u)\gamma_d(u,T_i)\Gamma_f(u,T_i)du$$

$$+ 2\int_0^{T_i}\rho_{df}(u)\gamma_f(u,T_i)\Gamma_d(u,T_i)du,$$

where $\gamma_{d,f}(t,T) = \sigma_{d,f}(t)e^{-\int_t^T \kappa_{d,f}(u)du}$, and

$$\Gamma_{d,f}(t,T) = \int_t^T \gamma_{d,f}(t,u)du.$$

Notice how we can rewrite the above as a quadratic equation in $\sigma_S(K,T_i)$, namely

$$a\sigma_S^2(K,T_i) + b\sigma_S(K,T_i) + c = 0,$$

where

$a = 1,$

$$b = -2\int_{T_{i-1}}^{T_i} \rho_{fS}(u)\gamma_f(u,T_i)du + 2\int_{T_{i-1}}^{T_i} \rho_{dS}(u)\gamma_d(u,T_i)du, \quad \text{and}$$

$$c = -\sigma_D^2(K,T_i) - 2\sum_{j=1}^{i-1}\sigma_S(K,T_i)\int_{T_{j-1}}^{T_j} \rho_{fS}(u)\gamma_f(u,T_i)du$$

$$+ 2\int_0^{T_i} \gamma_f(u,T_i)\Gamma_f(u,T_i)du$$

$$+ 2\sum_{j=1}^{i-1}\sigma_S(K,T_i)\int_{T_{j-1}}^{T_j} \rho_{dS}(u)\gamma_d(u,T_i)du$$

$$+ 2\int_0^{T_i} \gamma_d(u,T_i)\Gamma_d(u,T_i)du$$

$$- 2\int_0^{T_i} \rho_{df}(u)\gamma_d(u,T_i)\Gamma_f(u,T_i)du$$

$$- 2\int_0^{T_i} \rho_{df}(u)\gamma_f(u,T_i)\Gamma_d(u,T_i)du.$$

We could thus bootstrap $\sigma_S(K,T_i)$ by solving the quadratic equation for all strikes K at each point in time T_i, $i = 1,\ldots,N$, and hence obtain the local volatility $\sigma_S(S_t,t)$ for the spot FX process.

10.2.3   *The Pricing Partial Differential Equation*

The system of SDEs for local volatility spot FX and Gaussian interest rates as below

$$dS_t = (r_t - r_t^f)S_t dt + \sigma_S(S_t, t)S_t dW_t^S, \quad z_t = \log S_t;$$

$$dx_t = -\kappa_d(t)x_t dt + \sigma_d(t)dW_t^d, \quad r_t = \phi_d(t) + x_t;$$

$$dy_t = (-\rho_{fS}(t)\sigma_f(t)\sigma_S(S_t, t) - \kappa_f(t)y_t)dt + \sigma_f(t)dW_t^f,$$

$$r_t^f = \phi_f(t) + y_t; \quad \text{and}$$

$$dW_t^d dW_t^f = \rho_{df}(t)dt, \quad dW_t^d dW_t^S = \rho_{dS}(t)dt,$$

$$dW_t^f dW_t^S = \rho_{fS}(t)dt$$

gives rise to the following PDE for the price of a derivative V_t:

$$\frac{\partial V_t}{\partial t} + \left(\phi_d(t) + x_t - \phi_f(t) - y_t - \frac{1}{2}\sigma_S^2(S_t, t) \right) \frac{\partial V_t}{\partial z_t}$$

$$+ \frac{1}{2}\sigma_S^2(S_t, t)\frac{\partial^2 V_t}{\partial z_t^2} - \kappa_d(t)x_t\frac{\partial V_t}{\partial x_t} + \frac{1}{2}\sigma_d^2(t)\frac{\partial^2 V_t}{\partial x_t^2}$$

$$- (\rho_{fS}(t)\sigma_f(t)\sigma_S(S_t, t) + \kappa_f(t)y_t)\frac{\partial V_t}{\partial y_t} + \frac{1}{2}\sigma_f^2(t)\frac{\partial^2 V_t}{\partial y_t^2}$$

$$+ \rho_{df}(t)\sigma_d(t)\sigma_f(t)\frac{\partial^2 V_t}{\partial x_t \partial y_t} + \rho_{dS}(t)\sigma_d(t)\sigma_S(S_t, t)\frac{\partial^2 V_t}{\partial x_t \partial z_t}$$

$$+ \rho_{fS}(t)\sigma_f(t)\sigma_S(S_t, t)\frac{\partial^2 V_t}{\partial y_t \partial z_t} = (\phi_d(t) + x_t)V_t.$$

Being a three-factor PDE, the Craig–Sneyd ADI scheme [CS88] discussed briefly in Section 7.2.2 provides a practical and effective solution.

However, since in long-dated FX, expiries involved tend to be long (e.g. 30 years), if there is a significant interest rate differential between the two currencies, the forward FX rate can be very different from the spot FX rate with the differential growing with time, so that it may be necessary to construct a large grid for convergence. We could go for a transformation of variables that is driftless and has standard deviation of a Wiener process, however that could lead to numerical problems as evaluating numerical derivatives may be necessary.

A simpler approach is to scale based on typical levels of interest rates to hopefully neutralise (or at least reduce) the drift over the maturity. For example, if $\bar{r}$ is a representative domestic rate, $\bar{r}^f$ is a representative foreign rate and $\bar{\sigma}_S$ is a representative spot FX value up to the maturity of the deal, then a change of variable

$$\varsigma_t = \frac{z_t - \left(\bar{r} - \bar{r}^f - \frac{1}{2}\bar{\sigma}^2\right)t}{\bar{\sigma}\sqrt{t}}$$

could help improve convergence on a grid of the same size.

Another transformation to kill off the correlation components (if possible) and hence remove cross terms (for which we generally do not apply any implicit treatment) will improve upon stability as well.

10.3 Stochastic Foreign Exchange Volatility and Stochastic Interest Rates

In Chapters 5 to 7, we explored the implications of stochastic versus local volatility for the dynamics of forward smile for equities and foreign exchange. In particular, the smile under a local volatility model can sometimes flatten out over time, whereas that under a stochastic volatility model preserves its shape. In Chapter 8, we explained how forward volatility is important when pricing products with early exercise features, since we need to consider the value of options starting at different points in time. In Section 10.2, we have explained that for long-dated FX, as expiry increases the contribution of stochastic interest rates can become a lot more important to the dynamics of the forward FX rate. However, obviously adding stochastic volatility would better explain behaviour for shorter expiries, and hence improve overall capture of the model dynamics.

To this end, there has been interest in adding stochastic volatility to the spot FX process, giving the following system of SDEs:

$$dS_t = \left(r_t - r_t^f\right)S_t dt + \sigma_S(t)\sqrt{z_t}S_t dW_t^S,$$

$$df_d(t,T) = \mu_d(t,T)dt + \sigma_d(t,T)dW_t^d,$$

$$df_f(t,T) = \mu_f(t,T)dt + \sigma_f(t,T)dW_t^f, \quad \text{and}$$

$$dz_t = \kappa(1 - z_t)dt + \eta\sqrt{z_t}dW_t^z,$$

where

$$dW_t^d dW_t^f = \rho_{df}(t)dt, \quad dW_t^d dW_t^S = \rho_{dS}(t)dt,$$

$$dW_t^f dW_t^S = \rho_{fS}(t)dt, \quad dW_t^S dW_t^z = \rho_{Sz}(t)dt.$$

(Usually, we can treat $dW_t^d dW_t^z = dW_t^f dW_t^z = 0$.)

This gives us a four factor model which is not amenable to solution by PDEs, so we will have to accept the implications (in terms of stability of sensitivities) of treating early exercise via Monte Carlo.

An important question is how we can efficiently calibrate this model to recover the prices of FX options. After all, it would be prohibitively expensive if we have to calibrate our model via Monte Carlo pricing of FX options. We explore this next.

10.3.1   *Calibration via Fourier Transforms*

We note from Section 6.3.3 that in the absence of stochastic interest rates, the price of an FX option under a stochastic volatility model can be obtained via Fourier transform techniques. Can we utilise this somehow?

The following idea is due to Andreasen [Andr06]. Suppose we instead define the system of SDEs

$$dS_t = \left(r_t - r_t^f\right)S_t dt + \sigma_S(t)S_t(dW_t^x + \sqrt{z_t}dW_t^y),$$

$$df_d(t,T) = \mu_d(t,T)dt + \sigma_d(t,T)dW_t^d,$$

$$df_f(t,T) = \mu_f(t,T)dt + \sigma_f(t,T)dW_t^f, \quad \text{and}$$

$$dz_t = \kappa(1 - z_t)dt + \eta\sqrt{z_t}dW_t^z,$$

where

$$dW_t^d dW_t^f = \rho_{df}(t)dt, \quad dW_t^d dW_t^x = \rho_{dS}(t)dt,$$

$$dW_t^f dW_t^x = \rho_{fS}(t)dt, \quad dW_t^y dW_t^z = \rho_{yz}dt,$$

$$dW_t^x dW_t^z = dW_t^d dW_t^y = dW_t^f dW_t^y = dW_t^x dW_t^y = 0.$$

Note we now have split the Wiener process for spot FX into two component processes, with one correlated to the rates processes and another correlated to the stochastic volatility process. In this way, we have the value of spot at time T given by

$$S_T = \frac{S_0 D^f(0,T)}{D(0,T)}$$

$$\bullet \exp\left(-\frac{1}{2}\int_0^T \Lambda^2(u)du + \int_0^T \Lambda(u)dV_u - \frac{1}{2}\int_0^T \sigma_S^2(u)z_u du\right.$$

$$\left. + \int_0^T \sigma_S(u)\left(\rho_{yz}dV_u^1 + \sqrt{1-\rho_{yz}^2}dV_u^2\right)\right),$$

where

$$\Lambda^2(t) = \sigma_S^2(t) + \left(\int_t^T \sigma_d(t,v)dv\right)^2 + \left(\int_t^T \sigma_f(t,v)dv\right)^2$$

$$- 2\rho_{df}(t)\int_t^T \sigma_d(t,v)dv\int_t^T \sigma_f(t,v)dv$$

$$+ 2\rho_{dS}(t)\sigma_S(t)\int_t^T \sigma_d(t,v)dv - 2\rho_{fS}(t)\sigma_S(t)\int_t^T \sigma_f(t,v)dv,$$

and V_t, $V_t^1 = W_t^z$, V_t^2 are Wiener processes with $dV_t dV_t^1 = dV_t dV_t^2 = dV_t^1 dV_t^2 = 0$.

We note that we have the product of a lognormal component and a Heston component, both of which are independent.

We obtain

$$E^T\left[\left(\frac{S_T D(0,T)}{S_0 D^f(0,T)}\right)^\alpha\right] = e^{-\frac{1}{2}(\alpha-\alpha^2)\int_0^T \Lambda^2(u)du} E^T[e^{\alpha(x_T-x_0)}]$$

$$= H_{LN}(\alpha)H_{SV}(\alpha),$$

where

$$dx_t = -\frac{1}{2}\sigma_S^2(t)z_t dt + \sigma_S(t)\sqrt{z_t}(\rho_{yz}dV_t^1 + \sqrt{1-\rho_{yz}^2}dV_t^2)$$

and we have defined $H_{LN}(\alpha) = e^{-\frac{1}{2}(\alpha-\alpha^2)\int_0^T \Lambda^2(u)du}$, and $H_{SV}(\alpha) = E^T[e^{\alpha(x_T-x_0)}]$ is as per Section 6.3.3.

The price of European options is then given by

$$D(0,T)E^T[(S_T-K)^+]$$
$$= S_0 D^f(0,T) - D(0,T)\frac{K}{2\pi}$$
$$\times \int_{-\infty}^{\infty} \frac{e^{(-ik+1/2)\log\left(\frac{S_0 D^f(0,T)}{KD(0,T)}\right)}}{k^2+1/4}\hat{q}_{LN}(k)\hat{q}_{SV}(k)dk,$$

where

$$\hat{q}_{LN}(k) = H_{LN}\left(ik-\frac{1}{2}\right), \quad \text{and}$$

$$\hat{q}_{SV}(k) = H_{SV}\left(ik-\frac{1}{2}\right)$$

(by following similar logic to Section 6.3.3).

In this way, given the volatilities of interest rates and their correlations vis-à-vis spot FX, we have a convenient method to calibrate our remaining parameters to match the prices of FX options, and hence relate our model to market observables.

10.4   Consolidation

10.4.1   *Summary*

The context of our discussion is the long-dated FX markets, which came about largely due to interest rate differentials amongst various currencies. In particular, since Japanese yen interest rates tend to be much lower than US dollar interest rates, the FX forward implies a significant appreciation of the yen in 30 years' time, which investors are happy to bet against via structured notes, giving rise to the

PRDC market. Whereas interest rates products (e.g. bonds) tend to be much less volatile than equities and FX over short maturities, their variance grows proportional to T^3, whereas spot equity/FX variance grows proportional to T, so that the interest rates components can contribute significantly to an FX forward variance over a sufficiently long maturity (say over 10 years).

We proceeded to consider how stochastic interest rates affect the forward volatility of FX. In particular, we considered Gaussian interest rates and a lognormal spot FX process and calibrated spot FX volatilities to target variances at expiries T_1 and T_2; we then showed that the forward variance from T_1 to T_2 can be significantly different to the case of zero interest rates volatility. We further noted that correlations between spot FX and the interest rates processes affect this forward FX variance. This is relevant because callable products depend on forward volatility. We next explored how stochastic interest rates affect the terminal correlation of forward FX rates of different maturities. It is clear that in the absence of stochastic interest rates, the terminal correlations must be 100%. This again is relevant in that the prices of products with certain early termination features (e.g. triggers and tarns) are influenced by terminal correlations.

Thereafter, we proceeded to consider the implications of stochastic interest rates on forward FX skew. In particular, in a local volatility framework for spot FX, if we consider a CEV parameterisation, skew is generated by a beta of less than 1 (sub-lognormal). We noted that Gaussian interest rates (typically assumed for simplicity) contribute lognormally to the forward FX rate, so that they dilute the skew of the spot FX process. We further discussed an approach to calibration of local volatilities for spot FX in the presence of stochastic interest rates as presented by Bloch and Nakashima. This turns out to just involve solving a quadratic equation for the FX local volatility at each strike and expiry. We then discussed the PDE for long-dated FX (which at three factors is at the limit of feasibility), and suggested scaling variables for better convergence on the grid.

We finally moved on to stochastic volatility, and noted that this problem involving four factors is beyond the realm of PDEs.

We discussed Andreasen's approach to the pricing of vanilla FX options via a Fourier transform technique provided we have no correlation between the stochastic volatility process and the interest rates processes (although the interest rates and spot FX are allowed to follow a correlation structure and spot FX can also be correlated with stochastic volatility). This is particularly useful if we need fast pricing for calibration of the model to the prices of FX options.

10.4.2   *Exercises*

(1) Consider the following parameterisation based on Gaussian interest rates and lognormal spot FX: $dS_t = (r_t - r_t^f)S_t dt + \sigma_S(t)S_t dW_t^S$, $df_d(t,T) = \mu_d(t,T)dt + \sigma_d(t,T)dW_t^d$ and $df_f(t,T) = \mu_f(t,T)dt + \sigma_f(t,T)dW_t^f$, where $dW_t^d dW_t^f = \rho_{df}(t)dt$, $dW_t^d dW_t^S = \rho_{dS}(t)dt$, $dW_t^f dW_t^S = \rho_{fS}(t)dt$. Find the value of a quanto Libor rate, i.e. where the Libor rate L_T (set at time T, with accrual fraction τ and paid at time $T + \tau$) is in the foreign currency but paid in the domestic currency without conversion at the FX rate.

(2) Consider the same parameterisation as in Question 1 but to be more specific, say the HJM processes correspond to a Hull–White model with constant vol of 0.7% and mean reversion speed of 2%. Take lognormal spot FX vol as 15%. The correlation for the domestic–foreign rates is 30% and other correlations are 0%. Using the formula for forward vol in Section 10.1.1, determine how much of forward variance comes from the interest rates component and how much from the spot component for forward starting times 1y, 5y, 10y and expiries 1y, 5y, 10y, 20y, 30y.

(3) Use the same parameters as in Question 2 except where specified otherwise. Compute the 10-year forward starting volatilities for expiries 1y, 2y, ..., 10y. Now, increase the domestic-spot correlation to 20% and bootstrap spot FX vols so that forward FX variances for expiries 1y, 2y, ..., 20y are preserved. Again, compute the 10-year forward starting volatilities above. How do they compare? Try the same instead by increasing the foreign-spot correlation to 20%.

(4) Implement via Monte Carlo the CEV parameterisation of spot FX with Gaussian rates in Section 10.2.1. For spot FX, use 85, for CEV vol use $0.15 \times 85^{1-\beta}$. Try it with $\beta = 0.2, 0.5, 0.9$. What values of β would give a comparable skew if interest rates vols are 0%?

11

Forward Volatility
and Callability

"You put a cat in hot water. You measure if the temperature
is 63°C or 70°C. Does it matter? The cat is dead."

There tends to be a liquid market for vanilla options in various
assets. When selling a more esoteric product, a financial institution
attempts to offset the risk by hedging with the underlying and vanilla
options. To the extent that we calibrate our model to the prices
of vanilla options, we hope to have captured the implied dynamics of the underlying and reflected this in the price of our exotic
product.

However, the prices of vanilla products tend to give only a snap-
shot of the market. For instance, in equities and foreign exchange
(FX), liquid options are spot starting (i.e. they are for a given strike
at a future maturity). This gives us the implied terminal distribution of the underlying at that maturity. Consider however a forward
starting call option with maturity T_2 and strike αS_{T_1}, where α is a
constant multiplier and S_{T_1} is the value of the underlying set at a
future time $T_1 < T_2$ (see Figure 11.1 for a diagrammatic illustration).
To price this, we actually need to know the transitional probabilities
between T_1 and T_2. It is clear that knowledge of the terminal distribution of the underlying for all future times is inadequate. Instead,
as discussed in Chapters 5 to 7, whether we posit a local volatility
(LV) or stochastic volatility (SV) model has significant implications
for the forward volatility and hence the prices of such products.

T_1: strike is
fixed as αS_{T_1}

T_2: payoff is
$\max\left(S_{T_2} - \alpha S_{T_1}, 0\right)$

Today

Figure 11.1:   A forward starting option has strike that is determined at a future date T_1 before maturity T_2.

Continuing on from our earlier illustration of the effect of the forward volatility smile in the pricing of barriers and volatility swaps, in this chapter, we shall explore further various products dependent on forward volatility. In the equity world, cliquets that pay based on the return over a future time period, e.g. $\max(\frac{S_{T_2}}{S_{T_1}} - 1 - K, 0)$, are extremely popular, since investors tend to be interested in returns rather than in absolute levels of the underlying. We start by exploring the implications of local volatility versus stochastic volatility assumptions on cliquet pricing. We further consider how dVega/dSpot is a particularly relevant quantity in understanding such products.

We next consider forward volatility in the context of interest rates. In the simplest case, callable products (including the extremely popular Bermudan swaption) are forward volatility products in the sense that in evaluating whether to exercise now versus to exercise in a later period, we are comparing spot volatility against forward volatility. Interest rates have the peculiarity that since the underlying (the rates themselves) are not an asset (as opposed to say discount bonds), they are not constrained to grow at the risk-free rate. This allows us the flexibility to introduce mean reversion, which effectively provides for control of forward volatility growth. In equities and FX, we do not have that degree of freedom, so mean reversion can only be introduced into the stochastic volatility component if desirable to control forward smile evolution.

Finally, we consider the implications of stochastic interest rates on forward FX volatility evolution. As discussed in Chapter 10, the dynamics of stochastic interest rates heavily affect the smile of FX options over long expiries. In a similar way, stochastic interest rates may moderate the effect that the stochastic volatility on spot FX has on the forward FX smile dynamics. This is relevant when considering callable structures in long-dated FX.

11.1   The Cliquet

Retail investment in equities has been popular since the 1980s. This is due to the perception that they offer the best returns over a long investment horizon, at least in the US and Europe. However, even over a 10-year period, markets have been known to be subject to significant declines. And the past decade has not been particularly encouraging. Figure 11.2 should make the above clearer.

Options offer an investor the opportunity to participate in positive growth whilst limiting downside risk. However, what should one do if markets appear to be at risk of significant short-term decline but may thereafter recover? Suppose that today is 3 June 2002. A 4-year call option on the STOXX 50 index with a fixed strike of 3,700 would subsequently expire out-of-the-money because of the initial decline before the recovery (see Figure 11.3).

But investors are concerned with their returns over each period. After all, many portfolio managers are assessed against quarterly benchmarks on returns. So how about a portfolio of options with

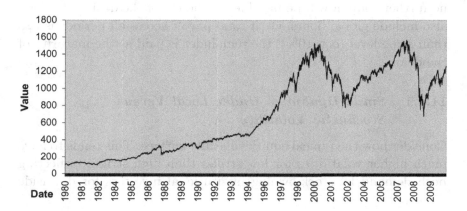

Figure 11.2:   History of S&P 500 index (1980 to 2010).
Source: Bloomberg data.

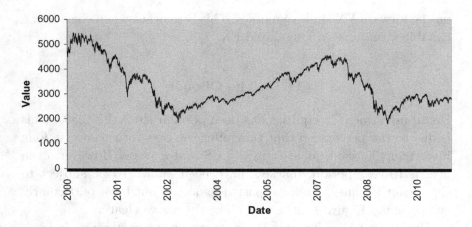

Figure 11.3:   History of Stoxx50 index from 2000 to 2010.
Source: Bloomberg data.

payment dates $\{T_i\}_{i=1}^N$ (say 1-year apart), and corresponding payoffs $\max(\frac{S_{T_i}}{S_{T_{i-1}}}-1-K,0)$, where S_{T_i} is the index level and K is the strike? This is the cliquet. Usually, to cheapen a cliquet, a local cap C (say 10%) is applied, so that the payoff is $\min(\max(\frac{S_{T_i}}{S_{T_{i-1}}}-1-K,0),C)$. In addition, typical structures can include global caps, i.e. if combined coupons paid across all prior periods exceed some level (e.g. 40%), no further coupon will be payable for the life of the deal.[1] They can also include global floors, i.e. if total payoff across all periods is less than some level (e.g. 10%), the remainder is paid at the maturity of the deal.

11.1.1   *Smile Dynamics Under Local Versus Stochastic Volatility*

Consider now the typical equity volatility surface. This tends to have much higher volatilities for low strikes than high strikes (reflecting both demand by stock-owning institutional investors for downside

---

[1]Note that the deal does not terminate and the investor must wait until maturity to get her principal back.

protection, and a non-negligible probability of collapse in stock prices due to adverse market or company-specific events). Further, volatilities tend to be higher for short expiries (as dealers seek compensation for discrete market shocks whose effects dissipate over longer horizons).

The cliquet is essentially a forward smile product. After all, its payoff depends on the return across two future points in time. As discussed in Section 5.2.1, under a local volatility model, the decline in volatility for long expiries is reflected by lower volatilities for future times, hence an overall decline in volatility levels over time. Further, the volatility smile will generally flatten over time to reflect the generally less pronounced smile for long expiry options under an LV model. So, all in all, the forward smile will be a lot flatter than the current smile. This is not just counter-intuitive but probably means we will underprice cliquet options in an LV model.

In contrast, in a stochastic volatility model, as discussed in Section 6.1.2, the volatility smile persists over time, so that the forward vol smile looks similar to today's smile. It is the growth of volatility as per the volatility of variance that leads to a pronounced volatility smile over time. In fact, as discussed in Section 6.3.1, it is necessary to have a large mean reversion to dampen the growth of volatility over time, so that the smile does not get too exaggerated over long expiries. This is coupled with a high volatility of variance so that we get a pronounced smile at the short end, in keeping with the prices of vanilla options.

If it is however felt that SV gives too pronounced a forward vol smile, then perhaps a mixture of LV and SV (per Section 7.2) is appropriate. This is usually the case in FX, although in equities typically stochastic volatility alone is adequate to capture the observed market dynamics.

11.1.2   *Relevance of dVega/dSpot*

Having first put in place an approximate overlay using vanilla options of similar characteristics to reduce risk, hedging of exotic products typically involves trying to trade in the underlying and vanilla options to manage the sensitivities with respect to various market quantities. Usually, one attempts to zero out the first order sensitivities (deltas) $\Delta = \frac{\partial P}{\partial S}$ (or $\Delta_i = \frac{\partial P}{\partial R_i}$ in interest rates), where P is the price of the derivative, S is the underlying value in equities or FX (and R_i is the interest rate for a standard instrument with a particular maturity, e.g. 5-year swap rate). There is an attempt to manage the second order sensitivities (gammas) $\Gamma = \frac{\partial^2 P}{\partial S^2}$ (or $\Gamma_i = \frac{\partial^2 P}{\partial R_i^2}$), by putting on an offsetting trade whenever they get too large. For options, there is also a need to control first order volatility sensitivities (vegas) $\nu_i = \frac{\partial P}{\partial \sigma_i}$, where σ_i is the implied volatility for an expiry bucket T_i (or an expiry and tenor bucket in the world of interest rates swaptions).

Higher order sensitivities and cross sensivities are sometimes ignored, either due to logistical difficulties[2] or because they can be unstable to compute.

However, for the cliquet, the cross sensitivity dVega/dSpot $\frac{\partial \nu_i}{\partial S} = \frac{\partial^2 P}{\partial S \partial \sigma_i}$ is particularly important, in addition to the vega itself. After all, dVega/dSpot is a measure that takes account of the correlation of the volatility with the underlying. As such, it determines the cost of volatility hedging as spot moves, the cliquet being primarily forward volatility dependent.

Local volatility and stochastic volatility give very different values of dVega/dSpot. As spot increases, in an LV model,[3] the volatility smile moves in the direction of lower spot values. In contrast, in an SV model (per Section 6.2.3), the volatility smile moves in the direction of higher spot values. This leads to different deltas for LV and SV models, since $\frac{\partial P}{\partial S} = \frac{\partial P^{BS}}{\partial S} + \frac{\partial P^{BS}}{\partial \sigma} \frac{\partial \sigma}{\partial S}$, where P^{BS} is the Black–Scholes price (per Section 5.2.2). As dVega/dSpot is also dDelta/dVol ($\frac{\partial \nu_i}{\partial S} = \frac{\partial^2 P}{\partial S \partial \sigma_i} = \frac{\partial \Delta}{\partial \sigma_i}$), it is thus clear that its value is affected by the choice of a local volatility or stochastic volatility model.

---

[2]E.g. there can be too many combinations of cross terms, especially when considering a basket of stocks.

[3]Per Section 5.2.2.

11.1.3 *Effect of Gamma Changing Sign*

Wilmott [Wil02] analysed a cliquet with a local cap and global floor. He noted that the payoff is not always convex and so gamma can change sign depending on the level of the underlying's fixing at the start of the period versus that at the end of the period. If vega is high when gamma is positive, then this benefits the product. In contrast, price will be lower if vega is high when gamma is negative.

Let us just focus on a single period cliquet with a local cap (i.e. payoff $\min(\max(\frac{S_{T_2}}{S_{T_1}} - 1 - K, 0), C)$). Suppose for now that we are at time t past the start of the period (i.e. $T_1 < t < T_2$) and S_{T_1} has fixed, so that this becomes a regular call spread. Under the Black–Scholes model, this has negative gamma if current spot is in some region where the payoff is affected (limited) by the cap (as seen in Figure 11.4). We could replicate a call spread by being long a call option and being short another with a higher strike, so the gamma dynamics are not important for a simple call spread. For a cliquet, however, up to the first fixing, we have forward volatility dependence. Naturally, we have to ask what our model gives for the volatility profile conditional on the realised fixing at the period start and current spot — and are we overestimating or underestimating the value of the capped cliquet?

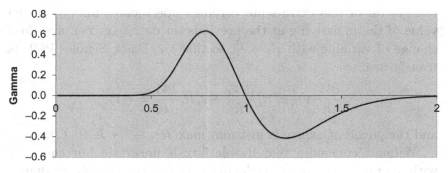

Current Spot / Period Start Fixing

Figure 11.4: We depict here the gamma of a capped cliquet if we are past the period start, so that the first fixing is known. We have used a cap of 10%, time to period end of 6 months, lognormal volatility of 30%, a flat interest rate of 3% and assumed no dividends are payable.

Wilmott suggests the following approach to give the lowest estimate for the value of a cliquet. Basically, he assumes that there are two states of volatility $\{\sigma^+, \sigma^-\}$ with $\sigma^+ > \sigma^-$. The state of higher volatility is realised when gamma is negative (i.e the most unfavourable outcome for the buyer). If you want the highest estimate for the cliquet's value, then you choose the state of higher volatility to coincide with positive gamma instead.

The above can be easily treated via a partial differential equation (PDE) framework, where the gamma condition can be readily computed. Let us work in a framework with only a lognormal diffusion process for the underlying and uncertain volatility as above. The Black–Scholes PDE is

$$\frac{\partial V_t}{\partial t} + \frac{1}{2}\sigma_t^2 S_t^2 \frac{\partial^2 V_t}{\partial S_t^2} + r_t S_t \frac{\partial V_t}{\partial S_t} = r_t V_t$$

with final condition $\min(\max(\frac{S_{T_2}}{S_{T_1}} - 1 - K, 0), C)$, and where

$$\sigma_t = \begin{cases} \sigma^+ & \text{if } \dfrac{\partial^2 V_t}{\partial S_t^2} < 0 \\[2mm] \sigma^- & \text{if } \dfrac{\partial^2 V_t}{\partial S_t^2} > 0 \end{cases}.$$

We have a dependence on S_{T_1} in addition to S_t (for $t > T_1$). We can get rid of this extra state variable. Specifically, take S_t' as the value of the underlying at the previous set date (e.g. T_1), and do a change of variable with $R_t = \frac{S_t}{S_t'}$ so that the Black–Scholes PDE is transformed to

$$\frac{\partial V_t}{\partial t} + \frac{1}{2}\sigma_t^2 R_t^2 \frac{\partial^2 V_t}{\partial R_t^2} + r_t R_t \frac{\partial V_t}{\partial R_t} = r_t V_t,$$

and the payoff at expiry is just $\min(\max(R_{T_2} - 1 - K, 0), C)$.

Wilmott concludes that if volatility is uncertain but can vary within a range (of say 10%), the impact on price is far bigger than if volatility is some constant level within this range (see Figure 11.5). So just using low and high values of volatility to estimate the bounds for a cliquet's price is unlikely to be adequate. Considering that forward vol dynamics are particularly model-dependent for a cliquet,

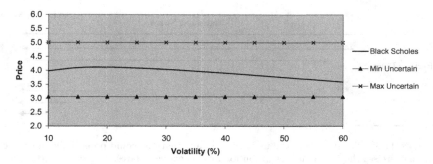

Figure 11.5:   Here we show the plot of the Black–Scholes price of a cliquet (1y between fixings, 10% cap) versus volatility. We have superimposed the price under the uncertain volatility model for the max and min cases (where vol is allowed to be either 25% or 40%). Notional is 100 and we assumed a flat interest rate of 3% and no dividends. (Time to first fixing does not matter, as it will cause period start and end prices to be multiplied by the same factor.)

and it is far from clear what dynamics volatility really has, the above uncertain volatility framework can give conservative bounds as to the price of a cliquet.

It is unlikely that a model where volatility is highest (or lowest) when gamma is positive is appropriate — after all, volatility is a feature of the underlying and should be independent of some esoteric contract. However, the above should make clear to the reader that the choice of model (local volatility, stochastic volatility, or indeed something else) can significantly affect the price of a cliquet.

11.2   The Bermudan Swaption

As discussed in Chapter 8, a Bermudan swaption entitles the holder to enter into a swap on a range of exercise dates. To be more specific, consider a Bermudan swaption which allows for exercise at annual intervals from 1 June 2010 to 1 June 2019 inclusive. If exercised, then the holder enters into a swap to pay a fixed strike of 5% annually and receive floating coupons based on Libor, from the exercise date to the maturity (end) date of 1 June 2020. See Figure 11.6 for an illustration.

A Bermudan swaption is popular because it serves as a natural hedge for callable bonds. Basically, callable bonds are those where

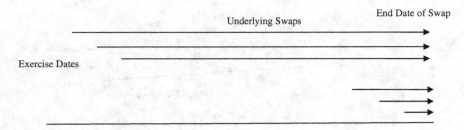

Figure 11.6:   We show here the underlying swaps that one could potentially enter into if he exercises the Bermudan swaption for various exercise dates. The swap starts when exercised and the end date is always the same.

the issuer has the right to repay the notional on coupon dates and hence avoid paying further coupons. The issuer will do so if interest rates fall, so that it is to its advantage to call the bond and refinance at lower interest rates (e.g. if the coupon is 5% and it is possible to refinance at 4%). From the investor's perspective, she has just sold an option to the issuer and so the callable bond is cheaper than an equivalent non-callable bond. For example, the non-callable bond might have paid a coupon of 4.5% instead.

A Bermudan swaption is also used to hedge interest rate risk for mortgage products in the US. US mortgages are typically of up to 30-year terms. Homeowners typically have the right to prepay their loan without penalty,[4] at any time of their choice. Indeed, homeowners can prepay when rates go down, although they do not always refinance when economically optimal but often do so for other reasons instead (e.g. sale of house when moving).

When valuing a Bermudan swaption, we need to determine if it is optimal to exercise the option. Its value is the maximum of the exercise value on any exercise date (intrinsic) versus the holding value (i.e. the value of future exercise opportunities). To price the holding value, we need the volatilities of swaptions as seen at future time points, i.e. the price is dependent on forward volatility. We further remark that assuming a Bermudan swaption has been issued a long time ago under different economic circumstances (e.g. when

---

[4]Penalty for prepayment when the homeowner wishes to sell his property is even prohibited by legislation in certain states.

rates were much higher), then its strike could make it deep out-of-the-money. For example, when 20-year swap rates were at 5% to 6% in the US in 2007, it would not be unusual to trade 20-year Bermudan swaptions with strikes at 6%. This would be deep out-of-the-money in the environment of 2010 when swap rates were hovering around 3.5% to 4%. In that sense, it can also be necessary to consider the forward volatility smile for pricing Bermudan swaptions.

11.2.1   *Effect of Mean Reversion on Forward Vol Growth*

In Section 8.2.1, we considered how mean reversion in a short rate model affects forward volatility of the short rate, and hence of other interest rate products. Basically, we calibrate to match terminal volatilities of options today. In a model with mean reversion, local volatility has to be increased so that terminal variance is maintained over a given period $[0, T]$, due to the volatility dampening effect of mean reversion.

Consider again the simplified Ornstein–Uhlenbeck process

$$dx_t = -\kappa x_t dt + \sigma dW_t$$

with variance $\mathrm{var}(x_T|x_t) = \frac{\sigma^2}{2\kappa}(1 - e^{2\kappa(t-T)})$ over the period $[t, T]$.

Having calibrated σ to match the variance over $[0, T]$, it follows that over a period $[t, T]$ (where $t < T$), the terminal volatility would be higher (since there is less time for volatility dampening).

In particular, caplet vols increase vis-à-vis swaption vols with higher mean reversion due to a shorter period for vol dampening compared with swaptions (as per our discussion in Section 8.2). Given a short rate model with a set of time-dependent local volatilities $\sigma(t)$ and mean reversion parameters $\kappa(t)$, we can simultaneously calibrate to at-the-money volatilities of caplets and co-terminal swaptions,[5] with expiries corresponding to the exercise dates of the Bermudan swaption.

Calibrating to caplets increases mean reversion, forward volatility, and the price of the callable product. There is a structural

---

[5]I.e. with maturity/end date being that of the Bermudan swaption.

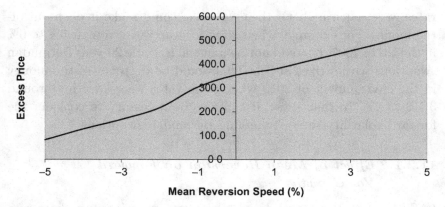

Figure 11.7:   We plot here the switch price of a 30-year (Non-call 1-year) at-the-money Bermudan receiver swaption (based on euro data representative of early 2011). Switch price is how much the Bermudan swaption is worth more than the value of the highest European swaption within the package. Notice how the switch price increases with mean reversion.

imbalance in the supply and demand of caplets and swaptions, since banks are net sellers of caplet volatilities due to corporations seeking protection from higher rates on their borrowings, whilst they are net buyers of swaption volatilities due to corporations selling their optionality from callable bonds. (Naturally, banks would bid up caplet vols and bid down swaption vols in the process of hedging.) In this way, caplet volatilities tend to be structurally higher than swaption volatilities. In practice, it turns out that the prices of Bermudan swaptions do not fully reflect the mean reversion levels implied by calibration to caplet prices. Figure 11.7 shows how mean reversion affects the price of a Bermudan swaption.

11.2.2   *Mean Reversion and Forward Vol in a No-arbitrage World*

In the previous section, we have discussed how mean reversion in a short rate model leads to higher forward volatility of interest rate instruments. Considering that forward volatility affects the prices of callable products, we would want to see how we could possibly increase or decrease forward volatility for other assets.

Let us consider the process for an FX rate X_t instead (expressed as number of units of domestic currency per unit of foreign currency) with SDE

$$dX_t = \mu(\{\theta_t\})X_t dt + \sigma(\{\theta_t\})X_t dW_t,$$

where $\{\theta_t\}$ represents state variables.

For no arbitrage, we require that

$$\frac{X_t B_t^f}{B_t} = E^Q\left[\frac{X_T B_T^f}{B_T}\right],$$

where B_t is the domestic money market account with SDE $dB_t = r_t B_t dt$, and B_t^f is the foreign money market account with SDE $dB_t^f = r_t^f B_t^f dt$.

From the process

$$d\left(\frac{X_t B_t^f}{B_t}\right)\bigg/\frac{X_t B_t^f}{B_t} = (\mu(\{\theta_t\}) + r_t^f - r_t)dt + \sigma(\{\theta_t\})dW_t,$$

which is a martingale under the risk neutral measure with numeraire B_t, we obtain

$$\mu(\{\theta_t\}) = r_t - r_t^f.$$

This means that the drift of our FX rate is fully specified by the domestic and foreign interest rate processes, so that there is no room to incorporate mean reversion into the spot FX process.

Similarly, the drift for an equity process is fully specified by the domestic interest rate and dividend processes. It follows that any mean reversion in equities has to be incorporated into the dividend process, which seems odd and in any case is not likely to give the required degree of freedom.

The reason for this difference is that an interest rate is not an asset,[6] so we can specify its dynamics without fearing that we breach no-arbitrage considerations. In contrast, a stock is an asset and

---

[6]Although a discount bond is an asset.

an FX rate (applied to a foreign asset) is a domestic asset, and so their dynamics are not freely specifiable. In commodities, however, it is often not possible to construct an arbitrage by holding the spot underlying as storage can be impossible or prohibitively expensive (e.g. agricultural products will go bad and electricity cannot be stored easily). In that sense, we can often model the forward process directly in commodities and mean reversion can be applied.

This is a relevant consideration because to control forward volatility dynamics in equities and FX, we are forced to introduce a stochastic volatility process. We can then apply mean reversion to the stochastic volatility and hence control the forward smile. Due to the possibility of controlling forward smile without stochastic volatility in interest rates and also because of the greater complexity of modelling the entire term structure versus a spot process, stochastic volatility modelling in interest rates has tended to be less advanced than in equities and FX.

11.3   Callable Long-Dated Foreign Exchange Structures

Callability allows the issuer to terminate a structure at his discretion, and as such makes a product cheaper from the perspective of an investor. Since investors typically seek products with higher yield, callability is often added, so that the issuer can offer a higher coupon on these products vis-à-vis comparable non-callable structures.

We have considered long-dated FX products in Chapter 10. In particular, the Power Reverse Dual Currency (PRDC) has been popular in Japan because the much higher dollar interest rates than yen interest rates implies that the USD/JPY[7] FX forward for a long expiry is much lower than the FX spot.[8] This leads to investor interest in products that benefit if the forward FX rate is not realised. Effectively, the coupons tend to be FX options with a fixed strike,

---

[7] Recall this means number of yen per dollar.
[8] E.g. the 30-year forward FX rate can be 50 whereas the spot FX might be 90.

e.g. the coupon might be $L \max(X_T - K, 0)$, where $L = 0.0025$ is a multiplier, $K = 75$ is the strike and X_T is the USD/JPY spot at the coupon payment date T.

Consider a 30-year PRDC. By introducing callability, so that the issuer can repay the bond on each coupon date, the investor can get a higher coupon on these products, typically in the form of a lower strike (e.g. 70) or a higher multiplier (e.g. 0.004) for the underlying FX options. Whereas a collection of FX options can be priced via Black's formula, we considered in Chapter 10 how callability requires us to have a term structure model involving stochastic interest rates and spot FX, since to evaluate the holding value, we need to determine the value of the rights of termination on future coupon dates. This evaluation depends on the forward volatility smile.

11.3.1 *Forward Foreign Exchange Vol Evolution in the Presence of Stochastic Interest Rates*

Hopefully, it should be clear from our earlier discussion that local volatility and stochastic volatility models lead to very different forward volatility dynamics. In particular, SV tends to perpetuate the current volatility smile over time, whereas in an LV model the volatility smile over time can flatten if the smile for long expiries is less pronounced.

As a consequence, an appropriate mixture of local volatility versus stochastic volatility can be necessary to capture the correct dynamics of the FX process.[9]

In Section 10.2.1, we have seen how stochastic interest rates following a Gaussian process can dilute the skew of the forward FX process under an LV model for spot FX, since Gaussian interest rates contribute lognormally to the forward FX process. Generalising, the dynamics of interest rates influence the dynamics of forward FX volatility. For a long expiry T, stochastic interest rates processes become increasingly more important to the FX forward, since interest rates vol contributions to FX forward vol grow

---

[9]As per our discussion in Section 7.1.

proportional to $\sqrt{T^3}$ whilst spot FX vol contribution grows proportional to $\sqrt{T}$.[10]

It should thus be noted that for long-dated FX products, the contribution to the forward FX dynamics of an SV process on the spot FX process will be moderated by the dynamics of the interest rates volatilities. After all, the SV smile will act on only a less significant volatility component (of the spot FX process rather than the forward FX process).

Of course, one could introduce stochastic volatility on the interest rates processes too if necessary, although the resulting model (of six factors) could be too unwieldy to effectively deploy in practice (as pertains the intuition behind the interrelation of the various parameters as well as the stability of calibration methodologies).

11.4   Consolidation

11.4.1   *Summary*

This chapter is a bit of a consolidation of the effects of various features on forward volatility. This is important as there are various products, dependent on forward volatility, three classes of which (the cliquet, the Bermudan swaption, and callable long-dated FX products) we examined here.

The cliquet pays the return over a period starting and ending in the future, and is interesting to investors as poor returns over past periods need not continue to burden the payoff. We examined how a local volatility model will underprice the cliquet since downward sloping volatilities over increasing expiries in equities translate to lower forward volatility in the LV model. The payoff of a locally capped cliquet is not always convex, and gamma can change sign. We considered an approach by Wilmott to have two states of volatility dependent on whether gamma is positive or negative if one wishes to price a cliquet conservatively or aggressively. Whilst not actually advocating this approach, we hope to have illustrated how

---

[10] As per Section 10.1.

important vol dynamics are for the cliquet. We further discussed why dVega/dSpot is important for the cliquet, accounting for the effect of correlation between the stochastic volatility and the underlying.

Next we explored the Bermudan swaption, where the investor can choose when to exercise amongst a series of exercise dates into a swap ending on a fixed maturity (end date). This is popular as a hedge for callable bonds as well as US (prepayable) mortgages. We discussed the importance of mean reversion in that it leads to higher forward volatility if the model is calibrated to the variance over fixed expiries. This is shown to increase the optionality value of future exercise, and hence the price of the Bermudan swaption. We contrasted the possibility of introducing mean reversion to an interest rates or commodities forward process (since these are not assets), versus why in equities or FX mean reversion to control variance growth can only appear in the stochastic volatility term.

Finally, we revisited the long-dated FX world. Here, we considered how interest rates contribute significantly to the forward FX process for long maturities. This means that the effect of stochastic volatility on the spot FX process is diluted over long maturities in the presence of stochastic rates.

11.4.2 *Exercises*

(1) Assume lognormal dynamics for the underlying $dS_t = rS_tdt + \sigma S_tdW_t$ and constant interest rates r. Compute the price of a cliquet with payoff $\max(\frac{S_{T_2}}{S_{T_1}} - 1, 0)$ at time $T_2 > T_1$.

(2) Consider the Hull–White model $dr_t = \kappa(\theta(t) - r_t)dt + \sigma dW_t$. Find $\text{corr}(f_{t,T}, f_{u,T})$ where $f_{t,T} = E_t^T[r_T]$ and $t < u < T$.

(3) Assume the following dynamics $dS_t = \mu S_tdt + \sigma(S_t, t)S_tdW_t$ for the underlying and deterministic interest rates r_t. Suppose we want to delta hedge (via the Black–Scholes approach) an at-the-money call option. Construct the relevant replicating portfolio and determine its cost. Hence, explain why forward volatility is not so important for a simple call option.

(4) Repeat the comparison in Question 3 of Chapter 10, except this time leave correlations constant (i.e. 0% between spot FX and

interest rates). Instead, increase both interest rates vols to 1%. Next decrease both interest rates vols to 0%. How do forward FX variances compare?

(5) Implement via Monte Carlo a long-dated FX model with stochastic interest rates and stochastic vol. The parameterisation in Question 2 of Chapter 10 is reasonable for interest rates and spot FX processes. Use a Heston-style stochastic vol. Take vol of variance of 100%, mean reversion speed of 100%, correlation of 0% as benchmark. Convince yourself by varying the stochastic vol parameters that the impact on smile for long-expiry options (i.e. over 20 years) is moderated by the stochastic interest rates.

12

Funding and Basis

"Suppose I can borrow an infinite amount of money, then a
doubling strategy is guaranteed to make me money."

Until now in this book, in developing the framework for derivatives
pricing, we have made the traditional assumption that financial institutions can lend and borrow at a common (almost) risk-free rate.
This forms the bedrock of derivatives pricing in that under such circumstances, financial institutions are free to pursue arbitrage opportunities heedless of funding implications.

Prior to 2008, the majority of AA-rated investment banks were
able to borrow and lend at the Libor rate (or Euribor rate for euros).
In that sense, Libor could be considered the 'risk-free' rate for pricing derivatives, since positions could be funded at Libor. And assuming banks were happy to pursue 'riskless' opportunities that yielded
above Libor, we could expect a fully hedged portfolio to yield Libor.

But the financial world has been rudely awakened from such idyl-
lic arrangements when the seismic shocks of the credit crisis of 2008
brought an end to the era of unlimited liquidity. These days it is
no longer possible to borrow at Libor in the absence of collateral
arrangements. Indeed, as Figure 12.1 demonstrates, even govern-
ments of Group of Seven (G7) economies are charged a premium for
borrowing, leading to government yields for long-dated borrowing
exceeding the long-term swap rate.

Is it so surprising that we should not be able to borrow unlimited
amounts at the same rate? Certain strategies would work if unlimited

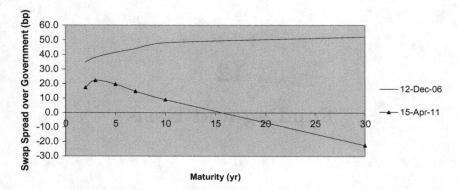

Figure 12.1: We show here the US swap spread over government (i.e. swap rate–government bond yield) prior to the crisis (December 2006) and after the crisis (April 2011). The pre-crisis spread was positive, reflecting the perceived risk-free nature of government borrowing. After the crisis, the negative spread for long maturities reflects the reluctance of institutions to lend to anyone in the absence of collateral arrangements. *Source*: Bloomberg data.

borrowing was allowed. For example, suppose you play a game that involves tossing a coin: If heads appear you get twice your bet; if tails appear you lose your bet. This is a fair game, since expected return from a bet of 1 is $\frac{1}{2} \times 2 + \frac{1}{2} \times 0 = 1$ (i.e. what you started out with). Consider a strategy where you start with £1, exit if you win, and double your bet indefinitely if you lose. This is guaranteed to make you £1 eventually. But in the (extremely unlikely) event that you have 29 (consecutive) unsuccessful runs, your 30th bet will be £1 × 2^{29} = £536,870,912 (beyond the means of most of us)!

In a more practical setting, a company's borrowing would be constrained by regulations pertaining to assets versus capital. Also, equity investors tend to demand return on capital far higher than prevailing interest rates. And when an institution's leverage gets too large, other institutions will be reluctant to lend it more capital, in the absence of a significant risk premium. So, unconstrained borrowing and lending at the same rate is clearly a simplification of reality.

Previously, considerations on funding were largely ignored. But this lack of discipline actually hurt institutions in the 2008 crisis, which had used up far too much of their balance sheets on deals that were expected to yield the tiniest of returns over Libor. Rather curiously, an institution with AAA-rating, which charged its desks for funding accordingly, would have incentivised them to do deals even if these were expected to yield under Libor[1] — this happened with some institutions and the resultant deals were not always sensible. Such profligate use of an institution's balance sheet is likely to be no longer possible in the days ahead.

In this chapter, we shall finally explore the implications of funding as pertains the pricing of derivatives. This has previously been of concern mainly in the long-dated FX markets, particularly as regards to yen borrowing because of the huge supply of yen loans due to persistently low interest rates, perpetuated by a surplus of Japanese exports over imports and an anaemic Japanese economy. But wider considerations on the implications of funding look likely to stay in the foreseeable future. And whilst they throw a spanner in the theory of derivatives pricing, it shall be seen that much of the framework can be salvaged.

12.1 Funding Assumptions of Derivatives Pricing

Recall that the fundamental assumption of derivatives pricing is that we could construct (possibly involving dynamic hedging) a replicating portfolio whose value equals that of the derivative. Clearly, this portfolio has to be funded. So, funding goes to the heart of the valuation of a derivative. In this section, we shall examine this in the single currency context.

12.1.1 *The Risk-free Rate Versus Libor*

In Section 1.1.2, we showed how a derivative $f(S_t, t)$ on an underlying S_t can be priced by constructing the replicating portfolio

$$\Pi(S_t, t) = \Delta(S_t, t)S_t - f(S_t, t)$$

---

[1]Libor only involves AA-rated counterparties after all and so will attract a higher interest rate than AAA-borrowing.

with $\Delta(S_t, t) = \frac{\partial f_t}{\partial S_t}$ so that its SDE is given by

$$d\Pi(S_t, t) = \left(-\frac{\partial f_t}{\partial t} - \frac{1}{2} \frac{\partial^2 f_t}{\partial S_t^2} \sigma^2(S_t, t) \right) dt.$$

At any point in time, this portfolio could have a negative or positive change in value. If negative, assuming we could borrow at r_t^B, then the change in value must be equal to $d\Pi(S_t, t) = r_t^B \Pi(S_t, t) dt$. Similarly, if positive, assuming we could lend at r_t^L, then the change in value must be $d\Pi(S_t, t) = r_t^L \Pi(S_t, t) dt$. It is the existence of a common rate for borrowing and lending $r_t = r_t^B = r_t^L$ that leads us to the Black–Scholes equation for the price of a derivative.

This was not a problem in practice since prior to 2007, the bulk of investment banks (being AA-rated financial institutions) could borrow and lend at Libor (or Euribor for euros). In that sense, they could agree on a single rate to use for pricing derivatives. It is the existence of this rate that leads to derivatives having a unique price.

Note that the rate to be used in pricing derivatives is the Libor rate (or Euribor rate for euros) and not the rate on government bonds, since the former reflects the cost of funding. In this sense, the often-used term 'risk-free rate' in the context of derivatives pricing is a misnomer.

12.1.2   *Funding in a Risky World*

Suppose we have two risky counterparties A and B whose discount curves are $D^A(0, T)$ and $D^B(0, T)$ for maturity T (see Figure 12.2), obtainable say by bootstrapping from the prices of their corporate bonds. Comparing with our risk-free discount curve $D(0, T)$, $D^A(0, T) < D(0, T)$ and $D^B(0, T) < D(0, T)$ since a risky payment is worth less than a risk-free one. Defining the continuously compounded zero-rate $r(0, T) = -\frac{\log D(0, T)}{T}$ and the equivalents for counterparties A and B, we have $r^A(0, T) = r(0, T) + s^A(0, T)$ and $r^B(0, T) = r(0, T) + s^B(0, T)$, where $s^A(0, T)$, $s^B(0, T)$ are the credit spreads of counterparties A and B.

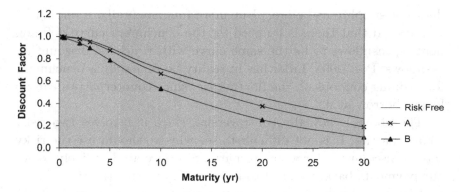

Figure 12.2: We illustrate how different funding names can have different discount factors and the effect tends to get more pronounced with increasing maturity.

Let us consider again a swap as discussed in Section 1.2.1. Suppose counterparty A pays the fixed leg and counterparty B pays the floating leg. The fixed leg pays rate R on coupon payment dates $\{T_i\}_{i=1}^N$ with accrual fraction τ_i. So, its value is given by

$$R \sum_{i=1}^N \tau_i D^A(0, T_i).$$

Suppose the floating leg has coupon dates $\{T_i^*\}_{i=1}^M$ with accrual fraction τ_i^*, and floating coupons are based on Libor. Note that counterparties still use Libor (or Euribor) as a reference for floating coupons (even if they could not fund at Libor). Thus, we still obtain floating coupons off the Libor curve via

$$f(0, T, T + \tau) = \left(\frac{D(0, T)}{D(0, T + \tau)} - 1 \right) \Big/ \tau,$$

so that the value of the floating leg is now

$$\sum_{i=1}^M f(0, T_{i-1}^*, T_i^*) \tau_i^* D^B(0, T_i^*) = \sum_{i=1}^M \left(\frac{D(0, T_{i-1}^*)}{D(0, T_i^*)} - 1 \right) D^B(0, T_i^*).$$

Notice that we are using a different curve to get our Libor cashflows and to discount the cashflows. Of course, the present value does not simplify as before.[2] But more fundamentally, it should be emphasised that there is no need for the benchmark curve defining floating cashflows to be the same curve with which we discount all cashflows. Post 2008, Libor has in reality become only a benchmark for defining coupons on the floating leg, since counterparties can no longer borrow at it.

The above is actually controversial, since it involves two risky counterparties. It is not difficult to see why we should use the risky rate of discounting for a counterparty. Since we are less likely to get our payments back, we need to be compensated for the risk.

However, should we allow a counterparty to take account of our own credit risk when pricing derivatives? To get a deal done, perhaps there is no other way, unless one counterparty is almost risk-free. But a firm is theoretically supposed to be governed for the benefit of shareholders, whilst improved credit standing mostly benefits bondholders. Perhaps a firm could monetise its own improved credit standing by borrowing more cheaply, but over-leverage can lead to a liquidity crisis that can ruin a firm, so such an idea has to be approached with care.

This controversy is even more acute for a dealer (say counterparty A), which is in the business of accepting positions from clients. Ideally, it wants to fully take account of its counterparty's credit risk and even charge its counterparty for its own (self) credit risk (since it will be charged to borrow), i.e. it wants to charge $r(0,T) + s^A(0,T) + s^B(0,T)$ to lend to counterparty B. But it does not want to have to be penalised by the counterparty for its own credit risk, and so wishes to discount its borrowings from counterparty B at $r(0,T)$, unless it needs the funds (and would otherwise have to issue bonds, for example). This cannot happen in practice as other financial institutions (with better credit rating) will undercut the dealer with more competitive pricing and win the business.

Such is the conundrum in a world where financial institutions no longer have unlimited liquidity, so that the law of one price (for a dealer at least) no longer holds!

---

[2]Compare the present value of the floating leg in Section 1.2.1.

12.1.3 *Collateralised Versus Non-collateralised Funding*

Financial institutions have since time immemorial been concerned with mitigating counterparty risk from exposure to other institutions. An arrangement that has developed over the past decades has been the posting of collateral. These days standard arrangements have been formalised with the Credit Security Annex (CSA) under the International Swaps and Derivatives Association (ISDA) Master Netting Agreement.

The basic idea is that you value all your positions[3] with a counterparty. If the net value is positive, the said counterparty has to post collateral to you equivalent to the net value.[4] If the net value is negative, then you have to post an appropriate amount of collateral instead to the same counterparty.

Let us assume that interest rates and dividends are zero for illustration. Suppose today Walmart's stock price is $30. I go long a forward contract to buy from you one stock of Walmart for $30 on 15 March 2011. The value of this forward contract is zero today. Suppose Walmart's stock price increases to $31 tomorrow. Then the forward contract is worth $1 to me. Consequently, you have to post $1 worth of collateral to me. If the day after, Walmart's stock price drops to $28, the forward contract is worth −$2, so now I have to post to you $3 (= $1 + $2) of collateral. As can be seen from this simple example, our net positions (after posting collateral) should be zero at the end of each day. (This works similarly to the daily margining of futures and options positions in a derivatives exchange.)

The effect of posting collateral means that in theory each counterparty should have negligible net exposure to the other at the end of each business day. In theory, this means that when dealing with a CSA-counterparty, you are subject to its credit risk for only 1 business day. In practice, valuation of exotic products can differ between two counterparties, and in addition disputes are often used

---

[3]Encompassing vanilla and exotic products under the scope of the agreement.
[4]Posting collateral often involves depositing cash or liquid and highly-rated securities like Treasury bills.

as tactical means of delaying posting of collateral by a few days for liquidity and other (e.g. interest saving) reasons. So, the exposure to a counterparty is usually greater than 1 business day. But still, a CSA arrangement provides significant reduction to a financial institution's credit exposure to a counterparty.

Due to a CSA arrangement providing for exposure to a counterparty to be reduced to almost 1 business day, dealers entering into a CSA arrangement can fund at the overnight index swap (OIS) rate.[5] This is currently significantly lower than the Libor rate. See Figure 12.3 for a recent history of the Libor-OIS spread. These days the preferred approach is to have a CSA arrangement with derivatives counterparties and then to fund at the OIS rate.

Whilst the risk of default of an AA-rated counterparty is likely to be much higher over 3 months than 1 day, the OIS spread versus Libor suggests an extremely high probability of default of AA-rated counterparties.

Morini [Mor10] provides a very useful insight into this puzzling circumstance. Specifically, he notes that Libor is the average of

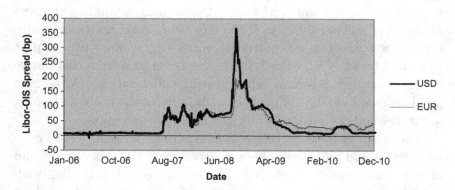

Figure 12.3:   Above is the history of the 3-month Libor–OIS spread (i.e. 3m Libor rate–OIS rate) from 2006 to 2010 for both the US dollar and the euro. It was stable at between 6bp to 8bp before August 2007, then spiked to frightening levels of 366bp for the dollar and 196bp for the euro during the height of the crisis, but has stabilised at about 16bp for the dollar and 24bp for the euro (higher than pre-crisis) these days. *Source*: Bloomberg data.

---

[5]Covered in Section 2.1.3.

quotes from AA-rated counterparties. When you do a swap however, you are dealing with a specific AA-rated counterparty. Notice that an AA-rated counterparty need not always remain AA-rated. The AA-rated counterparty today is very likely to be an AA-rated counterparty tomorrow. However, it is far from clear that an AA-rated counterparty today will remain AA-rated 3 months in the future. Lehman Brothers was a great example. Swift as was its demise, it certainly was not overnight. A floating rate based on Libor involves the quote of the same counterparties over the floating rate period (e.g. overnight, 3 months or 6 months). Clearly, the OIS swap based on daily resets involves the highest possibility of removing weak counterparties from the quote (on a daily basis), as compared to say the 3-month Libor rate.[6] This credit substitution phenomenon of the OIS rate means it represents far higher credit quality than the 3-month Libor rate. In this way, the OIS rate could truly be said to be 'risk-free' (or more correctly, subject to 1 business day of risk).

In the same way, if the floating rate of a swap was semi-annual, it would have to be higher than if it was quarterly, due to less frequent credit substitutions. Section 2.1.3 discussed basis swaps, where one leg paid a 6-month floating rate and the other paid a 3-month floating rate. The spread prior to 2008 used to be under 1 basis point, but now it is consistently over 10 basis points at the short end (see Figure 12.4).

This leads to the conclusion that we can no longer price swaps using a single curve. More specifically, we need a forecasting curve to obtain Libor rates of a given tenor (e.g. 6 months), which forms the reference rate for floating leg coupons. We then need another curve for discounting at the OIS rate.

When bootstrapping a yield curve, we need to reprice ordinary swaps and OIS swaps simultaneously.

Assuming that our benchmark swaps are of floating tenor Δ (e.g. 6 months in euros), we can construct the corresponding forecasting

---

[6]The quoted 3-month Libor rate applies for the interest payment over the next 3 months.

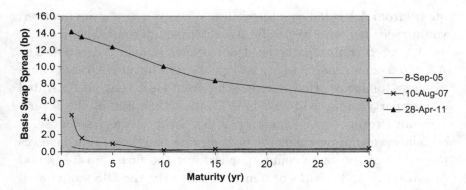

Figure 12.4: Above we see the 3-month versus 6-month basis swap spread. Notice how the spread was under 1bp long before the credit crisis (September 2005), reflecting how we can use one curve to forecast Libor rates of different tenors. Nowadays, the spread has stabilised at well over 10bp at the short end and about 6bp at the long end, so that forecasting using multiple curves has become inevitable.
Source: Bloomberg data.

curve $D^\Delta(0, T)$, i.e. where the Libor rate is

$$f^\Delta(0, T_{i-1}^*, T_i^*) = \left(\frac{D^\Delta(0, T_{i-1}^*)}{D^\Delta(0, T_i^*)} - 1 \right) \bigg/ \tau_i^*.$$

Let $D(0, T)$ be the discounting curve. To reprice a swap with maturity $T_N = T_M^*$ and coupon R_N^Δ, we require

$$\sum_{i=1}^{M} f^\Delta(0, T_{i-1}^*, T_i^*)\tau_i^* D(0, T_i^*) = R_N^\Delta \sum_{i=1}^{N} \tau_i D(0, T_i).$$

Since OIS swaps tend to be quoted as a spread over Libor[7], to reprice the corresponding OIS swap of maturity $T_N = T_M^*$ with spread s_N^Δ, we require

$$\sum_{i=1}^{M} (f^\Delta(0, T_{i-1}^*, T_i^*)\tau_i^* + s_N^\Delta) D(0, T_i^*) = D(0, T_0^*) - D(0, T_M^*).$$

Note that to obtain the above equation, we have used the following: For the OIS leg, we forecast and discount based on the same curve, so that its value is $D(0, T_0^*) - D(0, T_M^*)$ from Section 1.2.1.

---

[7]There are other conventions for quoting OIS Rates but the details do not affect the substance of the discussion, so we shall ignore them.

Notice that we have two free points $D(0, T_N)$ and $D^\Delta(0, T_N)$, and two targets R_N^Δ and s_N^Δ for each maturity $T_N = T_M^*$, so we indeed have enough degrees of freedom to reprice these instruments.

For different floating tenors (e.g. 3-month Libor versus 6-month Libor), we could either construct different curves or construct some curves as a spread over a chosen benchmark curve.

Since swaps are typically done between CSA-counterparties, they are fully collateralised and do not constitute a form of borrowing. In contrast, a government bond reflects borrowing by the relevant government, and an investor cannot get repaid her principal prior to maturity. For long-dated bonds, this is a huge loss of liquidity, and since 2010 with the preference for liquidity, swap rates for long expiries (e.g. 30-year term) are lower than government rates (even amongst G7 economies) of equivalent expiries (even though government bonds are theoretically risk-free in their own currencies).

12.1.4   *Correlation Between Funding Spread and the Underlying*

From our discussion earlier, it can be seen that funding is no longer an after-thought in the pricing of derivatives. It should be clear from the earlier graphs of the OIS spread and Libor basis spreads that funding spreads are not constant. Stochastic funding can lead to increased volatility of an underlying, and thus can increase the price of an option.

More interestingly, stochastic funding can even affect the forward price of an underlying, if the funding spread is correlated with the underlying. This is not a far-fetched point. Funding spreads (over the risk-free rate) are likely to be highest in times of financial crisis. In safe haven (e.g. G7) economies (that are not on the brink of default), central banks will attempt to stimulate economic growth by cutting interest rates. So, funding spreads can be quite negatively correlated with interest rates. Alternatively, in a non-safe haven economy on the brink of collapse, interest rates may need to be raised in times of crisis either as borrowers will no longer lend or because international bodies (e.g. the International Monetary Fund) demand such measures as a condition for financial assistance. So, correlation between funding spreads and interest rates can be positive instead.

Piterbarg [Pit10] shows that stochastic funding spreads can lead to a quanto effect on the forward price of an underlying. Let X_t be the value of an underlying, r_t be the risk-free rate for collateralised borrowing, r_t^A be the (risky) rate for uncollateralised borrowing by some counterparty A (which could but need not be Libor-eligible), and $s_t^A = r_t^A - r_t$ be the spread.

Consider a forward contract with maturity T and strike K with a CSA-counterparty. Its value at time t is

$$E_t^Q[e^{-\int_t^T r_u du}(X_T - K)],$$

so the fair value CSA-forward price of the asset is[8]:

$$F_{\text{CSA}} = E_t^Q[e^{-\int_t^T r_u du} X_T] / E_t^Q[e^{-\int_t^T r_u du}]$$

$$= E_t^T[X_T],$$

where we have changed from the risk-neutral measure[9] to the T-forward measure (with numeraire asset being the discount bond with maturity T given by $D(t, T) = E_t^Q[e^{-\int_t^T r_u du}]$, and discounting is based on the OIS curve).

Consider instead the same forward contract with counterparty A (for which no CSA arrangement is in place). The value of the forward is

$$E_t^Q[e^{-\int_t^T r_u^A du}(X_T - K)].$$

So the fair value forward price is given by

$$F_{\text{noCSA}} = E_t^Q[e^{-\int_t^T r_u^A du} X_T] / D^A(t, T)$$

$$= E_t^Q[e^{-\int_t^T r_u du - \int_t^T (r_u^A - r_u) du} X_T] / D^A(t, T),$$

$$= \frac{D(t, T)}{D^A(t, T)} E_t^T[e^{-\int_t^T s_u^A du} X_T]$$

---

[8]By setting the right-hand side to zero and solving for $F_{\text{CSA}} = K$.
[9]With money market account as numeraire.

where $D^A(t,T) = E_t^Q[e^{-\int_t^T r_u^A du}]$ is the discount curve for counter-party A, and we have again changed from the risk-neutral measure to the T-forward measure.

Then the quanto adjustment to the forward rate as a consequence of non-collateralised funding (from our counterparty A) is

$$F_{\text{noCSA}}(t,T) - F_{\text{CSA}}(t,T)$$

$$= E_t^T\left[\left(\frac{D(t,T)}{D^A(t,T)}e^{-\int_t^T s_u^A du} - 1\right)X_T\right]$$

$$= E_t^T\left[\left(\frac{D(t,T)}{D^A(t,T)}e^{-\int_t^T s_u^A du} - 1\right)(X_T - F_{\text{CSA}}(t,T))\right]$$

$$= E_t^T\left[\left(\frac{D(t,T)}{D^A(t,T)}(e^{-\int_t^T s_u^A du} - E_t^T[e^{-\int_t^T s_u^A du}])\right)\right.$$

$$\left.\times (X_T - F_{\text{CSA}}(t,T))\right]$$

$$= \frac{D(t,T)}{D^A(t,T)}\text{cov}_t^T(e^{-\int_t^T s_u^A du}, X_T),$$

since we have

$$E_t^T\left[\frac{D(t,T)}{D^A(t,T)}e^{-\int_t^T s_u^A du}\right] = 1 \quad \text{and} \quad F_{\text{CSA}} = E_t^T[X_T] \text{ (from earlier)}.$$

Thus, we see that the correlation between the funding spread s_T^A and the underlying X_T induces a quanto adjustment on the fair forward price in the non-CSA case (vis-à-vis the CSA case).

Considering that in the interest rates world, 30-year swaps and even those with longer maturities are common, this quanto effect can be large. If we posit a short rate model for interest rates (with mean reversion 2% and volatility 0.8%) and a corresponding short rate model for the funding spread (with mean reversion 5% and volatility 0.7%), then we see that over 30 years, a quanto adjustment in excess of 0.25% is quite possible. (This should be compared to a 30-year swap rate of just over 3% for euros in 2010.) Figure 12.5 shows the effect of stochastic funding on the fair value Libor rate for varying maturities.

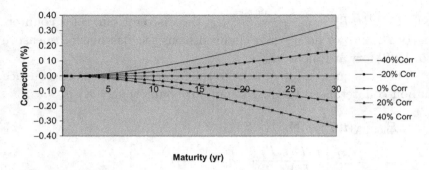

Maturity (yr)

Figure 12.5:   We show the absolute change in the fair value Libor rate for different maturities and correlation assumptions. We have assumed Hull–White processes with 0.7% vol, 1% mean reversion for interest rates and 0.5% vol, 5% mean reversion for the spread. The effect grows exponentially and can be quite significant over long maturities (e.g. −0.34% for the 30-year forward Libor rate assuming 40% corr). The effect on the swap rate is less pronounced (but still important at −0.10%).

Finally, we should remark that since stochastic funding influences the forward, it also influences the location of the at-the-money volatility. Further, the dynamics of the stochastic spread contributes to the dynamics of the underlying, and in that way influences the smile for options on the underlying.

12.2   Cross-Currency Funding

Cross-currency funding bias displayed the earliest systematic violation of the principle of lending and borrowing at an equivalent 'risk-free' rate across all currencies. Basically, it is possible to either fund in one's own currency, or borrow in a foreign currency and then enter into a cross-currency swap, so as to lock in one's funding in one's own currency. In theory, major AA-rated financial institutions should be indifferent to funding at the floating rate of any currency (with the offsetting cross-currency swap).

In practice, supply and demand reasons have led to significant variations in interest rate levels amongst different economies, so that certain currencies have been the funding currencies of choice. In particular, since the late 1990s, a prolonged period of recession in Japan has led to a protracted period of near zero interest rates, whereas interest rates in the dollar (or indeed any other major currency apart from the Swiss franc) have been much higher. As discussed in Chapter 10, this should theoretically imply that the yen should appreciate[10] over time. But the Japanese government has tended to adopt policies supporting a weak yen to promote exports. And Japan's continued economic stagnation for well over a decade has not supported a strong currency either. So, a rather voluminous carry trade (i.e. borrowing yen and investing in other currencies) has developed over the last decade.[11]

Naturally, this means that financial institutions are not indifferent to lending in different currencies. Indeed, with Japan's huge export-induced current account surplus and an ingrained culture of high household savings, there is a ready supply of yen as investors do not have many domestic alternatives for seeking higher yields. If you have a cross-currency swap[12] where one leg paid yen and the other paid dollars, this would imply that a negative spread must be added to the yen leg for the swap to price to par.

It should be remarked that prior to the credit crunch of 2008, the funding bias has been most pronounced in yen FX trades amongst developed economies (although it is also common for emerging markets FX), but it has not captured too much attention in the FX markets as a whole. Figure 12.6 illustrates the cross-currency basis spreads for some major currency pairs.

12.2.1   *Practical Funding in a World with Different Currencies*

When pricing cross-currency structures (especially involving the Japanese yen or emerging market currencies), it may be necessary to take funding bias into account. This means we need to construct curves that reprice cross-currency basis swaps. Standard cross-currency basis swaps are quoted vis-à-vis the US dollar.

---

[10]I.e. the forward FX rate in terms of number of yen per dollar should decline.
[11]The financial crisis of 2008 and its aftermath saw a huge appreciation of the yen, partly exacerbated by the unwinding of the carry trade. Ironically, this was not due to a significant change in the interest rate differentials of the US dollar versus the yen. Nevertheless, the interest in yen borrowing has probably waned as a result.
[12]See Section 2.3.1.

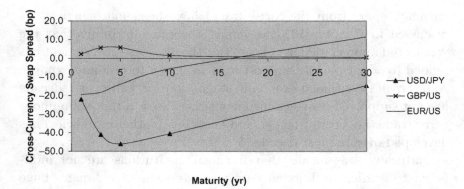

Maturity (yr)

Figure 12.6:　We show here the cross-currency swap spreads on the foreign leg (against the US dollar) as of 15 April 2011. Notice how the Japanese yen has the most pronounced spread for long maturities due to an inherent funding bias (i.e. there is a huge supply of yen).
Source: Bloomberg data.

Further, it is also necessary that we can reprice standard swaps in the domestic currency. For simplicity, for now, let us consider the world prior to 2008, where we can fund at Libor.

Specifically, for US dollars (i.e. the base currency), we can let the forecasting curve be the same as the discounting curve, and bootstrap our discounting curve $D^{\text{USD}}(0,T)$ by sequentially matching the prices of deposits, futures, and swaps as before. For example, having obtained prior discount factors, for a swap with maturity T_j and coupon R_j, we require $D(0,T_j)$ to satisfy

$$R_j \sum_{i=1}^{j} \tau_i D(0,T_i) = D(0,T_0) - D(0,T_j)$$

as we did earlier.

For other currencies, it is necessary to bootstrap by simultaneously matching the prices of swaps and cross-currency swaps for the same expiry. Specifically, we build a discounting curve $D^{\text{CCY}}(0,T)$ and a forecasting curve $D_f^{\text{CCY}}(0,T)$. For maturity $T_j = T_M^*$, the swap constraint given swap rate R_j^{CCY} is

$$R_j^{\text{CCY}} \sum_{i=1}^{j} \tau_i D^{\text{CCY}}(0,T_i) = \sum_{i=1}^{M} f^{\text{CCY}}(0,T_{i-1}^*,T_i^*)\tau_i^* D^{\text{CCY}}(0,T_i^*),$$

where the Libor rate is obtained from the forecasting curve via

$$f^{\mathrm{CCY}}(0, T_{i-1}^*, T_i^*) = \left(\frac{D_f^{\mathrm{CCY}}(0, T_{i-1}^*)}{D_f^{\mathrm{CCY}}(0, T_i^*)} - 1 \right) \Big/ \tau_i^*,$$

and the cross-currency basis swap constraint given cross-currency basis spread s_j^{CCY} is

$$-D^{\mathrm{CCY}}(0, T_0) + \sum_{i=1}^{M} (f^{\mathrm{CCY}}(0, T_{i-1}^*, T_i^*) + s_j^{\mathrm{CCY}}) \tau_i^* D^{\mathrm{CCY}}(0, T_i^*)$$

$$+ D^{\mathrm{CCY}}(0, T_M^*)$$

$$= -D^{\mathrm{USD}}(0, T_0) + \sum_{i=1}^{M} f^{\mathrm{USD}}(0, T_{i-1}^*, T_i^*) \tau_i^* D^{\mathrm{USD}}(0, T_i^*)$$

$$+ D^{\mathrm{USD}}(0, T_M^*).$$

Notice that there is no need to take account of the spot exchange rate X_0 (number of units of currency CCY per dollar) because we would do the swap based on notional 1 for dollars and notional X_0 for the other currency. (See Section 2.3.1 for a more detailed explanation.)

We have enough degrees of freedom since we have two constraints R_j^{CCY} and s_j^{CCY} at each time point $T_j = T_M^*$, and two free parameters $D^{\mathrm{CCY}}(0, T_j)$ and $D_f^{\mathrm{CCY}}(0, T_j)$. The above methodology extends to the deposit part of the domestic curve (which depends on $D^{\mathrm{CCY}}(0, T_j)$ only) and the futures part of the domestic curve (which depends on $D_f^{\mathrm{CCY}}(0, T_j)$ only), whilst we still have to match cross-currency basis swaps for the same maturities.

In this way, we have constructed a forecasting and discounting curve that could simultaneously reprice domestic interest rates instruments and cross-currency swaps against the dollar. Since standard cross-currency basis swaps are quoted against the dollar, our curves will now also reprice all other cross-currency swaps quoted consistently.

12.2.2   *Implications of Cross-currency Collateral*

As seen earlier in this chapter, since 2008, collateral arrangements have come to the fore regarding derivatives deals. As in the case of single currency deals, cross-currency deals can no longer be funded via Libor but instead if appropriate collateral arrangements are in place, then we can fund at the OIS rate.

This leads to further complications in that we need to have a curve for forecasting Libor for each of the tenors (1-month, 3-month, 6-month, etc.) of the floating rate, and a curve for discounting based on OIS. And we still have to account for the cross-currency basis in addition.

For deals in a single currency, it is (at least in theory) possible for collateral to be posted in the same currency. For FX deals, however, there is already a technical complication (since collateral can be posted in only one of the two relevant currencies). For FX deals, it is typical for collateral to be posted in the US dollar (regardless of the currencies constituting the deal).

Notice that if collateral is posted in a different currency from that of the deal, there is potential FX risk in the value of the collateral. And from our earlier discussion, it should be clear that it might be preferable to fund in certain currencies. As such, we need to distinguish funding by the currency of the collateral with risk-free funding only describing the situation where collateral is in the same currency as the deal.

In this way, we could boostrap our curves as before if we introduce another curve $D_{\text{USD}}^{\text{CCY}}(0,T)$ that reflects discounting for currency CCY under a USD-CSA arrangement. So, our equation for basis swaps is now

$$
-D_{\text{USD}}^{\text{CCY}}(0,T_0) + \sum_{i=1}^{M}(f^{\text{CCY}}(0,T_{i-1}^*,T_i^*) + s_j^{\text{CCY}})\tau_i^* D_{\text{USD}}^{\text{CCY}}(0,T_i^*)
$$

$$
+ D_{\text{USD}}^{\text{CCY}}(0,T_M^*)
$$

$$
= -D^{\text{USD}}(0,T_0) + \sum_{i=1}^{M} f^{\text{USD}}(0,T_{i-1}^*,T_i^*)\tau_i^* D^{\text{USD}}(0,T_i^*)
$$

$$
+ D^{\text{USD}}(0,T_M^*)
$$

whilst the equations for standard swaps and OIS swaps are respectively

$$\sum_{i=1}^{M} f^{\mathrm{CCY}}(0, T_{i-1}^*, T_i^*)\tau_i^* D^{\mathrm{CCY}}(0, T_i^*) = R_N \sum_{i=1}^{N} \tau_i D^{\mathrm{CCY}}(0, T_i)$$

and

$$\sum_{i=1}^{M}(f^{\mathrm{CCY}}(0, T_{i-1}^*, T_i^*)\tau_i^* + s_N^{\mathrm{CCY}})D^{\mathrm{CCY}}(0, T_i^*) + D^{\mathrm{CCY}}(0, T_M^*)$$

$$= D^{\mathrm{CCY}}(0, T_0),$$

where

$$f^{\mathrm{CCY}}(0, T_{i-1}^*, T_i^*) = \left(\frac{D_f^{\mathrm{CCY}}(0, T_{i-1}^*)}{D_f^{\mathrm{CCY}}(0, T_i^*)} - 1\right)\bigg/ \tau_i^*.$$

So, effectively, we now have three curves: $D_{\mathrm{USD}}^{\mathrm{CCY}}(0, T)$, $D^{\mathrm{CCY}}(0, T)$, and $D_f^{\mathrm{CCY}}(0, T)$ for discounting under USD-CSA, discounting under domestic CSA (of the currency CCY) and forecasting! And of course, as per Section 12.1.3, if we need to reprice swaps of other floating tenors (e.g. 3 months in euros) then we need even more curves.

Finally, as discussed in Section 12.1.4, the correlation between funding spreads and the underlying can lead to a quanto adjustment in the fair value forward price. Notice that in the cross-currency case, we cannot have domestic CSA arrangements for all trades. In particular, the standard is for USD-CSA to be used. This means that there will always be some sort of funding spread due to collateral mismatches.

As discussed in Section 12.1.4, funding spreads tend to be negatively correlated with the levels of interest rates for most G7 economies. Similarly, there can be a structural relation between funding spreads in USD-CSA versus the interest rates of some currencies. After all, some currencies are seen as a safe haven (e.g. the US dollar or the Swiss franc) and some yield-seeking trades get unwound in times of crisis-induced risk aversion (e.g. the carry trade where yen is borrowed to invest in other currencies). So, correlation between USD-CSA funding spreads and interest rates of G7 economies may not be negligible. This coupled with the prevalence of fairly long-dated cross-currency swaps in some markets (e.g. 30-year USD/JPY swaps are not uncommon), means the quanto effect can be sizeable.

A further complication is that since standard quoted cross-currency basis swaps are based on USD-CSA, there is already an in-built quanto adjustment in the pricing of cross-currency basis swaps, due to stochastic funding spreads. This quanto adjustment would have to be taken into account to even bootstrap curves to consistently reprice cross-currency basis swaps and domestic instruments, in a world of stochastic funding spreads. So, a cross-currency swap is no longer a trivial instrument to price!

12.3   Consolidation

12.3.1   *Summary*

In this final chapter, we explored the issue of funding, which has come to prominence after the financial crisis of 2008. In short, financial institutions can no longer fund at Libor, as the era of easy funding is over. Whilst we have avoided this topic in most of the book, completeness requires us to address how the framework for pricing derivatives is modified in light of this set of circumstances.

Starting by considering the meaning of the risk-free rate in the old world order, we established that it was really the cost of funding (i.e. Libor) rather than the true risk-free rate that we used in pricing derivatives. We then considered the situation where different counterparties had different funding costs, in particular where risky counterparties had to borrow at non-zero spreads over the risk-free rate. We proceeded with the market solution to this problem (the adoption of which accelerated with present funding woes) — collateralisation. Basically, under the CSA agreement, an institution must settle with each counterparty the net value of its position at the end of each trading day, hence reducing counterparty credit risk to one business day worth of market movements. This safety net allows firms to borrow at the overnight index swap (OIS) rate (much lower than Libor), whilst Libor becomes only a reference rate used for setting the floating rate contractually payable on derivatives.

With the Libor–OIS spread settling at much higher levels than prior to the crisis (say around 16 bp for the dollar and 24 bp for the euro now), we discussed Morini's theory that the spread is due to Libor being the rate payable by eligible counterparties over the period concerned, and how Libor is superior to Libor-eligible counterparties in that over long periods, the same counterparties need not be eligible to contribute to Libor. In this way, we established the OIS rate as the risk-free rate, since it is extremely unlikely for a Libor-eligible counterparty to be no longer Libor-eligible in one day's time. We proceeded to consider the implications of stochastic funding spreads. Borrowing from Piterbarg's analysis, we discussed how stochastic funding correlated to the value of the underlying induces an adjustment to the fair forward rate/price (akin to the quanto effect). This is relevant only for non-CSA counterparties however, since market quotes for standard instruments tend to be based on CSA counterparties, so that any such considerations are already accounted for.

We naturally proceeded to consider the multi-currency case. This had historically already violated the theory of borrowing and lending at the risk-free rate (across different currencies) in the sense that historically it had been desirable to fund in certain currencies, influencing funding spreads. An example is that the low interest rates of Japan made the yen a prime target currency for borrowing. This meant that cross-currency swaps involving floating rates of two different currencies have a non-zero fair value spread. In order to account for funding bias, it is necessary for us to have a separate forecasting curve (to project Libor rates) and discounting curve (to present value cashflows). This gives us the necessary degrees of freedom to simultaneously match the prices of instruments (e.g. swaps) in the currency concerned and cross-currency basis swaps (typically against the US dollar). In the post crisis world, there is a further complication: Collateral for cross-currency deals can only be posted in one of the currencies (in fact, it is typically posted in the US dollar regardless of the currencies involved in the trade). This means that our earlier discussion of how stochastic funding spreads can induce a quanto correction in the fair value forward is particularly relevant, since basis swaps with US dollar collateral and own currency instruments (e.g. swaps) with collateral in that currency require different quanto adjustments for consistency.

12.3.2   *Exercises*

(1) Consider the equation $\sum_{i=1}^{M} f^{\Delta}(0, T_{i-1}^*, T_i^*)\tau_i^* D(0, T_i^*) = R_N^{\Delta} \sum_{i=1}^{N} \tau_i D(0, T_i)$ for the par swap rate under OIS discounting in Section 12.1.3. If the OIS–Libor spread is zero, show that this reduces to the classical equation $D(0, T_0) - D(0, T_N) = R_N \sum_{i=1}^{N} \tau_i D(0, T_i)$. Suppose that the OIS–Libor spread is a constant s, i.e. $D(0, T) = D^{\Delta}(0, T)e^{-sT}$. Express the swap rate R_N^{Δ} in terms of the classical swap rate R_N and the spread s.

(2) Due to the huge supply of yen, the funding bias for USD/JPY is such that it is cheaper to borrow yen versus dollars (i.e. $s^{JPY} < 0$ in Section 12.2.1). There is also a significant funding bias for borrowing dollars versus an emerging market currency, e.g. USD/BRL (i.e. $s^{BRL} \neq 0$). Consider now a cross currency swap with one leg paying floating in yen (with no spread) and the other paying floating in Brazilian reais plus a spread s^*. What would the fair value spread s^* be?

(3) Consider a flat Libor discount curve given by $D(0, T) = e^{-0.03T}$. Suppose that the OIS discount curve is $D(0, T) = e^{-0.028T}$. Compute the swap rate (annual fixed coupons, semi-annual floating coupons) for different maturities (1 year, 5 years, 10 years, 30 years) and compare with that obtained via Libor discounting.

(4) Notwithstanding the discussion in Section 12.1.4, since we forecast based on Libor, the martingale equation only holds for risky discounting at the credit-worthiness of Libor counterparts. As such, OIS discounting induces a quanto correction. In the developed world, it is common for interest rates to be lowered in times

of crisis to simulate growth. As such, what should the direction of the quanto correction be? (Note that this is really just a theoretical discussion, since such a quanto correction is accounted for by market quotes which are based on Libor forecasting and OIS discounting.)

(5) Assume deterministic interest rates. Following our discussion in Section 12.1.4, derive the quanto effect of having a stochastic funding spread assuming that the asset follows a standard log-normal process $dX_t = r_t X_t dt + \sigma X_t dW_t^X$ and the funding spread follows a Hull–White process with constant parameters (except for time-dependent drift), i.e. $ds_t = \kappa(\theta(t) - s_t)dt + \lambda dW_t^s$ and $dW_t^X dW_t^s = \rho dt$. Hence, see that if the correlation between the asset and the funding spread is zero, there is no quanto adjustment.

Final Thoughts

At this point, the discussion draws to a close. I certainly hope that you have found the material presented in this book of some use.

In my earlier days, too often, I have come across books giving a general overview of the subject matter, or giving fairly thorough coverage of basic material. And then there are books that highlight specialised topics, or treat niche areas without setting out the general background. All these books have their uses, and some I still refer to this very day.

But a guide that helps a student to get a good working knowledge of quantitative finance — the limitations of various models, a practitioner's considerations and what drives the modelling agenda — I have found to be somewhat elusive. Far from being an encyclopaedic reference or a definitive text for certain subject areas, this book reflects my attempt to set out a framework from which a practitioner may understand the key considerations of derivatives pricing. By covering the three main traditional asset classes (equities, foreign exchange (FX), and interest rates), I hope to have shown that whilst respecting the uniqueness of each area, there are lots of useful tools that are common to them all, and that it is actually beneficial to consider how various concepts relate across different assets.

In a book as concise as this, I can only hope to present a framework for considering derivatives. To this end, I have tried to portray firstly the key idea of no arbitrage as captured (imperfectly) by replicating a payoff (even if dynamically). I have then tried to show how certain products can be priced without models (via replication) and others via an extension thereof (by adding correlation on top of implied marginals). Next, I have attempted to discuss how local and stochastic volatility models can both be used to capture skew, though the choice of which to use has implications as regard to different dynamics for the underlying and hence the prices of products dependent on forward volatility. I have then moved on to interest rates, covering both short rate models and the Libor Market Model, showing what they actually mean for simple products and considering their uses as relates interest rates exotics pricing. A discussion on long-dated FX shows the inter-relation between various asset classes that has become more important these days, as interest rates volatilities increase and we have to uncover the implications of previously ignored risk. And finally, funding is considered as a consequence of the credit crisis having thrown a spanner into the neat theoretical underpinnings of borrowing and lending with almost no constraints. Whilst this is not a complete list of things a practitioner should consider, it certainly should serve as a useful start.

I hope that this book will help you, the reader, see the wood from the trees. But this is only the beginning. Certainly there is a lot of specialised knowledge for any role a practitioner wishes to enter into: Be it better treatment of boundary conditions for partial differential equations (PDEs) in barrier pricing in FX; understanding the implications of various smile parameters on the dynamics of options and hence the risk of a book of products; or better parameterisation of volatility or correlation in local or stochastic volatility models.

It is with these thoughts that I wish to express my strong belief that whilst the market can and will evolve over time, various ideas and concepts are timeless. These serve as the building blocks essential to understanding derivatives pricing, for all its limitations. And hopefully, presenting them in a coherent manner could make it possible for a reader to grasp the key ideas, even if the details may be superseded by future research.

I hope that this book will speed up your understanding of the framework behind derivatives pricing. As for the details and their mastery, I leave it to other authors to contribute their part, and I wish you the best in the days ahead.

Glossary

Whilst new terminology has been defined when first encountered throughout the book, the following list of terms might nevertheless serve as a useful reference for the reader from time to time.

American Option: An option which can be exercised at any date up to and including its expiry.

Annuity: An instrument comprising a series of fixed payments over regular intervals.

Asymptotic Expansion: A method whereby one simplifies (and potentially changes the nature of) an equation by assuming certain variables are small enough for higher order terms to be ignored in a series expansion, so that a solution can be obtained.

At-the-Money (Atm): An option is at-the-money when strike is equal to spot or forward (subject to the convention for the given market).

Barrier: An instrument with a discontinuous change in payoff when some level is breached; a knockout becomes worthless if the barrier is breached prior to expiry, whereas a knockin will only pay out if the barrier is breached at some date prior to expiry.

Basis Point (bp): 0.01 of 1%.

Basis Swap: A basis swap involves two legs, each based on the Libor rate for a different tenor (e.g. 3 months versus 6 months) with a spread applied to one leg. A cross-currency basis swap involves two legs, each paying Libor in a different currency (typically one leg pays US dollar Libor) with a spread applied to one leg.

Basket: A collection of assets (e.g. stocks, rates products, and commodities).

Bermudan Option: An option where exercise is permitted on certain fixed dates (e.g. coupon dates of an instrument) prior to expiry.

Black–Scholes PDE/Formula: Black and Scholes illustrated the use of dynamic hedging via the underlying to eliminate risk in a derivative. The Black--Scholes model assumes the underlying follows a lognormal process, but the ideas can be generalised. Merton first solved the Black–Scholes equation, and the formula is still used to quote option prices.

Black–Karansinski Model: A short rate model which assumes the short rate follows a lognormal mean-reverting process. Developed by Black and Karasinski. Analytic formulae do not exist for the discount bond price as a function of the short rate.

Blend Distribution: A distribution involving a mixture of normal and lognormal components.

Calibrate: To choose model parameters such that the model recovers the prices of liquid market instruments.

Callable: A feature which allows the issuer the discretion to repay a note and hence no longer be liable for future coupons. The issuer will call when in his interest, so he would be willing to pay a higher fair value coupon on the note with this feature.

Cap: Used as a verb, to limit the amount payable; used as a noun, an instrument that comprises a portfolio of caplets.

Caplet: A call option on interest rates.

Cash-Settled Swaption: A type of swaption (the staple in euros and sterling) where the payoff is settled in cash, based on the cash annuity defined solely in terms of the swap rate. (Its payoff is not the cash value of a physically settled swaption.)

CEV Distribution: A distribution where the volatility is multiplied by the value of the underlying raised to some power (typically between 0 and 1 inclusive). The lognormal distribution corresponds to a power of 1. Absorption can lead to a huge point mass at zero.

Cheyette Model: A short rate/Heath–Jarrow–Morton (HJM) model where a convexity state variable is added. Developed by Cheyette. Discount bonds are Markovian in two state variables in a one-factor Cheyette model with local volatility (smile/skew). In the absence of smile/skew, the convexity state variable is redundant.

CIR Model: A short rate model where the short rate follows a mean reverting square root process. This assures positive interest rates. However, there can be a huge amount of absorption at zero. Developed by Cox, Ingersoll, and Ross.

Cliquet: An instrument with payoff based on the returns over future periods (e.g. between year 3 and year 4).

CMS Rate: A long-term swap rate (e.g. 10-year rate) paid over a single much shorter accrual period (e.g. 3 months).

CMS Spread: An instrument with payoff based on the difference in value between two CMS rates (e.g. 20-year rate versus 2-year rate). Typically, there is interest in options on the CMS spread.

Collateral: Cash or high quality instruments (e.g. Treasury bonds) that are posted with a counterparty to settle adverse market movements that have led to a mark-to-market loss versus that counterparty.

Constant Maturity Swap (CMS): A swap where over each coupon period, one leg pays the CMS rate (i.e. floating long-term rate, say 10-year swap rate, applied over the much shorter coupon period) set at the start of the period (e.g. every 3 months).

Contingent Liability: A position where one can be exposed to losses exceeding one's initial investment, as a consequence of unfavourable market movements.

Copula: A technique that involves producing a terminal joint distribution given two or more terminal marginal distributions and some correlation assumptions.

Correlation: A measure of linear co-dependence between two random variables.

Counterparty: The other institution with whom a party has conducted the transaction.

Coupon: An amount payable at certain dates as stipulated by the contract. This could be fixed or dependent on market conditions.

Craig–Sneyd Algorithm: A method for solving PDEs by acting on each dimensional variable separately. This provides for stability by allowing the necessary amount of implicitness and is fast as there is no need to invert matrices.

CSA: Credit Security Annex to ISDA Agreement. This is the arrangement whereby institutions agree to post collateral to settle mark-to-market profit and loss variations with respect to their counterparties at the end of each business day. In theory, this means that an institution is only subjected to overnight risk from counterparties with whom it has a CSA-agreement.

Delta: The sensitivity of an instrument with respect to a unit change in the value of the underlying. Hedging typically involves maintaining an amount of the underlying corresponding to the delta of the derivative.

Deposit: An instrument that accrues interest until maturity.

Derivative: An instrument whose value depends on that of an underlying (e.g. an option's value depends on that of a stock, interest rate or FX rate).

Digital: A digital option pays 1 if the underlying is above (call) or below (put) some level at expiry.

Discount Factor: The discount factor up to a maturity is the value today of a zero-coupon bond of that maturity with notional of 1.

Dupire's Formula: A formula to obtain the local volatility from the prices of European call or put options and their time and strike derivatives. Formulated by Dupire.

Dynamic Replication: A hedging strategy where one trades in the underlying and possibly options, to match a given payoff at a future time under any market condition. Model assumptions determine the amount of the underlying (and options) to hold at any given time.

Equity: A stock (also known as share).

Euribor: Euro Interbank Offered Rate — the average of quotes for lending in euros by major banks, sponsored by the European Banking Federation and ACI The Financial Markets Association. These days it is no longer possible to fund at Euribor, but it is nevertheless the benchmark for settling floating coupons in euros.

European Option: An option which can only be exercised on its expiry date.

Exchange: A regulated and organised market that brings together different market participants for trading various assets.

Exchange Traded Product: A product traded on a futures exchange, which acts as the central counterparty to both sides of the transaction.

Exercise: Acquire or dispose of the asset at the strike, or otherwise enter into a contract as per the terms of the option.

Expectation: An average computed based on probabilities of different outcomes. These may not be true probabilities but would correspond to the chosen measure.

Expiry: The exercise date for a European option and the last exercise date for an American option.

Feynman–Kac Theorem: A theorem that relates the martingale pricing equation with the Black–Scholes PDE.

Floor: Used as a verb, to ensure a minimum amount is payable; used as a noun, an instrument comprising a portfolio of floorlets.

Floorlet: A put option on interest rate levels.

Foreign Exchange (FX): Rates at which one may convert from one currency to another.

Forward: A contract to buy or sell an asset at a pre-agreed price (strike) at a future date (maturity). In contrast to a future, this is a private transaction between two counterparties.

Forward Price: The fair value strike of the forward, which gives a zero present value to the contract.

Forward Rate: The fair value of the interest rate between two future points in time (based on the current yield curve), so as to avoid arbitrage opportunities.

Forward Rate Agreement (FRA): A contract that pays the difference between the realised rate of lending between two future dates and an agreed level, in effect fixing the rate of lending for the period.

Forward Volatility: The volatility of an asset between two future points in time. When we reach the first time point, this becomes spot volatility again. However, the volatility can be very different conditional on different realisations of the underlying's value.

Fourier Transform: A technique for solving an equation by integrating over Fourier nodes (i.e. sine and cosine components).

FtSe 100: An index constructed from the prices of some of the largest 100 companies (by market capitalisation) in the United Kingdom.

Funding: In the real world, institutions must borrow to cover any cash shortfalls. Whereas financial derivatives theory was designed on the premises of large institutions being able to lend and borrow at a risk-free rate, this no longer holds after the credit crisis of 2008, and it is now necessary to consider the nitty-gritty of funding.

Futures: An exchange traded instrument where one agrees to buy or sell an asset at a pre-agreed price (strike) at a future date (maturity), with the exchange acting as central counterparty. Profit and loss on the position (based on the closing price of traded futures contracts) is settled daily in the form of margin posted.

Gamma: The sensitivity of the delta of an instrument with respect to a unit change in the value of the underlying. It determines the profit from delta hedging an option.

Girsanov's Theorem: This says that a change of measure actually just involves a change of drift whilst volatility is unaffected. The drift is actually the volatility of the Radon–Nikodym derivative.

Hedge: To protect oneself from adverse market moves by taking positions to offset one's exposure.

Heston Model: A stochastic volatility model developed by Heston. The volatility is assumed to follow a mean reverting square root process. This model benefits from the existence of a Fourier transform method for obtaining the prices of European options. However, absorption means there is a huge amount of mass at variance of zero.

HJM Model: An interest rate model which involves instantaneous forward rates. Developed by Heath, Jarrow, and Morton. Discount bond prices are given by an integral over instantaneous forward rates. This model has been shown to be equivalent to short rate models for most useful parameterisations, in a sense that we could formulate one in terms of the other.

Ho–Lee Model: A short rate model where the short rate is taken as a Gaussian process. Since it does not have mean reversion, it is not adequate for most interest rate products. However, it is still used in simple cases such as computing the futures convexity.

Hull–White Model: A short rate model where the short rate is taken as a mean reverting Gaussian process. Developed by Hull and White. Discount bond prices are given by a functional form involving an exponential of the realised short rate. Analytic and quasi-analytic formulae also exist for the prices of caplets and swaptions respectively, so that fast calibration is possible. However, negative interest rates are a real possibility.

Implied Volatility: The number (volatility) which when used in the Black–Scholes formula gives the market price of an option.

In-the-Money: An option where immediate exercise (if permitted) will yield a profit.

ISDA: International Swaps and Derivatives Association. An organisation representing the interests of some of the largest financial institutions in the derivatives markets.

Ito's Lemma: A relation between the SDE of a function of a stochastic variable and the SDE of the stochastic variable itself.

Libor: London Interbank Offered Rate — the average of quotes for lending by major AA-rated banks across various currencies (US dollar, sterling, Japanese yen, etc), as calculated by the British Bankers' Association. These days it is no longer possible to fund at Libor, but it is nevertheless the benchmark for settling floating coupons.

Libor-in-Arrears (LIA): An instrument which pays a Libor rate but where the fixing date is the same as the payment date. For a normal floating rate coupon, fixing is at the beginning of the reference period, whilst payment is at the end (e.g. 6 months later for the 6-month Euribor rate).

Libor Market Model: One of the three main classes of interest rate models. Developed by Brace, Gatarek, and Musiela. The idea is to directly model consecutive Libor rates that span the time period of interest. Whilst each Libor rate is a martingale under the measure corresponding to the discount bond with maturity equal to its pay date, a non-trivial drift term involving all Libor rates arises when bringing the Libor rates under one measure. This causes the Libor Market Model to be only Markovian in a large number of state variables (i.e. all the Libor rates of interest), and hence computations are slow.

Linear Swap Rate Model: A model where we approximate the ratio of a discount bond to a physical annuity via an affine function of the swap rate. This allows us to consider various simplifications in treating physically settled swaptions and related products together.

Local Volatility: A model where volatility is a function of the underlying and time. It has enough degrees of freedom to fit the prices of all vanilla options across all expiries and strikes in FX and equities. However, this is not a sufficient criterion when considering forward vol-sensitive products, and one must consider if the true dynamics are more attuned to a stochastic vol model.

Local Stochastic Volatility: A model which is a mixture between a local volatility and a stochastic volatility model. Since market dynamics for various assets are often between a local vol and a stochastic vol process, a mixture offers the necessary flexibility.

Lognormal Distribution: A distribution whose logarithm is normally distributed.

Long: To buy.

Margin: Collateral set aside to cover actual end-of-day and potential future losses from market movements, as required by exchanges for exchange traded instruments.

Marginal Distribution: The terminal distribution of an underlying. For a market variable, this can usually be obtained from the first and second derivatives of prices of vanilla options with respect to strike.

Markovian: A Markov process is one where the expectation depends only on the current value and not on its history. When we say a variable is Markovian in a small number of state variables, we mean that we could determine its current value from the current values of those state variables, without having to resort to any history.

Markov-Functional Model: One of the three main classes of interest rates term structure models. Developed by Hunt, Kennedy, and Pelsser. The definition is that discount bonds at future times are given by a function of a Markov process. Typically, the idea is to use a low dimensional Markov process, so that PDE solutions can be utilised.

Martingale: A variable whose expected value (under the appropriate measure) at a future point in time is its current value.

Martingale Pricing Equation: The no-arbitrage equation that states that the ratio of assets is a martingale under the measure whose numeraire is the asset in the denominator.

Maturity: The date when the principal of a bond or note is due, when cashflows of a swap end, and when a forward contract has to be settled.

Mean Reversion: A feature of a process, where the drift is pulled towards some long-run mean. Whilst economically one may justify this as due to markets tending to some equilibrium; in derivatives pricing, the main consideration is not about forward rates/prices (since they are given by no arbitrage) but about forward vols (since mean reversion leads to vol decay so that vols over longer periods are depressed relative to vols over shorter periods).

Measure: A measure corresponds to the choice of numeraire asset. The probabilities used in computing an expectation are based on the measure.

Moments Explosion: The phenomenon where a stochastic volatility model (with certain parameters) may give rise to infinite moments (including the important second moment) within finite time.

Monte Carlo (MC): A valuation method that involves averaging over the realised values of a security along different paths, as per generated random numbers.

Money Market Account: A fictional deposit, which is continuously compounded at the risk-free rate.

Nikkei 225: An index comprising the prices of some of the largest 225 companies (by market capitalisation) in Japan.

No Arbitrage: The main principle underlying derivatives pricing — since riskless profits should not exist, if you can construct a (possibly dynamic) portfolio that matches a payoff, then the portfolio must have the same value as the payoff.

Numeraire: A unit of measure of value. This must be a domestic asset whose value is always greater than zero. For example, a stock can be a numeraire, as can the money market account (assumed to represent risk-free growth).

OIS Rate: The rate applicable to an overnight index swap. This is the rate applicable for collateralised borrowing. Since collateralised borrowing involves daily posting of collateral to settle changes in the mark-to-market value of all positions with a counterparty, so that one is subject to only one business day's counterparty risk, this is seen as the risk-free rate.

One-Touch: A one-touch option pays 1 at expiry if at any time during the life of the option, the underlying breaches a barrier. The barrier is above spot for an upside one-touch and below spot for a downside one-touch.

Option: An instrument that gives one the right but not obligation to buy (call option) or sell (put option) an asset at a future date (expiry) at a pre-agreed price (strike).

Out-of-the-Money: An option where immediate exercise (if permissible) is worthless.

Overnight Index Swap (OIS): A swap where one leg pays the overnight rate, compounded over the accrual period.

Over-the-Counter (OTC): These are transactions done between private counterparties outside an organised exchange.

Par: When a note is worth par, its present value is equal to its principal.

Parameter Averaging: A technique where we approximate time-dependent parameters in a process with constant parameters which still preserve the distribution at a specified terminal time point.

Partial Differential Equation (PDE): An equation that relates partial derivatives. PDE methods of valuation involve constructing a lattice of points and moving forward or backward in time on the lattice. Their use tends to be limited to models with up to three factors plus time.

Power Reverse Dual Currency (PRDC): A very long-dated instrument whose coupons are linked to FX rates (usually in USD/JPY or AUD/JPY). Typically, the bet is that the yen will not appreciate to the extent implied by forward FX rates.

Premium: The price of an option.

Present Value (PV): The value today of an instrument or set of future cashflows.

Principal: The face value of a bond or structured note. At maturity, typically the principal is repaid in full, unless it is linked to market variables. Also, coupons tend to be quoted with reference to the principal (e.g. a 5% fixed coupon).

Probability: The likelihood of an event occurring. 100% means that an event is certain. Zero means that it is impossible.

Puttable: A feature where the investor has discretion to seek repayment of the note. This is a valuable right, since the investor will put the note when in her interest, so a puttable note tends to attract a lower coupon.

Quadratic Gaussian Model: A short rate model where the short rate is a quadratic function of a Gaussian process. Quasi-analytic formulae for the prices of discount bonds exist.

Quanto: An instrument where the payoff is in a non-natural currency of the underlying but where no FX conversion takes place (e.g. BMW stock paid in dollars rather than euros).

Radon–Nikodym Derivative: The ratio of the numeraire assets involved in a change between two measures. Change of measure is effected by multiplying the Radon–Nikodym derivative onto a payoff.

Range Accrual: An instrument with payoff proportional to the number of days in a reference period that an underlying stays above or below some barrier.

Reflection Principle: A property of Brownian motion relating the probability of the maximum or minimum attaining some value over the period to that of the final value of the process being at some level.

Risk-Neutral: Hedging is meant to eliminate risk, so that the drift of the underlying is irrelevant and one only needs to consider the cost of funding, hence the term risk-neutrality.

Risk Reversal: A package where one is long a call and short a put (or vice versa) of approximately the same moneyness (defined in accordance to market conventions). It gives an indication of the volatilities of low strikes versus high strikes (i.e. skew).

S&P 500: An index comprising the prices of some of the largest 500 companies (by market capitalisation) in the US.

SABR: Stochastic Alpha Beta Rho model. Developed by Hagan, Kumar, Lesniewski, and Woodward. It is a simple stochastic volatility model involving a CEV process for the underlying and a log-normal stochastic volatility component. The existence of an analytic formula (via an asymptotic expansion) for the prices of European options and the intuitive nature of the parameters in describing vol level, skew and smile, have led to this model becoming market standard for interpolation of swaption vols.

Self-Quanto (also Auto-Quanto): An instrument whose payoff is based on an FX rate quoted as ccy1/ccy2, but settled in ccy1 rather than the natural ccy2, with no FX conversion.

Short: To sell (possibly an asset one does not own by borrowing it).

Short Rate Model: One of the three main classes of interest rate term-structure models. Here the underlying is an instantaneous risk-free rate. Discount bonds are given by an expectation of an exponential over the integral of the short rate under the risk-neutral measure. The drift of the short rate is fully determined by the discount curve. Typically, it is desirable for the model to produce analytic prices of discount bonds for computational efficiency.

Snowball: A product that pays a put-like payoff plus the previous coupon (if greater than zero). Otherwise, coupon is zero and accumulation for the next coupon starts from zero.

Speculate: To seek to profit by betting on the movements of market variables.

Spread: The difference between two market quantities (e.g. the Libor rate versus the OIS rate).

Static Replication: Construction of a portfolio today to match a given payoff at a future point in time under any market condition. The value of the payoff today is then given by the value of the replicating portfolio. No model assumption is involved if market prices are available for all instruments used in the replication.

STOXX 50: An index comprising the prices of some of the largest 50 companies (by market capitalisation) in Europe.

Stochastic Volatility: A model where the volatility/variance is assumed to be a random process. This can lead to persistence of smile since the variance of volatility grows with time. The choice between local volatility and stochastic volatility models is important for forward volatility-sensitive products.

Strangle: A package where one is long a call and a put whose strikes are equidistant from the forward or spot in delta terms (or otherwise as specified by the convention of the market). This gives an indication of how much out-of-the-money vols trade at a premium to at-the-money vols (i.e. smile).

Strike: The exercise price of a forward or an option.

Structured Products: Instruments created by financial institutions and specially tailored to a client's market views and investment preferences, allowing the client better control over the risk-reward tradeoff.

Swap: An instrument that involves exchanges of cashflows. In a vanilla swap, one party pays a floating rate (based on some index like Libor or Euribor) and the other party pays a pre-agreed fixed rate on each coupon date. The fixed and floating legs need not have the same coupon dates. In a single currency swap, no exchange of notional takes place.

Swap Rate: The pre-agreed rate that applies to the fixed leg of the swap, which will cause the value of the swap today to be zero.

Swaption: An option that gives one the right to enter into a swap. A payer swaption is one where the underlying swap pays a fixed rate and receives a floating rate. A receiver swaption is one where the underlying swap receives a fixed rate and pays a floating rate.

Tanaka's Formula: Ito's Lemma as extended to include the derivatives of non-continuous functions via the theory of distributions.

Tarn: Target redemption note. A feature which leads to early termination of a note/swap, if the total coupons paid have exceeded some level. This makes the note cheaper as it limits the total coupons payable.

Terminal Distribution: The distribution of a variable as seen at one future point in time.

Theory of Distributions: An extension of calculus so that derivatives of the Heaviside and Dirac delta functions are defined (in terms of their integrals).

Transition Probability: The probability of moving from one state at a point in time, to another state at a future point in time.

Trigger (also AutoCall): A condition where the breach of some level will lead to early termination of a note/swap. Typically, this is designed to benefit the issuer, and hence increase the yield payable on the instrument.

Vanilla: Refers to simpler products. For options, these typically include European calls and puts and digitals, although the classification can vary according to different assets.

Variance: The square of volatility, although in derivatives pricing it usually is multiplied by the length of the period.

Variance Swap: A contract that pays the difference between realised variance and some strike.

Vega: The sensitivity of an instrument with respect to a unit change in the value of implied volatility.

Volatility (Vol): A measure of how much an underlying moves on average. Higher volatility increases the price of an option since it increases the cost of hedging.

Volatility Smile/Skew: A representation of implied volatilities for different strikes. Smile tends to refer to higher volatilities for out-of-the-money options (versus at-the-money options), whilst skew tends to refer to higher volatilities for low strikes versus high strikes (in equities) or vice versa (e.g. options on USD/BRL).

Volatility Swap: A contract that pays the difference between realised volatility and some strike.

Volatility Surface: A representation of implied volatilities for different expiries and strikes for equities and foreign exchange; and for different expiries, tenors, and strikes for interest rates.

Write: To write an option is to sell it.

Yield Curve: A representation of the rates of borrowing/lending for different maturities.

Zero-Coupon Bond: A bond that pays only the principal at maturity and no intermediate coupons.

Note on FX Quote Style

In the interbank market, the quote style is ccy1/ccy2. Rather unintuitively, this refers to the number of units of currency two per unit of currency one. For example, the exchange rate between the dollar and the yen is quoted as USD/JPY (i.e. number of yen per dollar) whilst that between the euro and the dollar is quoted as EUR/USD (i.e. number of dollars per euro).

In the futures market however (e.g. CME Group), some FX pairs are quoted as number of dollars per unit of currency (e.g. JPY/USD). It makes these currency futures similar to futures in any other dollar asset.

Bibliography

This book assumes foundational knowledge of financial mathematics, and takes the reader through a journey that hopefully will end in her understanding market practice derivatives modelling. With that in mind, I shall start by listing books that either deal with the basics (should the reader need to refresh her memory), or attempt more specialised coverage of various subject areas. Thereafter, I shall present a list of papers, which expand on much of the material covered in the text.

Books on Financial Modelling and Derivatives Pricing

[AV11] Andersen, LBG and VV Piterbarg (2011). *Interest Rate Modeling*. UK: Atlantic Press.

[Ben07] Benhamou, E (ed.) (2007). *Global Derivatives — Products, Theory, and Practice*. Singapore: World Scientific.

[BM06] Brigo, D and F Mercurio (2006). *Interest Rate Models — Theory and Practice; with Smile, Inflation, and Credit*. Berlin and Heidelberg: Springer Finance.

[BO10] Bouzoubaa, M and A Osseiran (2010). *Exotic Options and Hybrids*: *A Guide to Structuring, Pricing and Trading*. Chichester: John Wiley & Sons.

[BR96] Baxter, M and A Rennie (1996). *Financial Calculus*: *An Introduction to Derivative Pricing*. Cambridge: Cambridge University Press.

[BZ98] Brzezniak, Z and T Zastawniak (1998). *Basic Stochastic Processes*. London: Springer-Verlag.

[Chi04] Chisholm, AA (2004). *Derivatives Demystified — A Step-by-Step Guide to Forwards, Futures, Swaps and Options*. Chichester: John Wiley & Sons.

[Cla11] Clark, IJ (2011). *Foreign exchange option pricing — A Practitioner's Guide.* Chichester: John Wiley & Sons.

[Duf06] Duffy, DJ (2006). *Finite difference methods in financial engineering — A Partial Differential Equation Approach.* Chichester: John Wiley & Sons.

[dWe08] de Weert, F (2008). *Exotic Options Trading.* Chichester: John Wiley & Sons.

[Gat06] Gatheral, J (2006). *The Volatility Surface — A Practitioner's Guide.* New Jersey: John Wiley & Sons.

[Gla04] Glasserman, P (2004). *Monte Carlo Methods in Financial Engineering.* New York: Springer-Verlag.

[Hau07] Haug, EG (2007). *The Complete Guide to Option Pricing Formulas.* New York: McGraw-Hill.

[HK04] Hunt, PJ and JE Kennedy (2004). *Financial Derivatives in Theory and Practice.* Chichester: John Wiley & Sons.

[Hul11] Hull, JC (2011). *Options, Futures and Other Derivatives*, 8th Ed. New Jersey: Prentice Hall.

[Jos03] Joshi, M (2003). *The Concepts and Practice of Mathematical Finance.* Cambridge: Cambridge University Press.

[Kat01] Kat, HM (2001). *Structured Equity Derivatives: The Definitive Guide to Exotic Options and Structured Notes.* Chichester: John Wiley & Sons.

[KS01] Karatzas, I and SE Shreve (2001). *Methods of Mathematical Finance.* New York: Springer-Verlag.

[KS04] Karatzas, I and SE Shreve (2004). *Brownian Motion and Stochastic Calculus.* Berlin, Heidelberg and New York: Springer-Verlag.

[Lew00] Lewis, AL (2000). *Option Valuation Under Stochastic Volatility: With Mathematica Code.* Newport Beach: Finance Press.

[MM94] Morton, K and D Mayers (1994). *Numerical Solution of Partial Differential Equations.* Cambridge: Cambridge University Press.

[MR07] Musiela, M and M Rutkowski (2007). *Martingale Methods in Financial Modelling,* Stochastic Modelling and Applied Probability. Berlin, Heidelberg and New York: Springer-Verlag.

[Nef96] Neftci, SN (1996). *An Introduction to the Mathematics of Financial Derivatives*, 2nd Ed. San Diego: Academic Press.

[Oks98] Oksendal, B (1998). Stochastic Differential Equations, 5th Ed. Berlin: Springer-Verlag.

[Pel00] Pelsser, A (2000). *Efficient Methods for Valuing Interest Rate Derivatives.* London: Springer Finance.

[Reb02] Rebonato, R (2002). *Modern Pricing of Interest Rates Derivatives: The LIBOR Market Model and Beyond.* Princeton: Princeton University Press.

[Reb04] Rebonato, R (2004). *Volatility and Correlation — The Perfect Hedger and the Fox.* Chichester: John Wiley & Sons.

[RMW09] Rebonato, R, K McKay and R White (2009). *The SABR/LIBOR Market Model: Pricing, Calibration and Hedging for Complex Interest Rate Derivatives*. Chichester: John Wiley & Sons.

[Shr05] Shreve, SE (2005). *Stochastic Calculus for Finance: Binomial Asset Pricing Model v1*. New York: Springer Finance.

[Shr08] Shreve, SE (2008). *Stochastic Calculus for Finance: Continuous-time Models v2*. New York: Springer Finance.

[Tan10] Tan, CC (2010). *Demystifying exotic products — Interest Rates, Equities and Foreign Exchange*. Chichester: John Wiley & Sons.

[WHD95] Wilmott, P, S Howison and J Dewynne (1995). *The Mathematics of Financial Derivatives — A Student Introduction*. Cambridge: Cambridge University Press.

[Wil06] Wilmott, P (2006). *Paul Wilmott on Quantitative Finance*, 2nd Ed. Chichester: John Wiley & Sons.

[Wil07] Wilmott, P (2007). *Paul Wilmott introduces Quantitative Finance*, 2nd Ed. Chichester: John Wiley & Sons.

[Wil09] Wilmott, P (2009). *Frequently Asked Questions in Quantitative Finance*, 2nd Ed. Chichester: John Wiley & Sons.

[Wys06] Wystup, U (2006). *FX Options and Structured Products*. Chichester: John Wiley & Sons.

Papers on Financial Modelling and Derivatives Pricing

[AA00] Andersen, L and J Andreasen (2000). Volatility skews and extensions of the LIBOR market model. *Applied Mathematical Finance*, 7, 1–32.

[AA01] Andersen, L and J Andreasen (2001). Factor dependence of Bermudan swaption prices: Fact or fiction? *Journal of Financial Economics*, 62, 3–37.

[AAE00] Andersen, L, J Andreasen and D Eliezer (2000). Static replication of barrier options: Some general results. SSRN working paper.

[ABR05] Andersen, L and R Brotherton-Ratcliffe. Extended LIBOR market models with stochastic volatility. *Journal of Computational Finance*, 9(1), 1–40.

[And00] Andersen, L (2000). A simple approach to the pricing of Bermudan swaptions in the multi-factor libor market model. *Journal of Computational Finance*, 3(2), 5–32.

[And07] Andersen, L (2007). Efficient simulation of the heston stochastic volatility model. Working paper, Bank of America.

[Andr00] Andreasen, J (2000). Turbo charging the Cheyette model. Working paper, Gen Re Securities.

[Andr02] Andreasen, J (2002). Pricing simple exotics under stochastic volatility. Working paper, Nordea Markets.

[Andr06a] Andreasen, J (2006). Stochastic volatility for real. Working Paper, Bank of America.

[Andr06b] Andreasen, J (2006). Long-dated FX hybrids with stochastic volatility. Working paper, Bank of America.

[AP07] Andersen, L and V Piterbarg (2007). Moment explosions in stochastic volatility models. *Finance and stochastics*, 11(1), 29–50.

[As07] Assefa, S (2007). Calibration and pricing in a multi-factor quadratic Gaussian model. University of Technology Sydney, Quantitative Finance Research Centre, Research paper 197.

[Bax97] Baxter, MW (1997). General interest-rate models and the universality of HJM. Mathematices of Derivative Securities, Cambridge University Press, Cambridge.

[BDL10] Brauman, CA, J Dias and M Larguinho (2010). Speed and accuracy comparison of noncentral chi-square distribution methods for option pricing and hedging. 6th International Conference of the Portuguese Finance Network, Ponta Delgada, Azores, Portugal.

[BDT90] Black, F, E Derman and W Toy (1990). A one-factor model of interest rates and its application to treasury bond options. *Financial Analysts Journal*, 46, 33–39.

[Ben99] Benhamou, E (1999). Faster Greeks for discontinuous payoff options (A Malliavin calculus approach in black world). Working paper, London School of Economics.

[BGM97] Brace, A, D Gatarek and M Musiela (1997). The market model of interest rate dynamics. *Math Finance*, 7, 127–154.

[BGR08] Benhamou, E, A Gruz and A Rivoira (2008). Stochastic interest rates for local volatility hybrids models. Working paper.

[Bia09] Bianchetti, M (2009). Two curves, one price. SSRN Working paper.

[BK91] Black, F and P Karasinski (1991). Bond and option pricing when short rates are lognormal. *Financial Analysts Journal*, 47, 52–59.

[Bla76] Black, F (1976). The pricing of commodity contracts. *Journal of Financial Economics*, 3, 67–179.

[BN08] Bloch, D and Y Nakashima (2008). Multi-currency local volatility model. Working paper, Mizuho Securities.

[BS73] Black, F and M Scholes (1973). The pricing of options and corporate liabilities. *Journal of Political Economy*, 81, 637–654.

[Che92] Cheyette, O (1992). Markov representation of the Heath–Jarrow–Morton model. Working paper, BARRA.

[CIR85] Cox, J, J Ingersoll and SA Ross (1985). A theory of the term structure of interest rates. *Econometrica*, 53(2), 385–407.

[CL05] Carr, P and R Lee (2005). Robust replication of volatility derivatives. Courant Institute and Bloomberg.

[CM99] Carr, P and D Madan (1999). Option valuation using the Fast Fourier Transform. *The Journal of Computational Finance*, 2(4), 61–73.

[CM05] Castagna, A and F Mercurio (2005). Consistent pricing of FX options. Working paper, Banca IMI.

[CS88] Craig, I and A Sneyd (1988). An alternating implicit scheme for parabolic equations with mixed derivatives. *Computers and Mathematics with Applications*, 16(4), 341–350.

[CT07] Cont, R and P Tankov (2007). Constant Proportion Portfolio Insurance in presence of Jumps in Asset Prices. Columbia University Center for Financial Engineering, Report No. 2007-10.

[DK94] Derman, E and I Kani (1994). Riding on a smile (February 1994). *Risk*, 7(2), pp. 32–39.

[DK98] Derman, E and I Kani (1998). Stochastic implied trees: Arbitrage pricing with stochastic term and strike structure of volatility. *International Journal of Theoretical and Applied Finance*, 1, 61–110.

[Dup94] Dupire, B (1994). Pricing with a smile (January 1994). *Risk*, 7(1), 18–20.

[Dup97] Dupire, B (1997). A unified theory of volatility. Working paper, Banque Paribas.

[DY02] Dragulescu, AA and VM Yakovenko (2002). Probability distribution of returns in the Heston model with stochastic volatility. *Quantitative Finance*, 2, 443–453.

[EF10] Elices, A and J-P Fouque (2010). Perturbed Copula: Introducing the skew effect in co-dependence. arXiv Working paper (2010).

[EKGR95] Karoui, NE, H Geman and JC Rochet (1995). Changes of numeraire, changes of probability measures and option pricing. *Journal of Applied Probability*, 32, 443–458.

[EKVM91] Karoui, NE, R Viswanathan and R Myneni (1991). Arbitrage pricing and hedging of interest rate claims with state variables. Working paper, Universite de Paris IV and Stanford University.

[Eli07] Elices, A (2007). Models with time-dependent parameters using transform methods: application to Heston's model. arXiv working paper.

[Fri10] Fries, CP (2010). Discounting Revisited. Valuations under Funding Costs, Counterparty Risk, and Collateralization. SSRN Working paper.

[GBvWO08] Grzelak, LA, N Borovykh, S van Weeren and CW Oosterlee (2008). Incorporating an interest rate smile in an equity local volatility model. SSRN Working paper.

[GG06] Giles, M and P Glasserman (2006). Smoking adjoints: Fast Monte Carlo Greeks (January 2006). *Risk*, 88–92.

[GY04] Glasserman, P and B Yu (2004). Number of paths versus number of basis functions in American option pricing. *Annals of Applied Probability*, 14(4), 2090–2119.

[GZ99] Glasserman, P and X Zhao (1999). Fast Greeks by simulation in forward Libor models. *Journal of Computational Finance*, 3, 5–39.

[Hag03] Hagan, PS (2003). Convexity conundrums: Pricing CMS swaps, caps, and floors (March 2003). *Wilmott* magazine, 38–44.

[Hes93]   Heston, SL (1993). A closed-form solution for options with stochastic volatility with applications to bond and currency options. *Review of Financial Studies*, 2(6), 327–343.

[HJM92]   Heath, D, R Jarrow and A Morton (1992). Bond pricing and the term structure of interest rates: A new methodology for contingent claims valuation. *Econometrica*, 60, 77–106.

[HKLW02] Hagan, PS, D Kumar, AS Lesniewski and DE Woodward (2002). Managing Smile Risk (July 2002). *Wilmott magazine*, pp. 84–108.

[HKP04]   Hunt, P, J Kennedy and A Pelsser (2004). Markov-functional interest rate models. *Finance and Stochastics*, 4(4), 391–408.

[HL86]   Ho, TSY and SB Lee (1986). Term structure movements and pricing interest rate contingent claims. *Journal of Finance*, 41(5), 1011–1029.

[HP81]   Harrison, JM and SR Pliska (1981). Martingales and stochastic integrals in the theory of continuous trading. Stochastic Processes and their Applications, 11, 215–260.

[HW87]   Hull, JC and A White (1987). The pricing of options on assets with stochastic volatilities. *The Journal of Finance*, XLII(2), 281–300.

[HW90]   Hull, JC and A White (1990). Pricing interest rate derivatives securities. *The Review of Financial Studies*, 3, 573–592.

[HW94]   Hull, JC and A White (1994). Numerical procedures for implementing term structure models I: Single-factor models. *The Journal of Derivatives*, 2(1), 7–16.

[HW99]   Hagan, PS and DE Woodward (1999). Equivalent black volatilities. *Applied Math Finance*, 6, 147–157.

[Jam89]   Jamshidian, F (1989). An exact bond option pricing formula. *Journal of Finance*, 44, 205–209.

[Jam91]   Jamshidian, F (1991). Bond and option evaluation in the Gaussian interest rate model. *Research in Finance*, 9, 131–710.

[Jam97]   Jamshidian, F (1997). Libor and swap market models and measures. *Finance and Stochastics*, 1(4), 293–330.

[Kar11]   Karasinski, P (2011). What drives interest rates volatility? GARP Seminar.

[Lip02]   Lipton, A (2002). The vol smile problem (February 2002). *Risk*, 61–65.

[LS01]   Longstaff, FA and ES Schwartz (2001). Valuing American options by simulation: A simple least-squares approach. *The Review of Financial Studies*, 14(1), 113–147.

[LSSC99] Longstaff, F, E Schwartz and E Santa-Clara (1999). Throwing away a billion dollars: The cost of suboptimal exercise in the swaption market. Working paper, The Andersen School, UCLA.

[Luc08]   Lucic, V (2008). Boundary conditions for computing densities in hybrid models via PDE methods. Working paper, Barclays Capital.

[Mar78]   Margrabe, W (1978). The value of an option to exchange one asset for another. *Journal of Finance*, 33, 177–186.

[Mer09] Mercurio, F (2009). Interest rates and the credit crunch: New formulas and market models. SSRN Working paper.

[Mor10] Morini, M (2010). Solving the puzzle in the interest rate market. ICBI Global Derivatives Conference.

[MSS97] Milterson, K, K Sandmann and D Sondermann (1997). Closed form solutions for term structure of derivatives with log-normal interest rates. *Journal of Finance*, 52(1), 409–430.

[Ove02] Overhaus, M (2002). Himalaya options (March 2002). *Risk*, 101–104.

[Ped98] Pedersen, MB (1998). Calibrating libor market models. SSRN Working paper.

[Ped99] Pedersen, MB (1999). Bermudan swaptions in the LIBOR market model. SimCorp Financial Research Working paper.

[PP05] Pelsser, A and R Pietersz (2005). A comparison of single-factor Markov-functional and Multi-factor market models. SSRN Working paper.

[PPvR04] Pelsser, A, R Pietersz and M van Regenmortel (2004). Fast drift-approximated pricing in the BGM model. *Journal of Computational Finance*, 8(1), 93–124.

[Pit03a] Piterbarg, V (2003). Mixture of models: A simple recipe for a ... Hangover? SSRN Working paper.

[Pit03b] Piterbarg, V (2003). Computing deltas of callable LIBOR exotics in a forward LIBOR model. SSRN Working paper.

[Pit03c] Piterbarg, V (2003). A practitioner's guide to pricing and hedging callable libor exotics in forward libor models. SSRN Working paper.

[Pit05a] Piterbarg, V (2005). Stochastic volatility model with time-dependent skew. *Applied Mathematical Finance*, 12(2), 147–185.

[Pit05b] Piterbarg, V (2005). A multi-currency model with FX volatility skew. Working paper, Bank of America.

[Pit09] Piterbarg, V (2009). Rates squared (January 2009). *Risk*, pp. 100–105.

[Pit10] Piterbarg, V (2010). Funding beyond discounting: collateral agreements and derivatives pricing, (March 2010). *Risk*, pp. 97–102.

[Que02] Quessette, R (2002). New products, new risks (March 2002). *Risk*, pp. 97–100.

[RdG10] Rebonato, R and N de Guillaume (2010). A universal feature of interest rates: The CEV exponent, and its relevance for hedging. ICBI Global Derivatives Conference.

[RMJBN05] Rebonato, R, S Mahal, M Joshi, L-D Buchholz, K Nyholm (2005). Evolving yield curves in the real-world measures: A semi-parametric approach. SSRN Working paper.

[RS95] Ritchken, P and L Sankarasubramanian (1995). Volatility structure of forward rates and the dynamics of the term structure. *Mathematical Finance*, 5, 55–72.

[Sav00] Savine, A (2000). A theory of volatility. Working paper, Reech.

[Tez05] Tezier, C (2005). Short rate models. Linear and quadratic Gaussian models. Working paper, Barclays Capital.

[Vas77] Vasicek, O (1977). An equilibrium characterization of the term structure. *Journal of Financial Economics*, 5, 177–188.

[Wil02] Wilmott, P (2002). Cliquet options and volatility models (December 2002). *Wilmott magazine*, pp. 78–83.

Answers to Selected Questions

We present here answers to selected questions from the exercises section at the end of each chapter. These are by no means the only approaches to the problems, but hopefully should provide guidance for an interested reader.

Chapter 1

(1) We have

$$
\begin{aligned}
\mathrm{cov}(W_t, W_T) &= E[W_t W_T] - E[W_t]E[W_T] \\
&= E[W_t^2] + E[W_t(W_T - W_t)] - 0 \\
&= t - 0 \\
&= t.
\end{aligned}
$$

(2) We have

$$
\begin{aligned}
P\left(\min_{0 \le t \le T} W_t < m\right) &= P(\min_{0 \le t \le T} W_t < m \text{ and } W_T \ge m) \\
&\quad + P(\min_{0 \le t \le T} W_t < m \text{ and } W_T < m) \\
&= P(W_T < m) + P(W_T < m) \\
&= 2P(W_T < m),
\end{aligned}
$$

where the first term in the second equality comes from the Reflection Principle.

(3) We get

$$P_t = e^{-r(T-t)} \int_{-\infty}^{\infty} \max(K - S_t e^{(r-\frac{1}{2}\sigma^2)(T-t)+\sigma z\sqrt{T-t}}, 0)$$

$$\times \frac{1}{\sqrt{2\pi}} e^{-\frac{1}{2}z^2} dz$$

$$= e^{-r(T-t)} \int_{-\infty}^{z^*} (K - S_t e^{(r-\frac{1}{2}\sigma^2)(T-t)+\sigma z\sqrt{T-t}}) \frac{1}{\sqrt{2\pi}} e^{-\frac{1}{2}z^2} dz$$

$$= Ke^{-r(T-t)} N(z^*) - S_t e^{-\frac{1}{2}\sigma^2(T-t)} \frac{1}{\sqrt{2\pi}}$$

$$\times \int_{-\infty}^{z^*} e^{-\frac{1}{2}(z-\sigma\sqrt{T-t})^2} dz e^{\frac{1}{2}\sigma^2(T-t)}$$

$$= Ke^{-r(T-t)} N(z^*) - S_t N(z^* - \sigma\sqrt{T-t})$$

$$= Ke^{-r(T-t)} N(-d_1 + \sigma\sqrt{T-t}) - S_t N(-d_1),$$

where

$$z^* = \frac{\log(\frac{K}{S_t}) - (r - \frac{1}{2}\sigma^2)(T-t)}{\sigma\sqrt{T-t}}$$

and

$$d_1 = \frac{\log(\frac{S_t}{K}) + (r + \frac{1}{2}\sigma^2)(T-t)}{\sigma\sqrt{T-t}}.$$

(4) The portfolio is $\Pi_t = \Delta_t^S S_t + \Delta_t^P D(t,T) - f(S_t, r_t, t)$, so $d\Pi_t = \Delta_t^S dS_t + \Delta_t^P dD(t,T) - df(S_t, r_t, t)$.
But Ito's Lemma gives

$$dD(t,T) = \frac{\partial D}{\partial t} dt + \frac{\partial D}{\partial r_t}[\kappa(\theta(t) - r_t)dt + \lambda dU_t] + \frac{1}{2}\frac{\partial^2 D}{\partial r_t^2}\lambda^2 dt,$$

and

$$df = \frac{\partial f}{\partial t} dt + \frac{\partial f}{\partial S_t}(\mu(t)S_t dt + \sigma S_t dW_t) + \frac{1}{2}\frac{\partial^2 f}{\partial S_t^2}\sigma^2 S_t^2 dt$$

$$+ \frac{\partial f}{\partial r_t}[\kappa(\theta(t) - r_t)dt + \lambda dU_t] + \frac{1}{2}\frac{\partial^2 f}{\partial r_t^2}\lambda^2 dt$$

$$+ \frac{\partial^2 f}{\partial S_t \partial r_t}\rho\lambda\sigma S_t dt.$$

If we choose $\Delta_t^S = \frac{\partial f}{\partial S_t}$ and $\Delta_t^D = \frac{\partial f}{\partial r_t} / \frac{\partial D}{\partial r_t}$, then the resultant SDE for the portfolio is

$$d\Pi_t = \frac{\partial f}{\partial S_t}(\mu(t)S_t dt + \sigma S_t dW_t)$$

$$+ \left(\frac{\partial f}{\partial r_t} \bigg/ \frac{\partial D}{\partial r_t}\right)$$

$$\times \left(\frac{\partial D}{\partial t}dt + \frac{\partial D}{\partial r_t}[\kappa(\theta(t) - r_t)dt + \lambda dU_t] + \frac{1}{2}\frac{\partial^2 D}{\partial r_t^2}\lambda^2 dt\right)$$

$$- \frac{\partial f}{\partial t}dt - \frac{\partial f}{\partial S_t}(\mu(t)S_t dt + \sigma S_t dW_t) - \frac{1}{2}\frac{\partial^2 f}{\partial S_t^2}\sigma^2 S_t^2 dt$$

$$- \frac{\partial f}{\partial r_t}[\kappa(\theta(t) - r_t)dt + \lambda dU_t] - \frac{1}{2}\frac{\partial^2 f}{\partial r_t^2}\lambda^2 dt$$

$$- \frac{\partial^2 f}{\partial S_t \partial r_t}\rho\lambda\sigma S_t dt$$

$$= \left(\frac{\partial f}{\partial r_t} \bigg/ \frac{\partial D}{\partial r_t}\right)\left(\frac{\partial D}{\partial t}dt + \frac{1}{2}\frac{\partial^2 D}{\partial r_t^2}\lambda^2 dt\right)$$

$$- \frac{\partial f}{\partial t}dt - \frac{1}{2}\frac{\partial^2 f}{\partial S_t^2}\sigma^2 S_t^2 dt - \frac{1}{2}\frac{\partial^2 f}{\partial r_t^2}\lambda^2 dt - \frac{\partial^2 f}{\partial S_t \partial r_t}\rho\lambda\sigma S_t dt.$$

Since there is no more random component, this portfolio must grow at the risk-free rate, so

$$d\Pi_t = r_t \Pi_t dt$$

$$= r_t \left(\frac{\partial f}{\partial S_t}S_t + \left(\frac{\partial f}{\partial r_t} \bigg/ \frac{\partial D}{\partial r_t}\right)D(t,T) - f(S_t, r_t, t)\right)dt.$$

Thus, we get

$$r_t \left(\frac{\partial f}{\partial S_t}S_t + \left(\frac{\partial f}{\partial r_t} \bigg/ \frac{\partial D}{\partial r_t}\right)D(t,T) - f(S_t, r_t, t)\right)$$

$$= \left(\frac{\partial f}{\partial r_t} \bigg/ \frac{\partial D}{\partial r_t}\right)\left(\frac{\partial D}{\partial t} + \frac{1}{2}\frac{\partial^2 D}{\partial r_t^2}\lambda^2\right)$$

$$-\frac{\partial f}{\partial t} - \frac{1}{2}\frac{\partial^2 f}{\partial S_t^2}\sigma^2 S_t^2 - \frac{1}{2}\frac{\partial^2 f}{\partial r_t^2}\lambda^2$$

$$-\frac{\partial^2 f}{\partial S_t \partial r_t}\rho\lambda\sigma S_t.$$

But we can hedge with a discount bond with any arbitrary maturity T^*, so we require

$$\frac{r_t D(t,T) - \frac{\partial D(t,T)}{\partial t} - \frac{1}{2}\frac{\partial^2 D(t,T)}{\partial r_t^2}\lambda^2}{\frac{\partial D(t,T)}{\partial r_t}}$$

$$= \frac{r_t D(t,T^*) - \frac{\partial D(t,T^*)}{\partial t} - \frac{1}{2}\frac{\partial^2 D(t,T^*)}{\partial r_t^2}\lambda^2}{\frac{\partial D(t,T^*)}{\partial r_t}}$$

$$= A(t) + B(t)r_t,$$

for some $A(t), B(t)$.

From the SDE for the short rate, it is natural to set

$$r_t D(t,T) - \frac{\partial D}{\partial t} - \frac{1}{2}\frac{\partial^2 D}{\partial r_t^2}\lambda^2 = \frac{\partial D}{\partial r_t}(\kappa(\theta(t) - r_t)).$$

Thus, we end up with

$$r_t S_t \frac{\partial f}{\partial S_t} - r_t f(S_t, r_t, t) = -\frac{\partial f}{\partial t} - \frac{1}{2}\sigma^2 S_t^2 \frac{\partial^2 f}{\partial S_t^2} - \frac{1}{2}\lambda^2 \frac{\partial^2 f}{\partial r_t^2}$$

$$- \rho\lambda\sigma S_t \frac{\partial^2 f}{\partial S_t \partial r_t} - \kappa(\theta(t) - r_t)\frac{\partial f}{\partial r_t}.$$

(5) $X_t B_t^f$ is a domestic asset, so $\frac{X_t B_t^f}{B_t}$ is a martingale under the domestic risk-neutral measure. Then $d(\frac{X_t B_t^f}{B_t})/(\frac{X_t B_t^f}{B_t}) = (\mu + r_t^f - r_t)dt + \sigma dW_t$ gives $\mu = r_t - r_t^f$.

Chapter 2

(1) Swap rates involve averaging over different maturities. In the case of increasing swap rates, zero rates must therefore be higher than swap rates and forward rates higher still.

Consider

$$F_i = \left(\frac{D(0, T_{i-1})}{D(0, T_i)} - 1\right) \Big/ (T_i - T_{i-1}) = \frac{(1 + Z_i)^i}{(1 + Z_{i-1})^{i-1}} - 1 > Z_i$$

since

$$\left(\frac{1 + Z_i}{1 + Z_{i-1}}\right)^{i-1} > 1$$

for Z_i increasing.

Consider next

$$S_i = \frac{1 - D(0, T_i)}{\sum_{j=1}^i D(0, T_j)} \Rightarrow S_i \sum_{j=1}^i D(0, T_j) = 1 - D(0, T_i).$$

We can see that

$$S_{i-1} = \frac{1 - D(0, T_{i-1})}{\sum_{j=1}^{i-1} D(0, T_j)} \Rightarrow \sum_{j=1}^{i-1} D(0, T_j) = \frac{1 - D(0, T_{i-1})}{S_{i-1}}.$$

This gives

$$S_i D(0, T_i) + \frac{S_i}{S_{i-1}}(1 - D(0, T_{i-1})) = 1 - D(0, T_i)$$

$$\Rightarrow S_i D(0, T_i) + 1 - D(0, T_{i-1}) < 1 - D(0, T_i)$$

since S_i is increasing.

Thus,

$$S_i < \frac{D(0, T_{i-1})}{D(0, T_i)} - 1 = F_i.$$

(2) A lot of the material for this question will be more thoroughly covered in Chapter 8. The purpose of this exercise is just to give the reader a foretaste of futures convexity in practice.

Under the Ho–Lee model, the SDE for the short rate is $dr_t = \theta(t)dt + \sigma dW_t$. The fair value of a future is $E^B[L_T]$. For convenience, we approximate the Libor rate to be equal to the instantaneous forward $f_{t,T}$ rate applicable to time T as seen at time t. Thus, we have $E^B[L_T] \approx E^B[f_{T,T}] = E^B[r_T]$.

Based on the SDE of the Ho–Lee model, we have

$$r_t = r_0 + \int_0^t \theta(u)du + \sigma W_t,$$

so that

$$E^B[r_T] = r_0 + \int_0^T \theta(u)du.$$

And the price of a discount bond is given by

$$
\begin{aligned}
D(0,T) &= E^Q[e^{-\int_0^T r_s ds}] \\
&= E^Q\left[\exp\left(-\int_0^T \left(r_0 + \int_0^s \theta(u)du + \sigma W_s\right)ds\right)\right] \\
&= E^Q\left[\exp\left(-\int_0^T \left(r_0 + \int_0^s \theta(u)du + \sigma \int_0^s dW_u\right)ds\right)\right] \\
&= \exp\left(-r_0T - \int_0^T\int_u^T ds\theta(u)du\right) \\
&\quad \times E^Q\left[\exp\left(-\sigma \int_0^T\int_u^T dsdW_u\right)\right] \\
&= \exp\left(-r_0T - \int_0^T \theta(u)(T-u)du\right) \\
&\quad \times E^Q\left[\exp\left(-\sigma \int_0^T (T-u)dW_u\right)\right] \\
&= \exp\left(-r_0T - \int_0^T \theta(u)(T-u)du\right. \\
&\qquad\left. + \frac{1}{2}\sigma^2 \int_0^T (T-u)^2 du\right) \\
&= \exp\left(-r_0T - \int_0^T \theta(u)(T-u)du + \frac{1}{6}\sigma^2 T^3\right).
\end{aligned}
$$

This means that

$$\int_0^T \theta(u)(T-u)du = -\log D(0,T) - r_0T + \frac{1}{6}\sigma^2 T^3.$$

Differentiating with respect to T gives

$$\int_0^T \theta(u)du = -\frac{\partial}{\partial T} \log D(0,T) - r_0 + \frac{1}{2}\sigma^2 T^2.$$

Then

$$E^B[r_T] = r_0 + \int_0^T \theta(u)du$$

$$= -\frac{\partial}{\partial T} \log D(0,T) + \frac{1}{2}\sigma^2 T^2$$

$$= f(0,T) + \frac{1}{2}\sigma^2 T^2.$$

This gives the futures convexity as $\frac{1}{2}\sigma^2 T^2$.

(3) Buy one receiver swaption with 2% strike for 0.003 and sell two receivers with 1% strike for 0.004, hence netting 0.001 profit. If $R_T > 0\%$, then the payoff will be positive; if $R_T = 0\%$, then the payoff will be zero, hence this is an arbitrage assuming that rates cannot go negative.

Suppose now that rates can go negative. Notice that you only need to sell 1.5 receivers with 1% strike to cover the cost of buying the receiver with 2% strike. Thus, for breakeven, we seek R_T such that $2\% - R_T = 1.5 \times (1\% - R_T)$. This gives $R_T = -1\%$, i.e. we cannot lose money on the trade unless the swap rate falls below -1% (extremely unlikely).

(4) From Section 1.2.4, the price of a call option is

$$C_0 = S_0 N(d_1) - K e^{-rT} N(d_2),$$

where

$$d_1 = \frac{\log\left(\frac{S_0}{K}\right) + \left(r + \frac{1}{2}\sigma^2\right)T}{\sigma\sqrt{T}} \quad \text{and} \quad d_2 = d_1 - \sigma\sqrt{T}.$$

Define $n(x) = \frac{1}{\sqrt{2\pi}} e^{-\frac{1}{2}x^2}$, then the delta is

$$\Delta = \frac{\partial C_0}{\partial S_0}$$

$$= N(d_1) + S_0 n(d_1)\frac{\partial d_1}{\partial S_0} - K e^{-rT} n(d_2)\frac{\partial d_2}{\partial S_0}$$

$$= N(d_1) + S_0 n(d_1)\frac{\partial d_1}{\partial S_0} - Ke^{-rT}n(d_2)\frac{\partial d_1}{\partial S_0}$$

$$= N(d_1) + S_0 n(d_1)\frac{\partial d_1}{\partial S_0} - Ke^{-rT}n(d_1)\frac{S_0}{K}e^{rT}\frac{\partial d_1}{\partial S_0}$$

$$= N(d_1),$$

since

$$\frac{\partial d_2}{\partial S_0} = \frac{\partial d_1}{\partial S_0},$$

$$n(d_2) = \frac{1}{\sqrt{2\pi}}e^{-\frac{1}{2}(d_1-\sigma\sqrt{T})^2} = n(d_1)e^{d_1\sigma\sqrt{T}-\frac{1}{2}\sigma^2 T} = n(d_1)\frac{S_0}{K}e^{rT}.$$

The gamma is

$$\Gamma = \frac{\partial^2 C_0}{\partial S_0^2} = \frac{\partial \Delta}{\partial S_0} = n(d_1)\frac{\partial d_1}{\partial S_0} = \frac{1}{S_0\sigma\sqrt{T}}n(d_1),$$

since

$$\frac{\partial d_1}{\partial S_0} = \frac{1}{S_0\sigma\sqrt{T}}.$$

(5) From the Black–Scholes formula above, the vega is

$$\nu = \frac{\partial C_0}{\partial \sigma}$$

$$= S_0 n(d_1)\frac{\partial d_1}{\partial \sigma} - Ke^{-rT}n(d_2)\frac{\partial d_2}{\partial \sigma}$$

$$= -S_0 n(d_1)\frac{d_2}{\sigma} + Ke^{-rT}n(d_2)\frac{d_1}{\sigma},$$

since

$$\frac{\partial d_1}{\partial \sigma} = -\frac{\log\left(\frac{S_0}{K}\right)+rT}{\sigma^2\sqrt{T}} + \frac{1}{2}\sqrt{T} = -\frac{d_2}{\sigma}$$

and

$$\frac{\partial d_2}{\partial \sigma} = \frac{\partial d_1}{\partial \sigma} - \sqrt{T} = -\frac{\log\left(\frac{S_0}{K}\right)+rT}{\sigma^2\sqrt{T}} - \frac{1}{2}\sqrt{T} = -\frac{d_1}{\sigma}.$$

The price of a digital call option in the Black–Scholes world is given by $V_0 = -\frac{\partial C_0}{\partial K}$. Thus, its vega is given by

$$\frac{\partial V_0}{\partial \sigma} = -\frac{\partial \nu}{\partial K}$$

$$= -e^{-rT} n(d_2)\frac{d_1}{\sigma} + S_0 n(d_1)\frac{d_1 d_2}{K\sigma^2\sqrt{T}}$$

$$- S_0 n(d_1)\frac{1}{K\sigma^2\sqrt{T}} - Ke^{-rT} n(d_2)\frac{d_2 d_1}{K\sigma^2\sqrt{T}}$$

$$+ Ke^{-rT} n(d_2)\frac{1}{K\sigma^2\sqrt{T}}$$

$$= e^{-rT} n(d_2)\left(-\frac{d_1}{\sigma} - \frac{d_2 d_1}{\sigma^2\sqrt{T}} + \frac{1}{\sigma^2\sqrt{T}}\right)$$

$$+ \frac{S_0 n(d_1)}{K\sigma^2\sqrt{T}}(-1 + d_1 d_2),$$

since

$$\frac{\partial}{\partial K} n(d_1) = -d_1 n(d_1)\frac{\partial d_1}{\partial K} = n(d_1)\frac{d_1}{K\sigma\sqrt{T}}$$

and

$$\frac{\partial}{\partial K} n(d_2) = -d_2 n(d_2)\frac{\partial d_2}{\partial K} = n(d_2)\frac{d_2}{K\sigma\sqrt{T}}.$$

Chapter 3

(1) The gamma of call option is $\Gamma = \frac{\partial^2 C_0}{\partial S_0^2} = \frac{1}{S_0\sigma\sqrt{T}}n(d_1)$ per Question 4 of Chapter 2. The value of a digital option is $V_0 = -\frac{\partial C_0}{\partial K}$, so the gamma of a digital option is

$$\Gamma^D = -\frac{\partial \Gamma}{\partial K}$$

$$= \frac{d_1}{S_0\sigma\sqrt{T}}n(d_1)\frac{\partial d_1}{\partial K}$$

$$= -\frac{d_1}{S_0 K\sigma^2 T}n(d_1).$$

The payoff is discontinuous if spot is in the vicinity of strike as $t \to T$. So, gamma is extremely huge and it will cost a lot to delta hedge.

(2) Under a lognormal model, we have $dL_t = \sigma L_t dW_t$. Then

$$
\begin{aligned}
E[L_T^2] &= \int_{-\infty}^{\infty} (L_0 e^{-\frac{1}{2}\sigma^2 T + \sigma z \sqrt{T}})^2 \frac{1}{\sqrt{2\pi}} e^{-\frac{1}{2}z^2} dz \\
&= L_0^2 e^{-\sigma^2 T} \int_{-\infty}^{\infty} \frac{1}{\sqrt{2\pi}} e^{2\sigma z \sqrt{T} - \frac{1}{2}z^2} dz \\
&= L_0^2 e^{-\sigma^2 T} \int_{-\infty}^{\infty} \frac{1}{\sqrt{2\pi}} e^{-\frac{1}{2}(z - 2\sigma\sqrt{T})^2} dz e^{2\sigma^2 T} \\
&= L_0^2 e^{\sigma^2 T}.
\end{aligned}
$$

So, the convexity adjustment is

$$
\frac{L_0 + L_0^2 e^{\sigma^2 T} \tau}{1 + L_0 \tau} - L_0 = L_0 \left(\frac{1 + L_0 e^{\sigma^2 T} \tau}{1 + L_0 \tau} - 1 \right).
$$

Based on our numbers, this is 1.7046%.
Under a normal model with SDE $dL_t = \sigma_N dW_t$, we have

$$
\begin{aligned}
E[L_T^2] &= \int_{-\infty}^{\infty} (L_0 + \sigma_N z \sqrt{T})^2 \frac{1}{\sqrt{2\pi}} e^{-\frac{1}{2}z^2} dz \\
&= L_0^2 + 2L_0 \sigma_N \sqrt{T} \int_{-\infty}^{\infty} \frac{1}{\sqrt{2\pi}} z e^{-\frac{1}{2}z^2} dz \\
&\quad + \sigma_N^2 T \int_{-\infty}^{\infty} \frac{1}{\sqrt{2\pi}} z^2 e^{-\frac{1}{2}z^2} dz \\
&= L_0^2 + 2L_0 \sigma_N \sqrt{T} \left[-\frac{1}{\sqrt{2\pi}} e^{-\frac{1}{2}z^2} \right]_{-\infty}^{\infty} \\
&\quad + \sigma_N^2 T \left\{ - \left[\frac{1}{\sqrt{2\pi}} z e^{-\frac{1}{2}z^2} \right]_{-\infty}^{\infty} + \int_{-\infty}^{\infty} \frac{1}{\sqrt{2\pi}} e^{-\frac{1}{2}z^2} dz \right\} \\
&= L_0^2 + 0 + \sigma_N^2 T (0 + 1) \\
&= L_0^2 + \sigma_N^2 T.
\end{aligned}
$$

So, the convexity adjustment is

$$\frac{L_0 + (L_0^2 + \sigma_N^2 T)\tau}{1 + L_0\tau} - L_0 = L_0\left(\frac{1 + (L_0 + \sigma_N^2 T/L_0)\tau}{1 + L_0\tau} - 1\right)$$

$$= \frac{\sigma_N^2 T\tau}{1 + L_0\tau}.$$

Based on our numbers, this is a much smaller 0.1629%.

(3) Taylor's expansion gives

$$A_C(R_T) \approx A_C(R_0) + (R_T - R_0)A'_C(R_0) + \frac{1}{2}(R_T - R_0)^2 A''_C(R_0)$$

to second order. Thus, we have

$$E^T[A_C(R_T)] \approx A_C[R_0] + (E^T[R_T] - R_0)A'_C(R_0)$$

$$+ \frac{1}{2}E^T[(R_T - R_0)^2]A''_C(R_0).$$

Since

$$A_C(R_T) = \sum_{i=1}^{N} \frac{1}{\left(1 + \frac{R_T}{n}\right)^{ni}},$$

we get

$$A'_C(R_T) = -\sum_{i=1}^{N} \frac{i}{\left(1 + \frac{R_T}{n}\right)^{ni+1}}$$

and

$$A''_C(R_T) = \sum_{i=1}^{N} \frac{i(i + 1/n)}{\left(1 + \frac{R_T}{n}\right)^{ni+2}}.$$

We assume $E^T[A_C(R_T)] \approx A_C[R_0]$. (Note that the main problem with this assumption is that the cash annuity is not a proper numeraire as discussed earlier in the chapter.)

Thus, we get

$$E^T[R_T] \approx R_0 - \frac{1}{2}\frac{A_C''(R_0)}{A_C'(R_0)}E^T[(R_T - R_0)^2]$$

$$\approx R_0 - \frac{1}{2}\frac{A_C''(R_0)}{A_C'(R_0)}\sigma^2 R_0^2 T,$$

since $dR_t = \sigma R_t dW_t$.

Then the convexity adjustment for the CMS rate is approximately $-\frac{1}{2}\frac{A_C''(R_0)}{A_C'(R_0)}\sigma^2 R_0^2 T$.

(4) As per our approach in Question 2 of Chapter 2, we can obtain

$$E^Q[r_T D(T,S)]$$

$$= E^Q\left[r_T \exp\left(-r_T(S-T) - \int_T^S \theta(u)(S-u)du\right.\right.$$

$$\left.\left. + \frac{1}{6}\sigma^2(S-T)^3\right)\right]$$

$$= E^Q\left[\left(r_0 + \int_0^T \theta(u)du + \sigma W_T\right)\right.$$

$$\cdot \exp\left(-\left(r_0 + \int_0^T \theta(u)du + \sigma W_T\right)(S-T)\right)$$

$$\left. \cdot \exp\left(-\int_T^S \theta(u)(S-u)du + \frac{1}{6}\sigma^2(S-T)^3\right)\right].$$

Now we shall appeal to Girsanov's Theorem, in particular, we would like to change to measure Q^*, where $\frac{dQ^*}{dQ}(t) = \exp(-\frac{1}{2}(S-T)^2\sigma^2 t - (S-T)\sigma W_t)$, so that $dW_t^* = dW_t + (S-T)\sigma dt$. Then,

$$E^Q[r_T D(T,S)]$$

$$= E^{Q^*}\left[\left(r_0 + \int_0^T \theta(u)du + \sigma(W_T^* - (S-T)\sigma T)\right)\right.$$

$$\cdot \exp\left(-\left(r_0 + \int_0^T \theta(u)du\right)(S-T) + \frac{1}{2}(S-T)^2\sigma^2 T\right)$$

$$\cdot \exp\left(-\int_T^S \theta(u)(S-u)du + \frac{1}{6}\sigma^2(S-T)^3\right)\Bigg]$$

$$= \left(r_0 + \int_0^T \theta(u)du - \sigma^2 T(S-T)\right)$$

$$\cdot \exp\left(-\left(r_0 + \int_0^T \theta(u)du\right)(S-T) + \frac{1}{2}(S-T)^2\sigma^2 T\right)$$

$$\cdot \exp\left(-\int_T^S \theta(u)(S-u)du + \frac{1}{6}\sigma^2(S-T)^3\right).$$

Recall from Question 2 of Chapter 2 that $E^Q[r_T] = r_0 + \int_0^T \theta(u)du$. Further,

$$E^Q[D(T,S)]$$

$$= E^Q\left[\exp\left(-r_T(S-T) - \int_T^S \theta(u)(S-u)du\right.\right.$$

$$\left.\left. + \frac{1}{6}\sigma^2(S-T)^3\right)\right]$$

$$= E^Q\left[\exp\left(-(r_0 + \int_0^T \theta(u)du + \sigma W_T)(S-T)\right.\right.$$

$$\left.\left. - \int_T^S \theta(u)(S-u)du + \frac{1}{6}\sigma^2(S-T)^3\right)\right]$$

$$= \exp\left(-\left(r_0 + \int_0^T \theta(u)du\right)(S-T) + \frac{1}{2}\sigma^2(S-T)^2 T\right)$$

$$\cdot \exp\left(-\int_T^S \theta(u)(S-u)du + \frac{1}{6}\sigma^2(S-T)^3\right)$$

$$= \frac{D(0,S)}{D(0,T)}.$$

Thus,

$$E^Q[r_T D(T,S)] = (E^Q[r_T] - \sigma^2 T(S-T))\frac{D(0,S)}{D(0,T)}.$$

We therefore see that a payment delay from time T to time S causes the rate to decrease by $\sigma^2(S-T)T$. Notice that the formula is a product involving the term T, so if the rate is set in the near future (i.e. T is small), then the payment delay will be insignificant.

Chapter 4

(1) The Clayton distribution is $C(u, v) = (u^\theta + v^\theta - 1)^{\frac{1}{\theta}}$. So,

$$\frac{\partial C}{\partial u} = (u^\theta + v^\theta - 1)^{\frac{1}{\theta}-1} u^{\theta-1}$$

and

$$\frac{\partial^2 C}{\partial u \partial v} = (u^\theta + v^\theta - 1)^{\frac{1}{\theta}-2} u^{\theta-1} v^{\theta-1} (1 - \theta).$$

The Gumbel distribution is $C(u, v) = \exp(-\{(-\log u)^\theta + (-\log v)^\theta\}^{\frac{1}{\theta}})$. So,

$$\frac{\partial C}{\partial u} = C \left(\frac{1}{\theta}\{(-\log u)^\theta + (-\log v)^\theta\}^{\frac{1}{\theta}-1} \theta(-\log u)^{\theta-1} \frac{1}{u} \right)$$

$$= C \frac{1}{u} \left(\{(-\log u)^\theta + (-\log v)^\theta\}^{\frac{1}{\theta}-1} (-\log u)^{\theta-1} \right)$$

and

$$\frac{\partial^2 C}{\partial u \partial v} = C \frac{1}{uv}\{(-\log u)^\theta$$
$$+ (-\log v)^\theta\}^{\frac{2}{\theta}-2}(-\log u)^{\theta-1}(-\log v)^{\theta-1}$$
$$- C \frac{1}{u}\{(-\log u)^\theta + (-\log v)^\theta\}^{\frac{1}{\theta}-2}(-\log u)^{\theta-1}$$
$$\times \left(\frac{1}{\theta} - 1 \right) \theta(-\log v)^{\theta-1} \frac{1}{v}$$
$$= \frac{C}{uv}(-\log u)^{\theta-1}(-\log v)^{\theta-1}(\{(-\log u)^\theta$$
$$+ (-\log v)^\theta\}^{\frac{2}{\theta}-2} + (\theta - 1)\{(-\log u)^\theta$$
$$+ (-\log v)^\theta\}^{\frac{1}{\theta}-2}).$$

(2) The SDEs are $dS_t^{A,B} = rS_t^{A,B}dt + \sigma_{A,B}S_t^{A,B}dW_t^{A,B}$. The payoff is $V_T = \max(S_T^A - S_T^B, 0)$.

By the martingale equation, we have

$$\frac{V_t}{S_t^B} = E_t^B\left[\frac{V_T}{S_T^B}\right] = E_t^B\left[\max\left(\frac{S_T^A}{S_T^B} - 1, 0\right)\right].$$

Thus,

$$d\left(\frac{S_t^A}{S_t^B}\right) = \Lambda\frac{S_t^A}{S_t^B}dW_t, \quad \text{where } \Lambda^2 = \sigma_A^2 + \sigma_B^2 - 2\rho\sigma_A\sigma_B.$$

Then,

$$\frac{V_0}{S_0^B} = \int_{-\infty}^{\infty}\max\left(\frac{S_0^A}{S_0^B}e^{-\frac{1}{2}\Lambda^2 T + \Lambda\sqrt{T}z} - 1, 0\right)\frac{1}{\sqrt{2\pi}}e^{-\frac{1}{2}z^2}dz$$

$$= \int_{z^*}^{\infty}\left(\frac{S_0^A}{S_0^B}e^{-\frac{1}{2}\Lambda^2 T + \Lambda\sqrt{T}z} - 1\right)\frac{1}{\sqrt{2\pi}}e^{-\frac{1}{2}z^2}dz$$

$$= \frac{S_0^A}{S_0^B}e^{-\frac{1}{2}\Lambda^2 T}\int_{z^*}^{\infty}\frac{1}{\sqrt{2\pi}}e^{-\frac{1}{2}(z-\Lambda\sqrt{T})^2}dze^{\frac{1}{2}\Lambda^2 T} - N(-z^*)$$

$$= \frac{S_0^A}{S_0^B}N(-z^* + \Lambda\sqrt{T}) - N(-z^*)$$

where

$$z^* = \frac{\log\left(\frac{S_0^B}{S_0^A}\right) + \frac{1}{2}\Lambda^2 T}{\Lambda\sqrt{T}}.$$

Thus, the value of the option is $V_0 = S_0^A N(-z^* + \Lambda\sqrt{T}) - S_0^B N(-z^*)$.

If $\sigma_A = \sigma_B$ for $\rho = 1$, then we get $\Lambda = 0$, i.e. option has no volatility.

If further $S_0^A = S_0^B$, then $V_0 = 0$.

(3) The contract has payoff $V_T^* = \max(S_T^A, S_T^B) = S_T^B + \max(S_T^A - S_T^B, 0)$. Then, the value of this contract is $V_0^* = S_0^B + V_0$, where V_0 is as per the answer to Question 2.

(4) The convexity adjustment is given by $-\frac{1}{2}\frac{A_C''(R_0)}{A_C'(R_0)}\sigma^2 R_0^2 T$ (as per Question 3 of Chapter 3). For the 10-year CMS rate set in 30-years' time, this is 0.4028% (contrast this with the swap rate

of 4%). For the 2-year CMS rate, it is just 0.1380% — far smaller. Then, the spread option involves the convexity adjustment of 0.2648%.

So, even if correlation is 100%, a spread option whose strike is based on the forward swap rates (as opposed to the CMS rates and hence does not account for convexity) has a significant amount of intrinsic value.

Chapter 5

(1) A derivative with payoff $V(X_T)$ at time T has value

$$V(X_t) = e^{-r(T-t)} E[V(X_T)] = e^{-r(T-t)} \int_{-\infty}^{\infty} V(x)p(x)dx.$$

Ito's Lemma gives

$$dV_t = \frac{\partial V_t}{\partial x} dX_t + \frac{1}{2} \frac{\partial^2 V_t}{\partial x^2} (dX_t)^2$$

$$= \left(rX \frac{\partial V_t}{\partial x} + \frac{1}{2} \sigma^2 X^2 \frac{\partial^2 V_t}{\partial x^2} \right) dt + \sigma X dW_t.$$

We see that

$$\frac{d}{dt} V(X_t) = \frac{d}{dt} (e^{-r(T-t)} E[V(X_T)])$$

$$= e^{-r(T-t)} E \left[rV_t + rX \frac{\partial V_t}{\partial x} + \frac{1}{2} \sigma^2 X^2 \frac{\partial^2 V_t}{\partial x^2} \right]$$

$$= e^{-r(T-t)}$$

$$\times \int_{-\infty}^{\infty} \left(rV_t + rx \frac{\partial V_t}{\partial x} + \frac{1}{2} \sigma^2 x^2 \frac{\partial^2 V_t}{\partial x^2} \right) p(x)dx$$

$$= e^{-r(T-t)} \left\{ \int_{-\infty}^{\infty} rV_t p(x)dx + [rxV_t p(x)]_{-\infty}^{\infty} \right.$$

$$- \int_{-\infty}^{\infty} V_t \frac{\partial}{\partial x} (rxp(x))dx + \left[\frac{1}{2} \sigma^2 x^2 \frac{\partial V_t}{\partial x} p(x) \right]_{-\infty}^{\infty}$$

$$\left. - \int_{-\infty}^{\infty} \frac{\partial V_t}{\partial x} \frac{\partial}{\partial x} \left(\frac{1}{2} \sigma^2 x^2 p(x) \right) dx \right\}$$

$$= e^{-r(T-t)}$$

$$\times \left\{ \int_{-\infty}^{\infty} rV_t p(x) dx - \int_{-\infty}^{\infty} V_t \frac{\partial}{\partial x}(rxp(x)) dx \right.$$

$$\left. - \left[V_t \frac{\partial}{\partial x} \left(\frac{1}{2}\sigma^2 x^2 p(x) \right) \right]_{-\infty}^{\infty} \right\}$$

$$+ e^{-r(T-t)} \int_{-\infty}^{\infty} V_t \frac{\partial^2}{\partial x^2} \left(\frac{1}{2}\sigma^2 x^2 p(x) \right) dx$$

$$= e^{-r(T-t)} \left\{ \int_{-\infty}^{\infty} V_t \left\{ rp(x) - \frac{\partial}{\partial x}(rxp(x)) \right. \right.$$

$$\left. \left. + \frac{\partial^2}{\partial x^2} \left(\frac{1}{2}\sigma^2 x^2 p(x) \right) \right\} dx \right\}.$$

Further,

$$\frac{d}{dt} V(X_t) = \frac{d}{dt}(e^{-r(T-t)} E[X_T])$$

$$= re^{-r(T-t)} \int_{-\infty}^{\infty} V(x)p(x) dx$$

$$+ e^{-r(T-t)} \int_{-\infty}^{\infty} V(x) \frac{\partial p(x)}{\partial t} dx.$$

Thus,

$$\int_{-\infty}^{\infty} V_t \left\{ -\frac{\partial}{\partial x}(rxp(x)) + \frac{\partial^2}{\partial x^2} \left(\frac{1}{2}\sigma^2 x^2 p(x) \right) - \frac{\partial p(x)}{\partial t} \right\} dx = 0.$$

Since this holds for an arbitrary V_t, the integrand must be zero, i.e. we get the Fokker–Planck equation

$$\frac{\partial p(x)}{\partial t} = -\frac{\partial}{\partial x}(rxp(x)) + \frac{\partial^2}{\partial x^2} \left(\frac{1}{2}\sigma^2 x^2 p(x) \right).$$

(2) Start with $f(S_t, t) = e^{-\int_0^t r_u du}(K - S_t)^+$. Tanaka's formula gives

$$d[e^{-\int_0^t r_u du}(K - S_t)^+] = \{-r_t e^{-\int_0^t r_u du}(K - S_t)^+$$

$$- e^{-\int_0^t r_u du} 1_{S_t \le K} \mu(t) S_t\} dt$$

$$+ \frac{1}{2} e^{-\int_0^t r_u du} \delta_K(S_t) \sigma^2(S_t, t) S_t^2 dt$$

$$- e^{-\int_0^t r_u du} 1_{S_t \le K} \sigma(S_t, t) S_t dW_t.$$

Taking expectations and using the put price $P(K, t) = E[e^{-\int_0^t r_u du}(K - S_t)^+]$, we get

$$dP(K, t) = \left\{ E[-r_t e^{-\int_0^t r_u du}(K - S_t)^+ \right.$$

$$\left. - e^{-\int_0^t r_u du} 1_{S_t \le K} \mu(t) S_t] + \frac{1}{2} \frac{\partial^2 P}{\partial K^2} \sigma^2(K, t) K^2 \right\} dt$$

$$= \left\{ E[(\mu(t) - r_t) e^{-\int_0^t r_u du}(K - S_t)^+ \right.$$

$$\left. - e^{-\int_0^t r_u du} 1_{S_t \le K} \mu(t) K] + \frac{1}{2} \frac{\partial^2 P}{\partial K^2} \sigma^2(K, t) K^2 \right\} dt$$

$$= \left\{ (\mu(t) - r_t) P - \frac{\partial P}{\partial K} \mu(t) K + \frac{1}{2} \frac{\partial^2 P}{\partial K^2} \sigma^2(K, t) K^2 \right\} dt.$$

Thus, we obtain $\sigma^2(K, t) = 2 \frac{\frac{\partial P}{\partial K} - (\mu(t) - r_t) P + \frac{\partial P}{\partial K} \mu(t) K}{K^2 \frac{\partial^2 P}{\partial K^2}}$.

(3) From Section 1.2.4, the price of a call option under the normal model is

$$C_t = D(t, T) \left\{ (F(t, T) - K) N(-z^*) + \sigma \sqrt{\frac{T - t}{2\pi}} e^{-\frac{1}{2}(z^*)^2} \right\},$$

where $z^* = \frac{K - F(t, T)}{\sigma \sqrt{T - t}}$.

Thus, the forward delta is

$$\frac{\partial C_t}{\partial F(t, T)} = D(t, T) \left\{ N(-z^*) - (F(t, T) - K) n(-z^*) \frac{\partial z^*}{\partial F(t, T)} \right.$$

$$\left. - \sigma \sqrt{\frac{T - t}{2\pi}} e^{-\frac{1}{2}(z^*)^2} z^* \frac{\partial z^*}{\partial F(t, T)} \right\}$$

$$= D(t,T) \left\{ N(-z^*) + (F(t,T) - K)n(-z^*)\frac{1}{\sigma\sqrt{T-t}} \right.$$

$$\left. + \sigma\sqrt{\frac{T-t}{2\pi}}e^{-\frac{1}{2}(z^*)^2}z^*\frac{1}{\sigma\sqrt{T-t}} \right\}$$

$$= D(t,T) \left\{ N(-z^*) + (F(t,T) - K)n(-z^*)\frac{1}{\sigma\sqrt{T-t}} \right.$$

$$\left. + (K - F(t,T))n(-z^*)\frac{1}{\sigma\sqrt{T-t}} \right\}$$

$$= D(t,T)N(-z^*).$$

Note that this is a forward delta (as opposed to a spot delta). The equivalent forward delta for a lognormal model is $\Delta^{LN} = D(t,T)N(d_1)$, where $d_1 = \frac{\log(\frac{F(t,T)}{K}) + \frac{1}{2}\sigma^2(T-t)}{\sigma\sqrt{T-t}}$, which is obtainable by applying the same approach as in Question 4 of Chapter 1.

(4) Start with

$$N(x) = 0.5 + \frac{1}{\sqrt{2\pi}}\int_0^x e^{-\frac{1}{2}z^2}dz$$

$$= 0.5 + \frac{1}{\sqrt{2\pi}}\int_0^x \left(1 - \frac{1}{2}z^2 + \frac{1}{8}z^4 + \cdots\right)dz$$

$$= 0.5 + \frac{1}{\sqrt{2\pi}}\left(x - \frac{x^3}{6} + \frac{x^5}{40} + \cdots\right).$$

Under the lognormal model, the price of a call option is $C = D(0,T)(FN(d_1) - KN(d_2))$, where $d_1 = \frac{\log(\frac{F}{K}) + \frac{1}{2}\sigma^2 T}{\sigma\sqrt{T}}$ and $d_2 = d_1 - \sigma\sqrt{T}$. Using the above approximation, we get

$$C \approx D(0,T)\left(F\left\{0.5 + \frac{1}{\sqrt{2\pi}}\left(d_1 - \frac{d_1^3}{6} + \frac{d_1^5}{40}\right)\right\}\right.$$

$$\left. - K\left\{0.5 + \frac{1}{\sqrt{2\pi}}\left(d_2 - \frac{d_2^3}{6} + \frac{d_2^5}{40}\right)\right\}\right).$$

For the normal model, the call option price is

$$C^* = D(0,T)\left((F-K)N(z) + \sigma_N\sqrt{\frac{T}{2\pi}}e^{-\frac{1}{2}z^2}\right)$$

$$\approx D(0,T)\left((F-K)\left\{0.5 + \frac{1}{\sqrt{2\pi}}\left(z - \frac{z^3}{6} + \frac{z^5}{40}\right)\right\}\right.$$

$$\left. + \sigma_N\sqrt{\frac{T}{2\pi}}\left(1 - \frac{z^2}{2} + \frac{z^4}{8}\right)\right),$$

where $z = \frac{F-K}{\sigma_N\sqrt{T}}$.

If we equate C and C^* and ignore terms higher than order $O(d_1, d_2, z)$, we get

$$Fd_1 - Kd_2 = (F-K)z + \sigma_N\sqrt{T}.$$

Substituting for z, we get a quadratic equation in σ_N, namely

$$Fd_1 - Kd_2 = \frac{(F-K)^2}{\sigma_N\sqrt{T}} + \sigma_N\sqrt{T}$$

$$\Rightarrow T\sigma_N^2 - (Fd_1 - Kd_2)\sqrt{T}\sigma_N + (F-K)^2 = 0.$$

This has solution

$$\sigma_N = \frac{(Fd_1 - Kd_2) \pm \sqrt{(Fd_1 - Kd_2)^2 - 4(F-K)^2}}{2\sqrt{T}}.$$

Chapter 6

(1) With the above parameters, we get implied vols 20.26%, 15%, and 16.92% for strikes 0.8, 1, and 1.25 respectively. The reader can easily verify that increasing ν leads to higher vols for both the 0.8 and 1.25 strikes whilst increasing ρ to a positive number will change the direction of the skew.

(2) Take $\delta = 0.0001$ and compute prices of butterflies centred at strikes $K = \{0.01, 0.011, 0.012, \ldots, 0.019, 0.02\}$. You should get the following based on notional 10,000,000:

Strike K (%)	Butterfly Price
1.0	−0.74
1.1	−0.58
1.2	−0.44
1.3	−0.32
1.4	−0.21
1.5	−0.11
1.6	−0.02
1.7	0.06
1.8	0.14
1.9	0.22
2.0	0.30

Notice that prices of butterflies are negative for strikes less than 1.7%. But a butterfly always has non-negative payoff, being zero at $F_T \leq K-\delta$ or $F_T \geq K+\delta$ and positive for $K-\delta < F_T < K+\delta$, with a maximum payoff at $F_T = K$ of δ. So, this means there is arbitrage if the butterfly has a negative price.

(3) SABR cannot fit a pure skew once you have chosen the blend. The correlation needs a stoch vol to work off and the stoch vol generates a smile.

Chapter 7

(1) We start with

$$\frac{\partial V}{\partial t} + rS\frac{\partial V}{\partial S} + \frac{1}{2}\sigma^2 S^2 \frac{\partial^2 V}{\partial S^2} = rV.$$

Let $\tau = T - t$ and $x = \log S$. Then

$$\frac{\partial \tau}{\partial t} = -1, \quad \frac{\partial x}{\partial S} = \frac{1}{S} \quad \text{and} \quad \frac{\partial \tau}{\partial S} = \frac{\partial x}{\partial t} = 0,$$

so

$$\frac{\partial}{\partial t} = \frac{\partial \tau}{\partial t}\frac{\partial}{\partial \tau} + \frac{\partial x}{\partial t}\frac{\partial}{\partial x} = -\frac{\partial}{\partial \tau}, \quad \frac{\partial}{\partial S} = \frac{\partial x}{\partial S}\frac{\partial}{\partial x} + \frac{\partial \tau}{\partial S}\frac{\partial}{\partial \tau} = \frac{1}{S}\frac{\partial}{\partial x}$$

and

$$\frac{\partial^2}{\partial S^2} = \frac{\partial}{\partial S}\left(\frac{1}{S}\frac{\partial}{\partial x}\right) = -\frac{1}{S^2}\frac{\partial}{\partial x} + \frac{1}{S}\left(\frac{1}{S}\frac{\partial}{\partial x}\right)\frac{\partial}{\partial x}$$

$$= -\frac{1}{S^2}\frac{\partial}{\partial x} + \frac{1}{S^2}\frac{\partial^2}{\partial x^2}.$$

This transformation then gives the new PDE

$$-\frac{\partial V}{\partial \tau} + r\frac{\partial V}{\partial x} + \frac{1}{2}\sigma^2\left(-\frac{\partial V}{\partial x} + \frac{\partial^2 V}{\partial x^2}\right) = rV$$

$$\Rightarrow \frac{\partial V}{\partial \tau} = \left(r - \frac{1}{2}\sigma^2\right)\frac{\partial V}{\partial x} + \frac{1}{2}\sigma^2\frac{\partial^2 V}{\partial x^2} - rV.$$

Next, let $V = ue^{\alpha x + \beta \tau}$. Then

$$\frac{\partial V}{\partial \tau} = \beta V + \frac{\partial u}{\partial \tau}e^{\alpha x + \beta \tau},$$

$$\frac{\partial V}{\partial x} = \alpha V + \frac{\partial u}{\partial x}e^{\alpha x + \beta \tau}, \quad \text{and}$$

$$\frac{\partial^2 V}{\partial x^2} = \alpha^2 V + 2\alpha\frac{\partial u}{\partial x}e^{\alpha x + \beta \tau} + \frac{\partial^2 u}{\partial x^2}e^{\alpha x + \beta \tau}.$$

Thus, we have

$$\beta u + \frac{\partial u}{\partial \tau} = \left(r - \frac{1}{2}\sigma^2\right)\left(\alpha u + \frac{\partial u}{\partial x}\right)$$

$$+ \frac{1}{2}\sigma^2\left(\alpha^2 u + 2\alpha\frac{\partial u}{\partial x} + \frac{\partial^2 u}{\partial x^2}\right) - ru.$$

Ultimately, we seek to obtain $\frac{\partial u}{\partial \tau} = \frac{1}{2}\sigma^2\frac{\partial^2 u}{\partial x^2}$, which is possible only if

$$\beta u = \left(r - \frac{1}{2}\sigma^2\right)\left(\alpha u + \frac{\partial u}{\partial x}\right) + \frac{1}{2}\sigma^2\left(\alpha^2 u + 2\alpha\frac{\partial u}{\partial x}\right) - ru.$$

If we consider the terms in $\frac{\partial u}{\partial x}$ and u separately, we see that the required conditions are

$$0 = r - \frac{1}{2}\sigma^2 + \alpha\sigma^2 \quad \text{and}$$

$$\beta = \left(r - \frac{1}{2}\sigma^2 \right)\alpha + \frac{1}{2}\sigma^2\alpha^2 - r.$$

This gives

$$\alpha = \frac{1}{2} - \frac{r}{\sigma^2} \quad \text{and}$$

$$\beta = \left(r - \frac{1}{2}\sigma^2 \right)\left(\frac{1}{2} - \frac{r}{\sigma^2} \right) + \frac{1}{2}\sigma^2 \left(\frac{1}{2} - \frac{r}{\sigma^2} \right)^2 - r.$$

(2) The explicit scheme involves

$$\frac{u_j^{n+1} - u_j^n}{\Delta t} = \alpha \frac{u_{j+1}^n - 2u_j^n + u_{j-1}^n}{(\Delta x)^2}.$$

Consider the Fourier node $\hat{u}_j^n = \lambda^n e^{ik(j\Delta x)}$. Substituting this into our equation for the explicit scheme gives

$$\frac{\lambda - 1}{\Delta t} = \frac{\alpha}{(\Delta x)^2}(e^{ik\Delta x} - 2 + e^{-ik\Delta x})$$

$$\Rightarrow \lambda = 1 + \frac{\alpha\Delta t}{(\Delta x)^2}(2\cos k\Delta x - 2) = 1 - 4\frac{\alpha\Delta t}{(\Delta x)^2}\sin^2\frac{k\Delta x}{2},$$

since $\cos x = \frac{1}{2}(e^{ix} - e^{-ix})$ whilst $\cos^2 x + \sin^2 x = 1$ gives $\cos 2x = \cos^2 x - \sin^2 x = 1 - 2\sin^2 x$ so that $\cos x - 1 = -2\sin^2\frac{x}{2}$.

To avoid explosive growth, we need $|\lambda| \leq 1$, so the required condition is $-1 \leq 1 - 4\frac{\alpha\Delta t}{(\Delta x)^2}$ since $\sin^2 x \leq 1$, so that we finally get $\Delta t \leq \frac{(\Delta x)^2}{2\alpha}$.

If instead we consider the implicit scheme, then the equation is

$$\frac{u_j^{n+1} - u_j^n}{\Delta t} = \alpha \frac{u_{j+1}^{n+1} - 2u_j^{n+1} + u_{j-1}^{n+1}}{(\Delta x)^2},$$

so we get

$$\frac{\lambda - 1}{\Delta t} = \frac{\lambda \alpha}{(\Delta x)^2}(e^{ik\Delta x} - 2 + e^{-ik\Delta x})$$

$$\Rightarrow \lambda - 1 = -\frac{4\lambda\alpha\Delta t}{(\Delta x)^2}\sin^2\frac{k\Delta x}{2}$$

$$\Rightarrow \lambda\left(1 + \frac{4\lambda\alpha\Delta t}{(\Delta x)^2}\sin^2\frac{k\Delta x}{2}\right) = 1$$

$$\Rightarrow \lambda = 1\bigg/\left(1 + \frac{4\lambda\alpha\Delta t}{(\Delta x)^2}\sin^2\frac{k\Delta x}{2}\right).$$

Further, $0 \le \lambda = 1/(1 + \frac{4\lambda\alpha\Delta t}{(\Delta x)^2}\sin^2\frac{k\Delta x}{2}) \le 1$ since $\sin^2 x \ge 0$. So, we always have stability in an implicit scheme.

(3) The Craig–Sneyd scheme for a three factor PDE is

$$(1 - \theta\Delta t(q_{11}\delta_{x_1}^2 + r_1\delta_{x_1}))u^{(n+1,1)}$$

$$= \left[1 + \Delta t(1 - \theta)(q_{11}\delta_{x_1}^2 + r_1\delta_{x_1}) + \Delta t\sum_{i=2}^{3}(q_{ii}\delta_{x_i}^2 + r_i\delta_{x_i})\right.$$

$$\left. + \Delta t\sum_{i=1}^{3}\sum_{j=1}^{i-1}q_{ij}\delta_{x_i}\delta_{x_j} - f\Delta t\right]u^n,$$

$$(1 - \theta\Delta t(q_{22}\delta_{x_2}^2 + r_2\delta_{x_2}))u^{(n+1,2)}$$

$$= u^{(n+1,1)} - \theta\Delta t(q_{22}\delta_{x_2}^2 + r_2\delta_{x_2})u^n,$$

$$(1 - \theta\Delta t(q_{33}\delta_{x_3}^2 + r_3\delta_{x_3}))u^{n+1}$$

$$= u^{(n+1,2)} - \theta\Delta t(q_{33}\delta_{x_3}^2 + r_3\delta_{x_3})u^n.$$

Notice that

$$(1 - \theta\Delta t(q_{22}\delta_{x_2}^2 + r_2\delta_{x_2}))(1 - \theta\Delta t(q_{33}\delta_{x_3}^2 + r_3\delta_{x_3}))u^{n+1}$$

$$= (1 - \theta\Delta t(q_{22}\delta_{x_2}^2 + r_2\delta_{x_2}))u^{(n+1,2)}$$

$$- \theta\Delta t(1 - \theta\Delta t(q_{22}\delta_{x_2}^2 + r_2\delta_{x_2}))(q_{33}\delta_{x_3}^2 + r_3\delta_{x_3})u^n$$

$$= u^{(n+1,1)} - \theta\Delta t(q_{22}\delta_{x_2}^2 + r_2\delta_{x_2})u^n$$
$$- \theta\Delta t(1 - \theta\Delta t(q_{22}\delta_{x_2}^2 + r_2\delta_{x_2}))(q_{33}\delta_{x_3}^2 + r_3\delta_{x_3})u^n$$

and

$$\prod_{i=1}^{3}(1 - \theta\Delta t(q_{ii}\delta_{x_i}^2 + r_i\delta_{x_i}))u^{n+1}$$

$$= (1 - \theta\Delta t(q_{11}\delta_{x_1}^2 + r_1\delta_{x_1}))u^{(n+1,1)}$$
$$- \theta\Delta t(1 - \theta\Delta t(q_{11}\delta_{x_1}^2 + r_1\delta_{x_1}))(q_{22}\delta_{x_2}^2 + r_2\delta_{x_2})u^n$$
$$- \theta\Delta t(1 - \theta\Delta t(q_{11}\delta_{x_1}^2 + r_1\delta_{x_1}))$$
$$\times (1 - \theta\Delta t(q_{22}\delta_{x_2}^2 + r_2\delta_{x_2}))(q_{33}\delta_{x_3}^2 + r_3\delta_{x_3})u^n$$

$$= \left[1 + \Delta t(1 - \theta)(q_{11}\delta_{x_1}^2 + r_1\delta_{x_1}) + \Delta t\sum_{i=2}^{3}(q_{ii}\delta_{x_i}^2 + r_i\delta_{x_i})\right.$$
$$\left. + \Delta t\sum_{i=1}^{3}\sum_{j=1}^{i-1}q_{ij}\delta_{x_i}\delta_{x_j} - f\Delta t\right]u^n$$
$$- \theta\Delta t(1 - \theta\Delta t(q_{11}\delta_{x_1}^2 + r_1\delta_{x_1}))(q_{22}\delta_{x_2}^2 + r_2\delta_{x_2})u^n$$
$$- \theta\Delta t(1 - \theta\Delta t(q_{11}\delta_{x_1}^2 + r_1\delta_{x_1}))$$
$$\times (1 - \theta\Delta t(q_{22}\delta_{x_2}^2 + r_2\delta_{x_2}))(q_{33}\delta_{x_3}^2 + r_3\delta_{x_3})u^n.$$

Ignoring higher order terms, we get

$$(1 - \theta\Delta t\sum_{i=1}^{3}(q_{ii}\delta_{x_i}^2 + r_i\delta_{x_i}))u^{n+1}$$

$$= \left[1 + \Delta t(1 - \theta)(q_{11}\delta_{x_1}^2 + r_1\delta_{x_1}) + \Delta t\sum_{i=2}^{3}(q_{ii}\delta_{x_i}^2 + r_i\delta_{x_i})\right.$$
$$\left. + \Delta t\sum_{i=1}^{3}\sum_{j=1}^{i-1}q_{ij}\delta_{x_i}\delta_{x_j} - f\Delta t\right]u^n$$
$$- \theta\Delta t(q_{22}\delta_{x_2}^2 + r_2\delta_{x_2})u^n - \theta\Delta t(q_{33}\delta_{x_3}^2 + r_3\delta_{x_3})u^n$$

$$= \left[1 + \Delta t (1 - \theta) \sum_{i=1}^{3} (q_{ii} \delta_{x_i}^2 + r_i \delta_{x_i}) \right.$$

$$\left. + \Delta t \sum_{i=1}^{3} \sum_{j=1}^{i-1} q_{ij} \delta_{x_i} \delta_{x_j} - f \Delta t \right] u^n$$

which is the traditional formulation of the θ-scheme mixing explicit and implicit formulations.

(4) The diffusion equation is $\frac{\partial u}{\partial t} = \alpha \frac{\partial^2 u}{\partial x^2}$ and the boundary conditions are $u(x, 0) = \delta(x)$ and $\int_{-\infty}^{\infty} u(x, t) dx = 1$.
Let us define $u(x, t) = \frac{1}{\sqrt{t}} f(z)$, where $z = \frac{x}{\sqrt{t}}$. Then

$$\frac{\partial z}{\partial t} = -\frac{x}{2\sqrt{t^3}} = -\frac{z}{2t} \quad \text{and} \quad \frac{\partial z}{\partial x} = \frac{1}{\sqrt{t}},$$

so that

$$\frac{\partial u}{\partial t} = \frac{f'(z)}{\sqrt{t}} \frac{\partial z}{\partial t} - \frac{f(z)}{2\sqrt{t^3}} = -\frac{z f'(z)}{2\sqrt{t^3}} - \frac{f(z)}{2\sqrt{t^3}},$$

$$\frac{\partial u}{\partial x} = \frac{f'(z)}{\sqrt{t}} \frac{\partial z}{\partial x} = \frac{f'(z)}{t}, \quad \text{and}$$

$$\frac{\partial^2 u}{\partial x^2} = \frac{\partial}{\partial x} \left(\frac{f'(z)}{t} \right) = \frac{f''(z)}{t} \frac{\partial z}{\partial x} = \frac{f''(z)}{\sqrt{t^3}}.$$

Then our PDE becomes the ODE

$$-\frac{z f'(z)}{2\sqrt{t^3}} - \frac{f(z)}{2\sqrt{t^3}} = \alpha \frac{f''(z)}{\sqrt{t^3}}$$

$$\Rightarrow \alpha f''(z) = -\frac{1}{2} \frac{d}{dz} (z f(z))$$

$$\Rightarrow \alpha f'(z) = -\frac{1}{2} z f(z) + C \quad \text{for some arbitrary constant } C$$

$$\Rightarrow \frac{d}{dz} (f(z) e^{\frac{z^2}{4\alpha}}) = \frac{C}{\alpha} e^{\frac{z^2}{4\alpha}},$$

since

$$\frac{d}{dz} (f(z) e^{G(z)}) = (f'(z) + f(z) G'(z)) e^{G(z)}$$

where $G'(z) = \frac{z}{2\alpha}$ here, so that $G(z) = \frac{z^2}{4\alpha}$,

$$\Rightarrow f(z)e^{\frac{z^2}{4\alpha}} = \frac{C}{\alpha}\int_0^z e^{\frac{x^2}{4\alpha}}\,dx + D \text{ for some arbitrary constant } D$$

$$\Rightarrow f(z) = \frac{C}{\alpha}\int_0^z e^{\frac{x^2-z^2}{4\alpha}}\,dx + De^{-\frac{z^2}{4\alpha}}.$$

Take $C = 0$ and note that we still satisfy the boundary condition $u(x,0) = \delta(x)$. We obtain

$$u(x,t) = \frac{1}{\sqrt{t}}D\exp\left(-\frac{x^2}{4\alpha t}\right).$$

Using the other condition $\int_{-\infty}^{\infty} u(x,t)dx = 1$, we get

$$\frac{D}{\sqrt{t}}\int_{-\infty}^{\infty}\exp\left(-\frac{x^2}{4\alpha t}\right)dx$$

$$= D\sqrt{4\alpha\pi}\left(\frac{1}{\sqrt{2\pi}}\int_{-\infty}^{\infty}\exp\left(-\frac{y^2}{2}\right)dy\right) = 1$$

by substituting

$$y = \frac{x}{\sqrt{2\alpha t}} \Rightarrow dy = \frac{dx}{\sqrt{2\alpha t}}.$$

Hence, $D = \frac{1}{2\sqrt{\pi\alpha}}$, so

$$u(x,t) = \frac{1}{2\sqrt{\pi\alpha t}}\exp\left(-\frac{x^2}{4\alpha t}\right).$$

Chapter 8

(1) We have

$$dr_t = \kappa(t)(\theta(t) - r_t)dt + \sigma(t)dW_t.$$
$$\Rightarrow dr_t + \kappa(t)r_t dt = \kappa(t)\theta(t)dt + \sigma(t)dW_t$$
$$\Rightarrow d(r_t\phi(t)) = \kappa(t)\phi(t)\theta(t)dt + \sigma(t)\phi(t)dW_t,$$

where $\phi(t) = e^{\int_0^t \kappa(s)ds}$.

Thus,

$$r_t\phi(t) = r_\tau\frac{\phi(\tau)}{\phi(t)} + \int_r^t \kappa(s)\frac{\phi(s)}{\phi(t)}\theta(s)ds + \int_r^t \sigma(s)\frac{\phi(s)}{\phi(t)}dW_s.$$

Let $\Phi(t) = \int_0^t \frac{du}{\phi(u)}$. Then the value of a discount bond is given by

$$D(0,T) = E^Q\left[\exp\left(-\int_0^T r_u du\right)\right]$$

$$= E^Q\left[\exp\left(-r_0\int_0^T \frac{du}{\phi(u)} - \int_0^T\int_0^u \kappa(s)\frac{\phi(s)}{\phi(u)}\theta(s)dsdu\right.\right.$$

$$\left.\left. - \int_0^T\int_0^u \sigma(s)\frac{\phi(s)}{\phi(u)}dW_s du\right)\right]$$

$$= \exp\left(-r_0\Phi(T) - \int_0^T\int_s^T \frac{du}{\phi(u)}\kappa(s)\phi(s)\theta(s)ds\right)$$

$$\times E^Q\left[\exp\left(-\int_0^T\int_s^T \frac{du}{\phi(u)}\sigma(s)\phi(s)dW_s\right)\right]$$

$$= \exp\left(-r_0\Phi(T) - \int_0^T (\Phi(T) - \Phi(s))\kappa(s)\phi(s)\theta(s)ds\right.$$

$$\left. + \frac{1}{2}\int_0^T (\Phi(T) - \Phi(s))^2\sigma^2(s)\phi^2(s)ds\right).$$

Thus,

$$-\log D(0,T) = r_0\Phi(T) + \int_0^T (\Phi(T) - \Phi(s))\kappa(s)\phi(s)\theta(s)ds$$

$$- \frac{1}{2}\int_0^T (\Phi(T) - \Phi(s))^2\sigma^2(s)\phi^2(s)ds.$$

Differentiating with respect to T:

$$-\frac{1}{D(0,T)}\frac{\partial D(0,T)}{\partial T} = \frac{r_0}{\phi(T)} + \int_0^T \frac{\kappa(s)\phi(s)\theta(s)}{\phi(T)}ds$$

$$- \int_0^T (\Phi(T) - \Phi(s))\frac{\sigma^2(s)\phi^2(s)}{\phi(T)}ds.$$

$$(1)$$

Differentiating again with respect to T:

$$\left(\frac{1}{D(0,T)}\frac{\partial D(0,T)}{\partial T}\right)^2 - \frac{1}{D(0,T)}\frac{\partial^2 D(0,T)}{\partial T^2}$$

$$= -\frac{r_0\kappa(T)}{\phi(T)} + \kappa(T)\theta(T)$$

$$-\kappa(T)\int_0^T \frac{\kappa(s)\phi(s)\theta(s)}{\phi(T)}ds - \int_0^T \frac{\sigma^2(s)\phi^2(s)}{\phi^2(T)}ds$$

$$+\kappa(T)\int_0^T (\Phi(T)-\Phi(s))\frac{\sigma^2(s)\phi^2(s)}{\phi(T)}ds. \qquad (2)$$

From $(1) + (2)/\kappa(T)$:

$$-\frac{1}{D(0,T)}\frac{\partial D(0,T)}{\partial T}$$

$$+\frac{1}{\kappa(T)}\left\{\left(\frac{1}{D(0,T)}\frac{\partial D(0,T)}{\partial T}\right)^2 - \frac{1}{D(0,T)}\frac{\partial^2 D(0,T)}{\partial T^2}\right\}$$

$$=\theta(T) - \frac{1}{\kappa(T)}\int_0^T \frac{\sigma^2(s)\phi^2(s)}{\phi^2(T)}ds.$$

Hence,

$$\theta(T) = -\frac{1}{D(0,T)}\frac{\partial D(0,T)}{\partial T}$$

$$+\frac{1}{\kappa(T)}\left\{\left(\frac{1}{D(0,T)}\frac{\partial D(0,T)}{\partial T}\right)^2 - \frac{1}{D(0,T)}\frac{\partial^2 D(0,T)}{\partial T^2}\right\}$$

$$+\frac{1}{\kappa(T)}\int_0^T \frac{\sigma^2(s)\phi^2(s)}{\phi^2(T)}ds.$$

Note that we have derivatives of $D(0,T)$ with respect to T. In practice, differentiation should be avoided as we lose smoothness, and may not be able to recover discount bond prices exactly in our model.

(2) The instantaneous forward rate is given by

$$f_{t,T} = E_t^T[r_T] = r_t \frac{\phi(t)}{\phi(T)} + \int_t^T \kappa(s)\theta(s)\frac{\phi(s)}{\phi(T)}ds$$

based on the equation for r_T derived in Question 1.

Since $D(t,T) = e^{-\int_t^T f_{t,s}ds}$, we have from Ito's Lemma,

$$\frac{dD(t,T)}{D(t,T)} = r_t dt - \int_t^T \frac{\partial f_{t,s}}{\partial t}dsdt - \int_t^T \frac{\partial f_{t,s}}{\partial W_s}dsdW_t$$

$$+ \frac{1}{2}\left(\int_t^T \frac{\partial f_{t,s}}{\partial W_s}ds\right)^2 dt.$$

We note that the ratio of the discount bond over the money market account is a martingale under the risk-neutral measure, hence

$$\frac{dD(t,T)}{D(t,T)} = r_t dt - \int_t^T \frac{\partial f_{t,s}}{\partial W_s}dsdW_t.$$

From our equation for $f_{t,T}$, we have

$$df_{t,T} = \cdots dt + \frac{\phi(t)}{\phi(T)}dr_t = \cdots dt + \frac{\phi(t)}{\phi(T)}\sigma(t)dW_t.$$

This gives $\int_t^T \frac{\partial f_{t,s}}{\partial W_s}ds = \int_t^T \frac{\phi(t)}{\phi(s)}\sigma(t)ds$ as the volatility of the discount bond.

(3) We start with $dx_t = -\kappa_x(t)x_t dt + \sigma_x(t)dW_t^x$, $dy_t = -\kappa_y(t)y_t dt + \sigma_y(t)dW_t^y$, $r_t = \phi(t) + x_t + y_t$ and $dW_t^x dW_t^y = \rho(t)dt$.

From our discussion in the answers to Questions 1 and 2, it should be clear (using similar notation as before) that

$$r_T = \phi(T) + x_T + y_T$$

$$= \phi(T) + x_t \frac{\phi_x(t)}{\phi_x(T)} + \int_t^T \sigma_x(s)\frac{\phi_x(s)}{\phi_x(T)}dW_s^x$$

$$+ y_t \frac{\phi_y(t)}{\phi_y(T)} + \int_t^T \sigma_y(s)\frac{\phi_y(s)}{\phi_y(T)}dW_s^y$$

and

$$f_{t,T} = E_t^T[r_T] = \phi_T + x_t \frac{\phi_x(t)}{\phi_x(T)} + y_t \frac{\phi_y(t)}{\phi_y(T)}.$$

Then

$$df_{t,T} = \cdots dt + \frac{\phi_x(t)}{\phi_x(T)}dx_t + \frac{\phi_y(t)}{\phi_y(T)}dy_t$$

$$= \cdots dt + \frac{\phi_x(t)}{\phi_x(T)}\sigma_x(t)dW_t^x + \frac{\phi_y(t)}{\phi_y(T)}\sigma_y(t)dW_t^y.$$

So,

$$\mathrm{cov}(df_{t,T_1}, df_{t,T_2}) = \left(\frac{\phi_x(t)}{\phi_x(T_1)}\sigma_x(t)dW_t^x + \frac{\phi_y(t)}{\phi_y(T_1)}\sigma_y(t)dW_t^y \right)$$

$$\cdot \left(\frac{\phi_x(t)}{\phi_x(T_2)}\sigma_x(t)dW_t^x + \frac{\phi_y(t)}{\phi_y(T_2)}\sigma_y(t)dW_t^y \right)$$

$$= \frac{\phi_x^2(t)}{\phi_x(T_1)\phi_x(T_2)}\sigma_x^2(t)dt + \frac{\phi_y^2(t)}{\phi_y(T_1)\phi_y(T_2)}\sigma_y^2(t)dt$$

$$+ \rho(t)\phi_x(t)\phi_y(t)\sigma_x(t)\sigma_y(t)$$

$$\times \left(\frac{1}{\phi_x(T_1)\phi_y(T_2)} + \frac{1}{\phi_x(T_2)\phi_y(T_1)} \right) dt$$

whilst

$$\mathrm{var}(df_{t,T_1}) = \frac{\phi_x^2(t)}{\phi_x^2(T_1)}\sigma_x^2(t)dt + \frac{\phi_y^2(t)}{\phi_y^2(T_1)}\sigma_y^2(t)dt$$

$$+ 2\rho(t)\frac{\phi_x(t)\phi_y(t)}{\phi_x(T_1)\phi_y(T_1)}\sigma_x(t)\sigma_y(t)dt$$

and $\mathrm{var}(df_{t,T_2})$ can be similarly obtained.
Then,

$$\mathrm{corr}(df_{t,T_1}, df_{t,T_2}) = \frac{\mathrm{cov}(df_{t,T_1}, df_{t,T_2})}{\sqrt{\mathrm{var}(df_{t,T_1})\mathrm{var}(df_{t,T_2})}}.$$

(4) First, we construct the tree for x_t. At each node of the tree corresponding to time index n, we need to find α_n. Let A_j^n be the price of the Arrow–Debreu security corresponding to node x_j^n.

Then the value of a discount bond D_{n+1} with maturity corresponding to time index $n+1$ satisfies the equation

$$D_{n+1} = \sum_{j=1}^{N} A_j^n \exp(-g((\alpha_n + x_j^n))(t_{n+1} - t_n)),$$

being a sum of prices of all Arrow–Debreu states at time index n, discounted by the appropriate discount rate to time index $n+1$.

Supposing we know A_j^n, this gives us α_n (although it may involve a root-finding, depending on $g(\cdot)$). Once we have found α_n, we can then find the Arrow–Debreu prices for time index $n+1$ via

$$A_j^{n+1} = \sum_{i=1}^{n} A_i^n p(n, i, j) \exp(-g((\alpha_n + x_i^n))(t_{n+1} - t_n)),$$

where $p(n, i, j)$ is the transition probability of moving from node x_i^n to node x_j^{n+1} as per our original tree for x_t. (Note that since we have a trinomial tree, most of these probabilities will be zero.)

Note that at time $t_0 = 0$, we only have one Arrow–Debreu state $A_0^0 = 1$ corresponding to node $x_0^0 = 0$, so this determines $\alpha_0 = g^{-1}(-\frac{\log D_1}{t_1})$. We thus have all the information we need to build the tree by sequentially determining α_n one time index at a time.

(5) We note from the answer to Question 2 that $f_{t,T} = E_t^T[r_T] = r_t e^{\kappa(t-T)} + \int_t^T \kappa\theta(s)e^{\kappa(s-T)}ds$.

Thus, we get $df_{t,T} = \cdots dt + e^{\kappa(t-T)}dr_t = \cdots dt + \sigma(t)e^{\kappa(t-T)}dW_t$.

If we have piecewise constant vols with time points $\{T_i\}_{i=1}^{N}$, then we can determine the term vol Λ_j for expiry T_j via

$$\Lambda_j^2 T_j = \int_0^{T_j} \sigma^2(s)e^{2\kappa(s-T_j)}ds = \sum_{i=1}^{j} \sigma_i^2 \int_{T_{i-1}}^{T_i} e^{2\kappa(s-T_j)}ds$$

$$= \sum_{i=1}^{j} \frac{\sigma_i^2}{2\kappa}(e^{2\kappa(T_i-T_j)} - e^{2\kappa(T_{i-1}-T_j)}).$$

Keeping Λ_j constant for all T_j, we can then solve for our piecewise constant Hull–White vols σ_j. We get the following table of

Hull–White vols based on term vol of 0.7% and mean reversion of 1% and 10% respectively.

Time	Local Vol for MR = 1%	Local Vol for MR = 10%
1	0.704%	0.735%
2	0.710%	0.799%
3	0.717%	0.858%
4	0.724%	0.914%
5	0.731%	0.966%
6	0.738%	1.015%
7	0.744%	1.062%
8	0.751%	1.108%
9	0.757%	1.151%
10	0.764%	1.193%

It is left to the reader to attempt to implement the root-finding to obtain the prices of the swaptions.

Chapter 9

(1) For sake of notational clarity, let us define $dW_t^{i,j}$ to be the factor driving the i-th Libor rate based on numeraire being the discount bond maturing at the pay date of the j-th Libor rate. Then we have $dL_i(t) = \sigma_i(L_i(t), t)dW_t^{i,i}$.

The Radon–Nikodym derivative is given by

$$R(t) = \frac{dQ^{T_{i+1}}}{dQ^{T_i}}(t) = \frac{D(0, T_i)}{(1 + L_{i+1}(t)\tau_{i+1})D(0, T_{i+1})},$$

so

$$dR(t) = -\frac{\tau_{i+1}\rho_{i,i+1}(t)\sigma_{i+1}(L_{i+1}(t), t)}{1 + L_{i+1}(t)\tau_{i+1}} R(t)dW_t^{i,i+1}$$

in a similar spirit to our discussion in Section 9.1.1. (Note that the correlation term comes in because of the multi-factorness.) Girsanov's Theorem gives

$$dW_t^{i,i} = -\frac{\tau_{i+1}\rho_{i,i+1}(t)\sigma_{i+1}(L_{i+1}(t), t)}{1 + L_{i+1}(t)\tau_{i+1}} dt + dW_t^{i,i+1}.$$

Thus,

$$dL_i(t) = -\frac{\tau_{i+1}\rho_{i,i+1}(t)\sigma_{i+1}(L_{i+1}(t),t)\sigma_i(L_i(t),t)}{1 + L_{i+1}(t)\tau_{i+1}}dt$$

$$+ \sigma_i(L_i(t),t)dW_t^{i,i+1}$$

$$= \cdots$$

$$= -\sigma_i(L_i(t),t)\sum_{j=i+1}^{N}\frac{\tau_j\rho_{i,j}(t)\sigma_j(L_j(t),t)}{1 + L_j(t)\tau_j}dt$$

$$+ \sigma_i(L_i(t),t)dW_t^{i,N},$$

where we have sequentially changed measure (per Section 9.1.1) to the natural numeraire asset for the N-th (i.e. furthest) Libor rate.

(2) As $x = S\sqrt{D}z$,

$$xx^T = S\sqrt{D}z(S\sqrt{D}z)^T = S\sqrt{D}zz^T\sqrt{D}S^T,$$

since $(\sqrt{D})^T = \sqrt{D}$ for a diagonal matrix D.

Then $E[xx^T] = S\sqrt{D}E[zz^T]\sqrt{D}S^T = S\sqrt{D}I\sqrt{D}S^T = SDS^T = \Omega$, since $E[zz^T] = I$ (i.e. the identity matrix) for independent and identically distributed $N(0,1)$ variates z.
Also, $E[x] = S\sqrt{D}E[z] = 0$ since z are independent variates.
Thus, $\text{cov}(x) = E[xx^T] - E[x](E[x])^T = \Omega$.

(3) We have $dL_t^i = \cdots dt + \sigma_i L_t^i(a_{i1}dW_t^1 + a_{i2}dW_t^2)$, where $a_{i1} = \sin\theta_i$, $a_{i2} = \cos\theta_i$ and $dW_t^1 dW_t^2 = 0$.
So,

$$\text{cov}(dL_t^i, dL_j^t)$$

$$= \sigma_i\sigma_j L_t^i L_t^j(a_{i1}dW_t^1 + a_{i2}dW_t^2)(a_{j1}dW_t^1 + a_{j2}dW_t^2)$$

$$= \sigma_i\sigma_j L_t^i L_t^j(a_{i1}a_{j1} + a_{i2}a_{j2})$$

$$= \sigma_i\sigma_j L_t^i L_t^j(\sin\theta_i\sin\theta_j + \cos\theta_i\cos\theta_j)$$

and

$$\text{var}(dL_t^i) = \sigma_i^2 L_i^2 (a_{i1}^2 + a_{i2}^2) = \sigma_i^2 L_i^2 (\sin^2 \theta_i + \cos^2 \theta_i) = \sigma_i^2 L_i^2.$$

Thus,

$$\text{corr}(dL_t^i, dL_t^j) = \frac{\text{cov}(dL_t^i, dL_t^j)}{\sqrt{\text{var}(dL_t^i)\text{var}(dL_t^j)}}$$

$$= \frac{\sigma_i \sigma_j L_t^i L_t^j (\sin \theta_i \sin \theta_j + \cos \theta_i \cos \theta_j)}{\sigma_i \sigma_j L_t^i L_t^j}$$

$$= \sin \theta_i \sin \theta_j + \cos \theta_i \cos \theta_j.$$

If we wish to calibrate correlations, then we would have needed a constrained optimisation in general since correlations have to be between -100% and 100%. With the above parameterisation, we can do an unconstrained optimisation over θ_i.

(4) The relevant function is

$$f(x) = \sum_{i=1}^{N} f(x_i) \frac{\prod_{\substack{j=1 \\ j \neq i}}^{N} (x - x_j)}{\prod_{\substack{j=1 \\ j \neq i}}^{N} (x_i - x_j)}$$

(You can verify it by substituting $\{x_i\}_{i=1}^{N}$.)

The problem with a polynomial of degree n is that it has n roots in general and so has many turning points. Extrapolation is likely to be unrealistic and even interpolation is suspicious as most real phenomena are not like that.

Chapter 10

(1) We have $dS_t = (r_t - r_t^f)S_t dt + \sigma_S(t)S_t dW_t^S$, $df_d(t, T) = \mu_d(t, T)dt + \sigma_d(t, T)dW_t^d$ and $df_f(t, T) = \mu_f(t, T)dt + \sigma_f(t, T)dW_t^f$, where $dW_t^d dW_t^f = \rho_{df}(t)dt$, $dW_t^d dW_t^S = \rho_{dS}(t)dt$, $dW_t^f dW_t^S = \rho_{fS}(t)dt$.

The foreign discount bond is given by $D^f(t,T) = \exp(-\int_t^T f_f(t,s)ds)$, so Ito's Lemma gives

$$dD^f(t,T)/D^f(t,T)$$

$$= f_f(t,t)dt - \int_t^T \frac{\partial f_f(t,s)}{\partial t}ds dt - \int_t^T \frac{\partial f_f(t,s)}{\partial W_t}ds dW_t^f$$

$$+ \frac{1}{2}\left(\int_t^T \frac{\partial f_f(t,s)}{\partial W_t}ds\right)^2 dt$$

$$= r_t^f dt - \int_t^T \mu_f(t,s)ds dt - \int_t^T \sigma_f(t,s)ds dW_t^f$$

$$+ \frac{1}{2}\left(\int_t^T \sigma_f(t,s)ds\right)^2 dt.$$

Further, the foreign Libor rate is given by

$$L_f(t,T,T+\tau) = \left(\frac{D^f(t,T)}{D^f(t,T+\tau)} - 1\right)\bigg/\tau$$

$$= \left(\exp\left(\int_T^{T+\tau} f_f(t,s)ds\right) - 1\right)\bigg/\tau.$$

By no-arbitrage arguments, we require $\frac{D^f(t,T)S_t}{B_t} = E_t^Q[\frac{S_T}{B_T}]$, where $B_t = e^{\int_0^t r_u du}$ is the value of the domestic money market account at time t. This means that

$$d\left(\frac{D^f(t,T)S_t}{B_t}\right)\bigg/\frac{D^f(t,T)S_t}{B_t}$$

$$= \left(\frac{(D^f(t,T) + dD^f(t,T))(S_t + dS_t)}{B_t + dB_t}\right.$$

$$\left.- \frac{D^f(t,T)S_t}{B_t}\right)\bigg/\frac{D^f(t,T)S_t}{B_t}$$

$$= \left(1 + \frac{dD^f(t,T)}{D^f(t,T)}\right)\left(1 + \frac{dS_t}{S_t}\right)\left(1 - \frac{dB_t}{B_t}\right) - 1$$

$$= \frac{dD^f(t,T)}{D^f(t,T)} + \frac{dS_t}{S_t} - \frac{dB_t}{B_t} + \frac{dD^f(t,T)}{D^f(t,T)}\frac{dS_t}{S_t}$$

$$= r_t^f dt - \int_t^T \mu_f(t,s)dsdt - \int_t^T \sigma_f(t,s)dsdW_t^f$$

$$+ \frac{1}{2}\left(\int_t^T \sigma_f(t,s)ds\right)^2 dt$$

$$+ (r_t - r_t^f)dt + \sigma_S(t)dW_t^S - r_t dt$$

$$- \rho_{fS}(t)\sigma_S(t)\int_t^T \sigma_f(t,s)dsdt$$

$$= 0\,dt - \int_t^T \sigma_f(t,s)dsdW_t^f + \sigma_S(t)dW_t^S,$$

which gives

$$\int_t^T \mu_f(t,s)ds = \frac{1}{2}\left(\int_t^T \sigma_f(t,s)ds\right)^2 - \rho_{fS}(t)\sigma_S(t)\int_t^T \sigma_f(t,s)ds$$

so that differentiating with respect to T gives

$$\mu_f(t,T) = \sigma_f(t,T)\left(\int_t^T \sigma_f(t,s)ds - \rho_{fS}(t)\sigma_S(t)\right).$$

Note that from Section 8.1.2, the following equation holds regarding the drift for the domestic instantaneous forward:

$$\int_t^T \mu_d(t,s)ds = \frac{1}{2}\left(\int_t^T \sigma_d(t,s)ds\right)^2.$$

Since payment is at time $T+\tau$, the value of the quanto Libor is

$$E^Q\left[\frac{L_f(T,T,T+\tau)}{B_{T+\tau}}\right]$$

$$= \frac{1}{\tau}E^Q\left[\frac{\exp\left(\int_T^{T+\tau} f_f(T,s)ds\right) - 1}{B_{T+\tau}}\right]$$

$$= \frac{1}{\tau}E^Q\left[\exp\left(\int_T^{T+\tau} f_f(T,s)ds - \int_0^{T+\tau} f_d(s,s)ds\right)\right]$$

$$- \frac{1}{\tau}D(0,T+\tau)$$

$$= \frac{1}{\tau} E^Q \left[\exp\left(\int_T^{T+\tau} \left(f_f(0,s) + \int_0^T \mu_f(u,s) du \right. \right.\right.$$

$$\left.\left. + \int_0^T \sigma_f(u,s) dW_u^f \right) ds \right)$$

$$- \int_0^{T+\tau} \left(f_d(0,s) + \int_0^s \mu_d(u,s) du \right.$$

$$\left.\left. + \int_0^s \sigma_d(u,s) dW_u^d \right) ds \right] - \frac{1}{\tau} D(0,T+\tau)$$

$$= \frac{1}{\tau} \left\{ \exp\left(\int_T^{T+\tau} f_f(0,s) ds + \int_0^T \int_T^{T+\tau} \mu_f(u,s) ds du \right.\right.$$

$$\left. - \int_0^{T+\tau} f_d(0,s) ds - \int_0^{T+\tau} \int_u^{T+\tau} \mu_d(u,s) ds du \right)$$

$$\cdot E^Q \left[\exp\left(\int_0^T \int_T^{T+\tau} \sigma_f(u,s) ds dW_u^f \right.\right.$$

$$\left.\left.\left. - \int_0^{T+\tau} \int_u^{T+\tau} \sigma_d(u,s) ds dW_u^d \right) \right] \right\} - \frac{1}{\tau} D(0,T+\tau)$$

$$= \frac{D(0,T+\tau)}{\tau} \left\{ \frac{D^f(0,T)}{D^f(0,T+\tau)} \right.$$

$$\times \exp\left(\int_0^T \int_T^{T+\tau} \mu_f(u,s) ds du - \int_0^{T+\tau} \int_u^{T+\tau} \mu_d(u,s) ds du \right)$$

$$\cdot \exp\left(\frac{1}{2} \int_0^T \left(\int_T^{T+\tau} \sigma_f(u,s) ds \right)^2 du \right.$$

$$\left. + \frac{1}{2} \int_0^{T+\tau} \left(\int_u^{T+\tau} \sigma_d(u,s) ds \right)^2 du \right)$$

$$\cdot \exp\left(-\int_0^T \rho_{df}(u) \int_T^{T+\tau} \sigma_f(u,s) ds \int_u^{T+\tau} \sigma_d(u,s) ds du \right)$$

$$\left. -1 \right\}$$

$$
= \frac{D(0, T+\tau)}{\tau} \left\{ \frac{D^f(0, T)}{D^f(0, T+\tau)} \right.
$$

$$
\times \exp \left(\int_0^T \int_T^{T+\tau} \sigma_f(u, s) \left(\int_u^s \sigma_f(u, q) dq \right. \right.
$$

$$
\left. \left. - \rho_{fS}(u)\sigma_S(u) \right) ds du \right)
$$

$$
\cdot \exp \left(\frac{1}{2} \int_0^T \left\{ \left(\int_T^{T+\tau} \sigma_f(u, s) ds \right)^2 \right. \right.
$$

$$
\left. \left. -2\rho_{df}(u) \int_T^{T+\tau} \sigma_f(u, s) ds \int_u^{T+\tau} \sigma_d(u, s) ds \right\} du \right) - 1 \right\}
$$

$$
= \frac{D(0, T+\tau)}{\tau} \left\{ \frac{D^f(0, T)}{D^f(0, T+\tau)} \right.
$$

$$
\times \exp \left(\frac{1}{2} \int_0^T \left\{ \left(\int_u^{T+\tau} \sigma_f(u, s) ds \right)^2 \right. \right.
$$

$$
\left. \left. - \left(\int_u^T \sigma_f(u, s) ds \right)^2 \right\} du \right)
$$

$$
\cdot \exp \left(- \int_0^T \rho_{fS}(u)\sigma_S(u) \int_T^{T+\tau} \sigma_f(u, s) ds du \right)
$$

$$
\cdot \exp \left(\frac{1}{2} \int_0^T \left\{ \left(\int_T^{T+\tau} \sigma_f(u, s) ds \right)^2 \right. \right.
$$

$$
\left. \left. -2\rho_{df}(u) \int_T^{T+\tau} \sigma_f(u, s) ds \int_u^{T+\tau} \sigma_d(u, s) ds \right\} du \right) - 1 \right\}.
$$

Finally, we get

$$
E^Q \left[\frac{L_f(T, T, T+\tau)}{B_T} \right]
$$

$$
= \frac{D(0, T+\tau)}{\tau} \left\{ \frac{D^f(0, T)}{D^f(0, T+\tau)} \right.
$$

$$\times \exp \left(\int_0^T \int_T^{T+\tau} \sigma_f(u,s)ds \right.$$

$$\times \left\{ \int_T^{T+\tau} \sigma_f(u,s)ds + \int_u^T \sigma_f(u,s)ds \right\} du \right)$$

$$\cdot \exp \left(-\int_0^T \left(\rho_{fS}(u)\sigma_S(u) + \rho_{df}(u) \int_u^{T+\tau} \sigma_d(u,s)ds \right) \right.$$

$$\left. \times \int_T^{T+\tau} \sigma_f(u,s)dsdu \right) - 1 \right\}$$

$$= \frac{D(0,T+\tau)}{\tau} \left\{ \frac{D^f(0,T)}{D^f(0,T+\tau)} \right.$$

$$\times \exp \left(\int_0^T \int_T^{T+\tau} \sigma_f(u,s)ds \int_u^{T+\tau} \sigma_f(u,s)dsdu \right)$$

$$\cdot \exp \left(-\int_0^T \left(\rho_{fS}(u)\sigma_S(u) + \rho_{df}(u) \int_u^{T+\tau} \sigma_d(u,s)ds \right) \right.$$

$$\left. \times \int_T^{T+\tau} \sigma_f(u,s)dsdu \right) - 1 \right\}.$$

(2) We note from our earlier work (e.g. Questions 2 and 5 of Chapter 8) applying $f_{t,T} = E_t^T[r_T]$ that $df_{t,T} = \cdots dt + \sigma e^{\kappa(t-T)}dW_t$. Thus, $\sigma_d(t,T) = \sigma_f(t,T) = \sigma e^{\kappa(t-T)}$ in our case, with $\sigma = 0.7\%$ and $\kappa = 2\%$. Further, we have constant spot FX vol $\sigma_S = 15\%$.

In the absence of spot correlations and where the domestic-foreign rates correlation is $\rho_{df} = 30\%$, the components of forward FX variance between times T_1 and T_2 are:

(a) the spot part

$$\Sigma_S = \sigma_S^2(T_2 - T_1),$$

(b) the domestic rate part

$$\Sigma_d = \int_{T_1}^{T_2} \left(\int_u^{T_2} \sigma_d(u,v)dv \right)^2 du$$

$$= \int_{T_1}^{T_2} \left(\int_u^{T_2} \sigma e^{\kappa(u-v)}dv \right)^2 du$$

$$= \frac{\sigma^2}{\kappa^2} \int_{T_1}^{T_2} (1 - e^{\kappa(u-T_2)})^2 du$$

$$= \frac{\sigma^2}{\kappa^2} \int_{T_1}^{T_2} (1 - 2e^{\kappa(u-T_2)} + e^{2\kappa(u-T_2)}) du$$

$$= \frac{\sigma^2}{\kappa^2} \left\{ T_2 - T_1 - \frac{2}{\kappa}(1 - e^{\kappa(T_1-T_2)}) + \frac{1}{2\kappa}(1 - e^{2\kappa(T_1-T_2)}) \right\},$$

(c) the foreign part $\Sigma_f = \Sigma_d$, and

(d) the rates correlation part

$$\Sigma_{df} = -2\rho_{df} \int_{T_1}^{T_2} \int_u^{T_2} \sigma_d(u,v) dv \int_u^{T_2} \sigma_f(u,v) dv du$$

$$= -2\rho_{df} \int_{T_1}^{T_2} \left(\int_u^{T_2} \sigma e^{\kappa(u-v)} dv \right)^2 du$$

$$= -\frac{2\rho_{df}\sigma^2}{\kappa^2} \left\{ T_2 - T_1 - \frac{2}{\kappa}(1 - e^{\kappa(T_1-T_2)}) \right.$$

$$\left. + \frac{1}{2\kappa}(1 - e^{2\kappa(T_1-T_2)}) \right\}.$$

First notice that only $T_2 - T_1$ appears in the formula for the rate contributions, so considerations regarding forward start are irrelevant in the constant vol case.

If we apply the above formulae to the expiries in the question, then we get the following:

Expiry (y)	Spot Variance	Domestic Variance = Foreign Variance	Rates Correlation	Spot Contrib (%)	Implied Vol (%)
1	0.0225	0.00002	-0.00001	99.90	15.01
5	0.1125	0.0019	-0.0011	97.70	15.18
10	0.2250	0.0141	-0.0085	91.94	15.64
20	0.4500	0.0979	-0.0587	76.66	17.13
30	0.6750	0.2880	-0.1728	62.60	18.96

(3) Based on the calculations in Question 2, we have determined the forward FX variances that we wish to preserve for annual expiries.

The spot-domestic contribution between time points T_i and $T_j(> T_i)$, points where the piecewise-constant vol varies, is

$$
\begin{aligned}
\Sigma_{dS} &= 2 \int_{T_i}^{T_j} \sigma_S(u) \rho_{dS}(u) \int_u^{T_j} \sigma_d(u,v) dv du \\
&= 2\rho_{dS} \int_{T_i}^{T_j} \sigma_S(u) \int_u^{T_j} \sigma e^{\kappa(u-v)} dv du \\
&= \frac{2\rho_{dS}\sigma}{\kappa} \int_{T_i}^{T_j} \sigma_S(u)(1 - e^{\kappa(u-T_j)}) du \\
&= \frac{2\rho_{dS}\sigma}{\kappa} \sum_{k=i+1}^{j} \sigma_k^S \left\{ T_k - T_{k-1} - \frac{1}{\kappa}(e^{\kappa(T_k-T_j)} - e^{\kappa(T_{k-1}-T_j)}) \right\},
\end{aligned}
$$

whilst the spot-foreign contribution is

$$
\begin{aligned}
\Sigma_{fS} &= -2 \int_{T_i}^{T_j} \sigma_S(u) \rho_{fS}(u) \int_u^{T_j} \sigma_f(u,v) dv du \\
&= -2\rho_{fS} \int_{T_i}^{T_j} \sigma_S(u) \int_u^{T_j} \sigma e^{\kappa(u-v)} dv du \\
&= -\frac{2\rho_{fS}\sigma}{\kappa} \sum_{k=i+1}^{j} \sigma_k^S \left\{ T_k - T_{k-1} \right. \\
&\qquad\qquad \left. - \frac{1}{\kappa}(e^{\kappa(T_k-T_j)} - e^{\kappa(T_{k-1}-T_j)}) \right\}.
\end{aligned}
$$

Suppose we increase spot-domestic correlation to 20%, then bootstrapping to match the forward FX variances involves solving a quadratic equation for the time dependent spot FX vols σ_k^S as we step forward in time. We obtain

Time (y)	Spot Vol (Dom Corr = 30%) (%)	Spot Vol (For Corr = 20%) (%)
1	14.90	15.07
2	14.69	15.21
3	14.49	15.34
4	14.29	15.47
5	14.10	15.60

(Continued)

	(*Continued*)	
6	13.91	15.73
7	13.72	15.85
8	13.54	15.98
9	13.36	16.10
10	13.19	16.21
11	13.02	16.33
12	12.86	16.44
13	12.69	16.55
14	12.54	16.66
15	12.38	16.77
16	12.23	16.88
17	12.09	16.98
18	11.94	17.08
19	11.80	17.18
20	11.67	17.28

Using the spot FX vols thus computed, we can obtain the 10-year forward starting vols below.

Expiry (y)	Forward Vol (%) (No Spot-Rate Corr)	Forward Vol (%) Dom-Spot Corr = 30%	Forward Vol (%) For-Spot Corr = 20%
1	15.01	13.13	16.27
2	15.03	13.18	16.27
3	15.07	13.23	16.29
4	15.11	13.30	16.33
5	15.18	13.39	16.37
6	15.25	13.48	16.42
7	15.33	13.58	16.49
8	15.43	13.70	16.56
9	15.53	13.82	16.64
10	15.64	13.95	16.73

In particular, we see that increasing the domestic rate-spot FX correlation decreases forward vol, whilst increasing the foreign rate-spot FX correlation increases forward vol.

Chapter 11

(1) We have $dS_t = rS_t dt + \sigma S_t dW_t$, so

$$\frac{S_{T_2}}{S_{T_1}} = e^{(r - \frac{1}{2}\sigma^2)(T_2 - T_1) + \sigma(W_{T_2} - W_{T_1})}.$$

The value of our payoff is

$$V_0 = e^{-rT_2} E\left[\max\left(\frac{S_{T_2}}{S_{T_1}} - 1, 0\right)\right]$$

$$= e^{-rT_2} \int_{-\infty}^{\infty} \max(e^{(r-\frac{1}{2}\sigma^2)(T_2-T_1)+\sigma z\sqrt{T_2-T_1}} - 1, 0)\frac{1}{\sqrt{2\pi}}e^{-\frac{1}{2}z^2}dz$$

$$= e^{-rT_2} \int_{z^*}^{\infty} (e^{(r-\frac{1}{2}\sigma^2)(T_2-T_1)+\sigma z\sqrt{T_2-T_1}} - 1)\frac{1}{\sqrt{2\pi}}e^{-\frac{1}{2}z^2}dz$$

$$= e^{-rT_1-\frac{1}{2}\sigma^2(T_2-T_1)}$$
$$\times \int_{z^*}^{\infty} e^{\sigma z\sqrt{T_2-T_1}}\frac{1}{\sqrt{2\pi}}e^{-\frac{1}{2}z^2}dz - e^{-rT_2}N(-z^*)$$

$$= e^{-rT_1-\frac{1}{2}\sigma^2(T_2-T_1)}$$
$$\times \int_{z^*}^{\infty} \frac{1}{\sqrt{2\pi}}e^{-\frac{1}{2}(z-\sigma\sqrt{T_2-T_1})^2}dz e^{\frac{1}{2}\sigma^2(T_2-T_1)} - e^{-rT_2}N(-z^*)$$

$$= e^{-rT_1}N(-z^* + \sigma\sqrt{T_2-T_1}) - e^{-rT_2}N(-z^*),$$

where $z^* = -\frac{(r-\frac{1}{2}\sigma^2)\sqrt{T_2-T_1}}{\sigma}$.

(2) We have $dr_t = \kappa(\theta(t) - r_t)dt + \sigma dW_t$.

$$\Rightarrow d(r_t e^{\kappa t}) = \kappa\theta(t)e^{\kappa t}dt + \sigma e^{\kappa t}dW_t$$

$$\Rightarrow r_T = r_t e^{\kappa(t-T)} + \kappa \int_t^T \theta(s)e^{\kappa(s-T)}ds + \sigma \int_t^T e^{\kappa(s-T)}dW_s.$$

Then

$$f_{t,T} = E_t^T[r_T] = r_t e^{\kappa(t-T)} + \kappa \int_t^T \theta(s)e^{\kappa(s-T)}ds$$

$$= (r_0 e^{-\kappa t} + \kappa \int_0^t \theta(s)e^{\kappa(s-t)}ds + \sigma \int_0^t e^{\kappa(s-t)}dW_s)e^{\kappa(t-T)}$$

$$+ \kappa \int_t^T \theta(s)e^{\kappa(s-T)}ds$$

$$= r_0 e^{-\kappa T} + \kappa \int_0^T \theta(s)e^{\kappa(s-T)}ds + \sigma \int_0^t e^{\kappa(s-T)}dW_s.$$

This gives (for $t < u$):

$$\text{cov}(f_{t,T}, f_{u,T}) = \sigma^2 \int_0^t e^{\kappa(s-T)} dW_s \int_0^u e^{\kappa(s-T)} dW_s$$

$$= \sigma^2 \int_0^t e^{\kappa(s-T)} dW_s$$

$$\times \left(\int_0^t e^{\kappa(s-T)} dW_s + \int_t^u e^{\kappa(s-T)} dW_s \right)$$

$$= \sigma^2 \left(\int_0^t e^{2\kappa(s-T)} ds + 0 \right)$$

$$= \frac{\sigma^2 e^{-2\kappa T}}{2\kappa} (e^{2\kappa t} - 1),$$

whilst $\text{var}(f_{t,T}) = \frac{\sigma^2 e^{-2\kappa T}}{2\kappa}(e^{2\kappa t} - 1)$ and $\text{var}(f_{u,T}) = \frac{\sigma^2 e^{-2\kappa T}}{2\kappa}(e^{2\kappa u} - 1)$.

Thus,

$$\text{corr}(f_{t,T}, f_{u,T})$$

$$= \frac{\text{cov}(f_{t,T}, f_{u,T})}{\sqrt{\text{var}(f_{t,T})\text{var}(f_{u,T})}}$$

$$= \frac{\sigma^2 e^{-2\kappa T}}{2\kappa}(e^{2\kappa t} - 1) \Big/ \sqrt{\frac{\sigma^2 e^{-2\kappa T}}{2\kappa}(e^{2\kappa t} - 1)\frac{\sigma^2 e^{-2\kappa T}}{2\kappa}(e^{2\kappa u} - 1)}$$

$$= \sqrt{\frac{e^{2\kappa t} - 1}{e^{2\kappa u} - 1}}.$$

(3) We start with $dS_t = \mu S_t dt + \sigma(S_t, t)S_t dW_t$. Ito's Lemma gives

$$dC_t = \frac{\partial C_t}{\partial t} dt + \frac{\partial C_t}{\partial S_t} dS_t + \frac{1}{2}\frac{\partial^2 C_t}{\partial S_t^2}(dS_t)^2$$

$$= \left(\frac{\partial C_t}{\partial t} + \mu S_t \frac{\partial C_t}{\partial S_t} + \frac{1}{2}\sigma^2 S_t^2 \frac{\partial^2 C_t}{\partial S_t^2} \right) dt + \sigma S_t \frac{\partial C_t}{\partial S_t} dW_t.$$

To construct a replicating portfolio we follow the approach in Section 1.1.2 and let

$$\Pi_t = C_t - \frac{\partial C_t}{\partial S_t} S_t,$$

so that

$$d\Pi_t = dC_t - \frac{\partial C_t}{\partial S_t} dS_t$$

$$= \left(\frac{\partial C_t}{\partial t} + \frac{1}{2} \sigma^2 S_t^2 \frac{\partial^2 C_t}{\partial S_t^2} \right) dt$$

$$= r_t \Pi_t dt$$

$$= r_t \left(C_t - \frac{\partial C_t}{\partial S_t} S_t \right) dt,$$

giving the familiar Black–Scholes equation

$$\frac{\partial C_t}{\partial t} + r_t S_t \frac{\partial C_t}{\partial S_t} + \frac{1}{2} \sigma^2 S_t^2 \frac{\partial^2 C_t}{\partial S_t^2} = r_t C_t.$$

Notice how $\sigma(S_t, t)$ is multiplied by the (positive) gamma $\frac{\partial^2 C_t}{\partial S_t^2}$ in the equation. So, the larger the vol is, the more the cost of delta-hedging. Also, observe that it is not the forward vol with which we need concern ourselves here, so the actual vol dynamics are not that important.

(4) Based on the calculations in Question 2 of Chapter 10, we have determined the forward FX variances that we wish to preserve for annual expiries. The one difference is that we have time-dependent spot FX vols now. The components of forward FX variance between time points T_i and $T_j (> T_i)$ are thus:

(a) the spot part

$$\Sigma_S = \sum_{k=i+1}^{j} (\sigma_k^S)^2 (T_k - T_{k-1}),$$

(b) the domestic rate part

$$\Sigma_d = \frac{\sigma^2}{\kappa^2} \left\{ T_j - T_i - \frac{2}{\kappa} (1 - e^{\kappa(T_i - T_j)}) + \frac{1}{2\kappa} (1 - e^{2\kappa(T_i - T_j)}) \right\},$$

(c) the foreign part $\Sigma_f = \Sigma_d$, and
(d) the rates correlation part

$$\Sigma_{df} = -\frac{2\rho_{df}\sigma^2}{\kappa^2}\left\{T_j - T_i - \frac{2}{\kappa}(1 - e^{\kappa(T_i-T_j)})\right.$$
$$\left. + \frac{1}{2\kappa}(1 - e^{2\kappa(T_i-T_j)})\right\}.$$

We could bootstrap the time-dependent spot vols sequentially from the variances at annual expiries to obtain the following.

Time (y)	Spot Vol (Rate Vol = 1%) (%)	SpotVol (Zero Rate Vol) (%)
1	14.99	15.01
2	14.95	15.05
3	14.86	15.14
4	14.72	15.26
5	14.55	15.42
6	14.34	15.61
7	14.09	15.83
8	13.80	16.07
9	13.47	16.34
10	13.10	16.62
11	12.69	16.93
12	12.23	17.25
13	11.73	17.58
14	11.18	17.92
15	10.58	18.27
16	9.91	18.62
17	9.16	18.99
18	8.33	19.35
19	7.37	19.72
20	6.23	20.10

This gives us the following 10-year forward starting vols:

Expiry (y)	Forward Vol (%) (Rate Vol = 0.7%)	Forward Vol (%) (Rate Vol = 1%)	Forward Vol (%) (No Rate Vols)
1	15.01	12.69	16.93
2	15.03	12.50	17.11
3	15.07	12.30	17.31
4	15.11	12.11	17.52
5	15.18	11.93	17.74
6	15.25	11.75	17.98
7	15.33	11.58	18.23
8	15.43	11.40	18.49
9	15.53	11.24	18.75
10	15.64	11.08	19.03

In this case, we have higher forward vols the lower the interest rates vol contributions are. And the effect is particularly obvious for long forward starting times (i.e. 10 years here). This highlights the implication that the much faster growth of interest rate volatilities (than spot FX vols) with expiry has for long-dated FX products. It is insufficient to just recover the variance of the FX forward but the amount of volatility attributable to interest rates versus spot FX components matters a lot.

Chapter 12

(1) The starting point is

$$\sum_{i=1}^{M} f^{\Delta}(0, T_{i-1}^*, T_i^*) \tau_i^* D(0, T_i^*) = R_N^{\Delta} \sum_{i=1}^{N} \tau_i D(0, T_i).$$

If the Libor–OIS spread is zero, then $D^{\Delta}(0, T) = D(0, T)$, so

$$\sum_{i=1}^{M} f^{\Delta}(0, T_{i-1}^*, T_i^*) \tau_i^* D(0, T_i^*)$$

$$= \sum_{i=1}^{M} \left(\frac{D(0, T_{i-1}^*)}{D(0, T_i^*)} - 1 \right) D(0, T_i^*)$$

$$= \sum_{i=1}^{M} (D(0, T_{i-1}^*) - D(0, T_i^*))$$

$$= D(0, T_0^*) - D(0, T_M^*)$$

$$= D(0, T_0) - D(0, T_N).$$

Similarly,

$$R_N^{\Delta} = \frac{\sum_{i=1}^{M} f^{\Delta}(0, T_{i-1}^*, T_i^*) \tau_i^* D(0, T_i^*)}{\sum_{i=1}^{N} \tau_i D(0, T_i)}$$

$$= \frac{D(0, T_0) - D(0, T_N)}{\sum_{i=1}^{N} \tau_i D(0, T_i)} = R_N.$$

Now, instead let $D(0,T) = D^{\Delta}(0,T)e^{-sT}$. Then

$$\sum_{i=1}^{M} f^{\Delta}(0, T_{i-1}^*, T_i^*)\tau_i^* D(0, T_i^*)$$

$$= \sum_{i=1}^{M} \left(\frac{D(0, T_{i-1}^*)}{D(0, T_i^*)} e^{s(T_{i-1}^* - T_i^*)} - 1 \right) D(0, T_i^*)$$

$$= \sum_{i=1}^{M} (D(0, T_{i-1}^*)e^{s(T_{i-1}^* - T_i^*)} - D(0, T_i^*))$$

$$= \sum_{i=1}^{M} D(0, T_{i-1}^*)(e^{s(T_{i-1}^* - T_i^*)} - 1) + D(0, T_0) - D(0, T_N).$$

Thus,

$$R_N^{\Delta} = \frac{\sum_{i=1}^{M} D(0, T_{i-1}^*)(e^{s(T_{i-1}^* - T_i^*)} - 1)}{\sum_{i=1}^{N} \tau_i D(0, T_i)} + R_N.$$

(2) We have from Section 12.2.1,

$$-D^{\text{JPY}}(0, T_0) + \sum_{i=1}^{M}(f^{\text{JPY}}(0, T_{i-1}^*, T_i^*) + s^{\text{JPY}})\tau_i^* D^{\text{JPY}}(0, T_i^*)$$

$$+ D^{\text{JPY}}(0, T_M^*)$$

$$= -D^{\text{USD}}(0, T_0) + \sum_{i=1}^{M} f^{\text{USD}}(0, T_{i-1}^*, T_i^*)\tau_i^* D^{\text{USD}}(0, T_i^*)$$

$$+ D^{\text{USD}}(0, T_M^*)$$

$$= -D^{\text{BRL}}(0, T_0) + \sum_{i=1}^{M}(f^{\text{BRL}}(0, T_{i-1}^*, T_i^*) + s^{\text{BRL}})$$

$$\times \tau_i^* D^{\text{BRL}}(0, T_i^*) + D^{\text{BRL}}(0, T_M^*).$$

Thus,

$$-D^{\mathrm{BRL}}(0,T_0) + \sum_{i=1}^{M}(f^{\mathrm{BRL}}(0,T_{i-1}^*,T_i^*) + s^*)\tau_i^* D^{\mathrm{BRL}}(0,T_i^*)$$

$$+ D^{\mathrm{BRL}}(0,T_M^*)$$

$$= -D^{\mathrm{JPY}}(0,T_0) + \sum_{i=1}^{M} f^{\mathrm{JPY}}(0,T_{i-1}^*,T_i^*)\tau_i^* D^{\mathrm{JPY}}(0,T_i^*)$$

$$+ D^{\mathrm{JPY}}(0,T_M^*).$$

where

$$s^* = s^{\mathrm{BRL}} - s^{\mathrm{JPY}} \frac{\sum_{i=1}^{M} \tau_i^* D^{\mathrm{JPY}}(0,T_i^*)}{\sum_{i=1}^{M} \tau_i^* D^{\mathrm{BRL}}(0,T_i^*)}.$$

(3) Based on different rates for Libor and OIS, we get the following:

Maturity (y)	Float Leg	Annuity	Swap Rate (%)
1	0.0296	0.9724	3.0439
5	0.1400	4.6008	3.0439
10	0.2618	8.6005	3.0439
30	0.6092	20.0132	3.0439

If we had used Libor discounting, the results would have been

Maturity (y)	Float Leg	Annuity	Swap Rate (%)
1	0.0296	0.9704	3.0455
5	0.1393	4.5738	3.0455
10	0.2592	8.5104	3.0455
30	0.5934	19.4858	3.0455

(4) Take Libor as the base case and let $s = r_O - r_L$, i.e. the spread is given by OIS rate — Libor rate. We start with the observation that the Libor rate is generally higher than the OIS rate. In a developed economy, interest rates tend to be cut in the event of a crisis (to stimulate the economy), so the spread widens as OIS falls but Libor does not fall as much due to credit concerns; when

the economy is booming (and credit risk is less of a concern), rates are hiked (to cool off inflation), so the spread drops as OIS rises but Libor does not rise as much. This suggests a negative correlation, hence a negative quanto correction.

(5) We start with $dX_t = r_t X_t dt + \sigma X_t dW_t^X$ and $ds_t = \kappa(\theta(t) - s_t)dt + \lambda dW_t^s$ with $dW_t^X dW_t^s = \rho dt$.

Thus,

$$X_T = X_t \exp\left(\int_t^T r_u du - \frac{1}{2}\sigma^2(T-t) + \sigma(W_T^X - W_t^X)\right),$$

and

$$s_u = s_t e^{\kappa(t-u)} + \kappa \int_t^u \theta(v)e^{\kappa(v-u)}dv + \lambda \int_t^u e^{\kappa(v-u)}dW_v^s,$$

so that

$$\int_t^T s_u du = s_t \int_t^T e^{\kappa(t-u)}du + \kappa \int_t^T \int_t^u \theta(v)e^{\kappa(v-u)}dvdu$$

$$+ \lambda \int_t^T \int_t^u e^{\kappa(v-u)}dW_v^s du$$

$$= \frac{s_t}{\kappa}(1 - e^{\kappa(t-T)}) + \kappa \int_t^T \theta(v) \int_v^T e^{\kappa(v-u)}dudv$$

$$+ \lambda \int_t^T \int_v^T e^{\kappa(v-u)}dudW_v^s$$

$$= \frac{s_t}{\kappa}(1 - e^{\kappa(t-T)}) + \int_t^T \theta(v)(1 - e^{\kappa(v-T)})dv$$

$$+ \frac{\lambda}{\kappa} \int_t^T (1 - e^{\kappa(v-T)})dW_v^s.$$

We seek

$$\mathrm{cov}_t^T(e^{-\int_t^T s_u du}, X_T)$$

$$= E_t^T[e^{-\int_t^T s_u du}X_T] - E_t^T[e^{-\int_t^T s_u du}]E_t^T[X_T].$$

We have

$$E_t^T[X_T]$$

$$= E_t^T\left[X_t \exp\left(\int_t^T r_u du - \frac{1}{2}\sigma^2(T-t) + \sigma(W_T^X - W_t^X)\right)\right]$$

$$= X_t \exp\left(\int_t^T r_u du - \frac{1}{2}\sigma^2(T-t) + \frac{1}{2}\sigma^2(T-t)\right)$$

$$= \frac{X_t}{D(t,T)}$$

and

$$E_t^T\left[\exp\left(-\int_t^T s_u du\right)\right]$$

$$= \exp\left(-\frac{s_t}{\kappa}(1 - e^{\kappa(t-T)}) - \int_t^T \theta(v)(1 - e^{\kappa(v-T)})dv\right)$$

$$\cdot E_t^T\left[\exp\left(-\frac{\lambda}{\kappa}\int_t^T (1 - e^{\kappa(v-T)})dW_v^s\right)\right]$$

$$= \exp\left(-\frac{s_t}{\kappa}(1 - e^{\kappa(t-T)}) - \int_t^T \theta(v)(1 - e^{\kappa(v-T)})dv\right.$$

$$\left. + \frac{1}{2}\frac{\lambda^2}{\kappa^2}\int_t^T (1 - e^{\kappa(v-T)})^2 dv\right)$$

$$= \frac{D^R(t,T)}{D(t,T)},$$

where $D(t,T)$ is the value of a discount bond maturing at time T as seen at time t, whilst $D^R(t,T)$ is the corresponding value for a risky discount bond.
Then,

$$E_t^T\left[\exp\left(-\int_t^T s_u du\right) X_T\right]$$

$$= X_t \exp\left(-\frac{s_t}{\kappa}(1 - e^{\kappa(t-T)}) - \int_t^T \theta(v)(1 - e^{\kappa(v-T)})dv\right)$$

$$\cdot \exp\left(\int_t^T r_u du - \frac{1}{2}\sigma^2(T-t)\right)$$

$$\cdot E_t^T \left[\exp\left(-\frac{\lambda}{\kappa} \int_t^T (1 - e^{\kappa(v-T)}) dW_v^s\right) + \sigma(W_T^X - W_t^X) \right]$$

$$= X_t \exp\left(-\frac{s_t}{\kappa}(1 - e^{\kappa(t-T)}) - \int_t^T \theta(v)(1 - e^{\kappa(v-T)}) dv\right)$$

$$\cdot \exp\left(\int_t^T r_u du - \frac{1}{2}\sigma^2(T - t)\right)$$

$$\cdot \exp\left(\frac{1}{2}\frac{\lambda^2}{\kappa^2} \int_t^T (1 - e^{\kappa(v-T)})^2 dv + \frac{1}{2}\sigma^2(T - t)\right.$$

$$\left. - \frac{\rho\sigma\lambda}{\kappa} \int_t^T (1 - e^{\kappa(v-T)}) dv\right)$$

$$= X_t \exp\left(-\frac{s_t}{\kappa}(1 - e^{\kappa(t-T)})\right.$$

$$\left. - \int_t^T \theta(v)(1 - e^{\kappa(v-T)}) dv + \int_t^T r_u du\right)$$

$$\cdot \exp\left(\frac{1}{2}\frac{\lambda^2}{\kappa^2} \int_t^T (1 - e^{\kappa(v-T)})^2 dv\right.$$

$$\left. - \frac{\rho\sigma\lambda}{\kappa}\left(T - t - \frac{1}{\kappa}(1 - e^{\kappa(t-T)})\right)\right)$$

$$= E_t^T[e^{-\int_t^T s_u du}] E_t^T[X_T]$$

$$\times \exp\left(-\frac{\rho\sigma\lambda}{\kappa}\left(T - t - \frac{1}{\kappa}(1 - e^{\kappa(t-T)})\right)\right).$$

Thus, the convexity adjustment is

$$\text{cov}_t^T(e^{-\int_t^T s_u du}, X_T)$$

$$= \left\{\exp\left(-\frac{\rho\sigma\lambda}{\kappa}\left(T - t - \frac{1}{\kappa}(1 - e^{\kappa(t-T)})\right)\right) - 1\right\}$$

$$\times E_t^T[e^{-\int_t^T s_u du}] E_t^T[X_T]$$

$$= \left\{\exp\left(-\frac{\rho\sigma\lambda}{\kappa}\left(T - t - \frac{1}{\kappa}(1 - e^{\kappa(t-T)})\right)\right) - 1\right\}$$

$$\times \frac{X_t D^R(t, T)}{\{D(t, T)\}^2}.$$

Index